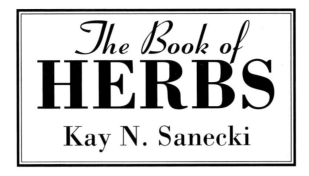

The Book of
HERBS

Kay N. Sanecki

A QUANTUM BOOK

Published by
Chartwell Books
A Division of Book Sales, Inc.
114 Northfield Avenue
Edison, New Jersey, 08837
USA

Copyright © 1996 Quantum Books Ltd

ISBN 0-7858-0672-5

This book was produced by
Quantum Books Ltd
6 Blundell Street
London N7 9BH

Produced in Australia by Griffin Colour

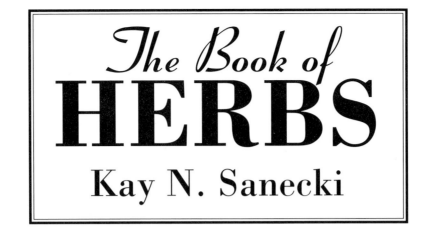

The Book of HERBS

Kay N. Sanecki

CHARTWELL
BOOKS, INC.

Culinary Herbs

ANY culinary traditions relying on herbs originated in the ancient world and reached northern Europe, including Britain, with the Romans. Forgotten during the Dark Ages, herbs were reintroduced into cultivation by the monks in the early Middle Ages and were the main flavouring, colouring and preserving agents. Even when the great spice markets of London flourished, herbs were cultivated, marketed and used in homes as very important items for the still room. Only the nineteenth-century industrial revolution brought a decline in their popularity with the mass production of synthetic flavourings.

Since the Second World War there has been a marked reawakening of interest in herbs and natural foods, which was initiated in America. When herbs are grown well the nutritional, digestive and preserving values are retained.

In the past, on both sides of the Atlantic, culinary herbs and vegetables were grown together in the kitchen garden. But twentieth-century gardeners have developed a love for decorative herb gardens, where 'sweet' herbs grow alongside 'pot' herbs and where numerous plants that had almost been forgotten have been brought back into cultivation.

All cooks have their own ideas about which herbs to use, but some herbs have an almost classical affinity with certain foods — these are listed in the following catalogue of culinary herbs. Often a small bunch of several sprigs of different herbs may be added to a dish, by tying them with cotton and allowing the bunch to float in the pan or dish during cooking time, and then removing it before serving. Chopped fresh herbs can be added to salads or sauces, or mixed into cream cheeses, or even be incorporated into herb butters. Vinegars may be flavoured with herbs, or in some instances coloured by them — chive flowers for example, turn vinegar a pretty pink.

A N G E L I C A

Angelica archangelica (Umbelliferae) B

An imposing and dramatic plant which, given good growing conditions, attains 2 m (6½ ft) in height, with large green-white mophead flowers held aloft. A good plant for the back of a border (especially when protected from rough winds) because the stout green ribbed stems stand up for themselves and hold the glossy green leaves about them like flounces.

Strictly speaking, angelica is a biennial plant, forming a good clump of foliage the first summer and dramatic flowers the second, dying after the seed has set. But by cutting back the growth in autumn (fall) and preventing the flower heads from seeding, the plant can be maintained as a short-lived perennial.

Angelica is cultivated mainly for its green stems which can be candied and used in confectionery. A chunk or two cut at flowering time makes a good addition to stewed fruit, or it can be used in jam-making as a substitute, especially for rhubarb. However, every part of angelica is useful. The dried root (when infused) makes a stimulating tonic reputed to encourage a dislike for alcohol. The ground roots are used for sachets, and an oil derived from the root is used in liqueurs. The juniper-flavoured seed can be substituted for real juniper berries in the making of gin. Leaves are edible as a vegetable when cooked and served with butter, offering a spinach-like flavour. In the past angelica was recommended for a wide range of ailments, and legend tells us that in medieval times an angel 'visited' a monk, directing him to use this plant to alleviate the sufferings of victims of a plague — hence the specific name *archangelica*.

CULTIVATION Angelica seed loses its viability so it is important to sow the seed when fresh. If this cannot be done, store it in a fridge or ice box throughout the winter, and then sow in the spring in tiny pinches, thinning out all but the best plants once germination has taken place. The seedlings do not transplant well, but it is worth trying when they are very small. Plant out at least 90 cms (3 ft) apart to allow the plants to develop uninhibited. A good rich loam ensures the most marvellous of all herb garden plants, otherwise growth will be restricted and poor in colour. Angelica dislikes hot, humid climates and appreciates a spot in gardens where it can be in the shade for some part of every day.

Basil / Sweet Basil

Ocymum basilicum (Labiatae) A

An ancient plant from the Pacific Islands which reached England via Asia and Europe in the sixteenth century, and was taken by early settlers to America.

A tender herb, several types of which are in cultivation. The large leaved, common or sweet basil, *Ocymum basilicum*, is the plant to choose for the kitchen with its strong, spicy, clove-like aroma. Dwarf or bush basil, *O. mimimum*, is hardier but has a weaker flavour.

Sweet basil bears tiny, white, purple-tinged flowers in midsummer and juicy aromatic leaves. It reaches 50 cms (1½ ft) in height. 'Dark Opal' has a gingery aroma, and when used shredded in salads adds a decorative air and exotic flavour. 'Dark Opal' was developed in 1962 at the University of Connecticut, and represents something of a breakthrough in herb cultivation, because, almost exclusively, herbs have escaped the attentions of the hybridist. Moreover, it was awarded the All-America medal by the seedsmen.

CULTIVATION In zones with a cold winter, sow basil in early to mid-spring in boxes or in frames, or later out of doors when all danger of frost has passed. The best results are obtained by starting off the seedlings with protection and maintaining a high temperature until they can be hardened off and planted out safely.

In warmer zones, sow directly into the beds, and thin out to about 20 cms (8 ins) apart, or transplant. Basil seedlings transplant easily. A plant can be potted up and kept indoors to maintain a fresh supply of leaves until late autumn, or it can be grown indoors where the plant will get at least five hours of sunshine each day. It is a good patio or window-box plant, and a happy inhabitant of a sunbaked yard.

B A Y / S W E E T B A Y

Laurus nobilis (Lauraceae) P

Bay, or sweet bay (the latter name being preferred in America) is a highly esteemed inhabitant of the herb garden. In classical times heroes and poets were adorned with garlands of bay leaves. The Latin name of the plant is honoured to this day in the title Poet Laureate.

Of Mediterranean origin, the bay is an evergreen tree. It is usually grown as a bush, and it hates cold winds. For this reason alone it has come to be cultivated habitually in large containers, its branches trimmed to some formal shape. It decorates porches, yards and balconies, and can be moved into shelter if necessary in the winter.

In warmer districts it is a good plant to grow as the surrounding hedge to the herb garden. The height and shape of the hedge, or of individual bushes, can be controlled by clipping or pruning. Bright green smooth oval leaves, punctuated by lovely fluffy-faced beige-yellow flowers at midsummer, make the bay easy to identify. (It is vital not to confuse it with cherry laurel — *Prunus lauroceracus* — which produces prussic acid.

In the kitchen a crushed leaf of bay added to prepared meats, stuffings, casseroles and chowders is almost traditional, and it is one of the vital ingredients of bouquet garni, the others being parsley and thyme. A few sprigs cut just before the flowers bloom, tied together and hung in a warm, dust-free place will provide dried leaves of bay for culinary flavouring. Bay is one of the very few herbs which is not used fresh as the flavour would be far too pungent.

CULTIVATION Cuttings taken with a heel in early summer (when the new spring growth has hardened a little) and made about 10-15 cms (4-6 ins) long are the most reliable method of propagation. Insert them in pans or pots, potting up separately once the roots are established, and keep them thus for a year or so before planting out. (Layering of established plants in summer is an alternative method of propagation.) Once plants are growing well, an occasional spray with water helps to keep the leaves clean and shining.

CARAWAY

Carum carvi (Umbelliferae) B

Caraway perpetuates itself in the garden by self-sown seed, ensuring a filmy greenness among the herbs. The leaves are thread-like and bright green; the stems are smooth, reach 60 cms (2 ft) in height and support dainty heads of purple-white flowers in high summer. These are followed by the familiar black, ribbed seeds used to flavour confectionery, cookies, bread and liqueurs (especially Kümmel).

A herb of ancient cultivation, legend endows it with the power to prevent lovers and doves from straying. It was thus a popular ingredient of love potions in medieval times and was fed to doves, pigeons and poultry to prevent them from wandering.

To harvest the seed, cut the flower head once the seed is ripe (and before it scatters) and either hang the heads up in a paper bag or folded in a clean cloth. This way the seed can fall naturally when it is fully ripe. Sieve out any pieces of stalk and store in an airtight container. One common practice is to scald the freshly collected seed with boiling water to rid it of insects which can then be dried off in the sun before storing.

CULTIVATION Seedlings do not transplant well, so sow *in situ* in spring or autumn (fall). Caraway thrives in all but the most humid warm regions, and does best from fall-sown seed because the germination is quicker from fresh seed. Subsequently the little plants need to be thinned so that they are about 15 cms (6 ins) apart, and may be grown in either groups or rows. But, when they are grown for their carrot-like roots it is best to do so in rows and treat them as a vegetable. They will grow in almost any well drained soil but need plenty of sun to produce seed of an acceptable flavour.

CHIVES

Allium schoenoprasum (Liliaceae) P

Chives (sometimes known as onion chives) are one of the most widely grown herbs. They resemble trim tufts of grass and are thus ideal for use as a path edging for both the kitchen garden and herb garden. As they mature the leaves become circular and hollow, and reach about 30-40 cms (12-15 ins) in length. (Giant chives grow a little taller). Their precise habit makes them excellent material for cultivation in pots for yards and balconies, or in window-boxes where good drainage can be assured.

The flavour is refined and onion-like and is best before the plants flower, or in plants that are prevented from flowering. When chopped as a garnish for cheese and egg dishes, soups, salads, sandwiches and quiches, the grass-like strips are added fresh just prior to serving. Chives are rarely used in cooking as the mild flavour is extinguished.

Chinese chives or garlic chives (*Allium tuberosum*) form clumps in the same manner as onion chives, the only difference being that the grass-like leaves are flat. The flavour is pleasant and nearer to garlic. They grow up to 60 cms (2ft) tall with upstanding, mauve-pink flower heads all summer. Both flowers and leaves may be incorporated in salads and herb butters.

CULTIVATION Divide established clumps of bulbs every three years in the spring, and transplant clusters from the outer edges of the clumps. Alternatively, chives can be raised afresh from seed. Although they thrive in any good garden loam, they show a marked preference for slightly acid soil and need to be kept moist throughout the growing season. Choose a place where they can enjoy some shade during the day and remove the flower heads to maintain a continuous supply of flavoursome leaves. The foliage dies down in the winter, so cover a plant or two with dry leaves to encourage a few early spikes for their fresh flavour. Alternatively, pot up a clump of bulblets in the autumn (fall) to keep in a porch or on the apartment windowsill for fresh early spikes. In those regions where the summer temperature remains above 32°C (90°F) clumps can be planted out afresh in the autumn (fall) to provide a winter supply of leaves.

In the garden allow at least two or three plants to flower for the sheer beauty of the purple-pink bobbed heads. Float these as a garnish in soups — especially consommé — or use them to decorate the cheese board or cold collations.

CORIANDER

Coriandrum sativum (Umbelliferae) A

The rounded beige seeds of coriander are best known as a flavouring for pickles and curries in both Europe and America. But in India and the Far East green coriander — or the fresh foliage — accounts for the distinctive curry flavours. This foliage happily is now becoming a market vegetable commodity much more widely available. In Indian cooking the seed is roasted before being ground for use.

A native of southern Europe and the Middle East, coriander used to be a popular herb in England up to Tudor times. The early settlers in America included coriander seed among the beloved items they took to the New World, as did the Spaniards in Mexico.

Today, coriander enjoys a wide popularity. However, among certain groups it still has mythical associations — the Chinese believe it to be endowed with the power of immortality and Jews include it in the bitter herbs prepared for the Feast of Passover. Today its unique flavour is being rediscovered. For the best flavour, seed should be freshly ground before use, when its slightly orange flavour lends itself to inclusion in breads, cookies and pastries.

The entire plant makes a decorative addition to the herb border — it may also be cultivated in pots quite successfully — and will reach a height of 45 cms (1½ ft). The lower leaves are fan-like (a distinguishing feature), the upper ones filigreed and the tiny flowers in high summer are a pinkish mauve. Before the seed ripens the entire plant can be distinctly odorous, but on maturity the rich aroma develops.

Sprigs can be frozen or preserved in salt and oil; coriander does not dry successfully.

CULTIVATION Coriander grows best in a dry atmosphere — in fact it is difficult to grow in damp or humid areas, and needs a good dry summer at the very least if a reasonable crop is to be obtained. Choose a sunny place and sow seed *in situ* once all danger of frost has passed. Alternatively, sow into decorative containers and continue to cultivate as a container plant on an apartment balcony, sunny patio or yard. The stems are weak and the plants tend to loll about and appear top heavy, so either add a twiggy stake or give it a companion to lean against!

DILL

Anethum graveolens (Umbelliferae) A

A native of the Mediterranean countries and Russia, dill has plumes of finely cut blue-green leaves and acid yellow flowers in flattish heads in mid summer. It grows to about 90 cms (3 ft) in height. However, the hollow stalks, when top heavy with flowers, can easily be knocked over by the wind, so it is advisable to try and find a sheltered spot for growing dill. Its reputation as a soothing herb is supported by the fact that both leaves and seeds contain a mild sedative, although the flavours vary considerably. Dill water was a remedy for restive infants 100 years ago and dill is still the sweet-tasting ingredient of the proprietary gripe water.

Its main use in the kitchen is as an addition to pickled cucumbers and gherkins; in America these are known as dill pickles. Dill vinegar is another popular condiment, made by macerating half a cup of dill seed in a quart of malt vinegar for three or four hours, then straining off the liquid and bottling. In central and eastern Europe chopped dill leaves are often used to garnish a dish of boiled potatoes or soured cream sauces, lending them a flavour which is nearer to parsley or anise than the sourness of the dill seed.

For the richest flavour harvest the leaves just before the plant flowers. Small sprigs wrapped in foil and sealed will keep for several weeks in the freezer. Alternatively, chop the leaves, add a little water and freeze in ice cubes.

CULTIVATION Sow seeds in a sunny spot, then thin the seedlings out so that they are about 20 cms (8 ins) apart. They resent being transplanted, and show their displeasure by bolting into flower prematurely. Sow in the spring as soon as the ground is warm, and follow with small sowings at fortnightly intervals throughout the summer to maintain a good supply of fresh leaves. Where winters are very mild seed can be sown in the autumn (fall) to overwinter and provide a good early crop the following spring, or self-sown seedlings will overwinter. Never sow near to fennel, as the two plants tend to cross and the subsequent seed is not as flavoursome as might be expected. The filmy foliage may be cut about six weeks after sowing and the seed collected when fully ripe.

FENNEL

Foeniculum vulgare (Umbelliferae) P

A superbly graceful and tall plant, fennel is easily recognized by its finely cut foliage which can be harvested and used fresh throughout the summer. It is far too sappy to dry. A mediterranean plant grown and used in northern Europe since Roman times, it was taken to America by the settlers for the digestive qualities of its seeds. They provide an anise-flavoured condiment which allays hunger and were used in Europe to mitigate the effects of Church-imposed fasts. More recently in American Puritan communities, seeds of fennel and dill were taken to church to nibble during long services and were known as 'meetin' seeds'.

Fennel is a traditional seasoning for fat meats like pork and, used with restraint, it makes a good accompaniment to poultry and lamb. It is delicious on herring and other oily fish, or to flavour yoghurt as a salad or vegetable dressing. Sometimes the seed is used to flavour bread.

Collect the seed heads just as they change colour and hang them up in a dry, airy, shaded place where the curved, ridged seed can fall onto paper or cloth beneath to be collected. The thick, glossy main stem reaches some 1.5 m (5 ft) in height with feathery soft, ferny foliage topped by dainty heads of yellow flowers in umbels, which bloom in midsummer. The Romans held fennel in high regard as a panacea for several ailments, and as the bestower of power and safe passage. In the Middle Ages in Europe it was sometimes stuffed into keyholes to stop the passage of evil spirits.

CULTIVATION Fennel is a tall plant suitable for the back of the herb border. Seed should be sown in the late spring. To maintain a continuous supply of fresh leaves throughout the season, sow a few seeds in succession with about a 10-day interval between sowings. It can be grown as an annual, although the established roots make good plants that overwinter easily. Divide such established roots in the autumn after the seed has been harvested.

LEMON BALM

Melissa officinalis (Labiatae) P

Lemon balm is a cottage garden plant which is grown for its lemon-scented leaves. It is also cultivated as one of the strewing herbs for its clean pervading fragrance.

It forms a dense round bush about 60-90 cms (2-3 ft) high, and as much across. In warmer climates it can reach 1 m (4 ft) in height. In its best forms the leaves are variegated with clear yellow; all forms dry well and are suitable for inclusion in *pot pourri* recipes.

In the kitchen, dried crushed leaves can be added to stuffings for poultry and meat; flower tips and young leaves can be floated in wine or fruit cups and may be used as a substitute for lemon juice in jam-making. Balm was the principal ingredient of *eau des carmes*, distilled by the Carmelite monks in seventeenth-century Paris as the forerunner of *eau de cologne*.

CULTIVATION Although slow to germinate, seed is otherwise easy to grow, and as it is so fine it hardly needs covering. A quicker method of propagation is to take cuttings in late spring and plant them out once they are established in warm districts, or in the following spring. A moist soil in a sunny spot enhances the essential oil of this plant, ridding it of the slightly musty overtones that develop during dry seasons or on light, dry soils. It is especially good, in both appearance and aroma, in the controlled conditions of containers. Cut back to soil level in the autumn (fall) to encourage young fresh growth and good fragrance.

Lemon balm is happiest in moderately warm regions, where it grows a little more lushly but it does not like great humidity and needs a cold winter to give of its best.

MARJORAM

Origanum onites (Labiatae) P

All the marjorams have a warm sweetly pungent aroma. Perhaps that of pot marjoram (*O. onites*) is somewhat rougher, but nevertheless it is one of the most popularly cultivated herbs, and flourishes in temperate climes. Its flowers are pink and white in high summer, and it forms good clumps of growth up to 60 cms (2 ft) in height.

The three kinds included here are the subject of some confusion, probably because until the 1940s common marjoram (*O. vulgare*), a red-stemmed perennial which spreads by tiny rhizomes, was called wild marjoram in American cookbooks. Today it is known as oregano. (Further confusion arises because in some countries, notably Mexico and the southern states of America, oregano is the colloquial name for totally unrelated plants with a similar flavour.)

Sweet or knotted marjoram (*O. majorana*) is a tender plant from north Africa which, in June, has mauve flowers almost hidden in knot-like clusters of leaves in little 'blobs' at the stem tips — hence the name knotted marjoram. It provides by far the best flavour for cooking. Except in hot climates, it is treated as a half hardy annual, producing bushy little plants about 20 cms (8 ins) high. An excellent herb to accompany meat (especially cold prepared meat) and bland vegetables like courgettes and potatoes.

All the marjorams dry well for winter use, and both flowers and leaves ought to be incorporated in *pot pourri*.

CULTIVATION Pot or wild marjoram is simple to raise from seed sown in spring or from summer cuttings or from root division in autumn (fall). On the other hand sweet marjoram needs to be treated as a half hardy annual. All three kinds can be started by sowing indoors or in cold frames early in spring, and are ready to transfer out of doors as soon as the temperature gets up to about 7°C(45°F). In very mild zones they can be treated as hardy.

Origanum dictamnus, dittany of Crete is grown as oregano in America, often as a pot plant and usually only for decoration — although its leaves can be added to salads.

M INT

Mentha species (Labiatae) P

Numerous mint species are grown almost everywhere, some wild, some cultivated forms, and all bearing a variety of vernacular and catalogue names which leads, inevitably, to some confusion. A further complication arises because the mints themselves hybridize and can vary in appearance according to environmental factors. But by examination of the essential oils, using chromatography, the identification and relationship of the whole range of mints has been made possible. But, as with all herbs, the country names persist.

Spearmint, the classic ingredient in mint juleps, was recorded as growing in Plymouth, Mass. in the early 1600s by Elder William Brewster. It appears, also, in Josselyn's seed list but is absent from the Winthrop seed order of 1631, for the simple reason that it was available locally and did not need to be imported. Mints have only one purpose in life — to walk about the plot and propagate themselves.

The kitchen garden mints are the most widely grown. Spearmint or garden mint (*Mentha spicata*, formerly *Mentha viridis*) used in the traditional English mint sauce to accompany roast lamb, is perhaps the commonest, with narrow pointed leaves, growing anything from 30-90 cms (1-3 ft tall). If left to flower in midsummer, it grows purple spikes, held well above the leaves. Apple mint (*M. rotundifolia*) has large, round, soft, rather downy leaves and, if left to flower, pink spikes growing up to 1 m (3¼ ft) high. The cream, variegated form with leaves bordered and overlaid with cream and young shoots often entirely cream is *M. rotundifolia variegata*, and is usually called pineapple mint. It is a good decorative garden plant often retaining its attractive foliage throughout the summer. Ginger mint or scotch mint (*M. gentilis*) is another decorative leaved plant, especially good in its *variegata* form when the golden variegation of the rather pointed leaves and its military trimness, often up to 40 cms (1½ ft) high, add greatly to the herb border. Raripila or pea mint (*M. raripila rubra*) with dark red stems and dark green rounded leaves with red-purple midribs, provides the most exquisite flavour.

All the foregoing are good culinary mints but the largest plant is Bowles's mint (*M. × villosa*) and its *alopecuroides* form is without doubt the connoisseurs' culinary mint. It is a vigorous plant, growing up to 1.5 m (5 ft) high, with broad leaves smeared with pale woolly down. The hairs disappear upon chopping or pounding.

Of the mints used in confectionery and the preparation of pharmaceutical products, peppermint (*M. × piperita*) is the most widely used. Two varieties, black and white, grow to about 1 m (3¼ ft), the former with black-purple stems and both produce a sharp clean oil. In the kitchen peppermint can be used to flavour fruit cups, sweets and puddings and to make a tisane from the dried or fresh leaves.

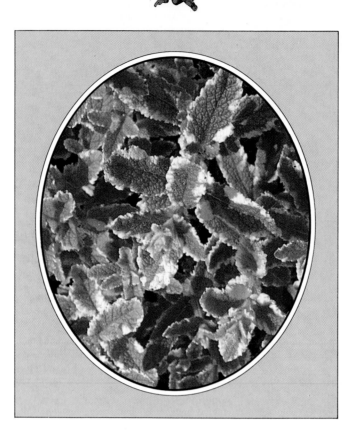

M I N T *CONTINUED*

Mentha species (Labiatae) P

The range of scent and flavour present in mints is a consequence of the barely perceptible variations in composition of the essential oils which can occur within a genus. A whole scale of scent is provided by the same oil; the minute chemical variations between one species and another are themselves affected by time of season, soil and weather — all contributing to the various overtones. Thus we can find mint described as gingery, lemony or peppery. Explore these slight variations in flavour by adding finely chopped mint just before serving to starters such as grapefruit or melon, or to citrus fruit desserts and chocolate mousse.

The smallest leaves of any of our cultivated plants belong to a mint, the Corsican mint (*M. requienii*). Unlike all other mints, this one seeds itself when it is well grown and provides ground cover. It is slightly peppermint scented, but is not a culinary mint.

The soft leaves of the mint are difficult to dry well — they tend to blacken and soon shatter. Try not to collect too many shoots at any one time unless the whole plant is being sacrificed. All mints can be included in *pot pourri*, especially the fruit-scented ones. Little sachets of dried leaves can be stored in cupboards and if rubbed occasionally will emit their aroma afresh.

CULTIVATION Mint is propagated by planting pieces of the rooted stem — known in Britain as Irishman's cuttings — about 5 cms (2 ins) deep in moist loamy soil, at almost any time during the growing season. Apple mint, sometimes called dryland mint in America, will tolerate less moist soil; they all like the sunlight. The plants need to be confined to their allotted space and this is best achieved by encircling the area with bricks or tiles, or pushing plastic strips into the ground to prevent their advance.

Container growing is possible provided regular watering can be assured — otherwise the containers need to be sunk into the ground. All mints can be grown indoors (although they tend to become scraggy) except for apple mint which sometimes makes quite a handsome plant.

A productive mint bed in the herb or kitchen garden should be remade and moved every three or four years to reduce the likelihood of mint rust disease.

Crowns of mint plants can be boxed or potted up in winter and taken to a warm greenhouse or conservatory to force succulent fresh shoots which become available within three or four weeks.

PARSLEY

Petroselinum crispum (Umbelliferae) B

All forms of parsley are grown as annuals, although strictly speaking they are biennial plants. By removing the flower heads the productive life of the plants can be extended and the quality of the foliage flavour maintained. The most familiar ones are the nicely curled-leaved sort (called French curly-leaved parsley in America) beloved of fishmongers as a garnish. The plain-leaved kind, *P. neapolitanum* called Italian plain-leaved parsley in America, has a more pronouced flavour and is preferred by some cooks, especially for long slow cooking. Nibble a sprig or two of this iron- and vitamin-rich plant to discover the refreshing flavour. It ought not to be known merely as the universal garnish and ingredient of parsley sauce for it has too fine a flavour. It is an ingredient of bouquet garni, sauce verte and sauce tartare. Parsley tea is a tonic and diuretic.

Hamburg parsley, *P. c.* 'Tuberosum' is a variety with plain unfrizzed leaves grown for its root which is used as a winter vegetable.

CULTIVATION Originating from the regions around the Black Sea, parsley is best sown in mid to late spring as an edging in the kitchen or herb garden or even to a flower border. Germination can be unbelievably slow, about six to eight weeks is the norm, but to encourage it try soaking the seed overnight and wetting the drill with water trickled from a kettle of boiling water immediately prior to sowing. (Legend has it that parsley seed goes nine times to the devil and back before germinating.) Subsequently thin the little plants with care during showery weather, or remove alternate plants for use until they are left standing about 30 cms (1 ft) apart. In all but the most northerly parts of America parsley can be sown in early spring, or even in the autumn (fall) before the ground freezes. Remove the flower stalks as they form to keep the plant buoyant and the leaves full of flavour.

Grow some in a container and keep it in a porch or on the kitchen window-sill for a fresh supply of leaves during the winter months, as parsley does not dry successfully. Although it will freeze, it loses its pert frilliness and is no longer attractive as a garnish.

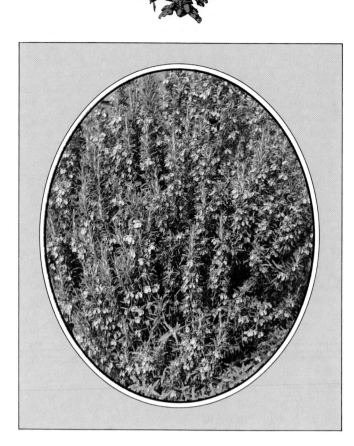

ROSEMARY

Rosmarinus officinalis (Labiatae) P

A very popular shrub with richly resinous evergreen foliage, which needs only to be brushed by the hand to release its fragrance, rosemary is said to be for remembrance. Its wonderful powder blue flowers bloom intermittently very early in mild localities until early summer when they enshroud the entire shrub. In happy circumstances it will rise to 1.6 m (8 ft). Culpeper recommended more than a dozen uses for rosemary and said 'The Flowers and Conserve made of them, are singular good comfort to the Heart.' Rosemary used to be burned in chambers to freshen the air; included in herbal tobacco; used in body cosmetics for its deodorant properties; included in *pot pourri*; and used in the treatment of many inner bodily complaints and as an external antiseptic and embrocation.

   As a culinary herb its flavour is pronounced, so exercise restraint in its use. Because the leaves are spiky, remove them before serving the dish. It is at its best as a flavouring for lamb or as a marinade ingredient for strong game.

CULTIVATION Take cuttings of the twisted wood of non-flowering shoots in early summer, or layer established branches in summer. Choose a sheltered position and well drained soil in which to plant it so that it can sunbathe. Where winters are cold, grow rosemary in containers that can be taken into shelter. The thick growth tolerates clipping, so it can be controlled.

SAGE

Salvia officinalis (Labiatae) P

Theré are several forms of the common or garden sage; all are reasonably hardy and keep their leaves in winter. In America leaves can even be harvested during the winter in the southern states, and we know from physic receipts that it was grown there for medicinal purposes in the seventeenth century.

The broad-leaved kind rarely produces its mauve flowers and is the best plant to use for its culinary purposes because the essential oil is rich. But for herb garden decoration use the purple-leaved or red sage (*S. o. purpurea*) and a daintier form, painted sage (*S. o. tricolor*), in which the young leaves are haphazardly splashed with cream, pale green and cherry pink; this is a less hardy plant. The narrow-leaved sage (*S. hispanica*) and the narrow-leaved golden sage (*S. icterina*) are all useful substitutes — the latter the sweetest and best of all for stuffings to accompany delicate meats. The whole range of flavours and aromas can vary even further when plants are cultivated on different soils and it is worth experimenting to find a plant that provides the most acceptable flavour, devoid of bitterness. Move it about the garden or try rooted cuttings elsewhere until the best flavour is produced. Sage tea made from fresh or dried leaves and flavoured with lemon juice has been used in the past in many forms as a headache remedy. Cold sage beer or ale is said to dispel depression.

Lax bushes of *Salvia officinalis* grow about 40-90 cms (1½-3ft) high and as much across, and ought to be replaced every four years or so, although many serve a useful life for much longer. Harvest sprays and hang them up in bunches to dry any time during the spring and summer. Once dry there is no fear of sage leaves reabsorbing atmospheric moisture, but nevertheless, store in containers.

Sage is supposedly the herb of eternal youth and is used in stuffings, cheeses, kebabs, leek pie and with gammon. Alternately, it can be used as a dentifrice, gargle and mouthwash, and when burnt as a deodoriser for animal and cooking smells.

CULTIVATION Select a sunny corner and alkaline soil for sage is a native of the Mediterranean shores and flourishes best when it is warm. Propagation is from summer cuttings taken with a heel or by layering established branches in spring and autumn (fall). Seed is unreliable and it rarely sets in Britain because sage is reluctant to flower. Where seed is available it is a slow and challenging method of perpetuating the plants. Keep the bushy plants well pruned to encourage young shoots with a strong flavour and because sage has a strong tendency to become leggy and twiggy.

S O R R E L

Rumex acetosa (Polygonaceae) P treated as A

The sorrel of herb gardens is a superior broad-leaved form of the wild plant native to the temperate regions of the Northern Hemisphere, including Britain and America. Distinguishable by the succulent leaves up to 10 cms (4 ins) in width, the upper ones with downward pointing lobes, it is known also as garden or broad-leaved sorrel and can reach 1 m (3¼ ft) high.

The main culinary attribute is the tangy flavour of the leaves, which is at its most refined just before the spikes of rusty pink flowers appear — so remove the flower buds to maintain a supply of tender leaves. It is useful for tenderizing meat: just wrap it around the steak, or add it pounded to the marinade. Alternatively, use it as a substitute for vine leaves, enfolding risotto mixtures. The French make sorrel soup from both sorts of sorrel.

CULTIVATION Raise new plants each season for the most refined flavour, sowing seed in spring in moist well-nourished soil where there is some shade during the day. Set in drills as for most salad crops; thin the little plants to about 30 cms (1 ft) apart. Prevent bolting by removing flower buds and pick the leaves frequently to maintain a supply of fresh succulent leaves.

Pinch out the flower heads to prevent flowering and seeding, or else be prepared to remove self-sown seedlings before they develop. Once sorrel establishes itself the roots plunge deeply and are difficult to eradicate. In really warm summers, or generally warm regions, sorrel leaves tend to become bitter. A mulch around the plants will help to keep the soil cooler, but once the season cools down the leaf flavour will improve.

TARRAGON/FRENCH TARRAGON

Artemisia dracunculus (Compositae) P

The true French tarragon or estragon is a superior herb, sometimes difficult to grow and reluctant to flower in the damp climates. It seems happiest in warm areas, but is difficult to grow in conditions that are both warm and humid.

With spiky bright green leaves and an upright stature, growing 70 cms (2½ feet) tall, tarragon produces little underground runners that creep about the garden. It is perhaps the most superior culinary herb, with a blunt flavour that adds a bite and enhances all other flavours.

Tarragon vinegar is made by steeping the fresh herb in wine vinegar for six to eight weeks, shaking the bottle occasionally. Sprigs to be used in this way ought to be picked early in the season when the essential oils are rich. A superb flavour to add to egg dishes, try to use the herb fresh as the flavour becomes stale when dried. It is better to quick-freeze tarragon to capture its wonderful flavour.

Russian tarragon (*A. dracunculoides*) has an inferior flavour, and is not generally recommended for culinary purposes.

CULTIVATION A plant for the sunniest driest places, tarragon is a lover of warmth and good drainage. The top growth needs to be cut back early in the autumn (fall). In colder parts it needs to be protected in some way to help it through the winter. Dry bracken or leaves or a peat mulch covered with plastic is usually sufficient, but in more extreme conditions apply the mulch after the ground has frozen solid, using dry straw or salt hay.

Try to pot up a young plant to grow indoors and keep through the winter. It will need a place where it gets whatever sunshine is available. Tarragon is not easy to keep in this way, so do not be too disheartened if it decides to go — nothing will persuade it to remain! Propagation is from root division or stem cuttings — seed offered is usually that of Russian tarragon.

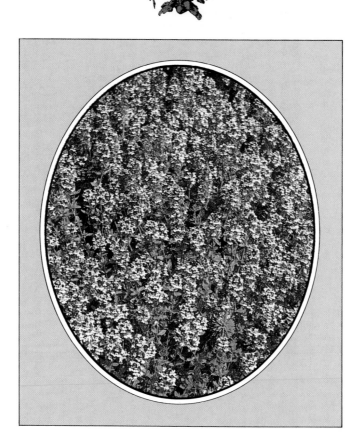

THYME

Thymus species (Labiatae) P

Thyme is one of the most important culinary herbs, and is used for its essential oil called thymol, which is a preservative. Garden thyme (*T. vulgaris*) is the main one grown for culinary purposes, although others offer variations of the true thyme aroma. Among the many decorative sorts are lemon thyme (*T. × citriodorus*) and caraway thyme (*T. herba-barona*) and one or two others, which are best used mixed with garden thyme. The nuances of flavour displayed among the thymes are not as varied as those of the mints, but the range is useful in cooking.

Garden thyme forms a cushion-like mound of growth; all the other thymes form a carpet-like growth covering the ground. Where the decorative value of a 'flowing' edge is needed, do not plant *T. vulgaris*, but select one of the others. A little hummock of garden thyme will reach about 30 cms (1 ft) in height and its cultivars are about the same size. The carpet-forming sorts are ground hugging and are no higher than 5-8 cms (2-3 ins).

Harvest thyme for drying before the plants flower and hang up to dry in a warm shaded place or lie the sprigs on a cloth or paper in a warm place.

Thyme has a powerful aroma and may be successfully dried or frozen. It is an ingredient of bouquet garni and always needs to be used with restraint as its overpowering strength can survive the longest cooking, and can become dominant. However, this lasting quality can be used to advantage in slowly simmered rich game dishes.

Its many uses include terrines, cooked meats and sausages, and as a preservative and flavouring in stews, vegetable broths, cream soups and stuffings. The lemony aroma of lemon thyme is a good accompaniment to fish dishes and makes an interesting addition to tea-breads and some desserts.

CULTIVATION Choose the sunniest part of the garden where the soil is well drained or even dry, and a little limy. Most plants will be either short-lived or need some protection from the cold and dampness in winter. In the drier and warmer maritime regions where winter temperatures do not fall too low or too quickly, it is always worth trying to keep thyme. It is a good plant for troughs and containers which can be brought indoors during the winter for protection.

Propagation is from seed sown in spring, and the tiny plants put out once they are big enough to handle at about 5 cm (1 in) intervals. Otherwise, take tip cuttings in summer before flowering starts.

Healing Herbs

HE medicinal value of plants is governed by their chemical composition, or active principle. From ancient cultures an intimate association has existed between man and his healing plants; botany and medicine stemming from very much the same source. The value of most of the physic plants used today must have been confirmed by trial and error over many centuries and varying cultures. Modern concepts relating to healing plants started in Europe in the sixteenth century with the printing of herbals, themselves based on the codices and practices of the classical world. Between those two cultures lay centuries when the use of physic plants became irrevocably linked with magic, emblems and superstitions. Primitive societies held curious ideas in which lay the origins of the folklore that surrounds the herbs today.

The sixteenth-century European medical schools were the first to establish botanic gardens, which were for the study of living plants. There are now more than 400 such gardens throughout the world, many of which conduct continuous research into medicinal plants.

In 1585 Raleigh organized the first colonizing expedition to the New World accompanied by men qualified to record the natural history of Virginia. There then began a great exchange of plants between the New World and Europe. Into Virginia came the plants Europe had cultivated and used for centuries, fruit, vegetables and more importantly, herbs — herbs for sustenance and herbs for healing.

AMERICAN MANDRAKE

Podophyllum peltatum (Saxifragaceae) P

A plant of shaded meadows and damp woodland indigenous to the Atlantic regions of America, mandrake, mayweed or wild lemon arrived in England c 1664. The drug obtained from the fleshy fibrous root was known to the American Indians as an emetic and vermifuge, and has a powerful and beneficial action on the liver, but must be used only in competent hands.

In English gardens it is seen as a semi-aquatic plant often incorporated in the decorative garden, but invaluable in the spacious bog/herb garden. Underground stems have many branches which are matted together with long fibrous runners. There are two kinds of stem, one bearing a single leaf, the other two leaves and a single white flower. Ultimately the plant attains 45 cms (1½ ft) in height, but it flowers early in the year before this height is reached. The leaves are broadly hand-shaped, roughly 30 cms (1 ft) across, rounded and deeply veined, and assume a deep, rich, red colour in late summer. The scented flower is followed by a large seed capsule which turns yellowish or red on maturity. Although the leaves and roots are poisonous this capsule — a fruit — is edible although somewhat acid in flavour.

CULTIVATION Divide established clumps in spring and plant in moist, humus-rich soil in a partially shaded spot. Twelve seeds form in each berry and may be sown when ripe. Where they are happy the plants spread once established, but the underground stems can be easily pulled apart.

BLACKROOT

Leptandra virginica (Scrophulariaceae) P

North American Indians knew this plant and used it to clear bile and to aid digestion. A native of eastern and southern America, it is known as Culver's root or Culver's physic. Erect stems up to 150-210 cms (5-7 ft) tall bear neat long spikes of white flowers in mid summer, rising above a good whorl of deeply lobed and ponted leaves. Rhizomes, the useful portion of the plant, are dark brown to purplish black and run horizontally just below the soil surface. They contain a volatile oil and when dried are used in the treatment of dysentery, enteritis and allied complaints. When fresh the root itself is an emetic, contradictory perhaps, but proof, if proof were ever needed, that plant drugs are best dealt with by trained herbalists.

CULTIVATION A plant seldom seen in herb collections in England, blackroot is now included in some National Trust gardens and is easy to cultivate. Propagation is by division of rhizomes in spring, setting them just below the soil surface in a well drained position where some organic material has been incorporated. The clumps need to be divided every three or four years. Hardy throughout America, it prefers higher altitudes and some shade.

COMFREY/COMMON COMFREY

Symphytum officinale (Boraginaceae) P

Comfrey is a plant with a predilection for dampish soils and waste ground near river banks where its black-skinned root can penetrate into the soft earth. It is chiefly for the rich mucilage which it contains that comfrey is prized pharmaceutically. The generic name *Symphytum* is derived from the Greek *symphuo*, meaning to be planted alongside.

Traditionally known as saracen's root, the common comfrey is believed to have been brought back to England by crusaders who had discovered its great therapeutic value in helping tissue to knit together. It served as a major healing herb, and its mucilagenous products were put to use as a bone-setting plaster. The early settlers took it to America and when Josselyn visited New England he declared that 'Compherie' grew well, in his book *New England Rarities Discovered* (1672).

Although the appearance of comfrey is unmistakable, there is a constantly discussed similarity between its young leaves and those of the foxglove. Comfrey has a rough hairiness; the veins of the leaves are closer together and there is a clamminess about it which is absent in foxglove.

The fresh leaves of comfrey form a good poultice or compress for sprained or twisted joints, and need to be wrapped in some sort of cloth as the hairy leaves can cause skin irritation. Dried leaves serve the same purpose but are not easy to dry without shattering. The mashed, sticky, creamy root also provides healing plasters and was used formerly in the relief of pulmonary and throat disorders, and in the healing of stomach ulcers.

Flowers appear in early summer in dangling coxcombs of bells — blue, white, mauve and pink — held on boldly arched stems. Comfrey grows to a height of 80 cms (2½ ft) and the stiff, angular, hollow stalks are covered with rough hairs. Fresh flowers and leaves produce a yellow dye. Contrary to the general rule, comfrey roots are harvested in the spring.

CULTIVATION When grown from seed, the plants are slow to reach maturity. More reliable plants are obtained by root division in spring. Select moisture-retentive soil, or even a poorly drained corner, and comfrey will thrive for many years. Plants have been known to span a generation.

Comfrey thrives happily in all but the very coldest regions where it can be propagated by root cuttings.

E VENING PRIMROSE

Oenothera biennis (Onagraceae) B

The oil of evening primrose is currently attracting considerable attention on both sides of the Atlantic for use in nervous disorders in general, and multiple sclerosis in particular.

It is called evening primrose because it transforms itself from its daytime bedraggled appearance into a fluttering pale yellow beauty in the evening, when its fragrance becomes increasingly powerful. Flowering begins in early summer and continues well into autumn; towards the end of summer the flowers tend to stay open all day. Older country names are moths, moonflower, primrose tree, and in North America, night willow herb.

An indigenous plant of America, extending from Labrador to the Gulf of Mexico and westward to the Rockies and flourishing in thickets and fence corners, it reaches 1.5 m (3½ ft) or more in height. A flat rosette of large pale green leaves develops the first year and the upright stem bearing the rather floppy yellow flowers in succession the following year. Frequently, particularly in America, the flowers are produced in the first summer, seed is set and the plant dies. But once introduced there is always a plentiful supply of fresh seedlings about the herb garden. The stem base is red, and as the leaves die they too assume the same colouring.

Evening primrose is thought to have arrived in Europe via Italy, and certainly as seed in ballast soil in England around 1621. It has become naturalized, particularly on sandy estuaries in the west country, and on sand hills in areas near ports. It is also at home on the dry soils of railway embankments. Now it is also a cultivated plant in gardens where its long flowering season is of value. (Several other species, all of them natives of America, are cultivated in British gardens and some are fragrant and hold their flowers open throughout the day, but *Oenothera biennis* is the true herb.)

The principles extracted from the stem bark and leaves were used for their astringent and sedative properties, and were used for digestive and nervous disorders. Today it is the essential oil that is of importance.

CULTIVATION Choose a dry, well drained soil and dry sunny corner for the best results and sow the seed *in situ* in late spring to produce flowers the following year. Alternatively, sow seed in early spring as soon as the soil warms up after the winter and transplant the seedlings — this will often encourage the little plants to flower the first year. The fleshy roots like to be able to forage, so a good depth of soil will give the best results. Once introduced into the garden, evening primrose will stay.

FOXGLOVE

Digitalis purpurea (Scrophulariaceae) B

No synthetic drug has replaced the cardiac glycosides that are obtainable from the foxglove. It therefore remains of immense importance in medicine and is an essential plant in the physic garden. One of the most poisonous plants of the British flora, it is a true biennial. The rosette of leaves is formed the first year and the flower spike the second; the plant then dies, but usually leaves a clutch of children around it. Occasionally a late-formed rosette may persist for the whole of the second year and flower in the third.

The tongue-shaped foliage is deeply veined, soft and dark green, but the real joy of the plant is in its spire of dangling purple-red bells spotted within, which hang on one side of the spike. It usually grows to 1-2 m (3¼-6½ ft) and flowers in early to mid summer.

A plant of ancient use and certainly recognized by the Anglo-Saxons in England, the value of foxglove in the regulation of heart activity was fully appreciated only in the eighteenth century following the work of Dr William Withering. Although Gerard grew foxglove in his garden it was only administered externally at that time in the treatment of wounds. Gerard quaintly recommends it for those 'who have fallen from high places'. No evidence exists of foxglove having been among the commonplace herbs required by the settlers in America and it is probable that it was not a European import there until its value was established. (Other *Digitalis* species do not contain digitalin.)

CULTIVATION Foxglove is easy to cultivate from seed, and once established there will always be some self-sown seedlings about. Somehow they always thrive best when allowed to select their own standing room, and foxglove has a pretty habit of showering its seed around so that a whole colony of the next generation plants stand within the same patch. Where the soil is good and enriched with leaf mould foxglove is abundantly happy. It tolerates dappled shade quite well, but in warmer regions it flourishes best in full sunshine, and often benefits from a first winter protection mulch of pine needles applied after the ground has frozen. In areas where the soil is damp, it is advisable to lift the plants in the first autumn (fall), harbouring them in a frame for the winter and replanting them the following spring.

G R O U N D   I V Y

Glechoma hederacea (Labiatae) P

A northern European plant that runs across the ground, rooting as it progresses and having wandered over most of Britain, ground ivy crossed the Atlantic and began its onslaught of the American continent from the East. Small pink flowers, minutely spotted with red, rise to about 25 cms (10 ins) at the most, above bountiful prettily marked leaves shaped like those of the ivy.

Gill tea is an old universal remedy for stubborn coughs and to stimulate the kidneys and clarify the blood. In America it used to be taken by painters as a remedy for 'lead colic' and to bathe sore eyes. The name 'gill' comes from the French *guiller*, meaning to ferment beer, the plant having been used to clear beers since Saxon times in Britain. The entire plant possesses a volatile oil bitter in flavour but balsam-like in aroma. Leaves stuffed into the nostrils were considered to relieve a headache; it has also been a component of snuff recipes, for the same reason.

CULTIVATION The trailing square stems root so easily that an 'Irishman's cutting' or piece pulled from an established plant will soon settle in. Specialist seedsmen offer the seed. Ground ivy prefers damper, heavier soils and some sunshine, and can be regarded as a weed suppressor because it tends to become dominant. It will repay careful attention by attracting butterflies to the garden.

HYSSOP

Hyssopus officinalis (Labiatae) P

An aromatic shrubby little evergreen with small blue flowers from mid to late summer and tiny leaves, hyssop is a good plant to grow in containers or as an edging. Hailing from southern Europe and cultivated in English gardens since about 1300, it was one of the herbs taken to the New World by the colonists to use in tea and in herbal tobacco, and as an antiseptic.

Pungently aromatic, it used to be used as a strewing herb in medieval days and a pinch or two of the dried herb added to *pot pourri* recipes lend a spicy tone to the mixture. Oil of hyssop was as highly prized in Europe as oil of lavender; it forms an important constituent of Chartreuse.

Hyssop tea made from a few flowers is claimed to relieve catarrh, and for the same reason it was often an ingredient of herbal tobacco. William Turner knew it when he wrote the first book ever to be written in English about English plants (1558) and said, 'The brethe or vapour of Hisop driveth away the Winde that is in the ears, if they be holden over it'. Medicinally, the healing virtues of hyssop are due to a volatile oil which renders it invaluable as a treatment for catarrh, but it also has a reputation for being effective against rheumatism.

CULTIVATION Hyssop is propagated by seed sown in spring, or by cuttings taken in the same season or very early in the summer, and rooted in damp peaty soil in a shaded place. For edging, plant out the rooted cuttings in late summer about 30 cms (1 ft) apart and do not clip for the following summer, but leave the job for 18 months.

Hyssop revels in light, fairly dry, warm soil and does especially well in window-boxes. It is far hardier than is generally realized. Cut growth down in the autumn (fall) to prevent rough winds ripping the plant from its foothold.

J ACOB'S LADDER

Polemonium caeruleum (Polemoniaceae) P

Polemonium was the name given by Linnaeus to this genus, commemorating a medicinal plant associated with Polemon of Cappadocia. This species grows sparsely over the whole of the temperate regions of the Northern Hemisphere, although nowhere near as prolifically as some of the other closely related species in America.

In cultivation it is appearing more frequently in representative collections of physic plants although it is no longer used in this way; it is a reasonably common decorative garden perennial. Flowering at midsummer with deep, rich blue flowers and soft, well divided green leaves, it stands up to 40-60 cms (1½-2 ft) high. A hundred years ago it was used as an anti-syphilitic agent and in the treatment of rabies.

False Jacob's Ladder or American Greek valerian is *P. reptans*, indigenous in America from New York to Wisconsin, on damp ground. As a cultivated plant it grows to 30 cms (1 ft) with similar pretty foliage, the blue flower heads nodding. The root of this species is bitter in flavour and is employed as an astringent and against snake bites.

CULTIVATION Choose a moisture-retentive soil in the sunshine to encourage the dainty soft growth of Jacob's Ladder, as this is the plant's main attraction. The flowers are somewhat fleeting, but they occur in succession over three to four weeks. Dead-heading is especially useful. There is a white-flowered form.

Propagation is by division of the creeping rootstock in the dormant season, and once established the plants themselves ensure a succession of generations by seed. It is beloved of cats who roll and rub among the clumps, so sometimes the young plants will need protecting.

LICORICE

Glycyrrhiza glabra (Leguminosae) P

One of the most widely used medicinal plants, licorice has been recorded in cultivation in England since 1562 and was taken to the New World in the following century. Juice from the well-developed root system — which can contain substantial lengths of tap root and stolons — provides the commercial licorice. It has long been used either to mask with its sweetness the unpleasant flavour of other medicines, or provide its own soothing action on troublesome coughs. Even the dried root, stripped of its bitter bark is recommended as a remedy for colds, sore throats and bronchial catarrh. It is the licorice stick of old-fashioned English sweet shops, which children purchased in order to chew the fibrous yellow root, held in the hand like a lollipop. Some heath food shops stock the dried sticks today.

A refreshing 'cure-all' beverage can be made by infusing pieces of the crushed or powdered root in water and adding fennel and lemon and allowing it to stand for 24 hours. The water itself, before the addition of fennel and lemon, makes a good mouthwash, and is especially recommended for a cracked or ulcerated tongue.

Known to the ancient world as *Radix dulcis* (sweet root), licorice does not appear in the wild, although it is thought to be a Middle Eastern plant which arrived in northern Europe via Italy. It is widely cultivated in southern Europe and the southwestern regions of the USSR. In Culpeper's day licorice was a commercially profitable crop, notably in the Pontefract district of Yorkshire in northern England, whence it assumed the name of Pontefract root. Black, hard, glossy 'boot laces' and straps of licorice were manufactured in the area as sweetmeats by concentrating the juice of the root through boiling. Even today, stamped out 'buttons' are sold as Pontefract Cakes in England, and are made in that area from imported licorice. These are thirst quenching and soothing to the digestion and act as a very mild laxative — a use to which licorice has been put for centuries.

A summer flowering plant, it reaches as high as 2 m (6½ ft) with very graceful dark green foliage and spikes of pale violet-blue flowers. Roots are harvested from established plants when three or four years old.

CULTIVATION Pieces of the root, each with a bud, should be planted about 15 cms (6 ins) deep and 1 m (3¼ ft) apart in spring or autumn (fall), or any time during the dormant season when the ground is workable and not frosty. Choose good sandy loam where some moisture is available. Licorice revels in hot summers.

L I L Y - OF - T H E - VA L L E Y

Convallaria majalis (Liliaceae) P

Country people used to make an infusion of May lily, as it was called, to administer to those suffering from a weak heart. As Gerard pointed out, 'The flower of the Valley Lillie distilled with wine . . . restoreth speech unto those that have the dum palsie and are falne into the Apoplexie'. He claimed also, that it strengthened the memory. Empiricism was well in advance of science for the drug convallamarin constitutes a very powerful cardiac remedy.

Dried flowers reduced to a powder are a powerful sternutatory, claimed to clear the head of nasal mucus, thus relieving ear noises, vertigo and chronic inflammation of the ears.

Richly scented, the flowers of the lily-of-the-valley make an attractive addition to *pot pourri*. Indigenous plants of the lowlands, especially wooded valleys of the temperate zones of the Northern Hemisphere, the far creeping rhizomes form colonies which are quite dense in some situations. Twin, broad, spear-like leaves guard the stiff lower spike of pretty dangling white bells in late spring. *Convallaria montana* of America is generally included with the species *majalis*, and some cultivars are available with superior flowers.

CULTIVATION In the herb garden the plants need to have a moisture-rich soil and some shade to give of their best. The crowns often take some time to become established and may even refuse to strengthen if they are not happy. Plant out corms or divisions of rootstock bearing a growth bud after flowering. (They are best purchased in the summer when the growth buds are plump.) Top dress with leaf mould occasionally when young.

Lily-of-the-valley can be forced in pots for indoor decoration and specially prepared crowns can be purchased for this purpose. Otherwise any good colony can be lifted from the garden in autumn (fall) and the plumpest crown selected for potting up, upright, in a peat compost. Keep the pot in a temperature of about 25 °C (75 °F) to hasten flowering. The plant is unsatisfactory in the warmer and humid zones, but even there it may be grown as a pot plant and kept in the shade.

LUNGWORT

Pulmonaria officinalis (Boraginaceae) P

Lungwort has a fortifying action on the respiratory system, soothing coughs, sore throats and congested tracts, and because of its additional virtue of promoting perspiration, is administered during influenza.

Indigenous to the shaded woodlands of Europe, lungwort has been known in gardens in England for centuries. The flowers resemble those of the cowslip in shade but are pink, mauve or blue according to the stage of development; the pink flowers turn blue after pollination, so intermediate shades can always be found. The vernacular 'cowslip' suggests the American native *Mertensia virginica*, abundant in the mid-west, also known as smooth lungwort and closely allied to the true lungworts. Another colloquial name for *P. officinalis* is spotted bugloss. It has a cucumber-like flavour and was used as a pot herb.

Flowering stems are hairy and grow to a height of 20-30 cms (9-12 ins) and are among the earliest herbs to flower in the spring. The leaves are oval, hairy, rough and spotted.

CULTIVATION Choose a lightly shaded spot with moist, well drained soil. Lungwort displays a slight preference for chalk. Propagation is by spring-sown seed, thinning the seedlings before autumn (fall), or by division of the roots in autumn (fall).

MILKWORT

Polygala species (Polygalaceae) B

Plants of this genus were named *Polygala* (meaning 'much milk' in Greek) because feeding cows on it is supposed to increase the flow of milk. Numerous species are sparsely distributed on dry banks, heathland and grassy pastures.

The plant cultivated in English herb gardens is *P. vulgaris* and rarely *P. amara*. In American herb gardens it is usually *P. senega*, indigenous to that continent and choosing drier rocky positions than its European counterparts.

The latter specific name commemorates the Seneca Indians who stored the root to treat rattlesnake bites. A Scottish doctor living in Pennsylvania in the 1730s recognized the snake bite symptoms as being very similar to pleurisy and pneumonia, experimented successfully, and introduced *P. senega* into England as an officinal plant in 1739. (Several other species have been cultivated in herb gardens and imported as dried root, indistinguishable from *senega*.)

A really pretty little plant that forms colonies, milkwort is admirably suited to the front of the border in a decorative herb garden. From late spring to mid summer dainty deep blue flowers (white in *P. senega*) dance above the basal foliage rosette. 'Dance' is an accurate description as they resemble tiny elaborately winged insects hovering not more than 5-30 cms (2-12 ins) above the ground-hugging leaves. Roots are small, knotted, often twisted and grey; these are harvested for use in general tonics. The bitter principle relieves chest congestion and acts as a mild laxative. (The supposed influence on lactation in nursing mothers is doubtful.)

CULTIVATION Alkaline soils where the drainage is good suit the milkworts best. The only way to propagate them is from root division of an established plant — unless a source of seed can be traced. (It is not readily available.) A decorative little plant, well worth tracking down to include in the herb garden.

MONKSHOOD/ACONITE

Aconitum napellus (Ranunculaceae) P

A highly poisonous plant indigenous to mountainous regions throughout northern temperate zones, monkshood has been cultivated as a healing plant for centuries. According to botanists it is strictly speaking a subspecies of *A. anglicum*. *Aconitum* species provided a poison used for tipping arrows and baiting wolves in medieval Europe, thus earning them the name of 'Wolf's Bane'. Later it became known as monkshood or helmet flower in recognition of its hooded flower. Winthrop's seed order from America in 1631 calls it 'munkhoods'.

A stately garden perennial reaching a height of 60 cms (2 ft) with distinctive deep green firm leaves held fairly horizontal and deeply divided. Deep rich blue flowers bloom in mid summer. Among the garden cultivars worth growing for herb garden decoration are 'Newry Blue' and 'Bressingham Spire'; both reach a height of 90 cms (3ft). The specific name *napellus* means 'little turnip' and describes the shape of the root tuber. Each root lasts only a year; a daughter formed alongside the parent tuber maintains the plant. All parts of the plant are used; the top growth is collected in summer and the root in autumn (fall).

Its toxicity demands that it be prescribed only under medical supervision. Homeopathic preparations are used in the treatment of sciatica and neuralgia as the drug acts upon the central nervous system.

CULTIVATION Sow the seed as soon as it is ripe, but do not expect spectacular results as the plants are slow to establish from seed. Separating a daughter tuber and planting it out in the autumn (fall) will be quicker and probably more successful. Planting can be carried out quite late into the winter, but it must be done before the stem bud bursts into growth — and this happens very early in the spring. Select a well-worked moisture-retentive soil somewhere where there is dappled shade. Monkshood prefers the less humid zones and is winter hardy, but it may need crown protection in low temperature areas.

Opium poppy

Papaver somniferum (Papaveraceae) A

Opium is a dangerous and addictive poison but it remains unsurpassed as a sedative administered for the relief of pain — a consequence of its two important alkaloids, morphine and codeine. Opium was a medicine known to the Greeks and Romans and the Egyptians before them, and the cultivation of the poppy spread to China more than 1,000 years ago.

The flowers vary considerably in appearance; they are sometimes double, sometimes single with flimsy mauve petals — occasionally white or pink. When the buds open the petals are like crumpled tissue paper balls, which very quickly unfold; this is a feature of the plant. Handsome in its stance, the plant attains perhaps 1 m (3¼ ft) in height, the blue-green-grey leaves sitting directly on the stem and held away from it, with jagged wavy margins.

Once the petals fall the seed head matures into the familiar smooth brown 'poppy head' with its lid of radiating ribs and little holes round the top through which the seeds escape. Opium is a form of latex which oozes out of the unripe seed heads when they are slit. Unripe poppy heads used to be infused to bathe swollen and sprained joints, and a fermentation made with hot barley meal as a binding agent was used in similar instances to relieve pain.

There are many types of poppy seed; the blue-grey tiny rounded ones are used in Europe and America to decorate and flavour bread and confectionery, and the smaller creamy ones are habitually used in India to thicken curries. Poppy seed oil, although a culinary oil (olivette), is commonly prepared for the industrial market and in the mixing of paints.

A native of the Middle East and the Mediterranean countries, the mauve flowers are a roadside feature of some southern counties of England. Poppies were taken as seed to America and appear in the 1631 order from John Winthrop Jr as 'popey seed'.

CULTIVATION Propagate from seed sown afresh each spring, although once introduced into the herb garden the plants will seed themselves. Lovers of sunshine, light warm soils and tolerant of chalk, the opium poppy ought to be in every representative collection of medicinal herbs.

R U E

Ruta graveolens (Rutaceae) P

This well-known member of the herb border, highly regarded in old country medicine all over Europe, is a native of the dusty soils of the Mediterranean regions. The Romans reputedly introduced it into Britain first, although it was probably reintroduced in the Middle Ages. It went to the New World with the European settlers, where it is now naturalized in some southern states on low quality soils. Herb of Grace, was one of its old names, and Parkinson explained it thus: 'The many good properties whereunto Rue serveth hath I think in former times caused the English name of Herbe of Grace to be given unto it'. Holy water was sprinkled as a preliminary to the celebration of High Mass in the medieval Church from switches made of rue twigs. Its reputation for repelling infection and poison made it customary for sprigs of rue to be placed near the judge before prisoners were brought from the pestilence-ridden gaols.

Just why it was held in such high esteem is difficult to assess; today its bitter flavour — dispersed by pulverizing or chopping — can be added, with discretion, to egg, fish or cream cheese dishes. In European wine-growing areas rue leaves are added to brandy to make a liqueur. The rather sombre little bushes were also thought to form an unfailing defence against witches and to grant a sixth sense. Renaissance painters in Europe are reputed to have consumed large quantities of rue tea to restore failing eyesight.

Rue is a dainty bushy plant 45-90 cms (1½-3 ft) in height with blue-green ferny leaves and greenish yellow spoon-shaped flowers during the summer. The entire plant emits a somewhat harsh aroma and has an equally harsh taste as a result of the volatile oil contained in the glands which are distributed over the whole plant. Medicinally rue is toxic in high doses and should be used with prudence, especially during pregnancy, as it has an ancient reputation for starting delayed periods. It is also used to treat bites and stings externally and, as a cold compress applied to the temples, it is said to relieve nervous headaches.

CULTIVATION Raised from seed sown in spring and thinned out to about 50 cms (1½ ft) apart, rue can make a good herb garden hedge and its evergreen nature lends itself to this use. Cuttings taken in summer will strike quite easily. Rue revels in a well drained soil and loves a sunny sheltered site. It benefits from being cut back in the spring to encourage new fresh growth.

S OLOMON ' S SEAL

Polygonatum multiflorum (Liliaceae) P

The hybrid *P. multiflorum* × *odoratum* is probably the most common representative of the genus in gardens, although *multiflorum* is the true officinal plant and is a native of Europe.

Solomon's seal was traditionally cultivated for its creeping rootstock which provided a tonic and astringent; the powdered root was applied to bruises and tumorous haemorrhoids to relieve pain. As an application for black eyes it was known to the battered wives of the fifteenth and sixteenth centuries, for Gerard wrote, 'The roots of Solomon's seal, stamped while fresh and greene and applied taketh away in one night or two at the most, any bruise blacke or blew spots gotten by fals or womens' wilfulness in stimbling upin their hastie husband's fists, or such like'. Gerard thought that for the knitting of broken bones 'there is not another herb to be found comparable to it'.

The plant has for centuries been employed as a cosmetic to clear freckles and as a skin tonic. In Turkey the young shoots, which are folded spikes of green, are harvested and cooked with asparagus.

Solomon's seal is a truly memorable plant. It has a fabulous aura with its pale green stems stretching up to a height of 60 cms (2 ft) arching over gracefully at the top. Large oval leaves alternate along the top half like wings above the dangling waxy white bell flowers.

CULTIVATION Given a well-worked, light and moisture-retentive soil where there is a little shade, Solomon's seal will soon establish sizeable colonies. An occasional top dressing of leaf mould is beneficial. The plants are best divided just after the stalks die down in the autumn (fall), although in dampish weather transplanting and division can be undertaken at any time of the year. Seed, when available, should be sown as soon as it is ripe in the late summer or early autumn (fall).

VALERIAN

Valeriana officinalis (Valerianaceae) P

Valerian is a native of the temperate zones of Europe and Asia, and is pretty indifferent to the soil and situation it selects. It is often found in dampish valleys and on dry stony elevated pastures. A plant for the back of the herb border, the flower stems reach a height of 1.5 m (5 ft) with pretty dark ferny leaves at the base and clustered heads of pink (and occasionally white) flowers in the summer. Roots are lifted in the second and third year in the autumn and are thick and clustered. After washing they need to be 'combed' before drying in the shade.

Valerian was formerly cultivated for its root, and was introduced into America in the eighteenth century. It was cultivated extensively in eastern Europe, the Netherlands and in America in New Hampshire, Vermont and New York. When grown for its root, the flowering stems are removed to encourage development of the rhizome. The ancient name was phu (or phew); a name that reflected the bad-smelling newly lifted root. It is reputed to be the charm the Pied Piper of Hamelin used to lead the rats away.

Valerian is administered as a painkiller and nervine, and is especially useful in calming nervous disorders and in treating insomnia.

CULTIVATION Propagation is by division of roots or stolons in autumn (fall) or spring. In the herb garden, plant it in a good moisture-retentive soil to obtain lush decorative plants. In America, where seed sets readily, seed can be sown in spring by just pressing it into the ground. Most gardeners buy their first plant, then depend upon the seed for a continued crop.

Witch Hazel

Hamamelis virginiana (Hamamelidaceae) P

The witch hazel from the woodlands of eastern America has much in common in appearance with the European hazel. Various explanations are proffered as to why the settlers called this shrub witch hazel. Perhaps the most acceptable is that they used the twigs for water divining in much the same manner in which they had used hazel at home — commonly called 'witching a well'. But they soon learned of its invaluable quality as an astringent, its ability to check bleeding, and as a treatment for bruises and bumps. The American Indians had used the bark to make an infusion to apply to sore eyes. Today, witch hazel remains a household remedy, as an extract that can be bought from pharmacies for use as a skin tonic and as an ointment to soothe sprains and bruises.

However, unlike those of the European hazel the seeds of the American plant are ejected with enough force to bombard passers-by, and this puckish quirk has gained it the name of snapping hazelnut. Witch hazel is a shrub which grows to a height of 3-3.6 m (10-12 ft). The leaves are more heavily veined than those of the European hazel, and once they have fallen in autumn the flowers appear on the bare wood within a month. These flowers are lovely little fluffy clusters of yellow which on inspection turn out to be bundles of tiny strap-shaped petals with a very faint scent. Seed ripens the following summer, the nuts containing two black seeds, oily and edible. Seed does not set in England.

Both leaves and bark have the astringent property for which the plant is renowned. In England the old nineteenth century Pond's Extract depended upon witch hazel for its effectiveness as a household panacea used in cases of burns and bruises.

CULTIVATION A shrub that makes a very welcome addition to the herb garden in areas free from early frosts, where it can be enjoyed unspoilt. However, the attractive foliage and curious strap-shaped petals will withstand the severest autumn (fall) quite well. Propagation is by cuttings taken in spring.

Pot Pourri

UTHORS of the early herbals expressed a widespread belief in the power of flower and leaf scents to alleviate all manner of ills of the flesh and spirit, and as unfailing protection against infections. Scented conceits such as *pot pourri* probably originated in England in Tudor times. Wands of aromatic plants were strewn on floors to absorb rubbish, alleviate strong smells and discourage vermin; it was merely a refinement to harbour together the sweet-smelling flowers and leaves of summer in jars or pouncet boxes (small containers with a perforated lid) or even open bowls.

Pot pourri translated literally from the French means 'rotten pot' because in the early days of *pot pourri* the mixtures were kept moist and the flowers virtually pickled. Brandy or some other spirit provided and maintained the moisture. Such a richly aromatic preserve was usually kept in closed containers, opened only infrequently when a room was to be perfumed.

Dry *pot pourri* is more popular today and is far less arduous to prepare, less rich in aroma and, naturally, not so long lasting. Essentially, *pot pourri* is a homogeneous mixture of dried aromatic leaves, scented flower petals with spices and perhaps a fragrant oil and some fixative to retain the scent. A captive mixture can be controlled to suit individual preference — herby, flowery, spicy or aromatic.

Scented powders in sachets, dried aromatic leaves or little bunches of scented plants were hung in cupboards or laid among clothes in chests to keep them fresh. Aromatic sprigs were burned on fires or in special censers, usually of bronze or copper, to set scented smoke pervading the room.

When the European colonists arrived in America they soon found that the berries of the wax myrtle, sweet gale or bayberry provided a fragrant wax which could be collected and burned to give a delicious aroma. Scented candles and wood chips are traditionally associated with religion, but the practice of scenting houses in this way goes back to classical times.

BERGAMOT

Monarda didyma (Labiatae) P

A handsome plant indigenous to South America and the eastern parts of America from New York to West Virginia, bergamot is an inhabitant of swampy stream borders in hilly areas. It was introduced into Britain around 1745 and is now well established as a decorative garden perennial, and is the parent of many cultivars.

The plant is quick to grow and forms clumps with numerous stolons. The flower stems grow to a height of 50-90 cms (1½-3 ft) and flower for many weeks from mid summer onwards. The entire plant is impregnated with a delightful fragrance even when the top growth has died down, and the roots remain sweetly aromatic with a suggestion of orange. This is why it has gained its name of bergamot, reminiscent of bergamot orange. The aromatic leaves dry well and retain their aroma so they may be included in *pot pourri*.

A tisane made from the leaves used to be drunk by the Oswego Indians — hence the country name Oswego tea. This infusion is recommended as a digestive and is helpful in treating cases of irregular and painful menstruation.

The flowers are a flamboyant red and are born in heads with red bracts between each floret, the whole resembling a sparkler firework. Reliable cultivars are available with pink, mauve and white flowers, all of which retain the aromatic attributes which make them extremely useful in the decorative herb garden — they all attract bees! The flowers make a decorative addition to fruit cups, but should be floated in water first to wash out the earwigs that love to hide in the little tubular florets.

The genus *Monarda* commemorates Nicholas Monardes, a doctor from Seville, who in 1569 wrote his reputable account of the economic plants, including medicinal, that he found in the New World. *Monarda fistulosa*, wild bergamot, was the first of the genus to reach England in 1637.

CULTIVATION Bergamot is best suited to moist soil, or any good garden soil to which moisture-retentive material has been added, and it loves to sunbathe. It is quite adaptable to a shaded position provided its feet remain damp. Chalky soils do not suit it at all well and it dislikes humid winters because its annual growth cycle is hindered.

A piece pulled from the outer edges of an established clump in spring will soon establish itself, and cuttings may be taken at the same time. The clumps form a mat-like growth and tend to become bare in the middle, so they need to be broken up and divided every three or four years.

CALAMINTHA

Calamintha nepetoides (Labiatae) P

The calamintha often found in herb gardens is *C. nepetoides*, although the true herb is *C. ascendens* — a European native, formerly the officinal plant, and at that time called *C. officinalis*. Both plants seem to have been used in the past without distinction.

A small, erect, bushy little plant 30-60 cms (1-2 ft) in height, calamintha has tiny, whitish mauve flowers in summer. Grown for its aromatic foliage reminiscent of the scent of thyme with pennyroyal overtones, it was mainly employed to relieve flatulence. The volatile oil, rather minty in flavour, enhances a tisane brewed from the dried leaves and which Gerard considered to take away 'sorrowfulness which cometh with melancholie, and maketh a man merrie and glad'. Culpeper described it as having a fierce and quick scent and called it mountain mint and, as usual, recommended its use for a wide variety of complaints ranging from shortness of breath, cramp, liver and spleen trouble, combined with salt to clear worms and as a contraceptive.

CULTIVATION Division of plants in spring, cuttings in spring and seed are all ways to start this little old-fashioned plant in the herb garden. Choose a dryish alkaline soil for the best results.

IRIS

Iris pseudacorus (Iridaceae) P

Two or three native European irises have been used in medicine, the best known, the yellow flag iris, is British and was the variety taken to America by the early settlers. In America this plant is called blue flag, the flowers being violet blue and variegated with yellow, and the flower stems attaining 60-90 cms (2-3 ft) in height. Iris has long been cultivated in America for its roots which are used to treat bumps and bruises, and as iridin (or irisin) for its action on the liver and bowels.

The true yellow flag bears small, elegant, golden yellow flowers in summer, and is a fairly common plant of waterway borders and marshy ground in Britain. Flowering stems and sword-like leaves reach a height of 60-150 cms (2-5 ft) and the plants can form extensive colonies. Universally known as *fleur de luce* or *fleur de lys* it was the heraldic emblem of the kings of France and legends abound on that score. The specific name *pseudacorus* acknowledges its resemblance when not in flower to the sweet sedge or sweet flag, *Acorus calamus*. However, the foliage and roots of iris are odourless whereas sweet sedge is aromatic.

The powdered root is an ingredient of snuff, and when sliced can provide a cure for toothache. Culpeper extolled its use, when distilled, as a remedy for weak and tired eyes and maintained that an ointment made from the flowers was good for treating ulcers or even syphilitic sores. The flowers produce a good yellow dye and the roots, with the addition of an iron mordant, produce a black dye.

CULTIVATION Yellow flag can only be grown successfully as a water plant. In the decorative herb garden it needs a boggy area where it can accompany water mints, sweet sedge, watercress, bogbean or brooklime. Settle the rhizomes into the borders of a muddy pool and, if necessary, tie some rhizomes together in a string or wire bag which can be weighted to prevent the clumps from floating away.

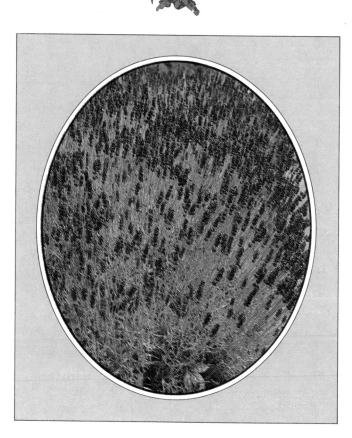

LAVENDER

Lavandula species (Labiatae) P

The best oil of lavender is obtained from *L. angustifolia*, which botanists recently seem to have included under the blanket name of *L. spica*. Gerard called it 'spike' which should settle the question because the old herbalists knew that spike lavender was the best one to grow. (Alternative names — and authorities differ — are *L. vera* and *L. officinalis*.)

For centuries the effectiveness of its clean sharp scent has been used to alleviate 'a light migram' as Gerard said, or for the falling sickness or giddiness of the brain according to Culpeper. Long before the world of manufactured deodorants and bath salts the Romans used lavender in their bath water; the name derives from the Latin *lavare*, to wash.

Lavender is one of the most popular plants in today's herb gardens and is particularly useful in borders to pathways, edges, internal hedges and on top of dry walls. Furthermore, it can be cultivated in large containers. Small grey abundant leaves, evergreen in Europe and England, form a rounded bush 90-180 cms (3-6 ft) high, and sometimes more in spread, which is punctuated with stiff-stemmed lavender-blue flower heads. The whole plant resembles a large pincushion. In America lavender is not regarded as a hardy evergreen because of the low winter temperatures, but if grown in containers in yards and tucked up for the winter its summer fragrance can be enjoyed.

Lavender is not really considered to be a culinary herb, but the odd leaf may be added to rich game stews. The flowers can be crystallized to decorate desserts and confectionery. Its most enduring quality is its perfume, and it is a marvellous *pot pourri* ingredient.

CULTIVATION Propagate from cuttings of strong new growth in summer or autumn (fall), and once rooted plant them out in a well drained rather poor soil. The bushes tend to look after themselves and respond to an annual haircut in autumn after flowering or in early spring. Bushes tend to straggle as they mature and it is often necessary to cut back severely in autumn (fall) to generate a strong growth the following spring. It is wise to maintain a supply of young plants.

ROSE

Rosa gallica officinalis (Rosaceae) P

Numerous mythological and romantic associations have surrounded the rose through the centuries and belief in its unfailing powers led to its uses in medicine and sweet-smelling confections.

Rosa gallica officinalis is the apothecary's rose, known somewhat misleadingly in England as the damask rose because it was brought back to Europe by the crusaders from Damascus. In America is is called the French rose, or rose of Provins. Because the dried petals hold their fragrance it has been widely used in the manufacture of various perfumes — especially in the area of the town of Provins, south of Paris, during the sixteenth, seventeenth and eighteenth centuries.

The plant is a bush some 60-120 cms (2-4 ft) in height, thick and spreading, and a good plant for an informal hedge around the herb garden. The leaves are a good dark green, composed of five leaflets, and the stiff bristly stems are virtually thornless. The petals are bright red with a golden cluster of anthers at the open centre.

In the past, rose honey, lozenges, rose scented snuff and rose scented candles, rose scented wine, rose vinegar and rose sauce were all widely available. Fresh or dried petals can be scattered on salads and desserts or floated in drinks and the hips can be gently boiled until soft, strained, and the liquid used as a tisane.

In perfumery, because the petals retain so strong a scent on drying, they were invaluable for sweet waters and sweet bags and they are the predominant ingredient of *pot pourri*.

CULTIVATION Roses love the sunshine and need some moisture at the roots. Basic cultivation is the same for all roses, although the complicated pruning routine associated with modern roses does not have to be followed for the apothecary's rose. Merely remove dead and old branches; if too much pruning is undertaken the energy of the plant will be directed into making growth rather than producing flowers.

In America this rose will thrive in all but the very northerly regions, and likes some winter cold in order to have its winter rest. Many gardeners consider its cultivation impractical, and it is certainly not for the southern and western seaboard states. (There the Cherokee rose, *R. laevigata* is a carefree grower.)

Choose good garden loam, and prepare the soil well before planting in the autumn (fall) or spring. It is advisable to buy small plants as propagation from cuttings can be a rather slow process. In areas where the winter temperature falls below − 12°C (10°F) bushes planted in autumn (fall) should be covered during their first winter with a protective mulch (which can be removed the following spring).

WORMWOOD

Artemisia absinthium (Compositae) P

A native of Europe including Britain, wormwood is one if the most magical plants of the herb garden. It has been introduced into America as a cultivated plant and is now naturalized in places.

Wormwood is primarily a flavouring for liqueurs and aperitifs — such as absinth and vermouth — because it has a unique fragrance. The pale green deeply cut leaves (which are silvery when young) provide a highly decorative foil in the herb garden. It is a little woody-based bush which glistens in the dew and rain. Rounded bushes grow up to 90-120 cms (3-4 ft) tall and produce green-yellow flowers in summer. The leaves are sweetest in aroma when gathered early in the summer.

In spacious herb gardens a splendid effect can be achieved by grouping several bushes together. It can be grown in containers and, where winter cold poses problems, taken into shelter during the winter. Add youngish leaves to *pot pourri* and herb sachets, and scatter dried sprigs in drawers and cupboards to keep the air fresh. The essential oil of wormwood is produced from this plant in both France and America.

CULTIVATION Propagate from summer cuttings or from seed sown as soon as it is ripe, and protect through the winter. Both dappled shade or full sunshine are suitable for wormwood, but bushes do appreciate some shelter from strong winds.

THE OFFICIAL

National Hockey League

STANLEY CUP

Centennial Book

THE OFFICIAL

National Hockey League
STANLEY CUP
Centennial Book

STANLEY CUP · 1893-1993

NHL

EDITED BY DAN DIAMOND

M&S

Canadian Cataloguing in Publication Data

Main entry under title:
The Official National Hockey League Stanley Cup centennial book

Includes index.
ISBN 0-7710-2803-2

1. Stanley Cup (Hockey)–History.   2. National Hockey League–History.
I. Diamond, Dan.

GV847.7.044 1992   796.962´648   C92-095045-0

Editor: Dan Diamond
Photo Editor: Ralph Dinger
Sidebars and Captions: James Duplacey
Additional Research: Ron Boileau (PCHA/WCHL/WHL), Al Kowalenko
Main Text: Bob Hesketh, Jack Sullivan, James Duplacey, Dan Diamond
Index: Janet Goodfellow
Coordinating Editor: Pat Kennedy for McClelland & Stewart
Design: Kong Njo

Printed and bound in the United States of America on acid-free paper.

McClelland & Stewart Inc.
The Canadian Publishers
481 University Avenue
Toronto, Ontario
M5G 2E9

For everyone whose dreams
are inscribed on the Cup

Contents

A Message
from the President

For athletes, all efforts focus on becoming a champion. For the men who skate in the National Hockey League, there is no greater accomplishment than winning the Stanley Cup, which, for one hundred years, has stood at the pinnacle of hockey excellence. Nothing in professional sports matches the feeling of holding the trophy aloft as a member of a Cup-winning team.

In fact, in the century since its first presentation, the Stanley Cup has become the most recognizable trophy in all of sports – a clear and immediate symbol of accomplishment that combines the past and the present. Look inside the bowl and you'll find the names of the 1907 Cup-champion Kenora Thistles. Or see Lester Patrick's name inscribed as part of the Cup-winning Montreal Wanderers in 1906 – and then read his grandson Craig's name inscribed twice as the general manager of the Cup-winning Pittsburgh Penguins of 1991 and 1992.

This is the magic of the Stanley Cup, the ability to bring together the game's great names and golden eras. The winners literally hold history in their hands.

I am honored to open this fine book, and join with you in celebrating the centennial of the Stanley Cup.

Gil Stein,
President,
National Hockey League

Introduction

by Milt Dunnell

I have, for some time, been thinking it would be a good thing if there were a challenge cup, which should be held, from year to year, by the champion hockey club of the Dominion. There does not appear to be any such outward and visible sign of a championship at present, and considering the interest the hockey matches now elicit and the importance of having the games fairly played under generally recognized rules, I am willing to give a cup that shall be annually held by the winning club.

– Excerpt from a letter by Lord Stanley, sixth Governor General of Canada to his aide, Lord Kilcoursie, and read at a dinner of the Ottawa Athletic Association, March 18, 1892.

YOUR LORDSHIPS, YOU HAVE NO IDEA OF WHAT YOU STARTED. GRANTED, you were somewhat aware of obvious dedication to the game of hockey in the frosty regions of the continent. Your hockey club, The Rebels, made up of sons and staff members and playing out of Government House, undoubtedly interrupted many debates on affairs of state to remind you of certain other issues that had to be settled on the rink.

Making allowance for all of that, you would have been absolutely astounded to discover that the modest rose bowl that Lord Stanley acquired upon payment of ten guineas ($48.67 Canadian) grew, not only in stature but in recognition as well, into the oldest and certainly one of the most coveted trophies for which professional athletes compete.

During the century since its presentation, it has become more than a symbol of athletic excellence and hockey supremacy. The playoffs to determine the Stanley Cup champion have become as much a rite of spring as the arrival of the robin or the swallow.

It took the first league-wide players' strike in the seventy-five-year history of the National Hockey League to make the public really aware of how much the Stanley Cup playoffs mean.

Players and owners alike agreed the games had to take place. Failure to play for the Stanley Cup would be a betrayal of those hardy Yukon gold miners who in 1905 came four thousand miles, by dog team, steamship, and

Opposite: Since 1893, Stanley Cup winners have had their names engraved on this much-recognized and much-modified trophy.

Chicago's Dirk Graham slips the puck past Pittsburgh goaltender Tom Barrasso to score the third goal of the 1992 finals. The Penguins scored four unanswered goals to erase a 4–1 Blackhawk lead and capture the series opener, 5–4.

rail, to challenge the Ottawa Silver Seven for a cup that already had become recognized as the biggest prize in hockey.

Not to play for the Stanley Cup would be to dishonor the memory of one-eyed Frank McGee, the Silver Seven's fabled star, who was ridiculed by the Yukon players after the first game of that famous two-game set because he had failed to live up to their expectations. McGee heard of the jibes. He scored fourteen goals in the second game, which the Silver Seven won by a score of 23–2. McGee was thirty-four when he was killed at the Somme in one of World War I's bloodiest battles.

Thousands of stories have been written about the Stanley Cup, without ever fully explaining the mystique that surrounds it. Clarence Campbell, the National Hockey League's third president, was a Rhodes Scholar. He may have come closest to understanding its appeal to the millions who eagerly await the playoffs each spring. Campbell referred to the sixty minutes of sustained speed and action that the modern game provides as the great motivating force that had caused the sport to overflow Canada's borders and be received with equal enthusiasm in the United States and Europe.

He didn't get around to discussing the passions aroused when the Stanley Cup is up for grabs, such as on that long-ago day in 1907, when the Kenora Thistles were enraged because the Montreal Wanderers, who were challenging for the Stanley Cup, had protested the addition of Alf Smith and Harry Westwick, both Ottawa Silver Seven stars, to the Thistles' roster.

The argument became so heated that a Thistles partisan tucked the Cup under his arm and headed for the town dock. He was going to throw the trophy into Lake of the Woods. Fortunately, he was intercepted. The squabble was settled, and the games were played in Winnipeg, with the Wanderers winning.

The truth is that the Stanley Cup has not always enjoyed the dignity that surrounds it today – dignity that befits its status as the premier prize in a sport that is rapidly gaining world-wide acceptance.

In 1904, officials from several senior leagues who were dissatisfied with the method in which Cup challenges were set up proposed replacing the Stanley Cup with a new trophy. In 1908, one Toronto newspaper said that the fifteen-year-old Cup was "a detriment to real sport."

Muzz Patrick, at that time general manager of the New York Rangers, once recalled how he and his brother, Lynn, had come across the Stanley Cup in the basement of their home in Victoria, British Columbia. Their father, Lester, was manager and coach of the Victoria Cougars, who had won it in 1925.

Being a couple of ambitious kids, they decided to be immortalized on the Cup. Using a nail, they etched their initials into it. Little did they know that official recognition was coming in the future: both their names were properly inscribed on the trophy, as members of the 1939-40 Stanley Cup-winning New York Rangers.

Then, there was the story that Léo Dandurand, a partner in ownership of the Montreal Canadiens, loved to tell about a night in 1924, when the Cup actually was abandoned. The Habs had been honored by the University of Montreal, where the Cup was on display, and Dandurand liked to point out that the Canadiens were the only professional team ever honored by the school, up to that time. With the dinner and the speeches out of the way, Georges Vezina, Sprague Cleghorn, and Sylvio Mantha decided they should proceed to Léo's house and drink some champagne from the Cup, so they all piled into Léo's Model T Ford, and Cleghorn, one of the toughest guys on skates, cradled the Stanley Cup as lovingly as if it were a baby.

Going up the Côte St. Antoine Road hill in Westmount, the car began to complain about its overload. Everyone except Léo, who was driving, got out to push. Cleghorn placed the Stanley Cup carefully on the curb, to lend his muscle. Then, having conquered the hill, they all climbed back into the car and proceeded to Léo's house. After providing an appropriate snack, Léo's wife finally asked, "Where's the Cup?" Léo and Cleghorn rushed back to the hill. There was the Cup, right where Cleghorn had left it.

Although he never actually witnessed a game for his Cup, Lord Stanley must have felt satisfaction over the passions that accompanied competition for his trophy. He would have particularly enjoyed a game that was played in 1904, between the Winnipeg Rowing Club and Ottawa, in the Aberdeen Pavilion on Ottawa's Exhibition Grounds. The pavilion, a makeshift rink, was used because of a rental dispute over the regular facility. The

The names of eight members of the Hockey Hall of Fame are inscribed on the Stanley Cup as members of the 1939-40 New York Rangers.

temperature was 20 below – and we're not talking about Celsius – but 2,500 spectators were crammed into the temporary quarters. Suddenly, there was an alarm. The city's post office was ablaze. Scarcely a soul left the pavilion.

Looking back, it is apparent that the history of Stanley Cup competition parallels the growth of the sport itself. First awarded in 1893, the trophy began its life at a time when an organized schedule of games was considered to be a progressive innovation in hockey. Any club could challenge for the trophy. Competition was controlled by two trustees who had been appointed by Lord Stanley to determine which challengers were deemed to be worthy opponents for the Cup holder.

In 1910, the National Hockey Association, forerunner to the National Hockey League, took over control of the Stanley Cup. The NHA champion accepted Cup challenges issued by the champions of other leagues. From 1914 through 1916, the NHA's top club met the champion of the western-based Pacific Coast Hockey Association to determine a Stanley Cup winner. With the formation of the National Hockey League in 1917, the NHL's champions played off with the western titleholders for the Stanley Cup each year until 1926.

Beginning in 1926-27, when top players from western teams were sold to newly established NHL franchises located in the northeastern United States, competition for the trophy has taken place exclusively within the NHL, and the NHL's playoff champion has been awarded the Stanley Cup each year. No club outside the NHL has played for the Stanley Cup since the Victoria Cougars were defeated by the Montreal Maroons in 1926.

Since the NHL made the Stanley Cup the grail of its orchestrated program in 1926, remarkable happenings have continued to occur en route to the crowning of a new Stanley Cup champion each spring. The 1950-51 semi-final between the Toronto Maple Leafs and the Boston Bruins provided one such event.

These teams were so evenly matched that further overtime, in a Saturday-night game, carried them into Toronto's Sunday curfew. Rather than risk prosecution, the teams abandoned the match, leaving a one-all draw, a rarity in Stanley Cup competition.

Game four of the 1988 finals was suspended as well when a power failure blacked out Boston Garden with the Bruins and Oilers tied 3–3 late in the second period.

More memorable is the legend of Lester Patrick, the forty-four-year-old silver-thatched coach of the New York Rangers, donning the goal pads after New York goalie Lorne Chabot was injured early in the second period of a game with the Montreal Maroons. The clubs carried only one goalie in those days, and the Maroons refused to permit the use of either of two goaltenders who happened to be in the stands. The Rangers won the game with Lester in goal, adding another footnote to one of the most illustrious careers in sports history.

It takes nothing away from the teams that defended or challenged in the early years to say that the greatest teams ever to wear skates have been seen in Stanley Cup tournaments under NHL jurisdiction. Don't try to rate these superb squads unless you're prepared for heated debate. But mention them? Yes.

Dynasties in any professional sport are becoming less likely because of increasing free agency and escalating salaries. So remember in awe the Montreal Canadiens crew, which Toe Blake coached to the Stanley Cup in five successive seasons, starting in 1955-56.

That hadn't been done before, and may not be done again, but give Scotty Bowman, Glen Sather, and Al Arbour credit for trying. Bowman coached a later version of the Canadiens to four consecutive Stanley Cup championships, beginning in 1976. Arbour's New York Islanders matched this feat with four Cups of their own, beginning in 1979-80. Sather, as general manager and coach or club president and general manager, put together an Edmonton Oilers club that was a dominant force, winning the Stanley Cup five times in seven years, beginning with a first victory in 1984. Hockey teams don't come much better than this one.

Detroit partisans are likely to inquire whether the early 1950s have faded from memory. The Red Wings of 1951-52 came close to perfection – as close as any team is ever likely to get in the heat of Stanley Cup competition. There were only six clubs in the NHL then, and the Red Wings won His Lordship's Cup in the minimum number of eight games. And get this: goalie Terry Sawchuk didn't allow a single goal on home ice. In fact, he allowed a total of only five goals in the playoffs.

Could that happen again? Not likely. But stay tuned. The unlikely and the unusual are what one should expect in Stanley Cup competition.

With so much color and drama in its past, one is inclined to speculate whether the Stanley Cup's future will ever be able to rival its glorious history. Try this: the biggest story in Stanley Cup hockey might still be in the dressing-room lacing up its skates.

How about a Stanley Cup final between Montreal and Moscow or Prague versus Philadelphia or Dusseldorf versus Detroit? Pure fantasy, you might say. Back there, on that night in 1892, Lord Kilcoursie would have said, "My good fellow, you must get more rest," if one had predicted that Lord Stanley's rose bowl would one day wind up in Boston, New York, Chicago, Detroit, Philadelphia, or Pittsburgh. And don't forget Kenora and Seattle.

So don't go away. The first hundred years have been wonderful, but the best hundred years could be coming up.

Defensive hockey was at its peak when Terry Sawchuk and the Red Wings' blueliners allowed just 0.63 goals-against per game in the 1952 playoffs.

The Beginning,

1893-1910

MEN HAVE GONE BROKE IN THE MAD SCRAMBLE TO GAIN TEMPORARY possession of the challenge cup donated in 1892 by the Earl of Derby, Lord Stanley of Preston, one of a long line of governors general of Canada who showed more than a passing interest in the sport.

Men with millions and a whim have spent fortunes in glittering bids to gain the squat, punch-bowl-shaped Stanley Cup. Some reached their goal. Others gave up the chase and turned to other mundane pursuits, such as making more money to pay for their folly.

The Cup, now perched atop a glistening 35 $\frac{1}{4}$-inch (90-centimeter) column of silver bands, has had a glamorous and storied career. It antedates tennis's Davis Cup by some seven years, and the long-forgotten Temple Cup, baseball's World Series emblem, by one.

Lord Stanley, who left Canada for his native England before the Cup was first won in 1893, couldn't have foreseen the intensity and heroism that the pursuit of his trophy would evoke. When Lord Stanley first spoke of a Dominion Challenge Cup to be awarded to the best hockey club in Canada, teams were strictly amateur. Gradually the players who filled the rinks decided that they should share in the profits, and, by the first years of the new century, many players were paid to play hockey.

Through the 1890s and as late as 1910, teams presumed to be purely amateur actually had anywhere from one to four professionals in their line-ups. No one was unduly alarmed by this, and each year's champion of the Amateur Hockey Association of Canada, complete with "shamateur" players, automatically inherited the Cup and with it the responsibility to defend the trophy against all comers.

Champions of recognized senior leagues in other parts of Canada could – and frequently did – challenge the AHA champion for the trophy. Challengers from leagues in Western Canada, the Maritimes, and Ontario often took on

Opposite: The brand-new Stanley Cup already shows evidence of extra silversmithing around its collar. Its is dwarfed by the Amateur Hockey Association of Canada's Senior Championship Trophy that stands behind it in this photo of the first Stanley Cup champions, the Montreal AAA of 1893. From left to right, seated: J. Lowe, forward; T. Paton, goaltender; Archie Hodgson, forward. Standing: Alex Irving, forward; Haviland Routh, forward; James Stewart, forward; Allan Cameron, coverpoint.

Lord Stanley of Preston, Canada's Govenor General from 1888 to 1893, returned to England to become the Earl of Derby without having seen a Stanley Cup game.

The Original Bowl

The bowl that currently sits atop the Stanley Cup is a carefully constructed copy of the original bowl purchased by Stanley in 1893. The original trophy was retired in 1969 because it had become brittle and easily damaged. It can still be viewed and studied at the Hockey Hall of Fame in Toronto.

the champion over the course of one season. With games played on natural ice, regular-season and Stanley Cup competition was packed into a fifteen-week period from late December to early March.

Challenges for the trophy were adjudicated by Sheriff John Sweetland and Philip D. Ross, two respected Ottawa residents who were appointed by Lord Stanley to act as trustees of the Cup. According to Lord Stanley's terms of Cup presentation, published in the Montreal *Gazette* on February 23, 1894, the trustees were requested "to suggest conditions to govern the competition. In case of any doubt as to the title of any club to claim the position of champions, the Cup shall be held or awarded by the trustees as they might think right, their decision being absolute. Should either trustee resign or otherwise drop out, the remaining trustee shall nominate a substitute."

Though the engraving on the bowl of the trophy reads "Dominion Challenge Cup" on one side and "From Stanley of Preston" on the other, it soon came to be called the Stanley Cup. Cup challenge matches mixed amateur, pseudo-amateur, and professional teams together from 1893 until 1910, when all-professional leagues like the National Hockey Association and the Ontario Professional Hockey League began to dominate the game.

This progression from amateur challenge trophy to top prize in an elite professional league did not occur smoothly, as the amateurs, of course, didn't hand the Stanley Cup over to the pros without a fight. The proponents of amateur hockey protested the infiltration of salaried players onto amateur teams and more or less demanded that the Stanley Cup should be theirs, as was originally intended. In many sports, amateur and professional athletes were uneasy compatriots in the first decades of the twentieth century. Gentleman amateurs, who played for pleasure and an ideal of good sportsmanship, did not adjust easily to the notions of play-for-pay and win-at-all-costs.

Amateur hockey's loss of the Stanley Cup was ameliorated by another titled gentleman, Sir Montagu Allan of Montreal, who, in 1908, donated the Allan Cup to serve as the top prize in senior amateur hockey. The Allan Cup is still awarded each year, but winning the Stanley Cup has endured as hockey's highest achievement; it is the game's glittering totem, the attainment of which supersedes any individual objective.

What was early Stanley Cup hockey like?

Games were played on poorly lighted, unheated rinks, and only with the cooperation of the weather, which had to be cold enough to produce ice...

Players supplied their own equipment, except jerseys and stockings, and the clubs made sure these were returned at season's end...

There were seven-man teams – goal, point (defense), cover point (defense), center, right wing, and left wing. The extra man was the rover...

There were no goal nets, just two poles mounted on a movable base that prompted endless shenanigans. It was the frequent practise of goaltenders to give the posts a sly boot just before a change of ends, leaving them seven or eight feet apart instead of the regulation six feet...

Games were made up of two thirty-minute periods, and no substitutions were allowed except in case of injury...

Penalized players were frequently visited by an officer of the law while "sitting on the fence," or penalty box as we know it today, and told to behave themselves in future...

Tobacco-chewing spectators frequently traded insults with referees, and the ladies, bundled up against the freezing temperatures, proudly wore the colors of their favorite team and looked upon opposing players as brutes...

Players had to be wary of debris thrown by spectators, and also had to avoid a crack on the skull from an opponent's stick or a smashing body-check, which hurt a lot more without the armor today's players wear...

There were no boards. The ice was ringed by a platform for spectators, and players who were body-checked or otherwise sent sprawling off the ice were booted back by fans...

Defensemen lined up in front of each other and relieved pressure in their own end by means of backhand lift shots that hoisted the puck to the other end of the rink...

Rush seats sold for 25 cents, reserved seats for 75 cents and a dollar...

Regulations governing the Cup bore no resemblance to those of today. Any club reserved the right to challenge, much in the style of the farm boy at the country fair who believes that he can last three rounds with the heavyweight prizefighter...

Cup matches were played on a sudden-death basis, or as either best-of-three or two-game, total-goal series. Challenges sometimes followed on the heels of one another, for there was no time interval required, the sole qualifications to challenge being the approval of the Cup trustees or, in some cases, the shortage of funds in the championship club's coffers. League games were played on Saturday nights, and Cup champions accepted challenges during the week...

Some Cup finals were played in December, some in January, February, or March...

This, then, was how it was in the beginning, when a bearded gentleman with a great fondness for an increasingly popular new winter pastime, spent a trifling sum for a trophy that money now can't buy.

Originally known as the Dominion Hockey Challenge Cup, the trophy purchased by Lord Stanley began to be identified by its donor's name by the mid-1890s.

(continued on p. 13)

Lord Stanley and Sons

by Phil Drackett

The pages of Stanley Cup history are liberally adorned with the names of famous brothers – the Patricks, the Cooks, the Bouchers, the Conachers, the Bentleys, the Richards, the Espositos, the Drydens, the Sutters, and many more. Yet the most formidable brotherhood of them all never saw a minute of Stanley Cup action.

The seven Stanley brothers were among the best hockey players of their time; they influenced the progress of the game both in North America and Great Britain, they brought about a Royal interest in hockey that has lasted nearly a hundred years, and it is their family name that is still proudly borne by hockey's trophy of trophies, the Stanley Cup, one of the most famous trophies in the sporting world.

They could skate, but they knew little or nothing about hockey when they sailed for Canada with their parents in 1888. Lord Stanley of Preston, later to become the sixteenth Earl of Derby, had been appointed Governor General of Canada.

Arthur, the third son, a born leader, was nineteen at the time. A keen all-round sportsman like his brothers (he excelled at rackets and cricket), he soon discovered ice hockey, and his brothers needed no encouragement to join him in taking up the game. Along with some new-found Canadian friends, they formed a couple of teams to play on a public rink. Unfortunately, the figure skaters who had had the rink much to themselves in the past resented the intrusion of the hockey players, and it was soon made plain to the "rough uncouth youths" that they could go and play on someone else's rink.

Which is just what they did. Arthur switched the action to a private rink on the grounds of Rideau Hall, the Governor General's residence, and formed a team called The Rebels, smartly turned out in red shirts and white trousers.

In 1890 he called a meeting of like-minded persons "to pursue the idea of forming an ice hockey association." It was a well-attended meeting, and eventually led to the formation of the Ontario Hockey Association, a powerful influence in the game from that day to this.

Arthur didn't let it rest there. He and brother Algy cornered their father and persuaded him to give a cup to be "an outward and visible sign of the ice-hockey championship." A Captain Colvill was entrusted with the task, and he purchased a squat, fluted silver bowl, a replica of which now sits on the top of today's trophy. Seven decades later, when thieves stole the Cup, they demanded $100,000 for its return.

There is some doubt about just how enthusiastic Lord Stanley was about hockey, although he was patron of the Ottawa Athletic Association. It was at a dinner for this group in March of 1892 that the new trophy was announced. However, there is no doubt that the pleas of Arthur and Algy played a major part in the Governor General's decision. One of the reasons given in the official announcement was "the interest that hockey matches now elicit."

The trustees were later instructed to hand the Cup over to the Montreal Amateur Athletic Association as the winner of the amateur hockey championship for the season that straddled New Year's Day, 1893. The Cup presentation took place in mid-May 1893, by which time the Stanley family was back in England, Lord Stanley having left Canada to tend to family business when his brother passed away.

The Montrealers defended the Cup in 1894, defeating the Ottawa Capitals, 3–1, before a record crowd of five thousand. A contemporary account reported, "The referee forgot to see many things."

It was a great pity that the Stanleys were not there to see their trophy begin its long and exciting history, but, nevertheless, the brothers' enthusiasm for the game was unabated. In the hard winter of 1895 when – as was unusual for England – there were three months of snow and ice, and the lake on the grounds of

Buckingham Palace froze over from January to March, the Stanleys interested members of the Royal family in a match.

On a day in January, the great match was played: Buckingham Palace versus Lord Stanley's team. The future King George V, Lord Mildmay, Sir Francis Astley Corbett, Sir William Bromley Davenport, and Ronald Moncrieff, most of them better-known on the turf, made up the Palace team; five of the Stanley brothers, plus Lord Annally, the opposition.

The Prince, who kept goal for the home side, was greatly impressed by the play of F. W. Stanley, who dribbled the puck at considerable speed "while skating backwards." This, remember, was some five years before Fred "Cyclone" Taylor amazed Canadian hockey fans by doing the same thing. Taylor always said he learned the art when world speed-skating champion and trick skater, Norval Baptis, visited Listowel, Ontario, where Taylor was playing at the time.

The Stanleys must have totally mesmerized the Prince. The Palace team scored one goal, while the Stanley team scored "numerous times." Presumably it

The Rideau Rebels of 1889. Comprised of senators, aides-de-camp, and members of Parliament, the team also included two of Lord Stanley's sons, Arthur (standing, second from left) and Edward (seated, far left).

was not thought diplomatic to record the exact number of times the Royal netminder fanned on shots.

Royal interest was maintained, however.

In 1904, King Edward VII and his Queen, Alexandra, took a party to an ice-hockey match at Hengler's (now the London Palladium theater) to see London play a team of Internationals. The game resulted in a narrow win for the latter. The Royal party included the King and Queen of Norway, the future King George V, and the Duke of Connaught, who had learned about the sport while stationed in Canada with the Army.

King George VI, when Duke of York, played regularly at the London Ice Club, and his younger brother Henry, Duke of Gloucester, was so keen that, in 1914, he once had a tour itinerary altered so that he could see two exhibition games between Ottawa and the Vancouver Millionaires.

Ted Kennedy, captain of the Toronto Maple Leafs, greets Princess Elizabeth at Maple Leaf Gardens, November 7, 1951. After staging an afternoon exhibition for the royal couple, Toronto and Chicago played a regularly scheduled game that evening, and the Leafs won, 1–0.

The present Queen and the Duke of Edinburgh have been interested spectators at matches in Canada and the United Kingdom, and the Royal princes have played the game. On the Royal Tour of Canada during the 1951-52 season, the Queen and her husband sampled hockey on two occasions, attending a game between the Canadiens and the Rangers at the Montreal Forum and a specially-arranged period of afternoon exhibition hockey at Maple Leaf Gardens between Toronto and Chicago. The following season, the Duke was at Wembley to see the Wembley Lions beaten, 2–1, by an All-Star team chosen by Britain's *Ice Hockey World* magazine.

The Stanleys did not confine the spread of the gospel of hockey to Royal circles. The Niagara Rink was the headquarters of the game in London at the time, shortly to be joined by the Princes and Brighton rinks. The Niagara club was the kingpin, but was no match for the rampaging Stanleys. Six of the brothers defeated Niagara easily, although Army duties restricted the ice time available to most of them. Another brother, Victor,

who became an admiral, could play only when on leave from the Navy.

Saddest of all, Arthur, best player of the seven, was forced to retire from the game in 1894 after a bout of rheumatic fever.

He turned to other activities. As chairman of the Automobile Club, he obtained Royal patronage for it and, during the First World War, was able, through the Duke of Connaught, then Governor General of Canada, to arrange for the club to become "home" for Canadian and other overseas officers on leave. He was also active in hospital work and became chairman of the British Red Cross.

There were plenty of people at the Royal Automobile Club to remind Sir Arthur, as he now was, of his hockey days. Aircraft designer and manufacturer T. O. M. Sopwith was in goal for England when they won the first championship of Europe in 1910 with an unbeaten record against Germany, Switzerland, and Belgium. It was a remarkable performance – they stopped off en route to the championship to play an exhibition match in Paris, which ended with three of their number injured. The two best players on the team were unable to turn out in the finals, while a third played with his shoulder strapped.

Another RAC member was Lord Brabazon of Tara, the first Englishman to fly, inventor of the Cresta bobsleigh run, and a government Air and Transport Minister. "Brab" played for the Princes club in the early days and was often on the team when it represented England in continental tournaments.

The RAC's competitions chairman, Earl Howe, a leading racing motorist, was vice-president of the Brighton Tigers Ice Hockey Club and, in modern times, the RAC has continued to play host to many hockey players, past and present. The RAC is also linked to another Stanley Cup, far less well-known than its hockey counterpart. It was put up by Sir Arthur for competition in motor trials.

The sport on both sides of the Atlantic owes a lot to the Stanley family. Lord Stanley is already in the Hockey Hall of Fame. Perhaps one day Sir Arthur Stanley, GCVO, GBE, CB, his third son, will join him there.

The Montreal Amateur Athletic Association's hockey team was the first winner of the Stanley Cup in 1893. Each of the club's players recived a gold ring from the association as a memento of the championship.

It was appropriate that the first winner of Lord Stanley's gift proved to be one of the three oldest hockey clubs in the world, the Montreal Amateur Athletic Association. The Montreal AAA, formed in November of 1884, won the Amateur Hockey Association of Canada title in 1893, and thus, under Lord Stanley's deed of gift, was the first to have its name inscribed on the Cup.

Differences abound in the historical accounts of events leading up to the awarding of this first Stanley Cup. In 1893, the Amateur Hockey Association of Canada ruled that the best team in the Dominion would be decided by a championship series in which five teams – Ottawa, Quebec, and three Montreal sides, the AAA, the Crystals, and the Victorias – would play each other twice, home and away. The winning side at the conclusion of this schedule earned the right to be called senior amateur champion. Prior to 1893, the championship was determined not by league standings at the conclusion of a regular schedule of games but by means of a succession of challenge matches. The Montreal AAA was hockey's first dynasty team, winning the title in seven consecutive seasons, often defeating the Ottawa club for the honor.

It captured the championship series of 1893 by finishing the schedule with a record of seven wins and one loss. The pivotal game of the season was held in Montreal on February 18, 1893, when the AAA met Ottawa. At this time both teams had lost only once during the season, and this match was considered by both the press and the players to be the championship game. The Ottawa newspapers carried numerous advertisements concerning the contest, and a special train was scheduled to enable Ottawa supporters to travel to Montreal for the game. Montreal defeated the Ottawa side 7–1, and, with the capital-city squad having only one game left in its portion of the schedule, Montreal seemed guaranteed to win the title. The AAA went undefeated in its remaining three games, although they were awarded a win against the Crystals by default when that club refused to play out a 2–2 tie. The Montreal AAAs thereby won the AHA title and were considered the champions of the Dominion.

After its defeat at the hands of the AAA, the Ottawa team defended its title as champion of the Ontario Hockey Association. Ottawa defeated Queen's University on March 1, 1893, by a count of 6–3 (or 6–4, depending on which newspaper you read). They then awaited a challenge from the Toronto Granites, who subsequently told the Ottawa team they were unable to find enough quality players to ice a team. They requested that a patched-together squad of players from other Toronto teams be permitted to take their place, and, although Ottawa agreed, the "All-Star" team couldn't muster enough players to make the journey to Ottawa either, so the team from Canada's capital retained its OHA title. Ottawa then played its final AHA game, defeating Quebec 14–0 on March 17. The Ottawa *Citizen*, in its summary of the game, addressed a challenge to the Montreal AAA team (AHA champions) to play Ottawa (OHA champions) in a game to determine the true Canadian champion, noting that the two sides had played each other twice during the year, with each team winning once. The challenge was dismissed, since Montreal, having captured the AHA championship series, had nothing to prove.

On May 1, 1893, Toronto and Montreal newspapers printed an item concerning the Stanley Hockey Championship Cup. The rules and regulations for the Cup's presentation were outlined in detail, and it was noted that the Montreal AAAs were to be considered the first holders of the trophy, since they had "defeated all comers during the late season, including the champions of the Ontario Association." The trophy was formally presented to executives from the Montreal AAA on May 15, 1893. However, internal bickering between the AAA hockey club and the association's executive resulted in the trophy not being "officially" accepted by the AAA's players until February 23, 1894.

It has been widely repeated in hockey folklore that the first Stanley Cup was awarded to the Montreal AAA hockey club because the Ottawa club refused to travel to Toronto to play a club from Osgoode Hall Law School. Numerous hockey historians have supported this theory in their treatments of the Stanley Cup story. However, original documents confirm that the Ottawa–Osgoode controversy took place not in 1893 but in 1894. It resulted in Ottawa's withdrawal from the OHA, a fact still reflected in the organization of amateur hockey in Ontario almost a hundred years after the historic split.

The Montreal AAA repeated as AHA champion again in 1894, and on March 22, at Montreal's old Victoria Rink, the first Cup game was played. Ottawa again provided the opposition before what one sports chronicler of the day described as "enthusiastic and fashionable spectators."

Montreal won 3–1 in a penalty-free game, one of the few in Cup history, and the accounts in the Montreal papers the next day were glowing and colorful.

"The Victoria Rink held the largest crowd ever packed into the rink," the Montreal *Gazette* said. It didn't, however, give attendance figures.

> There was "siss-boom-ah," "rah-rah-rah" and several other audible tokens of imbecility and enthusiasm mixed. Some kind people had extravagantly blown themselves on tin horns, which they blew afterwards with an apparent idea of getting square on the question of expenditure. The horns might have cost all the way up to five cents originally, but they made enough trouble to give a lucrative practice to any reputable ear doctor. This, of course, was only an outside part of the game and did not interfere with the play.

On the play itself, the reporter wrote that

> it may seem strange to anybody who knew the game to discover how the score came out as it did; but that fact is easily explained. Clever play and acquaintance with the rink accounted for it. . . .
> Nobody was ruled off, but James [George James of the MAAA] and Pulford [Harvey Pulford of the Capitals] ought to have been.

The *Gazette* reporter noted that "one of the pleasing features of the match was the display of ribbon. Every lady almost in the rink wore the favors of her particular club and never did belted knight in joust or tourney fight harder than the hockey men." It was a 1–1 game in the first half, with the first goal in Cup history being scored by Chauncey Kirby at the seven-minute mark. Archie Hodgson of Montreal tied it twelve minutes later, and nine minutes after the start of the second half, Billy Barlow scored what proved to be the winning goal. Barlow also scored the game's final goal.

Toronto's Osgoode Hall team challenged the Montreal AAA in late March, but Cup trustees Ross and Sweetland decided against staging a game, because there was a great possibility there would be no ice in the warm spring weather.

The Montreal Victorias gained possession of the Cup in 1895 by winning the AHA title, but they didn't bother to defend the trophy. Instead, the team went to New York for a post-season exhibition series with Ottawa.

Instead of a winner-take-all challenge match for the Stanley Cup, the Montreal AAA took on Queen's University at Montreal. It was agreed that if the MAAA won, the Cup would be turned over to the Victorias "without more ado." However, if Queen's won, the collegians would have to play the Victorias for the Cup. The MAAA prevailed by a 5–1 score, effectively securing the Cup for the Vics.

The Patriarch of the Pads

The first goalie to appear in a Stanley Cup game wearing leg pads was George Merritt of the Winnipeg Victorias in the 1896 challenge match between Montreal and Winnipeg. Merritt strapped on a pair of cricket pads and posted a 2–0 shutout over the Montreal Victorias.

One of the earliest known pieces of artwork featuring hockey action, this engraving shows action at the Victoria Rink in 1892 as the Montreal AAA battle the Montreal Victorias.

The Montreal Vics won the AHA championship the following year, but their march to a second consecutive Cup title was halted on February 14, 1896, at Montreal, by the Winnipeg Victorias, who won 2–0, for the first shutout and the first win by a western club in Cup history.

Dan Bain scored after ten minutes of the first half on a pass from Mike Grant, and Toat Campbell got the other goal at the nine-minute mark of the second. It was a stunning blow to the easterners, who grudgingly praised the Winnipeg players and panned the work of referee Alexis Martin of Toronto. According to the Toronto *Globe*, one play in particular displeased the easterners. Hartland MacDougall of Montreal opened the scoring in the first half and "while local rooters went wild with delight, their pleasure was premature. The referee had discovered an offside somewhere or other, and the puck was brought back."

"The visitors traveled East in search of wisdom and found victory, but they left a lot of wisdom mixed up with sadness behind them; and after awhile we Eastern remnants of an effete hockey civilization will arrive at

the conclusion that it is possible to extract some sort of good out of the Wild and Woolly West," one Montreal newspaper reported.

The Montreal Victorias won the Stanley Cup in each of the next three years.

The Vics traveled to Winnipeg and, on December 30, 1896, regained the trophy with a 6–5 victory over the westerners in a sudden-death final. Despite the fact that it took place place at the end of 1896, this game was accepted as an 1897 challenge.

In December of 1897, the Montreal Vics beat the Ottawa Capitals 14–2 in the first game of a total-goals series, before the outclassed Caps called the second game off "in the best interests of hockey."

No challenge was received in 1898. Ottawa apparently was still licking its wounds from the fearful beating it had taken the previous year and smarting from the rebuke of Montreal sportswriters who had said that the Caps had about as much license to challenge for the world's championship "as a team of cigar store Indians."

The Montreal Victorias, Stanley Cup champions from 1896 to 1899. The 1897 squad pictured here won seven of eight games. The 1898 edition of the club compiled a 8–0–0 record to become the first Stanley Cup champion to complete its season without a loss or a tie. The Vics captured their third Cup title by default, when no other club challenged them to defend the trophy.

It wasn't to be too many years before an Ottawa team – this time the Silver Seven – was to make up for all the indignities suffered by the Capitals.

The first bitter controversy in the Cup's short history came about in 1899 at Montreal. The Montreal Vics, who had again won the eastern title and, with it, the Cup, were challenged by the Winnipeg Victorias, who traveled east for a two-game total-goals series.

Montreal won the trophy for the third straight year, but it must, in all fairness, be pointed out that their victory didn't result solely from on-ice superiority. The series didn't finish. The westerners went home Cupless and angry.

Exactly twenty years later another Cup series would be halted, but the circumstances were in no way similar. In 1899 a referee decided to stop the series because the players refused to accept his decisions. In 1919 the proceedings were halted when a flu epidemic in Seattle left many players too weak to continue, and eventually claimed the life of Joe Hall.

Bill Findlay of Montreal was the referee of the 1899 series. Montreal won the opener 2–1 on late goals by Bob Macdougall and Graham Drinkwater after Tony Gingras had given Winnipeg a 1–0 lead early in the first half. The victory whipped up unprecedented interest for the second encounter. Ticket speculators made a killing, and a crowd of eight thousand crammed into Montreal's Arena Rink on Saturday, February 18, to see the westerners in action.

The Montreal Vics led 3–2 with twelve minutes to play when center Bob Macdougall received a two-minute penalty for whacking Gingras across the knee with his stick. Macdougall headed for the penalty box, and the Winnipeggers, incensed at such a light sentence, headed for their dressing room, directing very uncomplimentary remarks at Findlay as they went.

Findlay, apparently not accustomed to such treatment, left the scene abruptly and went home. A search party set out by sleigh, found Findlay, and convinced him to return to the rink. Upon his arrival, after what had already been a delay of sixty-five minutes, he gave the Winnipeg players fifteen minutes to suit up and continue play. But the Winnipeg Vics weren't appeased, and refused to return unless Findlay banished Macdougall from the game under an 1897 rule that said a referee could remove any player for ungentlemanly conduct.

Findlay refused. After the stipulated fifteen minutes, when there was no sign of the westerners, the game, the series, and the Stanley Cup were awarded to Montreal. The Cup's trustees upheld the referee's ruling.

As it turned out, the trustees' ruling was academic. The Winnipeg club couldn't have resumed play, as several of its players had not only already changed into their street clothes but presumably had launched themselves into Montreal's night life.

An elaborately inscribed hockey stick from the first great controversy in Stanley Cup play: the Montreal Victorias–Winnipeg Victorias match of February 18, 1899. There is a reference to "Fizzie the referee" on the shaft of the stick.

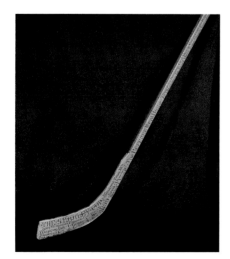

Such a farcical series of events, however, should not dull the luster of the names of some of hockey's earliest greats, who played in that era.

The Montreal Vics' line-up is a *Who's Who* of early hockey: Gord Lewis in goal; Mike Grant at point; Graham Drinkwater at cover point; at center, Bob Macdougall; at rover, one of the game's first superstars, 120-pound Russell Bowie, who would hang up his skates in 1910 after twenty-two years in the game; and on the wings Ernie McLea and Cam Davidson, with Shirley Davidson as spare.

The Winnipeg Vics featured Whitey Merritt in the nets, Charlie Johnston at point, Bob Benson at cover point, the famous Dan Bain at center, and Gingras at rover, with Toat Campbell and Addie Howard on the wings.

The Montreal Victorias' hold on the Stanley Cup was short-lived, however. Two weeks after defeating Winnipeg, they lost their league championship, and with it the Stanley Cup, to the Montreal Shamrocks, who successfully defended against Queen's with a 6–2 win in March of 1899.

Undaunted by the residue of bad feelings that still remained from their disqualification in February of 1899, the Winnipeg Vics took another swing at a Montreal club in 1900 and almost got their revenge. Playing the Montreal Shamrocks in a best-of-three series, the Winnipeggers won the opening game 4–3 but lost the second and third 3–2 and 5–4. No penalties were called in the second game for the second time in Cup history.

The new century also marked the birth of a more national interest in the Stanley Cup. In March of 1900, the Halifax Crescents flexed their muscles and traveled to Montreal in an effort to spirit the Cup away to the East Coast.

They returned to Halifax on the short end of 10–2 and 11–0 beatings.

By 1901, eastern fans may have suspected that the Winnipeg Vics were getting a discount from the railroad, for they arrived in Montreal again, with a few new faces, but with Bain, Gingras, and Campbell still forming the nucleus of the team. Art Brown was in goal, the Flett brothers, Rod and Magnus, were at point and cover, and Burke Wood, who was destined to carve out a fine career in hockey, was at rover.

This time Winnipeg returned home as winners. They swept the best-of-three series in two straight games, winning 4–3 in game one and 2–1 in game two, the first overtime match in Cup history. Bain was the hero of the playoffs, scoring three goals – one in the first game and both of Winnipeg's counters in the second. He opened the scoring in the first half of the second game, and after captain Harry Trihey of the Shamrocks tied it 1–1 in the second half, Bain potted the winner at four minutes of sudden-death overtime.

There were only two penalties in the first game, and a Montreal *Gazette* reporter described the lack of penalties by telling his readers that the referee "did not often use his powers of giving spectators' tickets away."

The Carriage Trade

In 1902, when the Toronto Wellingtons travelled to Winnipeg in search of the Stanley Cup, they were greeted on arrival by officials of the Winnipeg Victorias, and both teams rode through the streets in carriages. Between games of the best-of-three series, the Wellingtons were guests of the Vics at a theater party, and when the series ended with Winnipeg keeping the Cup with back-to-back 5–3 victories, the winners treated the Torontonians to a lavish banquet.

The Montreal Shamrocks, the third Montreal-based team to capture the Cup, included Art Farrell (standing, far right), who wrote the sport's first history, Ice Hockey: The Royal Game, *in 1899.*

The Toronto *Star* said the play was the "most scientific hockey ever witnessed in Canada." It reported also that Bain played "with a big mask over a sore eye."

In January 1902, at Winnipeg, the Winnipeg Vics turned back a challenge from the Toronto Wellingtons, known as the Iron Dukes, in the first Cup series played in western Canada. They won by identical 5–3 scores in a best-of-three series, and Winnipeg newspapermen wondered why the Wellingtons had traveled all that distance when they were obviously outclassed by the Vics. They presumably had forgotten that the Vics had made a few fruitless trips eastward themselves.

It was obvious by now that enthusiasm for Stanley Cup competition was burning brightly. In Toronto, thousands of citizens sat up well into the night waiting to hear blasts from the whistle on top of the Toronto Railway powerhouse. Two blasts would tell the Wellington fans that the Iron Dukes had won. Three blasts meant that they had lost.

The Winnipeg Victorias, who, in 1899, lost a controversial Cup match, in 1901 became the first team west of Ontario to win the Stanley Cup.

This series probably also set the style for the roving netminder – an innovation later credited to Hall-of-Famer Jacques Plante – when Wellington goalkeeper Dutch Morrison startled Winnipeg fans by darting from the net to check an opposing forward.

At any rate, eastern prestige, though tarnished by the defeat of the Iron Dukes, was restored by the Montreal AAA, who journeyed west two months later to give the Winnipeg Vics their comeuppance, two games to one.

And Montreal's system of getting the information to the populace was more colorful than Toronto's whistle blasts. A platform was erected in front of the Montreal *Star* branch office at the southeast corner of Peel and Ste. Catherine streets, and from there an announcer with a megaphone bellowed out the news to gathering crowds.

When the team returned, the players were mobbed at the railway station, bundled into sleighs from which the horses were detached, and dragged around the streets by celebrating fans.

Tony Gingras, whose injury in 1899 prompted the Winnipeg Vics to leave the ice in protest.

However, the Montreal AAA didn't have things all its own way at Winnipeg in 1902. On slushy ice and in a rugged game that observers said could hardly be called hockey, the Winnipeggers, with Gingras healthy and the game's only scorer, took the opener 1–0. The story was different in the second game, won by Montreal 5–0, and in the third, which the easterners took 2–1, Gingras again being the Winnipeggers' lone scorer. Art Hooper, who scored two of Montreal's goals in the second game, opened the scoring in the deciding contest.

The big boys for Montreal in the series, besides Hooper, were Jack Marshall and Charlie Liffiton. Twelve years later, Marshall was to lead the Toronto Blueshirts to the Stanley Cup, the first time that players from a Toronto club would taste champagne from the historic bowl.

The 1903 season marked the appearance on the Stanley Cup stage of one of hockey's most fabulous teams, the incomparable Ottawa Silver Seven.

The fabled Silver Seven were the main protagonists in an era that was to produce some of hockey's most unbelievable stories, some of its greatest moments, and many of its toughest, most combative – but best – hockey players.

The Silver Seven's triumphs were the beginning of nine Stanley Cup championships that Ottawa hockey clubs brought to Canada's capital city in a span of twenty-five years. The Seven stand as Ottawa's greatest team, and certainly the greatest the game had seen up until that time. In their three-year reign as Cup champions, they turned back the challenges of seven Canadian teams: the Rat Portage Thistles (twice), the Winnipeg Rowing Club, the Toronto Marlboroughs, the Brandon Wheat Kings, and the fabled Dawson City Klondikers. They met and conquered two others – Queen's University and Smiths Falls – in 1906, before yielding the trophy to the Montreal Wanderers in a pulsating two-game series.

(continued on p. 31)

Ottawa and The Stanley Cup

by Roy MacGregor

The site of one of the most fabled "incidents" in Stanley Cup play has nothing to mark its passing, and perhaps no one is alive who witnessed what really happened on that cold winter's night in early 1904 when the Toronto Marlboroughs, champions of the Ontario Hockey Association, came to Ottawa to challenge the Silver Seven for the Stanley Cup.

The Cattle Castle is in decay. It sits – windows broken, paint flaking – between the football field and the canal, a curious, slightly Moorish barn of a building that some people remember was once known as the Manufacturers' Building, but few recall as the glorious Lady Aberdeen Pavilion. State of the art in the 1890s, it is in a sorry state in the 1990s, with debate raging between those who would spend nearly $10 million to refurbish it and those who would pay a wrecker to knock it down. At the end of the twentieth century it is used only by the pigeons who nest along the rafters. Yet, when the century opened, these same rafters shook with the roars of a city so taken with hockey and skating it was said to have affected the very manner in which the people of Ottawa walked.

The night the Toronto Marlboroughs came to challenge marked the third time in less than a year that the Silver Seven had been forced to defend its claim to being the best hockey team in the entire Dominion. In the magnificently maintained Lady Aberdeen Pavilion, the ice was hard as rock, smooth as glass, and the Toronto team – composed of quick, hard-skating players – stunned the crowd by going ahead 3–1 in the first half. No one could believe it.

The home team, after all, was the famous Silver Seven, and though it would be decades before they would be voted Canada's outstanding hockey team of the first half-century, in early 1904 they were nonetheless renowned as the toughest, roughest hockey team in the world. Only a few weeks earlier, the Winnipeg Rowing Club had come to challenge and, with the hometown winning 2–0 and seven of the nine Winnipeg players requiring medical treatment, the Rowing Club's conveyance back West had been tabbed "the hospital train" by the daily newspapers.

Their pride as well as the Cup on the line, the Silver Seven came out for the second half against Toronto a changed team. But they were not the only part of the game that was different. The ice, so smooth and fast at first, was now soft and choppy. It slowed the Marlborough team down, and when the Silver Seven caught up to them, it was as if the hospital train had just rolled back into town. Ottawa scored five goals and went on to win, 6–3. When it was over, Henry Roxborough recorded in *The Stanley Cup Story*, one Toronto player could barely walk, one could no longer even grip a stick, and one had to be rushed off to the hospital with broken ribs.

"Ottawa players," reported Toronto's *Globe*,

> slash, trip and practise the severest kind of cross-checking with a systematic hammering of hands and wrists. They hit a man on the head when the referee isn't looking, and they body a man into the boards after he has passed the puck. The rubber is not the objective, but the man must be stopped at all costs; if he is put out altogether, so much the better.

Ottawa's Lady Aberdeen Pavilion, known today as the "Cattle Castle," played host to early Stanley Cup hockey in Canada's capital city.

"It was a case of shoot and duck," one of the Marlborough players was reported as saying. "The Ottawa defense didn't give a hang whether or not a goal was scored; they just walloped to teach you better manners during the next attack."

The Toronto players had even more to complain about than the rough play. Lame and aching, they were useless for the second game in the match, which Ottawa easily won 11–2, and went home convinced that they had been had by a bit of Stanley Cup trickery. After the crucial first game, the Toronto players claimed to a man – but could never prove – that Ottawa had salted the ice at the half-time interval instead of cleaning it.

Lady Aberdeen – Ishbel Maria Marjoribanks Gordon – was the wife of the Earl of Aberdeen, the seventh Governor General of Canada. That the city's first modern hockey arena was named after her rather than the Earl is appropriate, for she was, in fact, the true Governor General from 1893 to 1898, a large, strong-willed woman who offered advice freely to the prime ministers and established, among other matters, the Victorian Order of Nurses. Her husband, shy and slim, is remembered only for his ability to imitate train whistles and his love of skating. This viceregal approval of such an activity, however, had a profound effect on the community. People even began walking differently. "Skating," wrote Anson A. Gard, "gives grace and firmness of step, acquired in no other way, and since all Ottawans skate – as in no other

In 1904, a number of leagues, including the OHA and the CAHL, suggested replacing the Stanley Cup, but the venerable mug survived the coup attempt to become the oldest team trophy in North America.

THE HOCKEY LEAGUES WANT TO DO AWAY WITH THE STANLEY CUP

"CAST ADRIFT."

city is it so general – it follows that the Ottawa Step is unique."

Hockey's grand legacy comes from the Aberdeens' predecessor, Lord Stanley of Preston. The sixth Governor General was himself involved in one of the game's first recorded controversies when, according to J. W. Fitsell's *Hockey's Captains, Colonels and Kings*, Stanley strapped on the blades to join his two sons on the Government House rink and was roundly scolded by the New York papers for playing shinny on Sunday, the day of rest.

Stanley's two younger sons – Arthur and Edward – took to the new game with such passion that they became part of the Rideau Rebels, a team Fitsell credits with spreading the game west from its Montreal and Kingston hotbeds to new territory in Toronto, where, after a Rebels exhibition in 1888, the *Mail* reported: "It is a lively winter game and is the only one that can take the place of lacrosse, baseball, etc., for the enjoyment of spectators. If Montreal can attract thousands of spectators to see their games there is no reason whatever why Toronto should not support the game equally well."

Two years later, Arthur Stanley, now an aide-de-camp to his father, worked to establish an organization that could promote and organize the game. To further these ends, the Governor General agreed to donate the Cup that came to bear his name.

Lord Stanley's wish to see Ottawa's name engraved on the new bowl did not come true for ten years, long after he and his family had returned to England. The trophy's early years were, in fact, rather disappointing. The first winners, the Montreal Amateur Athletic Association, showed far more interest in the ornate Senior Amateur Trophy, which they also won in 1893. In 1900, Ottawa set out to capture the Cup, only to default when they couldn't ice seven players. The trophy came to the capital city only in 1903 when the Silver Seven defeated the defending champion Montreal Victorias in a two-game, total-goals series to win the championship of the Canada Amateur Hockey League (successor to the old AHA) and, with it, possession and the right to defend the Stanley Cup.

The Silver Seven were clearly the most powerful team of the day. They took their leadership from a mean right-winger, Alf Smith, who'd come back home from Pittsburgh to play, and the team found a name when manager Bob Shillington handed over a silver nugget to each player in recognition of their winning season. The "Seven," of course, referred to the manner in which the game was then played: seven men on a side with all seven going the full sixty minutes.

To gain a perspective on how much the way hockey is played has changed over the century, it is worth noting that Ted Patrick, the great Lester Patrick's younger brother, was generally considered a fine amateur player, despite the fact that he had lost a leg in a sledding accident and played on a wooden peg. Skating was far less important at first, with the puck being batted from player to player – but never in the form of a forward pass. The game was more akin to rugby than, say, lacrosse, with the ice surfaces considerably smaller and quick mobility less emphasized. Considering that the Wright brothers got off the ground the year the Silver Seven made their first defense of the Stanley Cup, it might be said that the game has changed almost as dramatically as flight itself has during this century.

That first challenge came from the Rat Portage Thistles of northwestern Ontario. The two-game, total-goals series was played in March 1903 at Dey's Rink, where hometown Ottawa – relying on what the *Globe* called "rough-house tactics" – won easily, 6–2 and 4–2. Attendance was so poor that the Thistles headed back to Rat Portage – soon to be renamed Kenora – $800 in the hole. Ten months later the challenge came from the Winnipeg Rowing Club, which left, bruised and bloodied, on the "hospital train."

It was during this time that the legend of the Silver Seven was born. Not only were they clearly the toughest hockey team in Canada, but indisputably they were the best. Alf Smith, who established the club and served as both manager and captain, was such a favorite of the fans that they wrote poetry about him. Smith's defense partner and fellow Hall-of-Famer, Harvey Pulford, also played on national championship teams in lacrosse and football, was the eastern Canadian boxing champion, the national rowing champion, and excelled in knocking hockey opponents into the second row of spectators. There were Arthur Moore, Dave Finnie, Billy Gilmour, and Harry "Rat" Westwick, who could play full-out for an entire thirty-minute half, and, of course, the talented Frank McGee.

In the photographs that are to be found in such treasures as Jim McAuley's *The Ottawa Sports Book*, the Silver Seven stare out with a certain cocky contentment that speaks of everything but violence. Five of the players part their hair dead center, Rat Westwick looks more like Oscar Wilde than a rugged hockey player, and Frank McGee looks too small to play. The photographs cannot do justice to the enigmatic McGee, however, a slight, handsome young man who was blind in one eye, yet was so adept at shooting that that he scored sixty-three goals in a mere twenty-two Stanley Cup playoff games.

There were other outstanding members of the team over the years – Bouse Hutton in goal, two more Gilmour brothers, Suddy and Dave – but it is McGee who will be remembered for as long as hockey survives for his part in a single game on the night of January 16, 1905. The Silver Seven were then at their height;

The 1905 Silver Seven defeated Dawson City and Rat Portage to keep the Cup in Ottawa.

the Brandon Wheat Kings had challenged them for the Stanley Cup in March of 1904, and the contest was so one-sided it is barely noted in the history of the Cup. But then came a challenge from a most unexpected source: Dawson City in the Yukon.

The challenge was issued by Colonel Joe Boyle, who had left Ontario in 1896 to join the Yukon gold rush and had struck it rich. Money was not the problem – $3,000 was raised to send the team – but finding players and just getting them to Ottawa certainly presented difficulties. Only one player had Stanley Cup experience. The goalie had just turned seventeen. A month before the puck would even drop, four of Boyle's players left by dogsled for Whitehorse, where they were joined by others for a single practice. Rail and steamer and rail again brought them to Ottawa, where they lost the first game, 9–2, and the ever-optimistic Boyle wired back to Dawson, "The beating is no disgrace. We have a good chance to win the Cup." The second game they lost 23–2, with McGee scoring fourteen goals. Boyle finally admitted defeat.

The Silver Seven, by this time, were already legendary figures, the first true national heroes of the game that had captured an entire country. When the Kenora Thistles came again to challenge in March of 1905, the fans, who had all but ignored the first Stanley Cup matches, were now scrambling for scalpers' tickets. In a contest so rough that the referee began wearing a hard hat in the second game, the Silver Seven again held the Cup, with McGee once more leading the way.

By 1906 the Silver Seven had defended successfully eight times, winning seventeen out of twenty Stanley Cup matches. But then came the challenge from the upstart Montreal Wanderers, suddenly a force to be reckoned with, thanks to a twenty-two-year-old marvel named Lester Patrick, a slick speedster who moved over the ice more like a sprinter than a skater. The Wanderers and the Silver Seven had tied for the league championship with identical 9–1 records, and a two-game series would settle the claim to the Stanley Cup.

Going into the first match in Montreal, the Silver Seven were 2–1 betting favorites, but the bookies sadly underestimated the new power of Montreal. With 4,200 fans watching, Montreal went ahead 7–0 and won 9–1, with Ernie Russell scoring four times, Pud Glass three, and Patrick twice. Game two was set for Ottawa on March 17 and, according to Eric Whitehead's *The Patricks: Hockey's Royal Family*, interest ran so high that the fans broke through the plate-glass windows at Allen & Cochrane's store to get at the tickets. In a rink built for 3,000, more than 5,400 were squeezed in for what, years later, the *Sporting News* would describe as "The Greatest Hockey Game in History."

It was a game that may have invented the "ringer," as well, for the Silver Seven had picked up Smiths Falls' remarkable stand-up goalie, Percy LeSueur, who promptly let in the first goal and then stopped Montreal cold. Frank McGee began Ottawa's comeback, and by the half, the Silver Seven were ahead 3–1, but still down 10–4 in the series. In the second half – without, apparently, any help from salted ice – Ottawa's Harry Smith took charge by scoring six goals. With the Seven now up 9–1, the series was suddenly tied 10–10. Smith's heroics so captivated the crowd that, at one point, play was suspended while Governor General Grey slapped him on the back. Montreal's Ernie Johnson "accidentally" managed to knock off the Governor General's stovepipe hat, and a Montreal fan ran off with it, but it did nothing to stop the Ottawa comeback. Smith scored yet again, and the goal might have gone down as the greatest comeback in history had not referee Bob Meldrum ruled the goal would not count. The play had been offside.

Play resumed and, when a frustrated Smith took a penalty, Lester Patrick scored twice to give Montreal the series, 12–10. With the Ottawa fans in shock and Montreal celebrating, the fan who'd made off with the top hat slipped into the dressing room and presented it to Johnson. Governor General Grey had lost his hat. The Ottawa Silver Seven, after three long years and eight successful defenses, had lost Governor General Stanley's bowl.

"You didn't change the lines too often, I'll tell you that."

Fearless Frank Finnigan, the last surviving member of an Ottawa Stanley Cup team, sat in his daughter Joan's living room one spring day in 1988 and looked back more than sixty years to the glory days of Ottawa hockey. Hair snow white and thick as ermine, the "Shawville Express" was going on eighty-seven, yet he seemed again a young man in his prime as he shot out a fist to show how he once knocked out Sprague Cleghorn, arguably the toughest player ever, with a single "lucky" punch.

"Don't you think a fellow has got to be on for three or four minutes to find himself?" he asked, shaking his head over today's thirty-second shifts. "You can be on for two minutes and not even touch the puck."

The man who scored the first goal of the game in which the Ottawa Senators won their last Stanley Cup – who scored, for that matter, the last goal the original team would count in Ottawa – perfectly mirrors what has happened to hockey in Ottawa over the twentieth century. At thirteen, Frank Finnigan played his first professional game, picking up $10 for helping the Quebec village of Quyon gain revenge on Fitzroy Harbour, its bitter Ontario rival just across the Ottawa River. A defensive specialist, he played fourteen years in the NHL and scored 115 goals and had 88 assists, his career beginning in Ottawa and ending in Toronto. It was, for decades, a hockey life to look back on, but recently it had become one to look forward to, for Frank Finnigan lived long enough to be on hand when the new Ottawa Senators were awarded their new NHL franchise. He lived to learn his old sweater, number eight, would be retired with glory. Had he not died on Christmas Day 1991, at the age of ninety-one, he would have dropped the first puck to open the second chapter in the history of his beloved Senators.

Team nicknames were employed much more casually in the early days of hockey than they are today, and so it was in the season following the Ottawa club's defeat at the hands of the Montreal Wanderers that "Silver Seven" began to be replaced by "Senators" to designate the Ottawa team. The club added a young twenty-

The 1909 Ottawa Senators, the first all-pro Stanley Cup champions, were one of four clubs that played in the Eastern Canada Hockey Association.

three-year-old from Renfrew, Fred "Cyclone" Taylor, and immediately set a league record for attendance, with 7,100 fans at their home opener. The new Senators did not disappoint, whipping the defending-champion Wanderers 12–2. The Ottawa *Citizen* reported, "Taylor proved to be the sensation of the night."

In 1908-09, the Ottawa Senators brought the Stanley Cup back to town. Peerless Percy LeSueur was in goal, Cyclone Taylor took care of the scoring, Bruce Stuart was team captain, and Marty Walsh – who may have originated the slapshot – was a star, as were Billy Gilmour and Fred Lake. Two seasons later, with most of the same players – Taylor excepted – they won again. And the Senators were widely expected to repeat in 1911-12, when the Ottawa team held a 5–4 lead against the Quebec Bulldogs with a mere twenty seconds left in the decisive match. Unfortunately for Ottawa, Quebec had a player named "Phantom" Joe Malone, who not

only tied it up in the final seconds but scored in overtime to give Quebec its first Cup victory.

These were times of enormous change in hockey. Instead of two thirty-minute halves, games switched to three twenty-minute periods. The seventh player – Frank McGee's rover position – was dropped, first in the East and much later in the West. Referees began dropping the puck instead of placing it on the ice for face-offs. Forward passing would begin in 1918, first in the neutral area and gradually in all zones. And on December 19, 1917, the newly formed National Hockey League – consisting of the Montreal Canadiens and Wanderers, the Toronto Arenas, and the Senators – played its first two regular-season games.

In the first seven years of the new league, the Senators placed first five times, in what were heady years for Ottawa fans. In 1921-22, Harry "Punch" Broadbent won the Art Ross scoring trophy with 46 points in 24 games, scoring in a record 16 consecutive games. In 1923-24, the Senators' Frank Nighbor – the player who perfected the poke check – was named the first winner of the new Hart Trophy as the league's most valuable player, and Cy Denneny won the scoring race with 22 goals and one assist in 21 games.

The Senators won the Stanley Cup four times in the NHL's first ten seasons – in 1920, 1921, 1923, and 1927 – for an official Senators/Silver Seven total of nine, though in fact Ottawa teams had successfully defended the Stanley Cup a total of fourteen times.

The popularity of hockey in Ottawa was then indisputable. When the Senators moved into the city's new Auditorium in 1924, a section behind the visitors' goal was set off to hold standing-room-only customers at fifty cents a ticket, and this "rush end" had to be caged off to keep the eager fans from pouring into the seats during the breaks. They came to cheer goaltender Clint Benedict and his sixteen playoff shutouts. They came to see Sprague Cleghorn, whose mean streak was so pronounced he was once charged with assaulting his wife with a crutch while he recuperated from a broken leg.

"Wonder Machine of Canada's Great Winter Pastime Gives City Prominence Everywhere," read a 1926 headline from the *Citizen*. "For forty years colors of the Ottawa hockey team have flashed up and down the ice, bringing kudos to the capital, and always proving the best drawing card on any circuit on which it has

Frank Nighbor, a member of four Ottawa Cup-winning teams, was the NHL's most valuable player and the first winner of the Hart Trophy in 1922-23.

played." How ironic that the city's last Stanley Cup glory was then only a year away.

That year, 1927, is remembered by most sports fans as the year Babe Ruth hit sixty home runs, but not by Frank Finnigan. To him, it was the year of his own greatest hockey glory and his city's last. He no longer played for the University of Ottawa team while pretending to work on "my degree in business administration – they rolled a piece of paper into a typewriter, typed out a sentence and I sat down and copied it, one finger, and that was that." Now he was twenty-six years old and a true professional, playing beside the likes of Alex Connell, "the Ottawa Fireman," who would record 12 shutouts in 44 games, Francis "King" Clancy, the little defenseman who would go on to become one of the game's true legends, George Boucher, a high-scoring rear guard who played professional football before joining the Senators,

When the Senators took a year's leave from the NHL, Ottawa star Frank Finnigan joined the Toronto Maple Leafs for the 1931-32 season and helped the Leafs to their first Cup title.

Frank Nighbor, Reginald "Hooley" Smith, Cy Denneny, Hec Kilrea, Alex "Boots" Smith, Milt Halliday, and Jack Adams.

They met Boston in the finals, a tough team that had Eddie Shore and former Senator Sprague Cleghorn on defense. Game one ended in a 0–0 tie, game two went to Ottawa, with Clancy, Finnigan, and Denneny all scoring and Boston managing but a single goal, and the third game also ended in a tie, 1–1. The fourth and decisive game, played at the "Aud" in Ottawa, went the hometown's way from the moment Frank Finnigan opened the scoring. Five players drew fines for fighting – Boston's Billy Couture was thrown out of the league for attacking the on-ice officials – but Ottawa won, 3–1, to claim the Stanley Cup for the last time.

Seven years later the Senators were gone, seemingly forever. The team was gutted, the owners broke, the fans no longer believing. "NO N.H.L. HOCKEY TEAM FOR OTTAWA NEXT WINTER," read black banners in the *Evening Citizen* of April 7, 1934. Inside, an editorial commented: "There will be genuine regret at the Hockey Association's decision [to not subsidize the clubs' losses], and not only in Ottawa. It cannot, however, go on losing money, and so, local fans must accept the situation as gracefully as they can."

"The last time the city of Ottawa had its name engraved on the Stanley Cup was in 1927," Jim McAuley recorded in 1987 when he published *The Ottawa Sports Book*. "In all likelihood it will never happen again."

Not in Frank Finnigan's lifetime, unfortunately. But suddenly, with Ottawa's new Senators beginning play in the NHL in 1992-93, anything is again possible in the city where the Silver Seven and the earlier Senators fashioned comebacks that have become the stuff of hockey legend.

The first club to challenge the Silver Seven was one that piqued the imagination of the hockey public. The Rat Portage Thistles from the town now known as Kenora, Ontario, challenged the Silver Seven in 1903 and 1905. Their popularity was due to the fact that Rat Portage/Kenora was the smallest community ever to ice a challenger for the Stanley Cup.

To the surprise of almost everyone, including the Silver Seven, the hardy men from the small railroad town 140 miles east of Winnipeg put up a respectable challenge in their first appearance on March 12, 1903, losing 6–2, and, two nights later, 4–2.

The Silver Seven overpowered three opponents in 1903-04. The Winnipeg Rowing Club lost the first game of a best-of-three series 9–1, won the second 6–2, and dropped the third 2–0.

Following the 9–1 beating, a *Winnipeg Free Press* writer said it was "the bloodiest game in Ottawa," and listed seven of nine Winnipeg players as casualties, two of whom had to retire from the game. "A team must be one-third better than Ottawa to win in the Capital," the writer added.

When the Toronto Marlboroughs challenged the Silver Seven six weeks later, they absorbed 6–3 and 11–2 beatings, as well as a severe working over. Captain Lal Earls said, on their return to Toronto, "By long odds, Ottawa is the fastest and dirtiest team in the country."

In those days, long before radio and television, newspapers had a significant influence on fans' perspectives on the game. An Ottawa *Journal* reporter, perhaps becoming accustomed to violence by this time, said offhandedly:

> The play wasn't any rougher than is usual and is expected in eastern hockey, but it was something new to the Marlboroughs who alleged that they had never before been treated in such an unladylike manner. The Ottawas blocked their opponents with precision and looked for the same treatment. They received it.

The Toronto *Globe*, on the other hand, was alarmed:

> The [Ottawa] style of hockey seems to be the only one known and people consider it quite proper and legitimate for a team to endeavor to incapacitate their opponents rather than to excel them in skill and speed . . . slashing, tripping, the severest kind of cross checking and a systematic method of hammering Marlboroughs on hand and wrists are the most effective points in Ottawa's style.
>
> In addition they have a habit of hitting men on the hand when the referee is not looking and body-checking an opponent into the boards when he has passed the puck. Even the Toronto goalkeeper [Eddie Geroux] didn't escape. He also was hit on the head. At various times, Marlborough players were so injured that the game had to be stopped until they recovered but all finished on the ice.

The Silver Seven players were inclined to regard Toronto's reaction lightly. "Marlboroughs got off very easily," one player remarked. "When Winnipeg Rowing Club played here, most of their players were carried off the ice on stretchers."

The Marlboroughs took more than a physical beating. When receipts were counted there wasn't enough money to go around, and the Toronto club lost $300 on the venture to Ottawa.

Two weeks after defeating the Marlboroughs, the Silver Seven began a two-game, total-goals series against the Brandon Wheat Kings, winning 6–3 and 9–3. The Wheat Kings returned to Manitoba, lamenting as they went that "Ottawa was the dirtiest club we've ever met." Goalkeeper Doug Morrison termed the Ottawa players "butchers."

In passing, it may be noted that a penalty to the same Morrison resulted in events that contradict the most popular folk tale concerning Lester Patrick, the immortal Silver Fox of hockey. In this era, goaltenders served their own penalties, so that a skater would have to fill in for a goalkeeper who had been banished to the penalty box. Patrick, then playing for the Wheat Kings as a rover, replaced Morrison in the Brandon nets, making one stop and having no goals scored against him. Nearly a quarter of a century later, on April 7, 1928, in Montreal, Patrick, then the coach of the New York Rangers, played in the nets for his club in a Stanley Cup playoff game. Most fans assume that this was the first time he had played goal in a Stanley Cup match. In fact, he had made his debut as a netminder in the 1904 series against Ottawa.

After already turning back the challenges of three teams in 1904, the Silver Seven were ready to take on a club from Amherst, champions of Nova Scotia, but the Cup's trustees said it was too late in the year – March 7 – to accept another challenge. They figured the ice would be too soft and slushy.

The Silver Seven's propensity for rough play has been largely forgotten with the passage of time, but the story of their first Stanley Cup opponent in 1905 – the Dawson City Klondikers, who traveled nearly 4,400 miles to Ottawa in search of the trophy – is a Stanley Cup legend in itself.

They were a bunch of rollicking customers from all parts of Canada who had been lured north by the smell of gold. Strong, wiry, confident young men like teenaged goalie Albert Forrest, the youngest player in Stanley Cup history, from Trois-Rivières, Quebec; Jim Johnstone, point, from Ottawa; Dr. Randy McLennan, cover point, from Cornwall; right winger Norm Watt from Aylmer, Quebec; left wing George Kennedy; center Hector Smith, from West Selkirk, Manitoba; rover Dave Fairbairn from Portage la Prairie, Manitoba; and spare A. N. Martin from Ottawa. They were reinforced by cover point Lorne Hanna from Brandon, Manitoba, who joined the team as they swept across the Prairies on their way to do battle with Ottawa.

The Klondikers left Dawson City on the afternoon of December 19, 1904, running behind dog teams and waving to the appreciative crowds that lined their route. The story of their twenty-day journey emerges in excerpts from contemporary accounts. Said the Ottawa *Journal*,

The Long Trip Home

After losing to Ottawa in 1904, the Klondikers from Dawson City in the Yukon went on a twenty-three-game barnstorming tour of the Maritime provinces, Quebec, and Ontario to earn money for the trip home. Goaltender Albert Forrest, at seventeen the youngest competitor in Cup history, on the return trip walked the last 350 miles from Pelly Crossing to Dawson City, alone.

The Dawson City Klondikers, photographed outside Dey's Rink in Ottawa, finished their barnstorming tour of Eastern Canada with a record of thirteen wins, nine losses, and one tie.

Their first day, they covered 46 miles, the second, 41. The third day saw them struggling along to cover 36 miles and some of them suffered with blistered feet. To proceed, these had to remove their boots. It may give an idea of the hardship they faced when it is recorded that the mercury went down to 20 degrees below zero during that trip from Dawson City to Skagway where they missed boat connections by two hours and had to fret at the dockside for five days. They went to Seattle and then Vancouver where they headed East by train.

Reporting their trip from Vancouver to Ottawa, the *Journal* said: "All along the route the Klondikers received expressions of good will from hockey enthusiasts who apparently are a unit in their desire to see the Yukon gentlemen beat Ottawa. Delegations met them at various places and cheered them on their way."

Unperturbed by all this hardship, the Klondikers arrived in Ottawa amid great fanfare on January 12, 1905, one day before the best-of-three series opened. They were weary but still confident, and asked that the series be postponed a week. The Silver Seven refused, citing conflicts with their regular league schedule.

This refusal may have prompted a Klondiker into a bit of bravado, for, when he saw Frank McGee play, he remarked, "He doesn't look like too much." This may have been an honest appraisal, for it was made after the first game, which the Silver Seven won 9–2 but in which McGee had scored only once, at the ten-minute mark of the first half of a penalty-filled contest.

It was a rough game, in which right-winger Norm Watt of the Klondikers banged Ottawa's Art Moore over the head, opening a four-stitch cut and

"One-eyed" Frank McGee scored sixty-three goals in twenty-two Stanley Cup games.

earning fifteen minutes in the penalty box. Later, he got into a hassle with Alf Smith. Both were banished for ten minutes.

The second game was tame – only four penalties called – and McGee exonerated himself in this meeting, which Ottawa took 23–2.

McGee, Ottawa's blond, heavily-muscled center-ice star was sometimes referred to by old-timers as the greatest player of all time. He established an all-time single-game Stanley Cup record in this contest, scoring fourteen goals, four in the first half and ten in the second, eight of them consecutively in the space of eight minutes and twenty seconds. He scored three – his sixth, seventh, and eighth – in ninety seconds and four goals in an even 140 seconds, setting new records at every turn.

His fourteen goals have never been approached, let alone matched, in any professional game, league, or Stanley Cup contest. Eight consecutive goals and four goals in 140 seconds are marks that remain untouched to this day.

As it turned out, the Klondikers made striking figures in their black, gold, and white uniforms, but these happy wanderers couldn't play big-league hockey. Thus it was recorded in Stanley Cup history that the team that traveled the farthest to win the silver grail was also the team that took the worst beating.

The high-scoring Rat Portage Thistles returned to challenge the Silver Seven in 1905 and walloped Ottawa 9–3 in game one of a best-of-three final. The Silver Seven's loss was only their second defeat in twelve Stanley Cup games. The Thistles, described as the fastest club in the country but lacking in strategy, paid dearly for their over-zealousness in the next two contests. Ottawa had played without Frank McGee and Billy Gilmour in the first game, but these two hearties returned to lead the Silver Seven to 4–2 and 5–4 victories in games two and three. Left-winger Tommy Phillips of the Thistles was the high scorer of the series with nine goals, six in the opener and three in the rubber game.

It didn't serve the Thistles to beat Ottawa in that first game. Descriptive passages from newspaper accounts of the second game indicate how tough it was. Reportedly, every Rat Portage player on the ice was hurt, including goaltender Eddie Geroux, who was cut on the face by McGee during a scuffle near the goal. McGee got four of Ottawa's six penalties and was convicted on four separate charges – cross-checking, kneeing, tripping, and holding.

An illuminating report by a Toronto *Globe* reporter, who may or may not have been prejudiced, read:

> The Silver Seven waded into the Thistles in butcher fashion and every forward who got near them was jolted good and plenty. McGee several times hit Thistle players over the head with his stick. Griffis and Bill McGimsie of the Thistles went on the ice fitter for the hospital than for the hockey game. They both had wrenched knees and were still rather weak from the fearful gruelling they took in the previous game. McGimsie was so done out that in the second half he fell down from sheer weakness in a scrimmage in the Thistle goal and was

The Stanley Cup—"Ticket for Montreal, please."
Railway Ticket Agent—"Return?"
The Stanley Cup—"No; I'm not coming back."

Editorial cartoons were a common feature on the sports pages during the early 1900s. The result predicted in this 1906 cartoon became reality when the Montreal Wanderers defeated the Ottawa Silver Seven, 12–10, in their two-game, total-goals series.

unable to get up for a few seconds. When he did rise to his feet, referee Grant ruled him off for five minutes for obstructing the goal.

Tom Hooper, cover point for the Thistles, had a nasty knee, too. He injured it early in the game when Harvey Pulford almost heaved him over the boards with a charge from behind. Tommy Phillips had his face cut open in three places and his eye closed, and he looked as though he had been in a railroad wreck. Griffis had a beautiful countenance, decorated by a swollen nose, split lips and a gash on the forehead. Captain Phillips complimented the Ottawas on their victory.

The games were played at Dey's Rink and boxes for six persons sold for $10, reserved seats for $1 and 75 cents, and standing room for 25 cents. Scalpers got $6 for $1 seats, sharing gleefully in the Silver Seven's string of successes.

The Silver Seven finally met their Waterloo in 1906 after having walloped Queen's University, 16–7 and 12–7, and Smiths Falls, 6–5 and 8–2.

The Montreal Wanderers, staffed by such stalwarts as Lester Patrick, who had changed clubs, goalkeeper Doc Ménard, Billy Strachan and Rod Kennedy at defense, center Pud Glass, and wingers Ernie Russell and Ernie

Lester Patrick, whose career as a player, coach, and general manager spanned forty-two years, played his finest hockey as a member of the Montreal Wanderers, leading the Redbands to a pair of Cup titles in 1906 and 1907.

"Moose" Johnston, finally lifted the Cup from the Silver Seven in a two-game, total-goals series.

The Wanderers, with the benefit of home ice and a supportive crowd, won the first game 9–1 and then, in Ottawa, lost the second, 9–3, to squeak out a win on a combined score of 12–10.

It was also one of the most spine-tingling finishes to a series. Going into Ottawa with an eight-goal lead and, according to newspaper reports of the first game, facing an Ottawa team that had "played pathetically round the nets," the Wanderers were almost assured of victory.

But the Silver Seven were far from dead. In the Montreal game, Wanderers' goalie Doc Ménard had been called upon to make only three stops in the first thirty minutes, but now the Silver Seven in Ottawa were bombarding him with five shots in the first sixty seconds. This fierce Ottawa attack forced Montreal into a defensive shell, and several times, to ease the pressure, the Wanderers lifted the puck into the crowd. Despite Ottawa's impressive attack, the Wanderers opened the scoring, with Lester Patrick breaking out with Pud Glass to give the Montrealers an almost insurmountable 10–1 lead on the series.

McGee, scoreless till now, finally cracked the Wanderers' defensive wall, and the spark was fanned into a flame. Led by Harry Smith, who scored five goals before it was over, Ottawa virtually snowed Montreal under to tie the series at ten goals each at 20:40 of the second half. Three of the Ottawa goals came in two minutes and thirty seconds of the second half, while Wanderers' point Billy Strachan was sitting in the penalty box.

While 5,500 fans shouted their excitement, Ottawa stormed the Montreal goal but couldn't break the deadlock. With five minutes to go, Lester Patrick spoke to each of his Wanderer teammates individually. It must have been one of the greatest pep talks ever given, for the Wanderers, throwing defense to the winds, charged the Ottawa net. Fittingly enough, Patrick himself scored two goals within two minutes to give the Wanderers the Cup and close out the fabulous reign of Ottawa's Silver Seven.

Writing of the Wanderers' strategy of attacking in the late moments of the game, the Ottawa *Journal* said: "It was a masterly stroke, the genius of a general."

"It was a scene never to be forgotten," said the Ottawa *Citizen*, "as Montreal defiantly hurled back the bounding beggars who charged the circle about Ménard in the last minutes of play. As the Ottawas charged and shot and scrambled and fell within a few feet of victory, the crowd behaved like inmates of a vast insane asylum, and the noise, deafening at times, grew with a fearful uproar."

Ottawa's Silver Seven, a talented, win-at-any-price team, compiled an amazing Stanley Cup record. Their methods may be questioned, but their statistics cannot be refuted. From 1903 to 1906, the Silver Seven won eight out of nine Stanley Cup series, outscoring their opponents 151 to 74.

In 1907, the Kenora (formerly Rat Portage) Thistles, reorganized after their defeats by the Silver Seven, made their third and final bid for a Stanley Cup, challenging the Montreal Wanderers. They won the trophy in mid-January in Montreal, with 4–2 and 8–6 victories for a combined score of 12–8 in this two-game, total-goals series. But the Thistles hardly had time to polish the Cup. Two months later, Montreal was back to reclaim it in one of the gaudiest, cross-country controversies in the history of the sport.

For their first series against the Wanderers, the Thistles had borrowed Art Ross from the Brandon Wheat Kings, paying this $50-a-month bank clerk $1,000 to play in the two Cup games. Apparently there was no objection to this by the Wanderers.

While the Wanderers were en route west for their second series against the Thistles, William Foran, who had replaced John Sweetland as a Stanley Cup trustee, responded to a protest filed by the Wanderers by announcing that there would be no imports or "ringers" allowed in the upcoming series. This met with great consternation in Kenora because, although the Thistles no longer had Art Ross in the line-up, they had further supplemented their roster with Harry "Rat" Westwick and Alf Smith from the Silver Seven and Fred Whitcroft from Peterborough of the OHA. The Thistles also claimed that

The series that saw the Kenora Thistles defeat the Montreal Wanderers in January of 1907 featured eleven future members of the Hockey Hall of Fame, including Lester Patrick, Art Ross, and Joe Hall.

the Wanderers had already benefited by importing a couple of players of their own, including goalkeeper Riley Hern and cover point Hod Stuart, both of whom played for Montreal in the first series between the two teams.

"No Westwick, No Smith, No game," the Thistles telegraphed Foran.

"Use Westwick and Smith," Foran wired back, "and neither team will get the Stanley Cup until decent regard for the sport prevails." No mention was made of Whitcroft.

After two postponements and several incendiary telegrams back and forth, the series was played despite the objections of the Cup's trustee. The Wanderers withdrew their protest when the Thistles agreed to shift the games to Winnipeg's much larger arena, guaranteeing a bigger gate for the clubs to share. The Wanderers won the first game 7–2 on the strength of a four-goal effort by Ernie Russell, but then lost the second game, 6–5, to win the round and the Stanley Cup by a combined 12–8 score.

Smith and Westwick played in both games for the Thistles, with Smith scoring twice and Westwick held goal-less. Whitcroft scored two goals, both in the second game, his final tally breaking a 5–5 deadlock with six minutes remaining. Cup trustee Foran relented and presented the Cup to the Wanderers on the basis that they were the team that had first protested the use of imported players. Besides, Foran realized that the Wanderers had to go ahead and play the Thistles: they couldn't afford to pass up the gate money.

For the next four years the Stanley Cup was to travel up and down the Ottawa River. In 1908 the Wanderers retained against three challengers. They defeated the Ottawa Victorias and the Winnipeg Maple Leafs by lopsided scores in January and March, and then bested the Toronto club that had won the championship of the newly established Ontario Professional Hockey League, by a 6–4 score on March 14.

Before the start of the 1909 season, the Wanderers successfully defended the Cup in a two-game, total-goals series against an almost all-import team from Edmonton. Ottawa took the Cup back at the end of the 1909 season by virtue of winning the Eastern Canada Hockey Association league championship with a record of ten wins and two losses. The Wanderers were runners-up, finishing with nine wins and three losses. The key game of the season was the final match-up between Ottawa and the Wanderers, which the Ottawa club – now known as the Senators – won 8–3.

During this time, protests were raised about the manner in which Stanley Cup challenge series were being conducted. Although the teams were still operating under the guise of amateurism, it was obvious to everyone that money had become increasingly important and that some of the athletes and some of the clubs were not playing solely for the joy of the game.

The hockey public, however, seemed to be little concerned with the mechanics of the Cup's presentation. What interested them was who won it

The members of the 1907 Stanley Cup-winning Kenora Thistles team were each presented with a silver cup in recognition of their outstanding play. The trophy pictured here belonged to Art Ross.

ERNIE JOHNSON   BERT LINDSAY   BRUCE STUART

and how. In 1909, for instance, in the Ottawa–Montreal Wanderers match in March, ticket scalpers received five times face value of a ticket, and four and a half hours before the face-off, huge crowds had gathered with the hopes of buying one. A crowd of 6,500 witnessed the game, described by an Ottawa hockey writer as "one of the greatest ever played on local ice."

The fans only took real exception when they were hit in their pocketbooks. In 1910, when Ottawa management raised the price of rush seats to 50 cents from a quarter, only 3,800 saw the final game against Edmonton.

Inflation, however, didn't keep people away for long. Two months later, when a game was being played against the Wanderers, one-dollar tickets were being sold on the street for seven dollars, and a crowd of 6,000 was on hand.

Ernie "Moose" Johnson (left), who is credited with developing the poke check, won four Cup championships as a member of the Montreal Wanderers. Bert Lindsay (center), father of Hall-of-Famer Ted Lindsay, finished his career with the NHL's Toronto Arenas. Bruce Stuart (right), won back-to-back Cups with the Montreal Wanderers in 1908 and the Ottawa Senators in 1909.

The Professional Leagues,

1910-1926

I N 1910, MAJOR-LEAGUE HOCKEY WAS OVERHAULED. THE EASTERN CANADA Hockey Association, successor to the original AHA, was dissolved, and two competing professional leagues were formed to take its place. However, poor attendance at early-season games quickly convinced team owners that too many clubs were competing for fan interest. The number of teams was quickly cut from ten to seven, with the surviving clubs all playing in the National Hockey Association. Thus started another colorful era in the history of the game.

The NHA proved to be a fantastic union. Up in the little valley town of Renfrew near Ottawa was a bearded millionaire, Ambrose O'Brien, who issued blank cheques in a grandiose bid to win the Stanley Cup. With magnificent disregard for expense, he gathered a glittering all-star team that included the peerless Fred "Cyclone" Taylor, one of the fastest skaters of all time; the two Patrick brothers, Lester and Frank; Bert Lindsay, who was the father of an all-star of the future, Ted Lindsay; Fred Whitcroft; the Cleghorns, Sprague and Odie; Jack Fraser of the 1903 Silver Seven; Bobby Rowe; and Newsy Lalonde, who, besides being a tremendous hockey player, would be named Canada's best lacrosse player of the half century in a 1950 Canadian Press poll.

The elastic bands were off the bankrolls, and hockey fever and the Stanley Cup chase spread to the silver-mining country of northern Ontario. Cobalt and Haileybury, two other wealthy boom towns that sprouted in the

Opposite: Pioneer player and builder Jack Adams played three seasons for the Vancouver Millionaires. He was the PCHA's scoring leader in 1921-22.

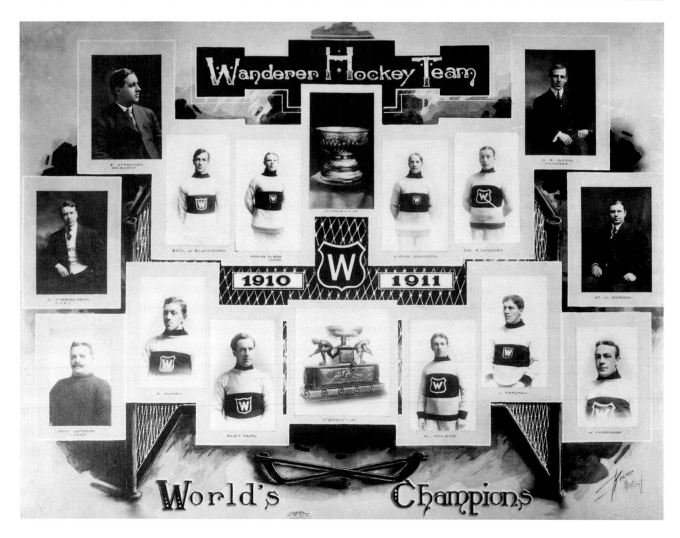

The 1910-11 Montreal Wanderers compiled a record of eleven wins and one loss to unseat the Ottawa Senators as Cup champions. It was the fourth and last championship for the club.

wilderness, also wanted major-league hockey – and got it. As well, the NHA boasted established clubs, including Ottawa, the Montreal Wanderers and the Shamrocks, and a new franchise, the Montreal Canadiens, which would prove to be the only survivor of that league. Though its history would be relatively brief, in 1910 the NHA opened the curtain on yet another of hockey's most noteworthy periods.

The Montreal Wanderers were the first club to win the Cup under the new NHA setup. Ottawa was still the Stanley Cup holder as the season began, having successfully defended its title against teams from Galt, Ontario, and Edmonton in January. But the Senators relinquished the Cup in March, when the Wanderers won the league title, clinching the crown with a 3–1 win over Ottawa on March 5.

The Wanderers accepted a post-season challenge issued by a team from Berlin (later Kitchener), Ontario, the champion of the Ontario Professional Hockey League. The Montrealers won the one-game contest by a 7–3 score. Within a span of two months, then, three Stanley Cup series had been played, involving Ottawa, Galt, Edmonton, Berlin, and the Wanderers.

Goalie Hugh Lehman matched the nomadic qualities of Percy LeSueur.

Lehman played in two Stanley Cup series with different clubs within two months, tending nets for Galt and then switching to Berlin for their challenge against the Wanderers. Earlier, in 1906, LeSueur had made a similar move when he left Smiths Falls, after it was defeated by Ottawa, to join the Silver Seven for the second game of their series against the Montreal Wanderers.

So with new blood, money, and ambitions, hockey launched itself head-long into another decade. Before it ended, it would see the Stanley Cup become the sole property of professional hockey and the centerpoint of a bitter rivalry between East and West. And the seeds would also be sown for the formation of the National Hockey League, which proved to be the sport's durable survivor, celebrating its seventy-fifth anniversary season in 1991-92. The very appearance of the game itself was to change, too. In place of two thirty-minute halves, three twenty-minute periods became the standard. As well, seven-man hockey, with point, cover point, rover, and three forwards would eventually be replaced by the six-man game we know today.

The Ottawa Senators captured the NHA's championship and the Stanley Cup in 1911 and fended off the challenges of Galt, the Ontario Professional League champions, and Port Arthur, the New Ontario League champions, in sudden-death games. Ottawa's Marty Walsh scored ten goals in the Senators' 13–4 win over Port Arthur. Walsh also scored three in Ottawa's 7–4 decision over Galt on water-covered ice, before only 2,500 fans. Galt also lost $20 on the deal. Its share of the proceeds was $375 and its expenses were $395.

Brothers Frank and Lester Patrick had moved to Canada's West Coast in 1910, and, in December of 1911, they established the new Pacific Coast

Marty Walsh (left), scored ten goals, including three in forty seconds, against Port Arthur on March 16, 1911. Paddy Moran (right), tended goal for fifteen seasons with Quebec. Jack McDonald (center), who scored nine goals in two Stanley Cup games for Quebec in 1912, later played for all four of the NHL's original clubs.

MARTY WALSH

J. MAC DONALD

P. MORAN

Hockey Association. Within two years, this new professional circuit would challenge for the Stanley Cup.

By 1912, the Renfrew Millionaires had decided to call it a day, having already lost a million dollars, thus reducing the NHA to four teams: the Quebec Bulldogs, the Ottawa Senators, the Montreal Wanderers, and the Montreal Canadiens, who finished in that order.

The Bulldogs brought the Cup to Quebec City for the first time in 1912, and repeated in 1913, receiving only feeble resistance from Maritime clubs. In 1912, at Quebec City, they defeated Moncton, New Brunswick, 9–3 and 8–0 in a best-of-three set, and in 1913 they would knock off the Sydney Miners, Maritime League champions from Nova Scotia, 14–3 and 6–2.

The Bulldogs' roster included an impressive list of names from goal out. Paddy Moran was in the nets, Harry Mummery and Joe Hall were on defense, Joe Malone played center, and the wingers were Tommy Smith and Rusty Crawford, with Bill Creighton, Walter Rooney, Jack Marks, and Goldie Prodgers as subs. Malone scored nine times against Sydney to become one of only three players to score more than eight goals in a Stanley Cup game.

In 1913 the Pacific Coast Hockey Association, under the guidance of the Patricks, first challenged the supremacy of the East. Though their competition was not sanctioned by the Stanley Cup trustees, Quebec's Bulldogs, having dispatched the Sydney Miners, traveled to the West Coast in late March for a best-of-three series against the Victoria Aristocrats, champions of the PCHA. These games were played using a combination of the seven-man rules still in force in the PCHA and the six-man system adopted by the NHA on February 12, 1913.

The six-man experiment in the East had first been tried in 1911, but initially was greeted derisively by the public and the press. The Ottawa *Citizen* called it "Hobble-skirted, bob-tailed, no-combination six-man hockey. It is slap-dash, ping-pong, every-man-for-himself hockey." The Toronto *Globe* said: "Individual rushes and the utter lack of team play is the trademark of the bob-tailed six-man game."

At the unofficial championship series in Victoria, the difference was split almost down the middle. The Bulldogs and the Aristocrats played the first game under seven-man rules, and the westerners won, 7–5. Under six-man rules, Quebec won, 6–3, and again, switching back to the seven-man hockey, Victoria won the rubber match, 6–1.

In 1914, NHA and PCHA governors agreed that the Stanley Cup playoffs would be played as a post-season best-of-five series between their champions. The prevailing feeling was that, if the Cup trustees didn't accept this arrangement, the two leagues were prepared to stop competing for the

Stanley Cup and let it pass out of elite professional hockey. The trustees recognized that the viability of Stanley Cup play now depended on the trophy's status as the top prize in the pro game, as senior amateur hockey, which rivaled the pros for fan support in these years, was now playing for the Allan Cup. The trustees were backed into a corner by the resolve of the two leading pro circuits. Unwilling to see the status of Stanley Cup competition diminished, they accepted the NHA–PCHA proposal.

The Quebec Bulldogs fell to third place in the 1913-14 NHA standings, leaving the Montreal Canadiens and the Toronto Blueshirts to play a two-game, total-goals series for the NHA title and, with it, possession of the Stanley Cup.

Although each team posted a shutout on its home ice, the Blueshirts, who later became the NHL's Maple Leafs, outscored the Canadiens 6–2 overall. The second game, which was played in Toronto, was the first Stanley Cup match ever played on artificial ice. This series also marked the Canadiens' first appearance in a Stanley Cup game.

After defeating the Canadiens, the Blueshirts and the Victoria Aristocrats hooked up in the first of thirteen consecutive East–West confrontations

Despite losing Goldie Prodgers, Eddie Oatman, and Jack McDonald to the rival PCHA, the Quebec Bulldogs easily retained their Stanley Cup throne in 1913, downing Sydney, Nova Scotia, in two one-sided games.

The Original Rocket

Although Maurice Richard is the most famous "Rocket" in Stanley Cup lore, he was not the first Rocket to win the Cup. "Rocket" Power was a member of the Stanley Cup-winning Quebec Bulldogs in 1913.

Frank Foyston, who finished his career with the Detroit Cougars in 1928, won his first championship with the Toronto Blueshirts in 1914.

for the Stanley Cup. Victoria of the PCHA traveled east to play Toronto, but overlooked the formality of submitting a challenge. Because of this, the Cup's trustees did not regard the series as legitimate, so, if the Aristocrats had won, some hurried backroom negotiation would have been required. As it was, controversy was avoided when the Blueshirts won three consecutive close games to successfully defend the title. Frank Foyston led the Blueshirts with three goals in the series, including the Cup-winner in the third game of this first best-of-five Stanley Cup series.

The strength of senior amateur hockey can be seen in attendance figures for the 1914 playoffs. The three NHA-PCHA Stanley Cup games drew 14,639 fans. By comparison, just two Ontario Hockey Association senior games between Toronto teams vying for a spot in the Allan Cup playdowns, drew more than 15,000 spectators.

Toronto slid to fourth place, with just eight wins in the twenty-game NHA season of 1914-15. Deadlocked with identical 14–6 records at the conclusion of the campaign, the Ottawa Senators and the Montreal Wanderers played a two-game, total-goals series for the NHA championship and the right to defend the Stanley Cup against the PCHA champions from Vancouver. Although the Wanderers had won three of the four regular-season meetings between the two clubs, in the playoffs the Senators recorded two shutout wins to take the series and earn a berth in the Cup final.

Fred "Cyclone" Taylor notched six goals in three games to lead the Vancouver Millionaires' team of superstars to a lopsided sweep of the best-of-five series. This was the first sanctioned, trustee-approved Stanley Cup final between NHA and PCHA clubs, the first victory for the upstart league from the West Coast, and the first Stanley Cup series to be played west of Winnipeg. More than 20,000 fans turned out for the series, generating $300 shares for each Vancouver player and $200 for each member of the Ottawa squad. The imposing skills of the Millionaires convinced many onlookers that the balance of hockey power had definitely swung West.

Beginning in 1915-16, military service brought about by the outbreak of World War I interrupted some players' hockey careers and increased competition to sign players between the NHA and PCHA. The Portland Rosebuds were easy winners in the PCHA that season, finishing four games up on Vancouver and Victoria. Despite the fact that the original terms of presentation for the Stanley Cup stated that it was to be awarded to the champion hockey club of the Dominion of Canada, the Oregon-based Rosebuds, upon clinching the PCHA crown, obtained the Cup from the previous year's champions, the Vancouver Millionaires, engraved their name on it, and headed for Montreal to meet the NHA champion Canadiens in the annual East-West challenge. Despite the Rosebuds' decision to place their name on the trophy, it was acknowledged that 1916's Stanley Cup

The 1913-14 Vancouver Millionaires finished in last place in the PCHA. One season later, in March of 1915, the first Stanley Cup games played on the West Coast saw the Vancouver Millionaires outscore the Ottawa Senators, 26–8, to sweep the best-of-five series.

champion would be the winner of the Portland–Montreal series.

For the first time since the best-of-five format was introduced in 1913-14, the Stanley Cup series came down to a fifth and deciding game. Portland's Tommy Dunderdale put the Rosebuds ahead early, but the Canadiens bounced back. Skene Ronan tied the game, and the seldom-used Goldie Prodgers netted the Cup-winner for a 2–1 Canadiens win. Goaltender Georges Vezina appeared in his first Cup final for the Canadiens, posting a 2.60 goals-against average en route to the club's first championship.

Competition for players between the PCHA and NHA had driven salaries up to the point that some clubs in both leagues were in financial trouble. Money was tight, and it wasn't long before rumblings of a fold-up of the National Hockey Association were heard. Gate receipts took a nose-dive when fans became tired of the hit-and-miss operations of the association and its teams. Sloppy organization, a by-product of the financial squeeze, resulted in games that often started one or two hours late.

Receipts in the first league game at Montreal in the 1915-16 season were less than $200. Sportswriters panned the league and its players. A Toronto *Globe* reporter noted that visiting clubs arrived for a game with only half a team, and sometimes without a goalkeeper, and declared that the "players have an impudent disregard of their obligations to the public."

Clubs with payrolls ranging from $4,000 to $8,000 had no assets except a

After defeating the defending Cup-champion Millionaires to win the PCHA title in 1916, the Portland Rosebuds engraved their club's name on the Stanley Cup, despite not being recognized as an official winner of the trophy.

The first Montreal Canadiens team to win the Stanley Cup in 1916.

The Stanley Cup Grand Slam

Jack Marshall played on four different Cup-winning teams, the only skater in the history of the trophy to accomplish that feat. He suited up with Winnipeg in 1901, the Montreal AAA in 1902, the Montreal Wanderers in 1907 and 1910, and completed his grand slam with the Toronto Blueshirts in 1914.

few hockey sticks, some well-worn uniforms, and trunks to store them in. Organized hockey in the East was on the skids. Teams were going broke fast.

On the ice, another U.S.-based club, the Seattle Metropolitans, skated to the PCHA title in 1916-17, its second season in the league. Since that season's Stanley Cup championship series was slated for the home rink of the PCHA champion, the Cup trustees moved with the times and acknowledged that a team from outside of Canada had the right both to host the championship and win the trophy. The Metropolitans faced the Canadiens, who had retained the NHA title and the Stanley Cup by defeating Ottawa, 7–6, in a close two-game, total-goals series.

In the first game of the East–West series, Montreal dominated, winning 8–4, with Didier Pitre scoring four times, but the Mets bounced back, winning the next three games while holding the Canadiens to just one goal in each contest. Seattle's Bernie Morris, who finished second in the PCHA's regular-season scoring race with 37 goals in 24 games, scored 14 times against Mon-

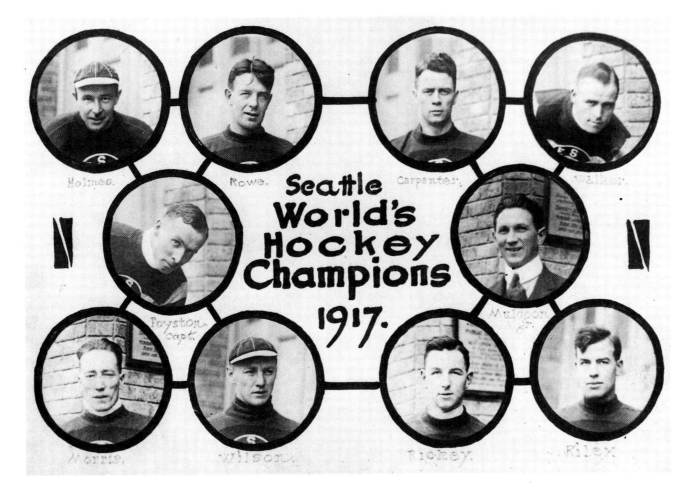

treal in the Cup series, including six goals in the 9–1 finale, enabling the Mets to become the first American squad to capture the coveted trophy.

The 1917 Seattle Metropolitans, the first U.S.-based team to win the Cup.

Financial problems and disagreements among club owners resulted in the formation of a new eastern professional league – the National Hockey League – in November of 1917. Four former NHA clubs – the Montreal Canadiens and the Wanderers, the Ottawa Senators, and the newly named Toronto Arenas – began play in the new league's inaugural season. The Wanderers were forced to withdraw from the league at mid-season when fire destroyed the Montreal Arena and, with it, the team's equipment, leaving just three clubs to complete the NHL's split schedule of 1917-18. The Canadiens, first-place finishers over the first half of the schedule, met the Arenas, who had finished on top in the second half of the campaign. Guided by rookie coach Dick Carroll, the Arenas won this grinding two-game, total-goals series by a combined score of 10–7, winning the NHL championship and the right to meet the PCHA champion for the Stanley Cup.

The PCHA adopted the two-game, total-goals format for its league championship playoffs for the first time in March of 1918. Defending Cup-champion Seattle met Vancouver in this low-scoring series that saw game one end in a 2–2 tie and game two result in a 1–0 shutout win for

First Time Lucky

A total of thirteen NHL coaches have won the Cup in their first year. Dick Carroll, who piloted the Toronto Arenas in 1918, was the first coach to accomplish the feat, while Jean Perron, who coached the Montreal Canadiens in 1986, was the most recent to capture the Cup in his rookie campaign.

Although he played for twenty seasons in five professional leagues, Hugh Lehman was a member of only one Cup-winning squad, the 1915 Vancouver Millionaires.

Bernie Morris, who scored fourteen goals in the 1917 Stanley Cup series against Montreal, including six in the decisive fourth game, never scored again in Stanley Cup play.

goalkeeper Hughie Lehman and the Vancouver Millionaires. Future Hall-of-Famer Barney Stanley scored the only goal in the final game.

The first NHL-PCHA Stanley Cup series was played in Toronto under the best-of-five format that had been in place since 1914, and it required all five games to determine a winner. Again, eastern (six-man) rules and western (seven-man) rules alternated, and this proved to be crucial to the outcome of the series. In every game, the winning team was the one playing under its own system of rules. Because the series was in the East, NHL rules were employed in the fifth and deciding game, helping Toronto to a 2–1 win. By comparison, in the series' two games played under PCHA rules, Vancouver had outscored the Arenas by a combined 14–5 count.

Montreal defeated Ottawa in the 1919 NHL playoffs. Defending champion Toronto had suffered through a demoralizing season, withdrawing from the

THE ARENA HOCKEY CLUB OF TORONTO

1918　1919

CHAMPIONS OF THE WORLD

The Arena Hockey Club of Toronto, the first NHL team to win the Stanley Cup. Jack Adams, who won seven Stanley Cups as a coach and general manager, won his first Cup as a player with this Toronto squad.

league on February 20, 1919. With only the Canadiens and the Senators left and several weeks to fill before the start of the NHL-PCHA finals in the West, the league decided to extend its finals from a best-of-five to a best-of-seven championship series. The Canadiens won in five games, with Newsy Lalonde leading all scorers with nine goals.

Vancouver finished first in the PCHA regular season and elected to play the first game of the league's two-game, total-goals championship in the home rink of the runner-up Seattle Metropolitans. This strategy backfired, as the Metropolitans recorded a commanding 6–1 win. Wingers Frank Foyston and Muzz Murray combined for five goals for the Mets. The Millionaires won game two on home ice but lost the series by a combined score of 7–5.

The Montreal–Seattle series had all of the hallmarks of a classic. Seattle used its mastery of western rules to win games one and three by lopsided scores. The Canadiens won game two, with Newsy Lalonde scoring all four of the NHL champion's goals. Game four was considered to be the finest contest ever played in a PCHA arena. The game ended 0–0 after twenty minutes of overtime. Finally, in game five, the Canadiens seemed to have mastered seven-man hockey. Newsy Lalonde scored two goals from the rover spot (the position of the extra man under western rules), and Montreal right winger Odie Cleghorn got the winner after more than fifteen minutes of overtime. A sixth and deciding game was scheduled for April 1, but a continent-wide epidemic of Spanish influenza intervened. With five Montreal players hospitalized or sick in bed, the series was abandoned just five and a half hours before the start of game six. No champion was declared.

From 1908 to 1926, superstar Newsy Lalonde scored twenty-seven goals in twenty-nine Stanley Cup games.

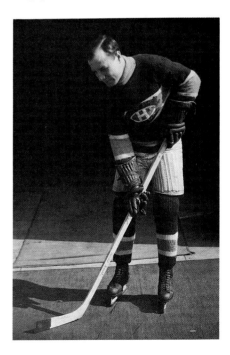

"Bad" Joe Hall was one of the NHA's finest defensemen. He played on two Cup-winners with the Quebec Bulldogs in 1912 and 1913 before joining the Canadiens. This photo was taken shortly before his death in 1919.

Jack Darragh played his entire career with Ottawa. He made his pro debut on the same evening that Georges Vezina first appeared in goal for the Montreal Canadiens.

Montreal defenseman Joe Hall never left hospital, succumbing to pneumonia brought about by the flu on April 5, 1919. Hall, who had played hockey for nearly fifteen years with Houghton, Michigan, Winnipeg, Kenora, Quebec, and the Canadiens, was buried in his adopted home town of Brandon, Manitoba.

Official lists of Stanley Cup winners state that there was no champion in 1919. This ignores an admittedly fading precedent established with the first Cup competitions of the 1890s. Throughout the first decades of Cup play, the Stanley Cup passed into the possession of any team winning its league championship – if the incumbent Stanley Cup-holder was a member of that league. By this criteria, the 1919 Montreal Canadiens became Stanley Cup holders when they captured the NHL crown from Toronto, the 1918 Cup champion, on March 6, 1919. While the annual NHL–PCHA series failed to produce a winner in 1919, using the standard of the day, the Canadiens had already won the Cup when they went west.

It appears that the Stanley Cup had evolved into a prize awarded solely for playoff supremacy. Though the Cup's trustees had made no specific ruling that changed the terms of competition, it is apparent that, by 1919, the Cup would be awarded only to the winner of the annual series between the NHL and PCHA champions.

In six of the next seven seasons, NHL clubs would go on to win the Stanley Cup. This apparent stability contrasted with significant changes in the structure of professional hockey that would prove to have a lasting effect on the terms of Stanley Cup competition.

The Ottawa Senators won both halves of the 1919-20 NHL regular-season schedule, earning the right to play the PCHA champion without having to contest a playoff. In the West, the Seattle Metropolitans again bested

Vancouver, winning by a combined score of 7–3 in a two-game, total-goals series. When the Mets arrived in Ottawa, it became apparent that their red, white, and green barber-pole uniforms were similar to the Senators' red, white, and black pattern. Ottawa agreed to play in white jerseys.

Ottawa won the first two games, but the Mets bounced back with a 3–1 win in game three. Warm weather resulted in poor ice conditions, which marred the first three games, so the series was shifted to Toronto to take advantage of the artificial-ice plant at the Mutual Street Arena. Seattle tied the series with a 5–2 win in game four, with Frank Foyston scoring twice. Jack Darragh, who had the game-winning goal in game one, lifted Ottawa to the championship with a three-goal performance in the decisive game, and Pete Green became the second rookie coach in the NHL to win the Cup, joining Dick Carroll of the 1918 Toronto Arenas.

For 1920-21, Ottawa and Vancouver were easy winners of their respective league-championship series. For the first game of the Cup finals, Vancouver's Denman Street Arena was packed with 11,000 fans, the largest crowd ever to see a hockey game anywhere in the world to that time. A record 51,000 tickets were sold for the series, which went to the five-game limit with each game being decided by one goal.

Jack Darragh was the hero for the second straight year, scoring both

Dapper dressers off the ice and flashy performers on it, the Ottawa Senators won back-to-back Cups in 1920 and 1921.

A Full Night's Work

Frank "King" Clancy is the only player to play all six positions in a single Stanley Cup game. On March 31, 1923, Clancy faced off as a center, played both sides of the defense, and skated up and down both wings. And, when goalie Clint Benedict was penalized for slashing, Clancy took a two-minute turn between the pipes.

The Regina Capitals, the first champions of the Western Canada Hockey League, a four-team professional circuit formed in 1921.

REGINA CAPITALS
CHAMPIONS WESTERN CANADA
HOCKEY LEAGUE
1921 - 1922

Ottawa goals in the 2–1 finale, as the Senators became the first NHL club to capture back-to-back Stanley Cups and the first team since the 1912-13 Quebec Bulldogs to repeat as Cup champions.

A third major hockey league began play in 1921-22. Made up of the Regina Capitals and the Saskatoon Shieks in Saskatchewan and the Calgary Tigers and the Edmonton Eskimos in Alberta, the Western Canada Hockey League and the PCHA agreed to match their league champions in a two-game, total-goals series to determine an opponent to meet the NHL champions in a best-of-five Stanley Cup final.

Regina won the WCHL's inaugural playoffs and faced the PCHA's Vancouver Millionaires in the western finals. The Capitals surprised Vancouver in game one, winning by a 2–1 score in a game played under the PCHA's seven-man rules. Regina's Dick Irvin got the winning goal. The series' second game shifted to Regina and used the WCHL's six-man rules. The Millionaires battled back, as defenseman Art Duncan scored three goals. Vancouver won 4–0, prevailing in the series by a combined score of 5–2.

In the NHL, the Toronto St. Patricks (the renamed Arenas club) defeated Ottawa 5–4 in the two-game, total-goals NHL playoffs. All the scoring in the series occurred in game one, as Corbett Denneny got what would prove to be the series-winning goal for the St. Pats. In the second game, played on slushy ice, the Senators dominated play, forcing Toronto to ice the puck frequently, but no goals were scored.

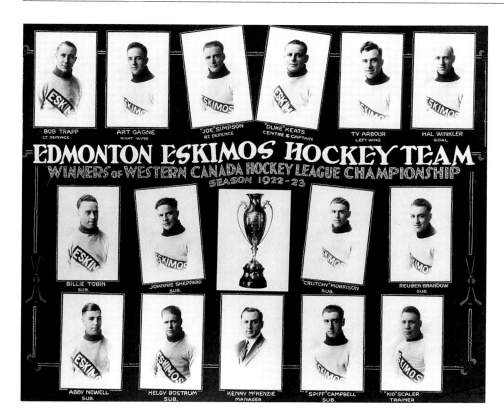

The Edmonton Eskimos, led by "Bullet" Joe Simpson, Gordon "Duke" Keats, and goaltender Hal Winkler, were WCHL champions and Stanley Cup finalists in 1923.

In the Stanley Cup finals, the St. Pats defeated Vancouver in overtime in game two and then captured the Cup with lopsided victories in games four and five. Cecil "Babe" Dye notched nine of the St. Pats' sixteen goals, including two game-winners, and goaltender John Roach, who in game four recorded the first Stanley Cup shutout by an NHL rookie, posted a 1.80 goals-against average as Toronto won its second Stanley Cup. Dye was also awarded the first penalty shot in Cup competition, but he didn't score, sending the puck high over the net. Center Jack Adams, who had been lured away from Toronto by Vancouver in 1920, returned to Stanley Cup play in impressive fashion, scoring six goals in the series.

Ottawa reclaimed top spot in the NHL in 1922-23, surviving a rugged playoff series with the Montreal Canadiens. The Senators won game one 2–0, despite persistent fouling by the Montreal defense pair of Sprague Cleghorn and Billy Couture. Both earned game misconducts and were suspended for the rest of the series by their own manager, Léo Dandurand. In game two, the revamped Canadiens took a two-goal lead before Cy Denneny notched a goal that gave the championship to the Senators. This series marked a changing of the guard for the Montreal club. It was the final appearance by nineteen-year veteran Didier Pitre and the first playoff action for superstar-to-be Aurel Joliat.

Edmonton defeated Regina for the WCHL championship on Duke Keats's overtime goal in game two of the playoffs, while in the PCHA, which had finally switched to six-man hockey, the renamed Vancouver Maroons

Cecil Dye, nicknamed "Babe" because he was a professional baseball player in the off-season, led all scorers in the Stanley Cup series of 1922, with eleven goals in seven games.

(formerly the Millionaires) defeated Victoria by a combined score of 5–3.

All three champions would play for the Stanley Cup in 1923, with all games taking place in Vancouver. The NHL and PCHA clubs met first, and the resulting series between Ottawa and Vancouver marked the first time in Stanley Cup history that two brothers opposed each other in the finals. In fact, two sets of brothers – Cy and Corbett Denneny and George and Frank Boucher – stood on opposite sides of the center line for the opening face-off. Cy and George skated with Ottawa, while Corbett and Frank suited up for Vancouver. Neither of the Dennenys scored in the series, but each of the Bouchers scored twice. Ottawa's Harry "Punch" Broadbent, who posted the only goal in game one, scored five times over the course of the four-game series to lead the Senators to the Cup. Vancouver coach Frank Patrick called this Senators team the greatest he had ever seen.

Three days after the end of their series with the Maroons, the Senators – still in Vancouver – played game one of a best-of-three series with the WCHL's Edmonton Eskimos. Ottawa's veteran defenseman Eddie Gerard had dislocated his shoulder in the last game against Vancouver and was replaced by young Francis "King" Clancy, who made his first start in Stanley Cup play in this game. Cy Denneny scored in overtime to give the Senators a 2–1 win. Gerard – sore shoulder and all – returned to the starting line-up for game two, which was won by Ottawa 1–0 on a goal by Punch Broadbent.

The Senators had won and defended the Stanley Cup all in the span of sixteen days.

The Montreal Canadiens, second-place finishers in the NHL's 1923-24 regular season, defeated Ottawa by a combined score of 5–3 to win the NHL championship, with twenty-one-year-old rookie Howie Morenz scoring the only goal in game one of the league finals. As the manager of the new champion of the league that held the Cup, Montreal's Léo Dandurand was much more assertive in claiming the Stanley Cup for his club than he had been in similar circumstances in 1919. Dandurand claimed that the western clubs weren't up to the caliber of his NHL champions and that his club was willing to play one western champion but not both the PCHA and WCHL winners. Frank Patrick, the PCHA's president, proposed a compromise: with the finals scheduled for Montreal, the Canadiens would play both western clubs, but the host team's customary contribution towards its opponents' travel expenses would be reduced by half.

Vancouver clinched the PCHA crown in a superb series with Seattle that was finally settled when Frank Boucher scored after fourteen minutes of overtime in game two. Calgary defeated Regina to win the WCHA championship, tying game one, 2–2, in Regina and then winning 2–0 at home.

Back-to-Back-to-Back

Eddie Gerard is the only player to appear on three consecutive Cup-winners with different teams. Gerard was a part of winning teams for Ottawa (1921), the Toronto St. Pats (1922), and Ottawa again (1923).

Both western clubs set off for Montreal. To generate additional money, the teams played a three-game series en route, the loser of which would face the Canadiens first upon arriving in Montreal. Games were played in Vancouver, Calgary, and Winnipeg, with Calgary dropping the first contest before rebounding to win games two and three. Cully Wilson, who had scored three goals in sixty-one seconds for the Tigers in a regular-season game, came off the bench to score three times in game two against Vancouver.

In Montreal, the Canadiens swept Vancouver with two one-goal wins. The second game, won by the Habs 2–1, was scoreless into the third period, until Vancouver's Frank Boucher opened the scoring and his brother Billy replied with two goals for the Canadiens. Two days later, Montreal and Calgary opened their series on a slushy ice surface. Howie Morenz paced the Montreal attack with three goals in game one and added another in the second contest. Game two was switched to Ottawa, but the slick artificial ice of the Senators' new home rink further favored the fast-skating Canadiens, who won the game 3–0 to complete a sweep of both 1924 series.

The 1923 Stanley Cup-champion Ottawa Senators were captained by Hall-of-Famer Eddie Gerard (center). Gerard, who made his first Cup appearance at the age of seventeen in 1908, played the final game of the series against Edmonton with a dislocated shoulder.

Although the 1923-24 Montreal Canadiens finished the regular season with an unimpressive record of thirteen wins and eleven losses, they blossomed in the playoffs, winning all six games and outscoring their opponents, 19–6. Sprague Cleghorn (left) and Billy Couture (right) were the Habs' starting defense pair on the 1924 Cup champs.

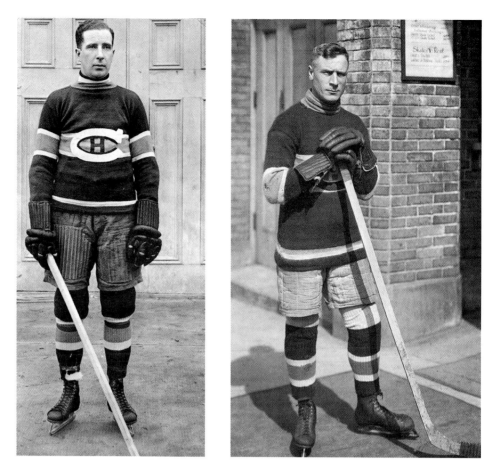

The Golden Goalie

Goaltender Harry "Hap" Holmes, who played from 1913 to 1928, played on four different Cup-winning teams: the 1914 Toronto Blueshirts, the 1917 Seattle Metropolitans, the 1918 Toronto Arenas, and the 1925 Victoria Cougars. Holmes's unique quartet of Stanley Cup championships is a record for goalies.

The NHL's supremacy in Stanley Cup play was interrupted in 1925 when the Victoria Cougars claimed what would prove to be the last Stanley Cup win by a team outside of the NHL.

Off the ice, western pro hockey was in trouble, while the NHL was on the verge of significant expansion. The Seattle Metropolitans franchise folded, leaving Vancouver and Victoria, the two surviving PCHA clubs, no choice but to join the WCHL for 1924-25. At the same time, the Boston Bruins began play as the NHL's first U.S.-based team. Art Ross, who had distinguished himself as a player with Kenora, the Wanderers, and the Senators, traded his shoulder pads for a suit and tie and accepted the post of manager of the newly formed Bruins. In Montreal, a syndicate headed by Jimmy Strachan obtained a franchise and formed a new club to be known as the Montreal Maroons.

Both the NHL and the WCHL Stanley Cup finalists in 1925 were third-place finishers in the regular season. In the NHL, the Montreal Canadiens faced second-place finisher Toronto for the championship. The first-place club, the Hamilton Tigers, had been suspended by NHL president Frank Calder after staging a post-season strike in an attempt to obtain bonuses as compensation for the extension of the NHL regular-season schedule from twenty-four to thirty games. Howie Morenz scored twice in game one, which was won by the Canadiens, 3–2. The Habs continued to roll in game

WESTERN CHAMPIONS
1924-25

WORLD CHAMPIONS
1924-25

W.C.H.L. CUP   STANLEY CUP

two, as goaltender Georges Vezina posted a 2–0 shutout to advance to the Cup finals.

In the West, the Victoria Cougars defeated Saskatoon by a combined score of 6–4 to earn the right to face regular-season champion Calgary for the WCHL crown. The two clubs tied 1–1 in game one of the two-game, total-goals series, and then Victoria followed up with a 2–0 shutout win to earn the right to host the Canadiens in a best-of-five Cup final.

The Cougars dominated the finals, needing four games to defeat the Canadiens. Victoria was very much the faster team, with scoring punch provided by defenseman Gordon Fraser, left wing Jack Walker, and center Frank Fredrickson. Victoria goaltender Harry "Hap" Holmes posted a goals-against average of 1.60 in eight post-season games.

The 1924-25 Victoria Cougars, the last non-NHL team to capture the Stanley Cup. This team featured five future Hall-of-Famers, including manager-coach Lester Patrick, Frank Foyston, and "Hap" Holmes.

(continued on p. 67)

The Stanley Cup Strike of 1925

by Myer Siemiatycki

The real drama of the 1925 NHL playoffs occurred not on but off the ice. For the first time in league history, an entire team – the first-place Hamilton Tigers – went on strike. All ten players on the Hamilton club refused to take part in postseason play without extra pay.

Few other events in NHL history have transformed the league more dramatically than the Hamilton Tigers' strike of 1925. The strike cost Hamilton its NHL franchise, and also cost a great team its chance at winning the Stanley Cup. The NHL's president, Frank Calder, disqualified the rebellious Hamilton squad from the playoffs – and the Hamilton Tigers of 1925 stand out among the best NHL teams never to win the Stanley Cup. But the strike also paved the way for the league's successful expansion into the United States. The Tigers' strike was pivotal in transforming the small, unstable NHL into the dominant league in the sport.

The Tigers joined the NHL for the 1920-21 season when Hamilton business interests paid $5,000 for the defunct Quebec City franchise that had played in the NHL as the Athletics in 1919-20. It must have seemed a steal for the vendors.

Hamilton inherited a doormat team in a struggling two-year-old circuit. The 1919-20 edition of the Quebec club ended the twenty-four-game season with four wins and not many more fans. Not for the first time since its formation in 1917, the NHL seemed on the verge of collapse, with its three surviving teams barely hanging on in Montreal, Toronto, and Ottawa.

Enter the marvelously named Abso-Pure Ice Company of Hamilton. The company had cornered the market on just about anything to do with ice in town, from home-refrigeration delivery to the construction of a spanking new 3,800-seat artificial-ice arena. The arena was to be open for paying pleasure skaters, but something – even a last-place club – was needed to fill the seats with ticket-buying customers. So Abso-Pure diversified into the hockey business. The firm bought and transferred the Quebec franchise to Hamilton, renamed it, and entrusted management of the team to Percy Thompson, who would coach and manage both pro and amateur hockey in Hamilton for decades to follow.

Unfortunately, neither a change of scenery nor some new player blood altered the Hamilton team's sorry on-ice record. The Tigers landed dead last in the four-team NHL in each of their first four seasons. Their "best" season saw them win nine of twenty-four games. This wasn't a team but a guaranteed loss-leader.

And yet in their fifth and final season (1924-25) the Hamilton Tigers leapt from losers to league-leaders, ending the regular season in first place. Percy Thompson had pulled the remarkable coup of wooing to Hamilton some of the country's premier amateur hockey players, who would take the NHL by storm. The wily Thompson traveled near and far to pluck future NHL Hall-of-Famers for his line-up.

Thompson's most fertile hockey harvest came from Sudbury, Ontario. As the hometown paper the Sudbury *Star* crowed, "This district is noted for its natural resources, but nickel, copper, gold, or silver pale into insignificance in the eyes of the athletic world when they are compared to the product which Sudbury has given to the hockey market."

During the early 1920s, the Sudbury Wolves had emerged as a hockey powerhouse. When they were invited to play exhibition games in the United States, the Pittsburgh *Dispatch* was duly impressed, writing, "The Sudbury six lived up to its reputation as being one of the best teams produced in Canada." Leading the Wolves were the Green brothers, Shorty and Red, playing forward, reinforced by Alex McKinnon on the forward line and Charlie Langlois on defense.

As early as 1920, the *Globe* in Toronto ran a headline wondering, "Who'll Land the Green Brothers?" Shorty was the fearless, rambunctious play-maker, while Red had the natural goal-scoring touch. Ironically, neither lived up to his moniker. Shorty wasn't diminutive, while Red wasn't red-haired. Red was simply short for Redvers. And neither was short on talent.

When the manager of Toronto's NHL team, Harvey Sproule, went north in 1920 to recruit Shorty Green, he was almost run out of town. As the Toronto *Telegram* repeated in a diplomatic headline, Sproule found himself, "Made To Feel Somehow that He Was an Unwelcome Visitor." Amateur hockey teams back then were home-grown expressions of community pride for town residents and commercial profit for club owners. The stars of the Sudbury Wolves were handsomely reimbursed as "employees" of local businesses in town, and saw no reason to formally turn pro until Percy Thompson came calling.

In 1923, the Tigers surprised the hockey world by signing both Green brothers to two-year contracts at twice the prevailing salary for top-notch players. King Clancy, for instance, was paid the princely sum of $1,500 by the Ottawa Senators for the 1923-24 season; that same year Shorty and Red Green earned $3,000 each in their rookie seasons. A year later, Thompson was back in Sudbury to snap up McKinnon and Langlois. So, four of ten players on the 1924-25 Hamilton Tigers were transplanted Sudbury Wolves.

President Calder was especially pleased by the league's good fortune in landing a player of Shorty Green's reputation. Congratulating Thompson on the signing, Calder noted, "It surely has never been for want of offers that Green has never played in the league before." Little could Calder know that, a year later, he and Shorty would be the leading antagonists in the Tigers' strike.

The Hamilton team's two other authentic stars had acquired their skills in Toronto's amateur-hockey system. Goalie Jake Forbes was a pioneer of the game in at least two respects. Standing barely five and a half feet tall, he was the first to prove that small could be terrific in an age that prized large goaltenders, who could obstruct a large portion of the net. Forbes had also demonstrated uncommon determination in standing up for what he felt he deserved. After playing two seasons for the NHL's Toronto St. Pats, Forbes sat out the 1921-22 season when the team rejected his $2,500 salary demand. Determined to play on his own terms, he proved receptive to Percy Thompson's offer.

The final piece of the Tigers' winning puzzle was the classiest. Center Billy Burch could have been a Hollywood heartthrob for all his charm and good looks. A Toronto newspaper described him during his amateur days as "one sweet player," while later in his professional career, a New York daily called him "a veritable cyclone on skates." Percy Thompson recognized that Billy Burch was just the center he needed between the relentless Shorty Green on right wing and goal-getter Red Green on left.

After leading the league in losses in consecutive seasons, goaltender Vernon "Jake" Forbes rebounded to top the NHL with nineteen victories in 1924-25. Like most of the Tigers, Forbes joined the New York Americans in 1925-26. He appeared in all thirty-six of the Amerk's games, allowing eighty-nine goals-against.

With four years of futility behind them, the Hamilton Tigers were finally poised to make waves in the NHL. After they defeated the Ottawa Senators 5–3 in the 1924-25 season opener, Hamilton scribe Paddy Jones felt safe in predicting that "Hamilton puck-chasers will not be the official door-mats, as they were in former seasons." In an era when wagering on athletic events was commonplace, Jones would have been wise to lay money on his hunch.

Interestingly enough, the rejuvenated Tigers were not the only big story in the NHL that season. The league itself had also undergone a major transformation prior to the start of play in 1924-25, adding two new franchises, and, ultimately, these changes would prompt the Hamilton Tigers' post-season strike. Since its formation in 1917, instability had been a hallmark of the four-team NHL. Through its first seven years, insolvent franchises, fire-damaged arenas, and competition from rival leagues conspired against the fledgling NHL. Particularly worrisome by the early 1920s was the prospect of a new international pro league, comprised of clubs in Canada and in major American cities.

The NHL's owners countered by developing expansionist plans of their own. By the early 1920s, it was clear that professional hockey's new frontier was in the United States. Fan interest in the sport was on the rise, and a number of American cities were building huge new sports facilities. Hockey was a natural winter event for these sport palaces, and the NHL's future now depended on whether it or a rival league capitalized on these opportunities. In 1922, the league sold to Montreal entrepreneur Thomas Duggan exclusive rights to establish two American franchises earmarked for New York and Boston. Duggan was to act as the league's emissary in selecting American owners to join the NHL.

Duggan proved to be a salesman *extraordinaire* for both the game and the NHL. Boston grocery magnate Charles Adams was Duggan's first taker, and, in the 1924-25 season, the Boston Bruins were the first American team to join the NHL. The league remained desperate to break into the biggest market of all – New York – but delays in construction of the new Madison Square Garden left the city without an appropriate playing site. The league's consolation prize for 1924-25 was the entry of a second Montreal franchise – the Maroons. The new club was designed to appeal to the city's English-speaking population, now that *les Canadiens* were ensconced as the embodiment of Francophone hockey.

Then, in a fateful decision, NHL owners decided that a bigger league needed a longer schedule. More games meant more revenue, which would make the NHL more appealing to new franchise owners. Each club would now play its five opponents six times each, extending the regular season from twenty-four games to thirty. Post-season playoff action was also expanded. Previously the top two regular-season clubs would face off for the league title in a two-game, total-goals series. The winner of this NHL playoff would then play for the Stanley Cup against the top team from Western Canada. Now, however, the NHL turned its playoffs into a two-stage affair. A semi-final round between the second- and third-place teams would determine the opponent that would challenge the first-place team in the league finals. Moreover, the league announced that profits from all playoff games were to be divided equally and exclusively among the six team owners. Unlike the modern NHL, no share was earmarked for the players.

From the players' standpoint, these changes in league format meant simply that they would be playing more games in a longer season with no guarantee of extra pay. Players on the league's first-place team in the 1924-25 season, for instance, would put in a seventeen-week season compared with the previous year's thirteen-week schedule. What would professional players make of such a proposition?

The Hamilton Tigers finished first in the 1924-25 regular season, edging out the Toronto St. Pats by a single point. Percy Thompson had proven himself an astute judge of hockey talent. Team captain Shorty Green and the flashy Billy Burch both had had the seasons of their lives. After a mid-season game in which Green scored a goal described by the Hamilton *Herald* as "the best bit of work and quick-thinking ever seen on the Hamilton rink," the paper ran the following headline over Shorty's photo: "Find His Equal!" Well, by the end of the season, close observers of the game felt they had. Billy Burch was named the second recipient of the recently donated Hart Trophy, awarded annually to the NHL's most valuable player.

Yet, as many commentators noted, the Hamilton Tigers' real secret weapon was their strong teamwork.

In an era when a team's six starters played most of the game, it helped that the Sudbury four had played together for years, and that Billy Burch and the Greens instantly struck up a life-long friendship. Tommy Gorman, manager of the Ottawa Senators' dynasty that had already captured three Stanley Cups in the 1920s, described the Tigers as "a magnificent hockey machine." Gorman would remember that assessment a year later when he was hired to manage New York's new NHL entry. Meanwhile, it was Hamilton sportswriter P. J. Jones who best captured the essence of the team when he wrote, "They have everything – speed, team play, and courage. Their unselfishness has been the big factor in their wonderful showing."

Once the regular season ended on March 9, 1925, the players' sense of mutual support quickly turned to solidarity and strike action. Assorted frustrations and the glimmer of great opportunity led all ten players to issue Percy Thompson with the same ultimatum. Unless every player received an additional $200, they would not play the winner of the Canadiens–Toronto semi-final series in the league finals.

After four consecutive finishes in the NHL's basement, the Hamilton Tigers reversed their standing, winning the 1924-25 regular-season crown with 39 points. The Tigers hiked their winning percentage from .375 in 1923-24 to .650 one season later. Despite playing six additional games in 1924-25, they reduced their goals-against from 68 to 60.

The players certainly had reason to believe they deserved more money. While the Hamilton club turned a record profit, the players had put out more than ever. Due to the extended season, they had all reported to training camp earlier than ever, played six extra regular-season games, and now were expected to wait through a week of semi-final action before they could play two more unpaid playoff games. It didn't help matters that Hamilton's owners had not followed the lead of other clubs in raising salaries or handing out generous Christmas bonuses as compensation for the extra games added to the schedule.

The Hamilton players recognized the consequences of their threat. Several spoke openly of their readiness to quit the sport rather than be taken advantage of. Un-

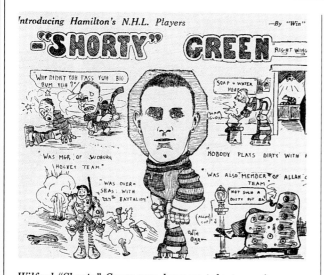

Introducing Hamilton's N.H.L. Players —By "Win"

Wilfred "Shorty" Green was long on talent, scoring eighteen goals for Hamilton in 1924-25. Green was one of the Tigers' talented transplants from Northern Ontario, where, along with his brother Red, he was part of the Sudbury Wolves, one of Canada's finest senior clubs.

doubtedly, the players sensed that timing was on their side. First, the league would be reluctant to cancel the finals and forego all its revenues. More important, the players knew that, with further NHL expansion in the offing and the possibility of rival leagues being discussed, the future for skilled professional hockey players was bright. Their talents would be in great demand, enabling them to take the risk of standing their ground.

Not surprisingly, it was fiery Shorty Green who became the players' spokesman once the dispute became public on March 11, 1925. As Green informed the press, the players were simply following the owners' logic and lead, declaring, "Professional hockey is a money-making affair. The promoters are in the game for what they can make out of it and the players wouldn't be in the game if they didn't look at matters in the same light. Why, then, should we be asked to play two games merely for the sake of sweetening the league's finances?"

League president Frank Calder provided the answer fast and straight. He countered that NHL contracts required players to make their services available from December 1 to March 31, regardless of the number of games played. Condemning the players' threat as a contract violation, Calder ordered the Tigers to play or face league suspensions and fines. Anything less, he feared, would invite repeated player rebelliousness.

Worse, Calder told the press, he feared that capitulation – even compromise – would jeopardize the owners' "large capital investment in rinks and arenas and this capital must be protected."

Battle lines were drawn, and neither side blinked. Shorty Green and Frank Calder held a fateful meeting in the Toronto Arena Gardens on Friday, March 13, during the deciding game of the Toronto–Canadiens semi-finals. By the end of the evening, two teams had been eliminated from Stanley Cup contention. Toronto lost the game. Hamilton was disqualified, and its players were suspended from the NHL and fined $200 each after Green informed Calder his teammates would not budge.

Calder considered a plan to salvage the playoff finals by allowing the fourth-place Ottawa Senators to meet the Canadiens, but ridicule from the press and resistance from the Canadiens players killed the idea. Instead, Calder announced on March 13 that, due to the Hamilton Tigers' strike, the NHL finals were canceled and the Canadiens would head west to represent the NHL in the Stanley Cup championship series.

The Canadiens proved no match against the Western Canadian Hockey League finalist Victoria Cougars. As Charles Coleman summed up the series in his classic book, *The Trail of the Stanley Cup*, "The Cougars were far too fast for the Canadiens and skated them dizzy." Managed by Lester Patrick and led by future Hall-of-Fame forwards Frank Fredrickson and Jack Walker, the Cougars handily defeated the Canadiens three games to one.

It was the last time a team outside the NHL ever won the Stanley Cup, and that may be the final legacy of the Tigers' strike. Certainly, Victoria would have had a much tougher time against the Tigers. More important, however, the Hamilton Tigers' strike had the long-term effect of establishing the NHL's undisputed supremacy as the dominant hockey league in the world.

Suspended for their strike action in March 1925, the ten members of the Hamilton Tigers were all back on the ice when the NHL began its landmark 1925-26 season. Now, however, the Greens, Burch, and company were transplanted and transformed into the New York Americans. The Hamilton franchise – team and players, right down to their striped Tiger sweaters – were sold to New York's most celebrated Prohibition bootlegger, "Big Bill" Dwyer. A New York franchise was viable now that Thomas Duggan had convinced promoter Tex Rickard to install artificial ice in his new eighteen-thousand-seat Madison Square Garden. Frequent visits to watch the Hamilton Tigers during their last winning season were part of Rickard's hockey conversion.

A tremendous amount was at stake in the NHL's first year in the Big Apple. Rickard was counting on hockey to make the Garden financially viable. The NHL was hoping that a strong showing in New York would forever end threats of rival leagues and woo other big American cities into the league. Having a rink and a team owner in place were all well and good, but it was players who would put fans in the seats. And Tommy Gorman, the team's newly recruited manager, knew exactly who he wanted.

The New York Americans began life with the class of the NHL's previous season on their side. Dwyer paid Percy Thompson and his Abso-Pure Associates $75,000 for the Hamilton franchise and players. It was clear

In response to demands for increased salaries by Hamilton players, NHL president Frank Calder disqualified the Tigers from Stanley Cup play.

to the Hamilton ownership that the NHL had outgrown small arenas. In the aftermath of the strike, moreover, the players served public notice that they would never play for Hamilton's owners again. The New York offer was simply far too good to refuse.

The Hamilton owners had no need of sympathy. They had made a whopping profit on their short-lived attachment to the NHL. Now the players, too, were about to cash in. They signed on for substantially higher salaries than they had earned in Hamilton. Shorty Green jumped from $3,000 a year to $5,000. Billy Burch proved to be the biggest winner, signing a three-year pact variously reported to be worth between $18,000 and $25,000. As a native of Yonkers, New York, and the most recent winner of the Hart Trophy, Burch would be the team's biggest marketing commodity in New York, where hockey promoters put him on a pedestal. "You've seen the Babe Ruth of baseball," huge billboards announced. "Now see Billy Burch, the Babe Ruth of hockey."

Before the New York Americans could ice their team, however, there was the outstanding matter of the players' suspension and fines, handed down the previous March. Prior to the 1925-26 season, league president Calder required every one of the ex-Hamilton Tigers to request readmission in writing, along with an explanation and apology for their strike action. Calder was miffed by the letters he received. As he informed Americans' manager Tommy Gorman, "most of these young players want to give me an argument," contending they were right to strike.

Calder held out until the players penned their *mea culpas.* Without expressions of transgression and regret, Calder instructed the players, their ban would not be lifted. Five weeks of correspondence and dozens of letters later, Calder finally had the apologies and promises of good behavior he deemed necessary for reinstatement. Yet, as Calder informed Gorman, the lifting of the players' bans had to be accompanied by both punishment and precautions. Gorman had to ensure that the players paid their $200 fines and, just in case the players considered any rebellious relapses, the league required Gorman to hold back $300 of each salary as a bond of dutiful conduct. The players would only get this money at season's end if they played in every game as required.

In their first season, the New York Americans proved to be a box-office success but a competitive disappointment. Injuries, poor playing conditions, and the temptations of Broadway life all contributed to the team's fifth-place finish. Still, fans flocked to see a sport that was promoted as much for its aggression as for its skill. Paul Gallico informed readers of the *Daily News* that hockey featured a confrontation between "men with clubs in their hands and knives lashed to their feet."

The curious flocked to see the New York Americans and the NHL's other new entry of the 1925-26 campaign, the Pittsburgh Pirates. A year later the NHL had three more American franchises. Chicago and Detroit both joined, and the financial success of the New York Americans convinced Tex Rickard that he should not only have an NHL franchise as a tenant in his arena, but should also own one as well. So were born the New York Rangers. Simultaneously, the Western Hockey League disbanded, freeing up its players to stock the new NHL teams.

Billy Burch captured the hearts of fans, and the Hart Trophy, in 1924-25, scoring twenty goals in twenty-seven games. Although he went on to have a superb career with the New York Americans, Boston, and Chicago, he appeared in only two playoff games.

With remarkable speed, then, the NHL had been completely transformed. Within three short years, it had grown from a four-city Canadian league into a ten-city North American circuit, flourishing in four of the largest cities in the United States. Unquestionably, the league now stood in a class of its own, and was synonymous with pro hockey at its best.

The turning point in the transformation was brought about by a troupe of ex-strikers from Hamilton, who proved that the sport and the NHL could thrive across international borders. The New York Americans drew more fans in 1925-26 than did any four franchises combined in hockey's other major professional circuit, the Western Hockey League.

Appropriately, it was Shorty Green who notched the first goal ever scored in Madison Square Garden. Both Green and Burch were later inducted into the Hockey Hall of Fame. To the end of his days, Shorty Green remained convinced that he and his Tigers teammates had done the right thing the year the Stanley Cup was within their grasp. Three decades after the event, Green told reporter Milt Dunnell, "I never regretted my part in the strike, even though it cost me a chance at the Stanley Cup. We realized hockey was becoming big. All we asked was the players be given some share of revenue. I'd do the same thing tomorrow."

The 1925-26 Saskatoon Shieks featured a number of players, such as Bill Cook, George Hainsworth, and Léo Reise, who went on to star in the NHL. Second-place finishers in the WHL, they lost a close inter-league playoff to the PCHA's Victoria Cougars.

Despite Victoria's Stanley Cup win, off the ice the gap between eastern and western big-league hockey continued to grow in 1926. In the West, the WCHL's foundering Regina franchise was transferred to Portland, Oregon, resulting in the league being renamed the Western Hockey League (WHL). In the NHL, growth continued. Most of the players from the Hamilton Tigers joined the newly established New York Americans. Another new club, the Pittsburgh Pirates, began play in 1925-26, and the regular-season schedule also expanded, growing from thirty to thirty-six games.

The Canadiens and the St. Pats, NHL finalists in 1924-25, occupied the bottom of the standings the following season. Ottawa finished in first place, followed by the Montreal Maroons and the Pittsburgh Pirates. In semi-final action, the Maroons outscored the Pirates 6–4 in a two-game, total-goals series. Center Bill Phillips's two goals in game two proved to be the margin of victory.

The Maroons then upset the Senators in an exceedingly low-scoring NHL final. King Clancy and Punch Broadbent exchanged goals in a 1–1 tie in game one. Albert "Babe" Seibert of the Maroons scored the only goal in game two, clinching the series for the Montreal club by a combined score of 2–1.

In the WHL semi-finals, third-place Victoria eliminated Saskatoon after eight minutes of overtime on a goal by Gordon Fraser in game two. In the

Hockey-hungry fans line up outside a Victoria sporting-goods store to purchase tickets for the last Stanley Cup series to feature a non-NHL team, the 1926 final between the Cougars and the Montreal Maroons.

finals, the Cougars upset Edmonton by a combined 5–3 score, with Frank Foyston coming off the bench to score a goal in both games.

The Maroons proved to be too powerful for the Cougars in the 1926 Stanley Cup finals. The series took place in the newly constructed Montreal Forum, where Nels Stewart, the Maroons' outstanding rookie, who had led the league in scoring with 42 points, showed further promise by scoring six goals against Victoria. Another star of the series was Montreal goaltender Clint Benedict, who had joined the Maroons from the Senators and shut out the Cougars in all three Montreal victories. Victoria's lone win came in game three by a 3–2 score.

The 1926 Stanley Cup was the end of a dynamic era in the history of hockey. It marked the conclusion of an intense inter-league East–West rivalry, as the WHL was disbanded just after the 1926 playoffs. With the NHL now hockey's pre-eminent league, Cup challenges from non-NHL clubs were reduced to no more than formalities. As it turned out, with the NHL now in control of the Cup and so many of the league's clubs based in the United States, the 1926 Cup final would prove to be the last between two Canadian teams until 1935.

Clint Benedict, the NHL's dominant goaltender in the league's early years, won three Cup championships with Ottawa before leading the Maroons to their first title in 1926 when he posted four shutouts in eight playoff games.

From 1893 to 1926, Stanley Cup competition had grown from challenge matches between amateur clubs in eastern Canada to a major-league professional championship followed by fans from coast to coast. Further expansion and a share of a booming market for professional sports in the United States lay just ahead.

The NHL
Takes the Cup,
1927-1942

BEGINNING IN 1926-27, MANY OF THE BEST PLAYERS FROM THE PCHA and its successor, the Western (Canada) Hockey League, found themselves playing for clubs in the newly expanded NHL. Big cities in the northern United States wanted major-league hockey and the league obliged, adding three new franchises: the Chicago Black Hawks, the Detroit Cougars, and the New York Rangers. This created a ten-team NHL with American and Canadian divisions.

Frank and Lester Patrick still held the contracts of numerous PCHA/WHL players and arranged several deals that brought these and other players east to fill out the rosters of both new and established NHL clubs. Players from the old Victoria Cougars were acquired by the new Detroit club of the same name, while members of the Portland Rosebuds joined the Chicago Black Hawks.

At least thirty top-ranked western players skated in the NHL in 1926–27, including Eddie Shore, Gordon "Duke" Keats, Perk Galbraith, Harry Oliver, and Harry Meeking with Boston; Dick Irvin, Mickey Mackay, George Hay, Charley "Rabbit" McVeigh, Percy Traub, and Jim Riley with Chicago; Frank Fredrickson, Frank Foyston, Clem Laughlin, Art Duncan, Jack Walker, and Harold "Slim" Halderson with Detroit; Art Gagné, Herb Gardiner, George Hainsworth, and Amby Moran with the Montreal Canadiens; Mervyn "Red" Dutton with the Montreal Maroons; Leo Reise, Laurie Scott, and "Bullet" Joe Simpson with the New York Americans; brothers Bill and Bun Cook and Frank Boucher with the New York Rangers; Jack Adams with Ottawa; and Jack Arbour with Pittsburgh. It would be a time of culture shock for some of the western players, who overnight went from playing in small communities like Saskatoon and Portland to the big-city life of places like New York and Chicago.

These were the years when the Roaring Twenties roared their loudest, and with the help of a new communications medium, radio, they have come to be

Opposite: Milt Schmidt, the classy center of Boston's "Kraut Line," spent sixteen years in the NHL as a player and another thirteen as a coach and general manager.

considered the first great Golden Era of sports in North America. The NHL, under the guidance of league president Frank Calder and its governors, was growing from a leaky-roof circuit into an international sports body. Gone were the hit-and-miss days of the NHA, complete with players changing teams at the drop of a contract and games that were as likely as not to start an hour late. In many ways, the roots of today's NHL can be traced back to the 1926-27 season.

Even the Stanley Cup playoffs underwent a radical face-lift that proved bewildering to old-timers who had lived through the days of simple, though indiscriminate, challenge matches, when a club threw its gauntlet on the ground if it thought it was good enough to dispute another's hold on the Cup. For 1926-27 and 1927-28, the first three finishers in each division at the conclusion of what was now a forty-four-game regular-season schedule qualified for the playoffs. In each division, the winner of a two-game, total-goals series between the second- and third-place clubs faced the first-place team in a two-game, total-goals series to determine the division champion. The two division winners would then meet in a best-of-five series for the Stanley Cup.

Out of this season of upheaval and change, the Ottawa Senators won the Stanley Cup. En route to the finals, the Senators, who finished first in the Canadian Division, defeated the Canadiens 4–0 and tied 1–1 to win the total-goals series.

Their foes in this milestone final series were the Boston Bruins, who, under Art Ross, finished in second place in the American Division. In the first round of the playoffs, the Bruins overwhelmed the Chicago Black Hawks 6–1 in the first game before tying 4–4 in the second to win the series. In the American Division finals, the Bruins held the first-place New York Rangers to a scoreless draw before defeating them 3–1 to earn a spot in the Cup finals.

The resulting best-of-five final was unique in that it ended after just four games, despite the fact that Ottawa had won only twice. The other two contests ended in ties after twenty minutes of overtime. Because the Bruins would be unable to catch Ottawa in the one remaining game, Frank Calder stopped the series to avoid the inference that the teams had played game five just to generate an extra gate.

Ill will between the teams simmered throughout the series. Billy Couture, a Boston defenseman who had previously been suspended when he was with the Canadiens in 1923, was expelled from the NHL and fined $100 for assaulting referees Gerry LaFlamme and Billy Bell following the final game of the series, which Ottawa took, 3–1.

Four other players, though not slapped as hard as Couture, were fined as a result of the wild contest. Hooley Smith of Ottawa was tapped for $100 and suspended for the first month of the following season for hitting Boston right-winger Harry Oliver just before the game ended. Lionel Hitchman and

Dick Irvin, who was the WHL's last scoring champion, moved on to the NHL and led all playmakers with eighteen assists in 1926-27, his first season with Chicago.

Jimmy "Sailor" Herberts of Boston and George "Buck" Boucher of Ottawa were assessed $50 each for "wild actions and intimidation" during the game. The fines, a total of $350, were collected from the players' playoff cuts, which amounted to $1,200 for each Senator and $800 for each Bruin, and were turned over to Boston and Ottawa charities.

If there was any doubt that the game was not appealing to American fans, it was dispelled by the 30,000 applications that the Bruins received for seats at the finals.

Notable players in the series included Jack Adams, King Clancy, Cy Denneny, and Frank Nighbor, who, with one-eyed Alex Connell in the nets, were part of what would prove to be Ottawa's last Stanley Cup-winning team. The Bruins were led by Eddie Shore, a bowlegged ex-cowboy, who was embarking on a gaudy fifteen-year NHL career as the league's outstanding defenseman and one of its most colorful personalities. Shore would later make a major contribution to the Bruins' Stanley Cup triumphs of 1929 and 1939. Manager Art Ross had also summoned such fine talent as Lionel Hitchman, Frank Fredrickson, Sprague Cleghorn, Billy Boucher, Perk Galbraith, Jimmy Herberts, Bill Stuart, and Harry Meeking, with the seasoned Hal Winkler in the nets.

The New York Rangers, now coached and managed by Lester Patrick, had been built into a formidable machine, and there was no denying them in the 1927-28 Stanley Cup playoffs. Conn Smythe, who preceded Patrick at the Rangers' helm, had laid the groundwork for a winner, signing Frank Boucher from Vancouver and Bill and Bun Cook from the disbanded Saskatoon Shieks before he left New York.

The Cup, however, didn't go to New York without a great deal of turmoil and strife. New York's final series opponent was the Montreal Maroons, and in the last game, on April 14, trouble broke out. In the third period, with the score 2–1 for the Rangers, Russ Oatman of the Maroons scored a goal that referee Mike Rodden disallowed on an offside. Fans managed to stay angry until after the game, which was won by the Rangers on two goals by Frank Boucher, with the Maroons managing only one – by Bill Phillips on a pass from Babe Siebert.

The end of the game was the signal for the outbreak. Rodden ducked out of the building by the back door, but NHL president Frank Calder, spotted by fans, had to be hustled into the rink's business office out of danger as the crowd closed in on him. The rumpus had started when someone in the crowd spotted the president and yelled that he was responsible for appointing Rodden as the referee.

One of the NHL's most dramatic events occurred in the second game of the finals. It involved the Rangers' forty-four-year-old manager-coach. For the second time in his illustrious Stanley Cup career, Lester Patrick, in a pinch, went into the nets in a final-series game.

Frank "King" Clancy, crown prince of hockey and one of its finest defensemen. When the Ottawa Senators sold him to the Leafs for $35,000 and two players in 1930, it was the highest price ever paid for a hockey player.

Joe Who?

In 1928, Joe Miller, a journeyman goalie with the New York Americans, was loaned to the Rangers for the rest of the final series after Lorne Chabot was injured. He backstopped the New Yorkers to their first title, allowing only a single goal in two Ranger victories. He never played in the post-season again.

Lester Patrick's forty-three-minute appearance in goal for the Rangers in the 1928 Stanley Cup finals was his longest stint between the pipes. In previous seasons, he had occasionally played in net when his club's regular goaltender was banished to the penalty box.

Patrick's heroics in the twine were performed in the second game of the final series. Lorne Chabot, an exceptionally talented goalie, who missed the playoffs only twice in eleven years, was injured after four minutes of the second period when Nels Stewart's backhander caught him flush in the left eye. He was taken to the hospital.

Because the Rangers did not have a spare goaltender in attendance, Patrick asked permission to use Ottawa goalie Alex Connell, who was in the rink, but Eddie Gerard, manager of the Maroons, refused. The Blueshirts then asked to use Hughie McCormick, a goalie from London, Ontario, in the minor Canadian Pro League, who was also in attendance, but Gerard, whose Montreal Maroons carried a substitute goaltender throughout the season,

Bill Cook (left) and Frank Boucher led the 1928 New York Rangers to the Stanley Cup in the team's second year of play.

Tiny Thompson starred for Boston during the 1929 playoffs, allowing only three goals in five games as the Bruins captured their first Stanley Cup crown.

was adamant, citing a league rule which stated that, if a team needed to replace its goaltender, the substitute must be a player under contract to the team.

The silver-thatched Patrick went into the nets himself and allowed only one goal for the remainder of the game, which was won 2–1 by the Rangers after seven minutes of overtime. Altogether he handled eighteen shots and was beaten only when Stewart took linemate Hooley Smith's rebound and drove it past him. Pittsburgh manager Odie Cleghorn took over from Patrick behind the Rangers' bench.

Chabot was out for the series and was replaced in goal by Joe Miller, who had played part of the season for the New York Americans. Miller proved equal to the task, allowing only three goals in three games, backstopping the Rangers to a five-game series win. Miller took his lumps, too. In the first period of the final game, he fell on an outstretched stick and finished the game with two black eyes and a badly cut nose.

Although the Bruins scored only nine goals in the 1929 playoffs, they won five consecutive games and their first title. Substitute goaltender Hal Winkler is seated at far right. (See below.)

Honorable Mention

Hal Winkler's name appears on the Stanley Cup with the 1929 Boston Bruins, even though he didn't play a single minute for the team that season. Winkler, who led the league in minutes played and shutouts during the 1927-28 campaign, retired before the 1928-29 season, and the Bruins honored him by placing his name on the Cup as their "sub-goaltender."

The NHL revamped its playoff format for 1928-29. Under the new rules, the first-, second-, and third-place teams would cross over to play their counterparts from the league's other division in the first round of the playoffs. The series between the two first-place teams was best-of-five. The others were two-game, total-goals affairs. The victorious first-place club advanced to the finals, to play the winner of a best-of-three series between the other two series winners. The final was reduced to a best-of-three contest.

Boston, first-place finisher in the American Division for 1928-29, had strengthened itself in the game's most vulnerable position, goaltender, by bringing up Cecil "Tiny" Thompson, who had played for Duluth and Minneapolis and was destined to spend ten spectacular seasons with the Bruins. During that time he won the Vezina Trophy four times, a record that was to stand until 1949, when Bill Durnan won his fifth with the Canadiens.

The Bruins polished off the Canadiens in the semi-finals and the Rangers in the finals in the minimum of five games, with Thompson racking up three shutouts and allowing just five goals-against. The series between the Bruins and the Rangers was the first all-American Stanley Cup final.

In Montreal, meanwhile, the Maroons and the Canadiens were involved in the greatest hockey rivalry the city has ever known. Elmer Ferguson of the *Montreal Herald* felt the pulse of Montreal hockey when he wrote:

"Canadiens had the brilliant Morenz and Joliat and [Alfred] Pit Lepine riding the crest. . . . Maroons had built up a great machine. Money was no object."

The Maroons had bought Hooley Smith for $22,500, purchased Dave Trottier for $15,000 and Dunc Munro for $8,000, and guaranteed Jimmy Ward $17,000 in bonus and salary for signing. They bought Reg Noble for $7,000 and paid big bonuses to get Nels Stewart and Babe Siebert to sign. Hockey passions flared between the two clubs, the English supporting the Maroons and the French the Canadiens.

The Maroons did everything they could to stay alive. But it was the Canadiens who would win two consecutive Stanley Cups, in 1930 and 1931, while the Maroons' popularity, by 1933, would irrevocably slide, never to recover – despite a Cup victory in 1935.

Hopes were highest for the Maroons' fans in 1930, when their club went down to the wire with the Canadiens for the lead in the Canadian Division standings. Both tied with fifty-one points over the forty-four-game schedule, but the Maroons took first place by virtue of having registered twenty-three victories, two more than the Canadiens.

The Maroons lost to the powerful Boston Bruins in the first round of the playoffs, losing a heartbreaker after forty-five minutes of overtime in game one. Boston was the NHL's best club, the first-place finisher by a thirty-point margin over Chicago in the American Division. The Canadiens advanced to the finals against the Bruins by beating Chicago and the New York Rangers.

The Canadiens, who had lost four straight to Boston in regular-season play, let out all the stops with the Cup on the line, winning 3–0 and 4–3 in the best-of-three final series. Sylvio Mantha scored for the Habs in both final-series games.

It was the Canadiens again in 1931, but this time a surprising Chicago Black Hawk club, which finished a distant second to the Bruins in the American Division, gave them plenty of trouble in the finals. The final series, which

George Hainsworth (right), here with Habs' defenseman Sylvio Mantha, backstopped the Montreal Canadiens to consecutive Stanley Cup victories in 1930 and 1931. He led all goaltenders in post-season minutes played, wins, and shutouts.

Les Canadiens sont lá! Despite losing three overtime games during the 1931 playoffs, including consecutive extra-session losses to Chicago in the finals, the Montreal Canadiens managed to become the first back-to-back Stanley Cup winners since the Ottawa Senators of 1920 and 1921.

now was a best-of-five, went the full distance, with the Black Hawks winning games two and three by 2–1 and 3–2 scores on overtime goals by Johnny Gottselig and Cy Wentworth.

The Canadiens took the opener 2–1 and the fourth game 4–2, and ended the series at Montreal with a 2–0 win in game five. Howie Morenz scored his first goal of the 1931 playoffs, and the final goal of the series, at 15:27 of the third period in game five.

The Canadiens had gone into the final series with four injured players. Armand Mondou had a broken rib; Albert "Battleship" Leduc, a slight concussion; Morenz, a badly cut face; and Pit Lepine, a cut hand. They did not ice a healthy club until the third game of the series.

Worthy of mention, in connection with the 1931 playoffs, was what was referred to as the "amazing maneuver" executed by Art Ross in the second game of the Boston–Canadiens semi-final playoff at Boston when he pulled his goalkeeper, Tiny Thompson, in the last minute of the game for an extra forward in an unsuccessful effort to erase a 1–0 deficit. This was the first time that a goalkeeper had been pulled out of the nets in a Stanley Cup playoff game.

In 1932, Toronto had not won a Stanley Cup since the old St. Pats, under manager Charlie Querrie and coach Eddie Powers, had defeated the Vancouver Millionaires a decade before. In 1927 the St. Pats franchise had become the Maple Leafs, when it was purchased by a group headed by Conn Smythe, who had previously been manager of the New York Rangers.

King Clancy (center), seen here with teammates Red Horner (left), and Hap Day, joined the Leafs in 1930 and remained an invaluable member of the organization for most of the next fifty-six years, serving faithfully as a player, coach, scout, adviser, and good-will ambassador. The NHL's award for leadership and community service is named in honor of Clancy.

In the fall of 1929, Smythe industriously set about the task of building a showplace arena where his team could play. When some people despaired, due to the stock-market crash of 1929, Smythe went out and solicited support for his dream. He found a sympathetic listener and just as good a salesman as himself in J. P. Bickell, a mining man, who heard Smythe's story and then telephoned several friends to inform them, "You have just bought ten thousand dollars worth of stock in Maple Leaf Gardens Limited."

Smythe's tactics in assembling a hockey team were just as forthright. He bought King Clancy from the Ottawa Senators for the unheard-of price of $35,000 and two players. By 1931 he had assembled the fabulous Kid Line of Joe Primeau at center, Charlie Conacher at right wing, and Harvey "Busher" Jackson at left wing. He got Lorne Chabot from the Rangers to play goal and added defenseman Reginald "Red" Horner and Clarence "Hap" Day, a pharmacist who was thinking about drugstores when Smythe told him to drop the pills and think about the puck. Jackson, Conacher, and Horner were all members of the Toronto Marlboroughs, Canadian junior champions in 1928. Dick Irvin, who had been fired as coach of the Black Hawks, was summoned from Regina to replace Art Duncan, and the Leafs were in business.

Toronto finished behind the Canadiens in 1932, then knocked over Chicago, 6–2, and the Maroons, 4–3, in a pair of two-game, total-goals series, before walloping the Rangers in three straight games, 6–4, 6–2, and 6–4. It marked the first time that a team had won a Stanley Cup final in three straight games.

The 1931-32 Maple Leafs were Toronto's fourth Stanley Cup-winning team.

The Leafs trailed only once in the entire series, in the second game when Bun Cook and Doug Brennan gave New York a 2–0 lead after one minute of the second period. The Leafs responded with six straight goals, with a member of the Kid Line in on each one.

A ghost from the past came back to haunt Conn Smythe in 1933, for Boucher and the Cook brothers, whom he had signed when he managed the Rangers, were instrumental in wresting the Cup from the Leafs in a best-of-five series that went four games. Right winger Bill Cook's overtime goal in the fourth contest gave the Rangers a 1–0 decision and the Cup. Two Toronto players, Alex Levinsky and Bill Thoms, were in the penalty box when the thirty-five-year-old master craftsman scored.

Cecil Dillon, though, was the standout for the Rangers. The man Patrick once called perhaps the greatest he had ever seen scored eight goals and counted two assists in helping the Rangers win the Cup. Three of these goals were scored against the Leafs.

The defeat at the hands of the Rangers was an anti-climax for the Leafs, for this was the year of a spine-tingling playoff game against Boston in Toronto, which lasted until nearly two o'clock in the morning before tiny Ken Doraty of the Leafs scored the goal that ended it.

Every respectable hockey fan in Toronto stayed up that night listening on radio to the longest game on record up to that time. At the end of one hundred minutes of overtime, managers Conn Smythe and Art Ross asked NHL president Frank Calder if he would stop the game and resume it the following night. Their request was refused.

The Bruins suggested tossing a coin. Smythe informed his players of this overture, and they were in agreement, but when the coin-tossing ceremony

Extra Strength in Extra Time

Bill Cook of the Rangers is the only player to score a Cup-winning power-play goal in overtime. During the 1933 finals, Cook scored the winner for New York with two Leafs in the penalty box.

GENERAL MOTORS HOCKEY BROADCASTS

"HE SHOOTS.....HE SCORES!"(Story under Pad.)

Ken Doraty slides the puck past Tiny Thompson at 4:46 of the sixth overtime period to end the second-longest game in NHL history. Eighteen hours later, the Leafs were in New York playing the Rangers in the 1933 Stanley Cup finals.

was about to take place at center ice, 14,539 fans were almost unanimous in urging the Leafs to go on with the game. This is one of the few times that fans can be credited with winning a game for any team. Calder suggested that, to bring about a quick conclusion, the teams remove their goaltenders, but this was also vetoed.

Doraty took a pass from Andy Blair, who had intercepted Eddie Shore's clearing pass, scoring finally at 164:46. The record for longevity of a playoff game stood until March 24, 1936, when the Detroit Red Wings defeated the Maroons at Montreal in a semi-final game when the winning goal was scored by Moderre "Mud" Bruneteau on a pass from Hec Kilrea at 16:30 of the sixth overtime period – after 176:30 of play.

The Stanley Cup in 1934 belonged to the Chicago Black Hawks. Or perhaps it would be more correct to say that it belonged to goaltender Charlie Gardiner. Chicago hockey fans will never forget this five-foot-eight-inch 155-pound swashbuckler, who was born in Edinburgh, Scotland, and began his hockey career in Winnipeg. He joined the Hawks in 1927 and played his first game before a crowd of 9,000, including the great Babe Ruth, who sat behind the Hawks' bench. Through his first two years in the NHL, he played the nets for a club that could win only 13 times and tie 10 in 88 games.

If Gardiner hadn't died at the age of twenty-nine, after helping the Hawks win their first Stanley Cup, there is little doubt that he would have been ranked among the game's greatest goaltenders. His record in the 1934 playoffs, which concluded with a final-series showdown against Detroit, was spectacular. In eight games of Stanley Cup action, the Black Hawks lost only one game and tied one other. Gardiner recorded two shutouts while posting a 1.32 goals-against average.

Cecil Dillon, who scored eight goals in the 1933 playoffs, fired the winning goal in the Rangers' 4–1 victory over the Maple Leafs in game one of the finals.

The Chicago Black Hawks rebounded from a last-place finish in 1933 to win their first Stanley Cup in 1934, thanks in large part to the heroics of goaltender Charlie Gardiner.

Crease Captain on the Cup

Charlie Gardiner, captain of the Stanley Cup-champion Chicago Black Hawks in 1934, is the only goaltender to have his name appear on the Cup as the captain of a Cup-winning team.

The Hawks, who hadn't won a game at Detroit since February 2, 1930, opened the final series with a 2–1 overtime decision. And to prove that was not a fluke, they made it two straight at the Olympia two nights later, winning 4–1.

The series then switched to Chicago and, before 17,700 fans, Detroit, with its big line of Larry Aurie, Herbie Lewis, and Marty Barry leading the parade, whipped the Hawks, 5–2.

The next game, which turned out to be the last for Gardiner, went to the Hawks, 1–0, after thirty minutes of overtime. Detroit defenceman Ebbie Goodfellow was in the penalty box when Harold "Mush" March scored the goal that won the Cup on a pass from Elwyn "Doc" Romnes.

The next day, teammate "Broadway" Roger Jenkins paid off a good-natured bet by pushing Gardiner through Chicago's Loop district in a wheelbarrow.

Two months later – on June 13 – Gardiner died in a Winnipeg hospital of a brain hemorrhage, which had caused his collapse three days earlier.

(continued on p. 90)

Brief Garland – Charlie Gardiner's Last Season

by Antonia Chambers

Requiescat in Pace

When Charlie Gardiner died in a Winnipeg Hospital [in June of 1934] the National Hockey League lost one of the best liked figures in the game. Wherever the Black Hawks played while on the road you could always count on seeing lots of action and hearing plenty of smart repartee if your seat happened to be close to the Chicago goal during any part of the contest.

For more than three seasons Gardiner was recognized as the best net guardian in hockey. He had unlimited faith in his own ability to outguess the league's best snipers, but with it all never tossed aside his infectious smile, nor failed to have a snappy comeback for those who sat back of his goal, making smart wise cracks about some of the close ones he just managed to clear.

Readers should know that while this smile was from the heart, it really cost Chuck a great deal to appear jolly in the face of defeat, because it hurt him deeply to have anyone score on him, even in his team's practice sessions. Dick Irvin often stated that in a practice Gardiner would work so hard to shut out his teammates that some of the quick tempered fellows would become quite annoyed with the Canny Scot. [Born in Edinburgh, he came to Canada at age seven.]

It is rather ironical that after striving so hard to win hockey's hardest honors Gardiner could not live long enough to enjoy the fruits of his victory....

There is no doubt but that he will be allotted a place in hockey's Hall of Fame, alongside his starry predecessor, Georges Vezina. Like the latter he gave his best for the game he loved, and all who knew him will cherish a memory of one who was as fine in every personal attribute as he was great in hockey. So, once again, Charlie – Rest in Peace – a phrase as universal as your popularity wherever hockey is known.

– Obituary for Charlie Gardiner
from a scrapbook kept by Ace Bailey

Howie Morenz called him "the hardest man I ever had to beat."

"To know [him] was to have acquaintance with one who stood for everything that is ideal in sport," wrote the *Montreal Star*.

"He was a real man," said Eddie Shore.

They were talking about Charlie Gardiner, the five-

Charlie Gardiner, circa 1931.

foot, seven-inch, one-hundred-and-forty-seven-pound goaltender of the Chicago Black Hawks from 1927 to 1934. Twice a Vezina Trophy-winner and four times an All-Star, he had 42 shutouts and a goals-against average of 2.02 in 316 regular-season games. In Stanley Cup play, his goals-against average dropped to a miniscule 1.61. He was a charter inductee of the Hockey Hall of Fame.

But statistics – however impressive – provide only a glimpse of Gardiner's greatness and reveal nothing of his personality. He played with true competitive fire and equally great *joie de vivre*. He rarely lost his composure; his only penalty came as the result of a tangle with Eddie Shore. His teammates enjoyed socializing with him, even though he never smoked or drank. He was devoted to his wife, Myrtle, and his son, Bobby. He had no use for gamblers; when they offered him money to throw games, he angrily refused and told the police. He always had time for fans, both young and old. He was loved by the people of his community, whether in Chicago or in his off-season home of Winnipeg, the town where he learned to play the game. He ran hockey instructional clinics and found time for charity events. He was an all-round sportsman, excelling in baseball, golf, trapshooting, and motor-boating. His hobby interests included singing, photography, and flying. He planned for his life after hockey, having established a sporting-goods business as well.

In the 1932-33 season, Gardiner was stricken with tonsillitis, an infection that he would never be able to defeat. Despite repeated hospitalization, he played every game. This infection grew steadily worse, and, in 1933, spread to his kidneys. His last season in hockey – 1933-34 – was a testament to his skill and to his great courage. He had ten shutouts in a forty-eight-game regular season, was named to the league's First All-Star Team, and backstopped his team to its first Stanley Cup, all the while enduring a painful and debilitating illness that would claim him on June 13, 1934.

This is the story of Charlie Gardiner's last season.

On November 6, 1933, Major Frederic McLaughlin, owner of the Chicago Black Hawks, announced Gardiner's selection as team captain, an honor and responsibility seldom accorded to a goaltender. "He was selected unanimously by the players," recalled Art

Coulter. "He was a real team man. Very popular. Inspirational. The guy deserved to be captain."

After Major McLaughlin came out on the ice to offer Gardiner congratulations on his new responsibility, he made a statement which drew gasps from those present and derision from the media in their next editions. "Never have I made such a pre-season prophecy," said the Major, "as I am about to make now. I am confident that this team will bring Chicago its first Stanley Cup."

The 1933-34 season began with a twenty-three-day training camp at the University of Illinois. Every day the Black Hawks spent about two and a half hours on the ice, followed by road drills and running, as well as sessions in the sweat room for players who were overweight. By the end of this ordeal, everyone was down to playing weight except Clarence "Taffy" Abel, the largest player in the NHL; he weighed in at 262 pounds.

The Black Hawks' season opened on November 9, 1933, with a 2–2 tie against the New York Americans. Even this early in the campaign, talk began to circulate that the Black Hawks would resume their cellar-dwelling ways of 1932-33. But after they beat the defending-champion Rangers, the mood on the train to the club's next game in Montreal was upbeat and relaxed.

Donnie McFadyen and Mush March played gin rummy; when March lost, his "You big lucky so-and-so" could be heard the length of the car, and, as he pretended to lunge at McFadyen, those sitting nearby erupted into laughter. Johnny Gottselig sat across from Rosie "Lolo" Couture, smoking cigarettes and cracking jokes. Two seats ahead, Lionel Conacher contentedly puffed on his pipe and enjoyed the scenery. Taffy Abel and Elwyn "Doc" Romnes absorbed themselves in a serious game of their beloved cribbage. Gardiner was engrossed in his usual game of checkers, and, after finishing off his opponent, turned to reporter John Carmichael. "I don't always beat him," joked Gardiner. "I'm not especially good at the game." One of his teammates hollered, "Hear, hear," to the laughter of the group.

The Hawks enjoyed success on the ice, staying near the top of the standings for much of the first part of the season. "Since his elevation to the captaincy, Gardiner has been the spark plug of the squad, rallying his defense at critical moments, calling plays for the wings," noted the *Daily News*.

In December, a rivalry that had developed between the Black Hawks and the Boston Bruins after several close, tough games led Chicago's Lionel Conacher to issue a defiant warning: "Listen, I'm not looking for trouble, but I said that any hockey player who took a punch at one of the Black Hawks would get the second smack from me, and that still goes. You can quote me as saying so." Conacher's former club, the Montreal Maroons, must have had second thoughts about having traded him to Chicago: attendance was down in Montreal, and over five hundred season-ticket holders had cancelled their subscriptions.

The Black Hawks traveled on to Boston for a pre-Christmas showdown with the Bruins, who were without Eddie Shore. Boston's all-star defenseman had been suspended because of an incident ten days earlier that left Maple Leaf left-winger Ace Bailey in a

Boston hospital, hovering near death with a fractured skull, after having been checked from behind by Shore. Compulsory use of helmets was suggested, but Chicago coach Tommy Gorman didn't think much of the idea. "We don't believe in them," he said. "And unless ordered to wear them by the league, we will not use them."

In spite of the Black Hawks' reluctance to be in the forefront of helmet-wearing, they were surprisingly receptive to another innovation: player committees, the function of which was to assist the coach in decision-making. Gardiner and Conacher were chosen to assist Gorman.

The Black Hawks beat the Bruins 3–1 on December 23, 1933, again putting them into first place. A victory

Gardiner's position as one of the league's best goaltenders was confirmed when he was selected to participate in the Ace Bailey Benefit Game in 1934.

over the Americans boosted the Hawks into a three-point lead, but Detroit pulled to within one, as the Black Hawks returned home to entertain Boston on January 11, 1934.

A dismally small crowd of nine thousand came out to watch the still-Shore-less Bruins, but they weren't able to tell the players without a scorecard, as the Bruins were, for the first time, wearing leather hockey helmets, designed by manager Art Ross. Gardiner made forty-five saves, but the game ended in a scoreless tie. The Black Hawks were now tied for first with the Rangers. Next, against the Americans, Gardiner chalked up his seventh shutout of the season in a 4–0 win.

Gardiner was racked with pain as he tried to sleep that night in his berth on the train, pain shooting downward from his head into his kidneys. When he awoke the next morning, he could see only black blotches. Horrified, he returned to sleep. When he awoke again, he saw normally, and the pain had subsided.

Chicago lost its next two games, 6–5 and 5–0. Meanwhile, Gardiner continued to feel the effects of his illness. He was dizzy whenever he lunged to the side of the net, and felt a sharp twinge through his head when he dove to the ice.

On January 20, the Black Hawks faced the Maple Leafs in a rough contest that ended in a 2–2 tie. Lionel Conacher, who had a reputation as a tough hockey player and who had played a prominent role in the game against the Leafs, was later corralled in the

Lionel Conacher's on-ice skills were often overshadowed by his other athletic abilities, but he played a major role in Chicago's first championship.

Hawks' hotel lobby by boxing star Kingfish Levinsky. The boxer, appearing to size him up, commented, "I got to hand it to you for tonight. You're good – you'd probably last a whole round with me." Conacher, discussing the game the next day, said, "They were going to give it to us before a hometown crowd and look good. Well, they got some in return. But I hate it, hate that fighting. I'd rather play hockey."

In late January of 1934, Gardiner recorded back-to-back shutouts against Toronto and Ottawa, giving him at least one shutout that season against every team except the Canadiens.

Charlie Gardiner was selected as the goaltender for an NHL all-star team that would face the Toronto Maple Leafs in an exhibition game that would raise almost twenty-one thousand dollars for Ace Bailey, whose injuries had ended his playing career. The day of the game, a Chicago newspaperman asked several of the players on the All-Stars if they planned to take it easy in the upcoming match. Gardiner replied,

> The Leafs won't get a single goal to-night if there is anything I can do to prevent it. This game may be the fore-runner of an annual affair . . . and it would be a matter of life-long pride with me if I were the winning goaler in the first game. Ace Bailey will be out of hockey for life, but he at least had the satisfaction of once leading the league in scoring and being on a Stanley Cup-winning team. My life's ambition is to win the latter honor.

Gardiner's gallant words couldn't keep the puck out of his net, as the Leafs won this inaugural NHL All-Star game by a score of 7–3.

Gardiner also used the three days between the end of the Bailey benefit and the Black Hawks' next regularly scheduled game to set up a hockey clinic with a few other players, and to design and order a new set of goaltending equipment for himself.

The February 1934 issue of *North American* magazine featured on its cover a little boy in makeshift goalie equipment, standing in a "net" made of two branches and a piece of twine, visualizing himself as Charlie Gardiner. It was a testament to Gardiner's huge popularity.

On one of the Hawks' many train trips back to Chicago, a lively discussion broke out about the cost of outfitting a hockey player. Finally Gardiner – who was, after all, a sporting-goods wholesaler in the off-season – took pen in hand and jotted down the following list:

Skates	$27.50
Socks	2.00
Pants	6.00
Jersey	7.50
Shoulder Pads	5.00
Gloves	10.00
Elbow Pads	3.50
Hockey Stick	2.00
Accessories	5.00
TOTAL	$68.50

February ended on a down note for the Black Hawks, with three losses and a 0–0 tie (Gardiner's tenth shutout). In their first game in March, they lost again, and fell into third place. Then they played the division-leading Red Wings, and lost 3–0. A mood of simmering frustration settled on the Black Hawk dressing room. "Would you please tell me," one player asked a reporter, "why we can't lick those guys?" Paul Thompson took a long drag on a cigarette and blew the smoke aimlessly into the gloom, murmuring, "Ain't it hell?"

Gardiner's illness flared up again during the Black Hawks' 6–2 loss to the Maroons on March 13. Since Chicago was trailing the Rangers by three points, second place looked hopelessly out of reach, as the club had only two games left in the season, both with the Leafs, who had scored a league-leading 171 goals in 42 games.

However, Gardiner's skill and leadership sparked the team to a pair of wins, 2–1 in Toronto and 3–2 at home. "Time after time we knew we were outplayed," said coach Tommy Gorman, "and on each occasion, Gardiner would rise to great heights and pull Chicago out of the fire." Combined with two consecutive losses by the Rangers, Chicago's strong finish enabled them to finish in second place in the American Division, one point ahead of New York.

On March 19, the day after the regular season ended, Charlie Gardiner was selected as the goaltender on the NHL's First All-Star Team, with 80 per cent of the participating sportswriters voting for him; he was also voted to other all-star teams, selected not by beat writers, but by the league's managers and coaches. In addition, he also won the Vezina Trophy for the second time; his margin over his nearest rival was the largest

Harold "Mush" March, a seventeen-year NHL veteran, scored at the 10:05 mark of the second overtime period in game four of the 1934 finals to secure Charlie Gardiner's only Cup victory. Note the fringe on the gloves and triangles on the pants of this, the only Art Deco uniform of the 1930s.

since the trophy was first awarded.

The playoff system in the two-division NHL of 1933-34 was very different from today's: The first playoff round saw the league's two second-place teams (the Black Hawks and the Canadiens) play a two-game, total-goals series, as did the two third-place clubs. The winners then played a third two-game, total-goals series, and the winner of that series would meet the winner of a best-of-five between the two first-place clubs, Toronto and Detroit.

Chicago's series with the Canadiens began in the Montreal Forum on March 22. Gardiner was playing despite a severe sty in his right eye. Montreal scored two goals early on, but for the last forty-five minutes of play, Gardiner let nothing in the net, even though his right eye was almost swollen shut. The Black Hawks won, 3–2.

In the Black Hawks' dressing room, owner Major McLaughlin was so excited he could hardly light his cigarette. Tommy Gorman walked around yelling, "Did we do it or did we do it?" Gardiner, Johnny Gottselig, and Lionel Conacher merrily sang in the showers; Gardiner's clear baritone voice could be heard blending with the off-key rendition of his teammates, to the amusement of the others. The three of them had to scramble wildly to make the train back to Chicago.

The Black Hawks returned to the Chicago Stadium, to an overflow crowd of seventeen thousand, on Sunday, March 25. Johnny Gagnon scored for the Canadiens to make it a 1–0 game and a 3–3 total-goals tie in the first period. Neither team scored again in regulation time. Early in the first overtime period, the Black Hawks received a major penalty, giving the Canadiens a five-minute power play. Gardiner played strongly, stopping Aurel Joliat on a breakaway. After the Black Hawks returned to full strength, Mush March beat Montreal goaltender Lorne Chabot on a waist-high shot to win the series, 4–3, catapulting the Black Hawks into the semi-final round.

When the Black Hawks returned to Montreal to play the Maroons in the semi-finals, Gardiner was suffering from a raging fever, but tried to conceal how ill he was. The Black Hawks took an early 1–0 lead, and Gardiner worked diligently to protect that margin, as the Black Hawks did not score again until the third period. They won 3–0; the *Montreal Star* noted that he played despite "suffering agony," and spent the time between periods flat on his back, attended by a doctor.

In the second game, the Black Hawks struck quickly, on a Paul Thompson goal twenty-five seconds into the first period. Not long afterwards, Harold Starr, leading a Maroons charge, drove into the Black Hawks' goal. Starr's skate blade caught Gardiner squarely in the forehead, gashing him just above his right eye. His face covered with blood, he was helped off the ice and into the dressing room. A doctor closed up the wound with seven stitches. Ten minutes later, he returned.

As the game continued, the combined effects of a too-warm arena, his injury, and tonsillitis sapped Gardiner's strength. With the score tied 2–2 early in the third period, an exhausted Gardiner withstood the Maroons' onslaught. The Black Hawks won, 3–2, on a goal by Tommy Cook, eliminating the Maroons.

The stage was now set for a final showdown between Chicago and Detroit. A game-within-the-game saw childhood friends – Gardiner and Detroit's Wilf Cude – tending goal for the opposing teams. "He lived near my place over on William Street [in Winnipeg], and for years we went back and forth to school together," said Gardiner.

In game one, the Hawks took the lead at 17:50 in the first period; Detroit countered with a power-play goal in the third, sending the game into overtime. Paul Thompson won it for the Hawks, two minutes into the second overtime period.

The second game began much like the first, with a Black Hawk goal at 17:52. Detroit tied the score, but Chicago took the lead early in the third period on goals by Doc Romnes and Art Coulter. Johnny Gottselig's goal near the game's end completed a 4–1 Black Hawk victory.

On the evening of game three, Gardiner dragged himself into the dressing room. As he bent over to lace up his skates, a wave of pain overcame him, and he had to stop for a moment. Gorman noticed, and told Conacher, "He's bad. What do you think we should do?" Gardiner, overhearing, forced himself to his feet and told them, "Listen, I want to play. Let me play – for the Cup."

For about five minutes he was able to play his normal game, but by the end of the period Detroit took a 2–1 lead. He managed to hold the Wings off in the second period, but by the midpoint of the third he had nothing left. Detroit won, 5–2. Gardiner collapsed on a bench. As his dejected teammates gathered, Gardiner rose on one elbow and told them, "Look, all I need is one goal in the next game. Just give me one goal, and I'll take care of the other guys."

On April 10, Gardiner took his place in the Black Hawks' goal crease. The first period was scoreless, but early in the second, Herbie Lewis took a high, hard shot, which made Gardiner reach, pain surging through him.

He caught the puck, but weak as he was, he could not hold onto it. Lewis was almost able to knock it into the net, but failed to make his move in time. Larry Aurie fired a blistering shot, but Gardiner blocked it with his pads, making what was normally an easy save only with great exertion. The Black Hawks tried another rush, but Lewis stole the puck and again raced in. Gardiner stopped the shot as the second period ended.

By the start of the third period, Gardiner was in almost constant pain, even when he was still. A rolling shot from Cooney Weiland nearly slipped over his stick, but he recovered in time to keep it out of the net. Gord Pettinger intercepted a Black Hawk pass and fired at the Chicago goal. Gardiner painfully dropped to his knees to halt the puck. Louis Trudel and Leroy Goldsworthy tried to score for the Black Hawks, but Pettinger and Ebbie Goodfellow struck back for the Red Wings; Gardiner somehow managed to fend off the attack. Hap Emms came back for Detroit, and Gardiner went down to block the puck. Goodfellow almost drove the rebound over the exhausted goaltender, but Black Hawk defenseman Roger Jenkins cleared the puck away as regulation time ended.

At the start of overtime, an exhausted Gardiner smiled, waved to the crowd, and shouted encouragement to his teammates. Goodfellow slammed a shot at him. Weiland picked up on the rebound and shot from the other side. Gardiner again dropped to his knees to make the save. As the twenty minutes of overtime wore on, he battled not only Detroit's onrushing forwards but wave after wave of pain. Every dive after a puck, every lunge with his stick, brought with it extreme discomfort. He could no longer smile. He could no longer yell to his teammates. But he could still play, and by the end of the first overtime, the game was still scoreless.

Play resumed in the second overtime period. With every move Gardiner made, pain tore through him; still he let nothing get by. There he stood, playing for the Stanley Cup, tending goal in double overtime on strength of will alone.

Finally at 10:05 of the second overtime period, Mush March's forty-footer found the Red Wings' net, giving the the Black Hawks the game and their first Stanley Cup. Exultantly, Gardiner threw his stick in the air, then collapsed, surrounded by congratulating teammates.

A panel on the barrel of the Stanley Cup, featuring the names of the Chicago Black Hawks of 1934. Manager Tommy Gorman, who led the Montreal Maroons to the Cup the next season, is the only coach to have won back-to-back Cups with different teams.

Two months later, at his home in Winnipeg, Gardiner canceled a singing lesson, telling his teacher that he felt poorly. Soon after, he lost consciousness. He was rushed to hospital, but efforts to revive him were unsuccessful. Ravaged by infection, he suffered a brain hemorrhage that emergency surgery was unable to control. Twenty-nine-year-old All-Star and Stanley Cup champion goaltender Charlie Gardiner was dead.

Tommy Gorman of the Montreal Maroons hockey club accepts the ever-growing trophy from NHL president Frank Calder.

By 1935, the handwriting was on the wall for the Montreal Maroons. They were losing the battle for fan support with the Canadiens, as it became obvious that the city was not big enough to sustain two NHL teams. The Maroons would drop from sight in 1938, but in 1935 they made one last attempt to regain favor with a three-straight final-series victory over the Toronto Maple Leafs, by scores of 3–2, 3–1, and 4–1. This was the first time in ten years that two Canadian teams had played for the Cup. It wasn't until 1947 that it happened again.

The Maroons were under the guidance of manager Tommy Gorman, who had won a Stanley Cup in Chicago the previous year. The club, at that time, was staffed by stalwarts such as Lionel Conacher, who had started his pro career with the Pittsburgh Pirates, Cy Wentworth, Hector "Toe" Blake, who later gained fame with the Canadiens, Jimmy Ward, Lawrence "Baldy" Northcott, Reginald "Hooley" Smith, and Dave Trottier, backed up in the nets by Alex Connell, "the Forgotten Fireman," who had been ousted from his job at Ottawa two years previously.

The year 1936 marked the beginning of Detroit's dynasty as one of hockey's greatest powers. With former PCHA and NHL star Jack Adams in the manager's chair and also coaching the team, Detroit was bound for a remarkable prosperity, which, through the 1940s and 1950s, would see them out of the playoffs only twice.

The Maple Leafs, who met the Red Wings in the 1936 finals, weren't given much chance by the pre-series handicappers. Indeed, they reached the finals

The Totem Trophy

Following their defeat at the hands of the Detroit Red Wings in the 1936 finals, the Toronto Maple Leafs went on a West Coast exhibition tour with the Chicago Black Hawks. In Vancouver, they defeated the Hawks in two straight games to capture an impressive new piece of silverware, the Totem Trophy. Shaped like a totem pole, the trophy was rediscovered during renovations at Maple Leaf Gardens in 1989.

more on Eddie Shore's temper and King Clancy's tongue than on plain ability.

This strange alliance came about in the semi-finals between Toronto and Boston, a two-game, total-goals affair. The Bruins had won the opener 3–0 and appeared to be headed for the finals. In the second game, however, Red Horner had scored while standing on the edge of the crease. The Bruins protested vehemently, and the roguish Clancy skated close to Shore, who had never been noted for his placid nature, and said: "Lousy break, Eddie. You're being robbed. Don't let him get away with it."

Whereupon the incensed Shore shot the puck at referee Odie Cleghorn, hitting him on the backside. For this felony, Shore was banished for two minutes, but en route to the penalty box he picked up the puck and threw it into the crowd. That meant a ten-minute misconduct penalty. This was quite long enough for the gleeful Clancy to drive his teammates to a pitch that resulted in an 8–3 victory in the game and an 8–6 triumph in the series.

The final series was played with no such shenanigans. The Red Wings opened the series at home and beat the Leafs, 3–1 and 9–4. Toronto stayed in the running with a 4–3 overtime win in Toronto before yielding the Cup to Detroit, 3–2, in the final game.

Injuries dominated playoff predictions in 1936-37. Charlie Conacher of the Maple Leafs and Toe Blake of the Canadiens both suffered broken wrists. Frank "Buzz" Boll of Toronto had broken his arm, and Eddie Shore had injured his hip. The Red Wings, who reached the finals against the New York Rangers, did so without Larry Aurie, one of the league's leading scorers, and

Eddie Shore excelled at dropping to his knees to block shots and smother loose pucks.

Earl Robinson followed up his finest NHL season by helping the Maroons win the Stanley Cup in 1935.

defensemen Doug Young and Orville Roulston, both of whom had suffered broken legs. Goaltender Normie Smith also injured his elbow in the third game of Detroit's semi-final win over the Canadiens, and though Smith started the first game of the finals, it was rookie netminder Earl Robertson who played strongly the rest of the way. Ebbie Goodfellow, Detroit's oak-like defenseman, also missed game four of the finals with a sore knee.

The Rangers were a formidable crew, with Frank Boucher, brothers Neil and Mac Colville, Alex Shibicky, Lynn Patrick, Ivan "Ching" Johnson, and others of that rollicking company flying high. It was little wonder that manager Jack Adams excused himself from dressing-room revelries and fainted dead away after the Wings won the series and the Stanley Cup in five games by scores of 1–5, 4–2, 0–1, 1–0, and 3–0. Detroit's Marty Barry was the top scorer in the playoffs, with four goals and seven assists for eleven points in ten games.

The year 1938 marked the second time that the Chicago Black Hawks would have their names inscribed on the silver bands of the Stanley Cup – and they did it as perhaps the greatest longshots ever to win the trophy. Based on regular-season form, the Hawks had outperformed expectations by even being in the finals against Toronto, let alone winning. It proved to be a series noted for its roughness, slashing, charges of double dealing, and fist fights between club officials.

The Hawks finished third in the American Division, with a sad season's record of 14 wins and nine ties in 48 games, and were a distant 30 points behind Boston, the division leader. They upset the Canadiens in the first

The 1936 Stanley Cup-champion Detroit Red Wings, coached by Jack Adams, included Hec Kilrea, a teammate of Adams's on the 1927 champion Ottawa Senators.

round of the playoffs, getting a goal from Paul Thompson at 11:49 of overtime in the third game of the series. (Two-game, total-goals series had been replaced by a best-of-three format in 1937.) The Black Hawks earned a spot in the finals by coming back to defeat the New York Americans two games to one. Chicago's Cully Dahlstrom scored the only goal of game two after thirteen minutes of overtime to enable the Hawks to get back into the series.

The Leafs had an easier path to the final, needing just three games – two of them going into overtime – to sweep the Bruins. The sequence of events in the Toronto–Chicago final reads like a melodramatic movie script.

First game, Toronto, April 5: Mike Karakas, the Chicago goalie, had an injured toe. Chicago coach, Bill Stewart, wanted to use Dave Kerr of the Rangers, but Toronto manager Conn Smythe said no. A desperate search unearthed Alfie Moore, property of the New York Americans, who had been on loan to Pittsburgh. He donned the pads after his eligibility was decided a half-hour before the game, but not before Bill Stewart and Conn Smythe indulged in jostling outside the dressing room. Result: Chicago 3, Toronto 1. Moore thumbed his nose at the Toronto bench.

Second game, April 7: President Frank Calder of the NHL ruled Moore ineligible. Paul Goodman, property of the Hawks, whom Stewart had never seen in his life, was found finally in a movie house two and a half hours before the game. He played goal. Result: Toronto 5, Chicago 1.

Third game, Chicago, April 10: Karakas returned for the Hawks, wearing a steel-toed boot. Everyone breathed a sigh of relief. Doc Romnes broke a 1–1 deadlock at 15:55 of the third period. The Leafs claimed his shot hit the post, but were overruled by referee Clarence Campbell, who would later become NHL president. Result: Chicago 2, Toronto 1. A crowd of 18,497 screaming fans cheered the Hawks, booed the Leafs, and applauded Campbell.

Fourth game, Chicago, April 12: The Hawks opened scoring at 5:52 on a goal by Cully Dahlstrom, marking the first time in the series that Chicago had scored first. Gord Drillon replied in short order for the Leafs. Carl Voss then took a pass from Johnny Gottselig, who finished as the leading point scorer in the series, and put Chicago ahead to stay late in the second period. Jack Shill put it out of reach, and Mush March wrapped it up. Result: Chicago 4, Toronto 1. The Black Hawks fans, still unbelieving, rose to their feet at the final gong, while the players congratulated each other.

Chicago players rushed to their goal, where Karakas was leaning to ease his swollen foot. The little goalie was mobbed and carried off the ice. Behind him pranced Bill Stewart, hanging on Mush March's neck, his bald head shining in the lights as 17,205 fans roared in acclaim. Stewart – a rookie behind the bench – became the first American-born Stanley Cup-winning manager, and his club, with eight Americans on the roster, set a new record for U.S. talent on a Cup-winning team. End result: Bill Stewart learned that there is nothing like success. He was fired the next season.

From Worst to First to Worst

The Detroit Red Wings, who rebounded from a last-place finish in the American Division in 1935 to finish first and win the Cup in 1936 and 1937, fell to last place and the worst record in their division in 1938.

Herb Lewis of the Detroit Red Wings says: "I go for Camels in a big way!"

THE lightning-quick camera eye caught *Herb Lewis* (*above, left*) in this slashing set-to before the goal. Next split-second he scored! After the game (*right*), Herb said: "You bet I enjoy eating. And I'll give Camels credit for helping me enjoy my food. Smoking Camels with my meals and afterwards eases tension. Camels set me right! And they don't frazzle my nerves."

Camel smokers enjoy smoking to the full. It's Camels for an invigorating "lift" in energy. At mealtimes it's Camels again "for digestion's sake." Thanks to Camel's gentle aid, the flow of the important digestive fluids — *alkaline* digestive fluids — speeds up. A sense of well-being follows. So make it Camels — the live-long day.

While it is doubtful that today's athletes would advertise tobacco products, endorsements like these were common in the 1930s. Left-winger Herbie Lewis combined with Marty Barry and Larry Aurie to form Detroit's top line in 1935-36 and 1936-37. Lewis and Aurie were the NHL's top two playoff scorers in 1937.

For the second time in its history the NHL went through a world war without a single interruption in its schedule. Men went to war, both players and executives, but all through the dark years from 1939 to 1945, not a game was postponed. Despite the league losing many players to military service, the gaps were filled, and the game carried on and even flourished. As happened during World War I, some of the NHL's more famous players, including Syl Apps, Maurice Richard, and Ted Kennedy, came to the fore at this time.

But the careers of others were deterred, and the farm and scouting systems that were bringing up new talent were disrupted. Players such as Lynn Patrick, Sid Abel, Max Bentley, Jim Conacher, Milt Schmidt, Woody Dumart, the Reardon brothers, Terry and Ken, Howie Meeker, whose hockey career, the doctors said after he was wounded, was at an end, "Sugar Jim" Henry, Jack Stewart, Chuck Rayner, Bobby Bauer, Ken Mosdell, Jimmy Peters, Floyd Curry, Bill Juzda, Bob Goldham, Tony Leswick, Johnny Mariucci, Wally Stanowski, and Harry Watson all lost potentially productive years.

From 1940 to 1946, when the post-war rebuilding process started, the Cup

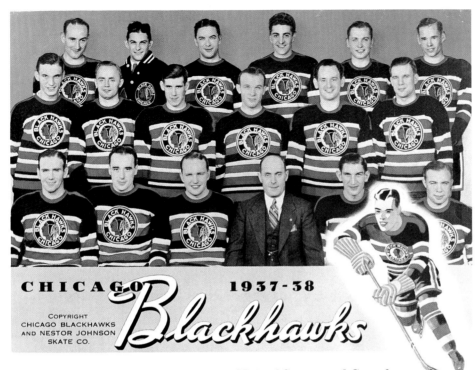

CHICAGO 1937-38 Blackhawks

COPYRIGHT
CHICAGO BLACKHAWKS
AND NESTOR JOHNSON
SKATE CO.

The Chicago Black Hawks, pictured here shortly before the 1937-38 campaign was about to begin. By season's end, eight new players were in the line-up, including former Calder Trophy-winner Carl Voss, who played for eight teams in eight years.

traveled back and forth between the United States and Canada on a regular basis.

With the withdrawal of the Montreal Maroons before the start of the 1938-39 season, the NHL was reduced to a single seven-team division. The playoff system was modified so that the first- and second-place teams would play a best-of-seven series to determine one Stanley Cup finalist. The third- and fourth-place teams would play a best-of-three, as would the fifth- and sixth- place clubs. The winners of these two series would meet in another best-of-three, the winner of which would go to the finals. For the first time, the Stanley Cup finals would be played using the best-of-seven format that is still used today.

Boston won the Cup in 1939 after being the runaway winner in league play. The Bruins had to endure five overtime games en route to the Cup – four in their semi-final series against the New York Rangers and one in the finals against Toronto.

These playoffs belonged to Mel "Sudden-Death" Hill, who came back to haunt Lester Patrick's Rangers after being turned down by the New Yorkers years before. During the season, he had been the almost anonymous right-winger on a line with the great Bill Cowley, but the spotlight was his in post-season play.

A ten-goal scorer during the forty-eight-game season, he netted three overtime goals that beat the Rangers by scores of 2–1, 3–2, and 2–1. The Bruins also took another game in regulation time, 4–1, while the Rangers

The Growth of the Cup

In the early days, players used to add their names to the trophy by scratching them onto the original bowl with a knife or a nail. From the 1890s to the 1930s, various bands were added to the bottom of the bowl to hold the names of the winning teams and their players. Throughout this time, the appearance of the Cup kept changing almost from year to year. In 1939, the Stanley Cup was given a standardized form as a long, cigar-shaped trophy. It stayed this way until 1948, when it was rebuilt as a two-piece trophy with a wide barrel-shaped base and a removable bowl and collar. The modern one-piece Cup was introduced in 1958.

salvaged 2–1 and 3–1 victories. In the seventh and deciding game of the semi-finals, his goal after forty-eight minutes of overtime sent the Bruins into the finals.

The Bruins and Hill, with a full head of steam, went on to eliminate Toronto in five games, losing 3–2 in the only overtime game of the set. Toronto got two of its goals while Hill was in the penalty box. The Bruins won 2–1, 3–1, 2–0, and 3–1. It was the first time that Boston fans had the opportunity to see Art Ross's team win the Cup on home ice.

The Bruins were riding high in these days. In 1935, Ross had scouted a sixteen-year-old named Milt Schmidt, who was to be turned down by the Leafs because he was too scrawny. Schmidt received his bid to try for the big time when Ross sent him a letter inviting him to attend the Bruins camp at Saint John, New Brunswick. Schmidt's reply was classic in its unpretentiousness. "Thank you very much for your invitation," he wrote back. "I shall be very happy to attend your camp and will start working immediately to save money for my transportation."

Schmidt turned down his first pro contract because he thought, at seventeen, he could stand another year in junior hockey. "After all," he said years later, "I was only a punk kid of seventeen. Mr. Ross gave me a brand new pair of skates, told me to put on some weight, and come back next year." He did, and made the club, to be joined by Bobby Bauer, a teammate of his from the Kitchener juniors, and another Kitchener-born player who had worked for the London juniors, Woody Dumart. The three spent part of the 1936 season with Boston's Providence farm club and joined the Bruins in 1937 to stay.

Even with Providence, Schmidt wasn't at all sure that he was good enough

The 1939 Boston Bruins and friends gather for a Stanley Cup supper following the Beantowners' five-game victory over Toronto in the first best-of-seven Stanley Cup final.

The defense never rested for the 1940 New York Rangers, thanks to the efforts of (left to right) Muzz Patrick, Art Coulter, Ott Heller, and Babe Pratt.

to play. When he got his first cheque from the Bruins as a member of the Providence club, Schmidt sent it right home to his mother with an enclosed note that said: "Please bank this for me. I'll need it fairly soon because I won't last long in this league."

Schmidt, Bauer, and Dumart together formed the Kraut Line, one of the greatest and most colorful forward combinations in NHL history. The Krauts were instrumental in winning four straight league titles for the Bruins, from 1938 through 1941. The first came while the league was still split into Canadian and American divisions, the remainder after the clubs formed one seven-team league in 1938.

They were on two Stanley Cup-winning teams within a span of three years and, in 1940, they lost a semi-final series to the second-place Rangers in six games.

In 1940, the New York Rangers defeated Toronto in a bitterly contested final that went six games, three of which were decided in overtime.

The Leafs at this time featured a line with Syl Apps at center, Bob Davidson at left wing, and the sharpshooting Gord Drillon at right. The Rangers' big guns were Phil Watson, Bryan Hextall, and Wilfred "Dutch" Hiller, with the Patrick brothers, Lynn and Muzz, at center and defense, along with the Colvilles, Neil and Mac, and high-scoring Alex Shibicky.

The Rangers won at home, 2–1 in overtime and 6–2, lost the next two, 2–1 and 3–0, and wrapped up the series on 2–1 and 3–2 overtime decisions.

Despite their success in 1940, the Rangers were on the verge of hard times. Noted for "growing their own" players, the Rangers club that won the Cup had only two players, Dave Kerr and Art Coulter, who had not come up through their own system. During the war their farm system would

Milt Schmidt won a First All-Star berth and the NHL's scoring championship with 52 points in 48 games in 1939-40.

Mainstays of the 1941 Stanley Cup-champion Boston Bruins, gathered in the dressing room following another victory. Left to right: Terry Reardon, Herb Cain, Bobby Bauer, Woody Dumart, and Flash Hollett.

disintegrate, and it did not show signs of reaching its former proportions until the mid-1950s.

The Rangers finished first in the league in 1942, but over the next thirteen years, until 1956, they made the playoffs only twice, in 1948 and 1950, when, as the league's Cinderella team under the guidance of coach Lynn Patrick, they were defeated in the finals by Detroit.

The 1940-41 season would also prove to be the last time that Boston would have its name engraved on the Cup until 1970. The line of Schmidt, Bauer, and Dumart – now called the Kitchener Kids Line, since "Kraut" was an unpopular expression at that time – played an important role in Boston's victory and then, as a unit, joined the Canadian armed forces. They came back following the war but never achieved their former greatness. Bauer broke up the combination when he retired to go into the skate business in Kitchener.

The Bruins won the Cup by defeating Detroit and recording the NHL's first four-game sweep since the seven-game format was introduced in 1939. Schmidt, who scored three goals and had four assists in the final round, was the leading scorer in Cup competition, with five goals and six assists.

Eight years after the 1942 Stanley Cup finals, Canadian sportswriters voted the series as the comeback of the half-century. The Leafs, down three games to none to Detroit, came back to win it all.

A beautifully bitter rivalry had sprung up between the clubs after the Maple Leafs won a pair of semi-final meetings in 1939 and 1940. Against this backdrop, the clubs met again in the 1942 finals, and the Wings overpowered the Leafs in the first three games.

The experts, who had favored Toronto, jumped off the Leaf bandwagon before the fourth game and announced that the Wings were unbeatable.

No one believed Billy Taylor of the Leafs when he told a group of resigned Toronto newspapermen in a Detroit hotel lobby on the eve of the fourth game: "Don't worry about us. We'll take 'em four straight." Taylor, who as a child had been a Leaf mascot, was dead right. With almost impossible determination, the Leafs, with a couple of unknowns named Don Metz and Ernie Dickens swinging the tide in their favor, won the next four games 4–3, 9–3, 3–0, and 3–1, the finale taking place in Maple Leaf Gardens.

The 16,218 fans, the largest audience to see a hockey game in Canada up until that time, exploded in spontaneous applause for one of sport's greatest comeback performances.

The 1941-42 Toronto Maple Leafs featured scoring punch throughout their line-up. They were the first team in NHL history to boast nine forwards with ten or more goals.

(continued on p. 109)

The Comeback to End All Comebacks

by Stan Fischler

The most remarkable thing about the "miracle" Stanley Cup playoffs of 1942 was the fact that there were so many remarkable things going on between April 4 and April 18 of that year, as super-plots crowded sub-plots and sub-sub-plots for space. Now, let's get something straight right from the start. The expression "miracle" has been abused in the realm of sport almost as much as the overused term "great." But when it comes to the 1942 Toronto Maple Leafs, the assertion that they were a miracle hockey club borders, if anything, on understatement. Just think about coach Hap Day's team in this context: never in the history of major professional sports – not in baseball, football, or basketball – has a team lost three straight games in a championship final series and then rebounded to win the next four and the title.

"We stand alone," said defenseman Wally Stanowski, one of the fourteen-carat heroes of that epic comeback. "Nobody else can make that statement." And how many Stanley Cup playoffs can make these statements:

- A letter from a fourteen-year-old girl proved the inspiration to the bedraggled Maple Leafs after they had lost the first three games.
- A pair of stars – high-scorer Gordie Drillon and veteran defenseman Wilfrid "Bucko" McDonald – were benched and replaced by non-entities Don Metz and Ernie Dickens at their respective positions.
- The club's founding father, Conn Smythe, was virtually banned from the Maple Leafs' dressing room for game seven.
- Disregarding orders to stay out, Smythe twice in-

vaded the club's locker room to deliver passionate speeches.

- Detroit Red Wings' general manager Jack Adams punched a referee and was suspended for the series.
- Under Adams, the Red Wings introduced a completely new strategy that eventually became *de rigueur* for contemporary hockey.
- For the first time in National Hockey League history, a playoff series was profoundly affected by a world war.

These are among an infinite number of emotional swerves and counter-swerves that pulled at the nerve endings of fans throughout the seven-team circuit at a time when many observers truly believed that the 1941-42 campaign would be the NHL's last for the duration of World War II.

Nazi Germany's Panzers had laid a carpet of terror across Europe by the time the NHL held its annual meeting in Toronto on September 12, 1941. Less than three months later, the Japanese completed their sneak attack against the Americans' Pearl Harbor naval base, drawing Uncle Sam into the war, and, before season's end, Boston's superb Kraut Line (Milt Schmidt, Woody Dumart, and Bobby Bauer) had enlisted en masse in the Royal Canadian Air Force.

The Kraut Line's departure, while noble of spirit, would prove a demoralizing blow for the defending-champion Bruins. In the spring of 1941, the Schmidt–Bauer–Dumart trio had catapulted Boston to a Stanley Cup championship, during which they ousted the Leafs four games to three in a preliminary round. "Boston had an excellent team," says Stanowski of the Leafs, who played in all seven games. "But we weren't too bad either. We finished second in 1940-41, only five points behind the Bruins. And we even led them in game seven, until they caught and passed us [2–1] at the end. So we approached 1941-42 in not bad shape."

To put it mildly. During the off-season, manager Conn Smythe executed some deft deals that would have long-term reverberations on the Maple Leaf psyche in April of 1942. He signed rookie defenseman Bob Goldham, who would become one of the game's best shot-blockers, as well as a heavy-bearded backliner named Ernie Dickens. His last move was the signing of Winnipeg right wing Johnny McCreedy. "We're pretty well stocked," Smythe allowed, as his Leafs prepared for the season-opener on November 1, 1941, at Maple Leaf Gardens. The Rangers beat them, 4–3, but then Smythe's club reeled off six straight wins by November 22, and the little manager felt he could go off to war himself with a clear conscience.

Although Smythe was fifty-six at the time, there was absolutely no hesitation on his part when it came to enlisting in the Canadian Armed Forces. Quite the contrary; the man who would become renowned as "the Little Major" was as chauvinistic as the most jingoistic military poster. He had been this way in World War I, when he enlisted in the Sportsmen's Battery, and he was no less enthused now in 1941.

"I thought, if I could go out and form my own battery, hustle for recruits and get it organized," noted Smythe in his autobiography, *If You Can't Beat 'Em in the Alley*, "they'd have to let me take it overseas." While his Leafs were preparing for training camp, Smythe's 30th Battery was formed, and he was named the major and commanding officer. With exceptional foresight, Smythe had planned for his military commission, even as far as allowing Dick Irvin (whom he said was "not tough enough") to depart to take the Canadiens' coaching job so that he could put his former defenseman Clarence "Hap" Day behind the bench. "Hap was everything I wanted," said Smythe. "He could do things I couldn't; fire people; bench them; live always on what a man could do today, not what he had done a few years ago."

Apparently the high command that would fill Smythe's vacuum was only concerned with what Conn could do tomorrow, which, for them, was nothing. With incredible speed, Maple Leaf Gardens directors, Ed Bickle and Colonel Bill MacBrien, along with assistant manager, Frank Selke, Sr., began making plans to reshape the club to their liking. Before leaving the Gardens for the Army base at Petawawa, Ontario, Smythe barked at them, "My God, don't you wait until the corpse stops breathing?"

Smythe may not have been at Maple Leaf Gardens, but his memory lingered on, thanks to Day, a faithful aide who implemented all the moves his boss had suggested. As an added fillip, Smythe had wangled crack right wing Lorne Carr from the last-place New York Americans, by now a decrepit club which had just changed its name to the Brooklyn Americans for the

Canny Conn Smythe was renowned for scouting athletes on the football field and the baseball diamond as well as in the hockey arena. His Leaf teams won the Stanley Cup five times in the 1940s.

1941-42 season, although it still played at New York's Madison Square Garden.

As the schedule moved into the home stretch, Day's Leafs engaged the Rangers in a neck-and-neck run for first place. The New Yorkers came out on top, but not by much. A strong second, Toronto boasted a well-balanced roster with two threatening forward units. The front line included the distinguished captain, Syl Apps, a 1936 Olympic track-and-field star, as well as a collegiate football ace. Tall and handsome, Apps was the quintessential all-Canadian athlete. He was a strong skater, possessed a powerful shot, and could stickhandle with the best.

Apps, a center, was flanked by right wing Gordie Drillon and left wing Bob Davidson. Drillon ranked with the league's foremost sharpshooters, while Davidson was one of the NHL's best two-way players.

No less effective was the second line, which had two refugees from the New York Americans, Carr and Dave "Sweeney" Schriner, the latter of whom was admired for his ability to play well in important games.

Day juggled his third line. He could choose from the rookie Johnny McCreedy, Pete Langelle, Hank Goldup, and Nick Metz, one of the finest penalty-killers to come down the pike. Although little was thought of him at the time, Nick's kid brother, Don Metz, was also around.

Little did anyone imagine what the fourth-stringer could do. "My brother, Nick, had been with the Leafs since 1934," recalls Don. "He had become a regular long before I ever made the big club. I got my first shot in 1939-40, and again in 1940-41. I wasn't considered good enough to be a regular in 1941-42, but I did score a couple of goals, and I was around for the finish." The 1941-42 Leafs finished with twenty-seven wins, eighteen losses, and three ties, for fifty-seven points, three behind the first-place Rangers. Turk Broda had established himself as a premier goaltender, fronted by a well-balanced defense. Bucko McDonald and Rudolph "Bingo" Kampman were, as their nicknames suggested, devastating checkers in an era when hip- and chest-checks were routine bulwarks of the defense.

"You couldn't say we were favorites to win the Cup," says McCreedy, "because the last time Toronto turned the trick was back in 1932. But we had a solid club, and we'd get a really good test in the opening series against New York."

The Rangers featured hockey's most prolific scoring line in Lynn Patrick, Bryan Hextall, and Phil Watson, who had accounted for 71 of the 177 goals New York had scored in topping the league. Hextall was the league scoring champ. The team was well-balanced, from Sugar Jim Henry's goaltending to the defense corps, and nobody was surprised when a headline in a Toronto newspaper blared HEAVY SCORING RANGERS RULE AS FAVORITES OVER HAP'S BOYS.

In no time at all, the Leafs demolished the forecasts. They won the first two games, dropped the third, but won the fourth to take a commanding three-games-to-one lead. The Rangers won game five, 3–1, setting the stage for game six on March 31 at Maple Leaf Gardens. For a time it appeared that the Leafs would blow the Rangers out of the rink on that night. Johnny McCreedy scored a fluke goal in the first period, and Pete Langelle beat Henry early in the second. Broda was indomitable through the end of the second period and half of the third. Then the Leafs momentarily dropped their guard, and the Rangers quickly tied the score. Reeling under the relentless pressure, Broda just barely prevented New York from taking the lead, and it appeared that the period would wind down with the score tied. Toronto had the puck, with less than a minute left in the period.

There were thirty seconds remaining, and the Leafs had to make a decision. They could remain in a defensive shell and keep possession of the puck until the bell sounded, ending the period, or they could attempt to score, risking a Rangers counter-attack. The decision was made by Nick Metz, who nursed the puck on his stick as he skated away from the Toronto net.

Logically, Metz should have circled back to Broda and reorganized the attacking formation, because Apps was on the right side and Drillon on the left – the wrong position for both players. Yet Metz imperturbably moved forward, crossing into the Rangers' defensive zone with only fifteen seconds remaining in the period. His flankers were both better scorers, and the New York backliners realized this as they prepared for the period's final thrust. Who, they wondered, would get the pass – Apps or Drillon? The Rangers moved back, but the pass was never delivered. Metz swiftly snapped his wrists, and before Sugar Jim Henry could move, the webbing of the net had bulged behind him with only six seconds left in the period.

Pandemonium gripped Maple Leaf Gardens. A conscientious team-player, Metz was penitent about his "mistake," and he headed for the bench to apologize. "Coach," Nick said to Day, "I know I should have passed off to Syl or Gordie."

"That's one apology I'll accept without an argument," laughed Day, whose club had catapulted its way to the Stanley Cup finals on the strength of Metz's goal.

The Leafs had fully expected to meet the defending-champion Bruins in the finals, but somehow, a spunky Detroit Red Wing club got in the way. Fifth-place finishers, the Wings upset Montreal, two games to one, in the quarter-final round, and then erased the Bruins in two straight games to reach the finals. It had been a decade since Toronto had last captured the Cup. Would this be the year? Maple Leafs' publicist Ed Fitkin wondered along with the others. "Nobody could say for sure," said Fitkin. "So many times the Leafs had appeared to be title-bound and disappointed. They had gone ten long years without winning the darn thing."

In an era when videotape was only a dream, scouting was in its infancy. Yet Red Wings' coach Jack Adams had detected a flaw in Toronto's otherwise solid fuselage – slow-footed defenseman Bucko McDonald, who could be beaten by speed along the boards. Adams devised a new tactic, which was unheard of in an epoch when teams routinely carried – or passed – the puck over the enemy blue line. "In the opening game," said Fitkin, "Detroit completely crossed us up. Instead of carrying the puck over the blue line, the way everyone else did, they would shoot it past our defensemen and then skate like hell after the puck and often get to it before we did. Bucko, who had been terrific all season and especially strong against the Rangers, found his effectiveness marred by these tactics." Detroit won game one, 3–2, employing Adams's new system to perfection. Not surprisingly, the Red Wings' room was oozing jubilation and confidence.

"We've got the team to beat the Leafs," ventured Adams. "We'll take them in six games."

The second game of the series at Maple Leaf Gardens was virtually a clone of the opener. Don "Count" Grosso once again opened the scoring for Detroit and, as he had done before, scored a second decisive goal. Only the score – 4–2 for the Wings – was different.

Incredibly, the Leafs were collapsing at every corner like a house of cards. The redoubtable Broda, later immortalized as a consummate big-game goaltender, played the worst game of his Stanley Cup career in game three. Despite the loss of young center Sid Abel with an injured jaw, the Red Wings poured five goals past Broda and skated out of Olympia Stadium to a cacophonous cheer, embellished by a 5–2 victory. "We had hit rock bottom," recalled McCreedy. "The dump-and-chase business really had us confused."

To put it mildly.

From his Petawawa outpost, the livid Major Smythe was on the phone with Day. "Hap told me that he was planning to shake up the team for the fourth game." But how? Day's options were limited. He studied his reserve list and evaluated the play of his veterans. Drillon, his leading scorer in the regular season, hadn't had a single point in three games. McDonald was constantly being duped on defense. "Hap made a bold move," says Don Metz, who had been watching the games in civvies from the stands. "He benched Gordie and Bucko. That's when I found out I was moving into the rotation."

It seemed that everyone in the Toronto high command was anxious to do something to help the team, including Maple Leaf Gardens director Bill MacBrien, who resorted to a propaganda gambit worthy of a World War II counterspy.

Stanowski recalls,

> The first thing MacBrien did was meet with all the guys in the dressing room after we had lost the third game. He said, Just don't pay any attention to what you read in the newspapers tomorrow.
>
> Sure enough, the next day we picked up the papers and there was a statement from MacBrien, "the Maple Leafs are going to accept defeat." The Detroit players also read it and became overconfident. They were all set to have a champagne party.

In addition to Don Metz, inexperienced Ernie Dickens was inserted into the line-up, leaving the Leafs with two rookie defensemen, Dickens and Bob Goldham. No wonder a headline in the *Detroit Times* proclaimed, WINGS RULE HOT FAVORITES TO DEAL KNOCKOUT BLOW.

The Detroit Olympia's largest crowd up to then, 13,694, filled the arena, expecting Don Grosso and company to apply the *coup de grâce*. By this time, Day was not above pulling out every stop, even if it meant stooping to the maudlin level. Prior to the game, he gathered his troops in the dressing room and read a letter he had received from a fourteen-year-old fan. Unlike the majority of Toronto followers, the lass expressed her conviction that, yes, the Leafs still could rally and save the series. Somehow her belief actually moved the normally laconic Day, and when he read the letter, he virtually oozed conviction out of every pore. The message touched a nerve among the players, and Sweeney Schriner rose from the bench and said, "Don't worry about this one, Skipper. We'll win it for the little girl!" Billy "The Kid" Taylor added, "We're not licked yet."

The results after half a game indicated otherwise. Detroit held a 2–0 lead on goals by Mud Bruneteau and Sid Abel. The Leafs rallied with a pair of late second-period goals, but Detroit again forged ahead at 4:18 of the third period on Carl Liscombe's goal.

"We may have been behind," says Stanowski, "yet there were some positive signs. Don Metz and Ernie Dickens fit in without a problem, and Hap kept harping on the fact that we only had to win one shift at a time."

As it happened, Toronto won the third period with a little help from Stanowski. The twenty-two-year-old defenseman, who would emerge as a playoff hero, helped arrange the tying goal by captain Apps at 6:15. The game's next goal would likely be the winner – and it was.

In his flights of fancy, Day had imagined that a line featuring the two Metz brothers – Nick and Don – would mesh neatly with Apps. He put them on the ice at about twelve minutes of the third, and, within forty-five seconds, Nick Metz had beaten Red Wings' goalie Johnny Mowers. Apps and Don Metz got the assists. From that point on, the Leafs stalled the Detroit scoring machine. Broda would not be beaten, and Toronto finally had a victory, 4–3.

Perhaps the tantalizing early-third-period lead had lured the Wings into a state of mistaken complacency. Perhaps the frustration of blowing the advantage was seen as a portent of things to come. Whatever the reason, an incident late in the third period detonated an explosion on the Detroit bench that would have reverberations for the remainder of the series. It also would alter the course of the finals, allowing the Maple Leafs to swim downstream for a change after having flailed against the tide for the first three matches.

The uprising occurred at the tail end of the game, with Toronto leading 4–3. Referee Mel Harwood gave Detroit veteran Eddie Wares a misconduct penalty. Furious, Wares refused to leave the ice and, instead,

The Metz Brothers, Nick (left) and Don, were key contributors in the Leafs' amazing comeback in the 1942 Stanley Cup finals.

skated to the Red Wings' bench, where he picked up a hot-water bottle. He then attempted to give the bottle to Harwood. Unimpressed with this curious gesture, Harwood slapped Wares with a $50 fine, and this time ordered him to the penalty box. Wares complied. On the ensuing face-off, Harwood almost immediately whistled the Wings for having too many men on the ice. The Olympia roared with revolt, but the stoical referee merely ordered Detroit to send a player to the penalty box. Grosso was the designated sitter. He headed for the penalty area, stepped in, but then bobbed out again and dropped his stick and gloves at the referee's feet. Harwood fined him $25 and ordered him back into the box. Grosso acceded to the demand, and the game continued to its conclusion, a tumultuous and unexpected Maple Leafs' victory.

Under normal conditions, it didn't take much to unnerve Jack Adams, but the defeat, coupled with Harwood's officiating, caused a terrible post-game reaction. Adams jumped the boards and pursued the referee across the ice, punched him several times, and finally was restrained by linesmen Don McFayden and Sammy Babcock. When the dust had cleared, the repercussions were severe. League president Frank Calder announced that Adams was "indefinitely suspended and prohibited from taking any further part in the bench management of the Detroit Red Wings. For their part in the affair, Wares and Grosso are each fined $100."

Day's benching of Drillon and McDonald paid off, but the coach had one more move on the drawing board. He dropped tall forward Hank Goldup, a three-year veteran, and replaced him with eighteen-year-old Gaye Stewart, who would be relief man for Schriner and Davidson. Stewart proved significant in one respect, having been the first player ever to make the jump from junior hockey to the senior ranks to minor professional and then to the NHL in one season.

"I was still in high school in the fall of 1941," Stewart remembers.

When the hockey season started, I was playing for the Junior Marlboros in Toronto. In December they promoted me to the Senior Marlies, and in March I moved up to the Hershey Bears of the American League. I stayed with them until the Calder Cup playoffs were over, and then I got word to report to Detroit and meet the Leafs. They told me to keep my skates warm, but didn't dress me for the fourth game, and a lot of people thought there wouldn't be a fifth game, so I figured I might miss the big show after all. Then we won that big fourth game and Hap put me in the line-up for game five. He alternated me, sometimes with Apps, other times with Taylor. What a thrill for a kid still going to high school in Toronto.

The Toronto brain trust decided to enter game five (April 14 at Maple Leaf Gardens) with Don Metz and Ernie Dickens still in the line-up, along with newcomer Stewart. Could so many inexperienced players in key positions help maintain the Maple Leafs' momentum? That was the question that permeated the Gardens before the opening face-off. In three hours the answer was resoundingly in the affirmative. Don Metz scored three goals and added two assists for five points out of nine Maple Leaf goals. They ran up a 7–0 lead after two periods, and cruised to a 9–3 victory. "A lot of people tried to make me out to be a hero," Don Metz recalls, "but I didn't look at it that way. My brother had been playing a lot more than me, and when Hap put me in the line-up, I had had the benefit of being rested in the first three games." Gaye Stewart adds, "Don was one of the quietest guys on the team; in fact he and his brother, Nick, were those typical silent Westerners. He wasn't the type to brag about himself. But I can tell you, that was Don's greatest night." Metz's modesty notwithstanding, he *was* a hero, if for no other reason than his unflappable performance during the intense comeback that remained incomplete.

Detroit still led the series three games to two with game six to come on Olympia ice. "The 9–3 win in Toronto was the turning point in the series," says Stewart. "Up until then, we had some doubts, but after that win, going to Detroit didn't bother us at all. From the fifth game on, nobody on our club thought we were going to lose."

The first period of game six at the Olympia was scoreless, although the Wings dominated, only to be thwarted by Broda's superb goaltending. No sooner had period two begun, than Don Metz struck again. He required only fourteen seconds of the second period to bang the puck past goalie Johnny Mowers, and the Leafs were off and running en route to a 3–0 shutout for Broda. This was especially ironic, since the Turk had made his debut at the Olympia in 1936 as a Red Wings'

Gaye Stewart, the last Toronto Maple Leaf to lead the league in goals, made his NHL debut during the 1942 finals. Stewart earned a regular spot with the Leafs in 1942-43, winning the Calder Trophy with a twenty-four-goal performance.

farmhand before moving on to the Maple Leafs.

"I give Hap Day a lot of credit for turning the team around," says Stewart.

> What he stressed with me and some of the younger guys was disciplined defensive checking. He figured that the goals would eventually come, and they did. Another thing about him was special: Hap was the first coach that I can remember who always kept a notepad handy near the bench; something like what Bob Johnson did with the Penguins in 1991.
>
> We didn't have video then, so the notes were very important. Every time an idea came to Hap, he'd reach back for his pad, jot it down, and then refer to it with us between periods.

The Red Wings, like the Maple Leafs, had one more chance. The seventh and final game was played on the night of April 18, 1942, at Maple Leaf Gardens, where 16,218 spectators came to see what the Maple Leafs were made of. They remembered the collapses of the past, and they wondered if it would happen again. One who certainly remembered was Major Conn Smythe, who took the train to Toronto from the Petawawa army base. But instead of being hailed at the Gardens by the general staff, Smythe, as he put it, "was welcomed by Bickle, MacBrien, and Selke the way a skunk is at a garden party." Bickle, then in charge, actually barred Smythe from the Leafs' dressing room.

"I knew what I could do in the dressing room," said Smythe in his memoirs. "I was good at touching the raw spots, even with people I trusted. I'd give them as much as I knew they could take, send them out hating me, and they'd go and destroy the enemy, just to show me up."

Day, who also knew the power of Smythe's barbed rhetoric, urged him to talk to the players, adding that he, Day, would punch Bickle in the face if he got in the way. Smythe entered the dressing room and said his piece, but the results weren't evident at first.

Syd Howe put Detroit ahead, 1–0, and Toronto's attack suddenly fizzled, as it had in the first three games of the set. At one point goalie Mowers turned back the Leafs with his team two men short, and when the second period ended, the teams returned to their dressing rooms with the Red Wings still nursing a 1–0 lead. The little major entered the Leaf locker room for another talk.

As he recalled:

> I could see that the game had slowed down because both sides were tired. That lessening of the speed made the game exactly right for old Sweeney Schriner and old Lorne Carr and young Billy Taylor. I walked over to the corner where they were and gave it to them hard, one at a time and then all three. I'll never forget Sweeney looking up at me with a grin. "What ya worrying about, boss? We'll get you a couple of goals."

Truer words were never spoken.

The Leafs needed a break, and they got it early in the third period, when referee Bill Chadwick whistled Jimmy Orlando into the penalty box for two minutes. Coach Day sent the Schriner line out for the power play, instead of Apps and the Metz brothers. "Sweeney was a big man," wrote hockey historian Charles Coleman, "a fast skater and very nimble in his play."

Never was Schriner more nimble than he was in front of the Detroit net with his Maple Leafs on the brink of defeat. Sweeney awaited the pass, but the puck rolled to him on its side, instead of moving like a pancake. In order to handle the rubber, Sweeney had to turn his back to the cage. He did just that, and rapped the puck past the startled Mowers to tie the score. The Maple Leafs were alive again! Spectators crumpled programs in excitement; others leaned so far forward in their seats that they jammed their knees into the backs of those in the rows ahead of them. Everyone waited and hoped for the moment when Toronto could pull the string that would drop Detroit out of contention. But they worried about the Red Wings' propensity for coming from behind.

In the next two minutes, the Red Wings' forwards attempted to puncture the Maple Leafs' blue-line corps, but Day's "substitutes" came through nobly. Rookies Ernie Dickens and Bob Goldham would not be breached, and Don Metz checked zealously on the forward line.

A whistle was blown, and Day changed squads. He sent in young center Pete Langelle, with veteran Bob Davidson on left wing and thirty-year-old rookie Johnny McCreedy on the right side.

Immediately they stormed into the Red Wings' zone, with McCreedy leading the way with a shot on Mowers. The Detroit goalie moved far out of his cage to deflect the drive, but the puck rebounded back into play, and Mowers was stranded away from the gaping net. In a desperate lunge, the Detroit defense tried to cover Mowers's abandoned net, but Langelle pounced on the puck like a leopard seizing his prey and smacked it into the cage.

"The puck happened to bounce ten feet from Mowers," says Langelle, "and I kinda banged at it. Next thing I knew, the red light was on and we were ahead." With less than five minutes remaining, Schriner also scored, giving Toronto a two-goal lead. The Wings were thoroughly demoralized as the clock ticked down the final seconds of the game.

Recalls Ed Fitkin: "Pandemonium broke loose on the ice and in the stands at the final bell. Every player on the Leaf bench leaped over the boards and rushed out on the ice to grab and hug a teammate, while the crowd roared with the ecstacy of the moment. Broda, grinning and whooping, was mobbed by every Leaf at the final bell." In those pre-television days, celebrations were

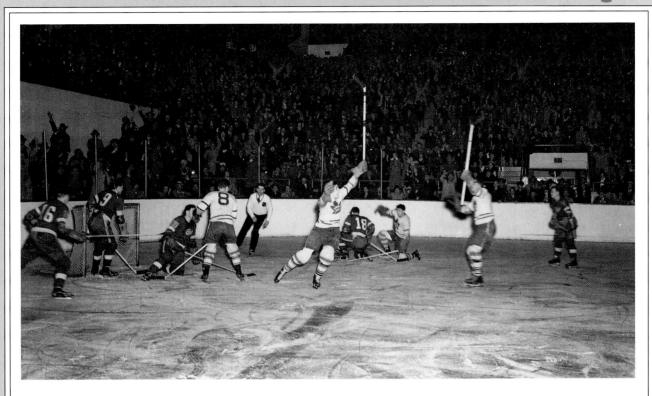

more spontaneous and certainly more modest than they are in the 1990s. "After we dressed, I went back to the old Westminster Hotel, where I was staying, and had a beer with Bucko McDonald," says Stewart. "Toronto was a very conservative town in those days, so you couldn't just go out and do a lot of celebrating."

Smythe stayed long enough to pump a few hands and then caught a train back to Petawawa. One of his soldiers, the Toronto *Telegram* columnist Ted Reeve, remembered Smythe "feeling so good we got away with only two hours gun drill and the route march was cut down to ten miles!"

Toronto formally honored its heroes with a luncheon the following day at the Royal York Hotel. Obvious aces such as Broda, Apps, and Schriner were duly acknowledged, as well as the unlikely stars – Don Metz, Dickens, and Stanowski. Perhaps captain Apps said it best when he nodded towards the coach and said, "We wouldn't be celebrating the championship today if it hadn't been for Hap and his faith in us. He won the Cup more than anybody."

In fact, there was an endless number of contributors, from the letter-writing fourteen-year-old girl, who proclaimed her faith in the Leafs when they were down by three, to Major Conn Smythe, who inspired his troops, to peach-faced rookie Gaye Stewart, who

The Shot that Shook the Walls. Pete Langelle (arms raised, center of picture) has just fired the puck into the vacated Detroit net to give the Leafs a 2–1 lead in game seven of the 1942 finals.

stepped into the breach without missing a step.

"I still look back," says Stewart, "and think about that club winning four after losing three in the finals, and only one word comes to mind – phenomenal!"

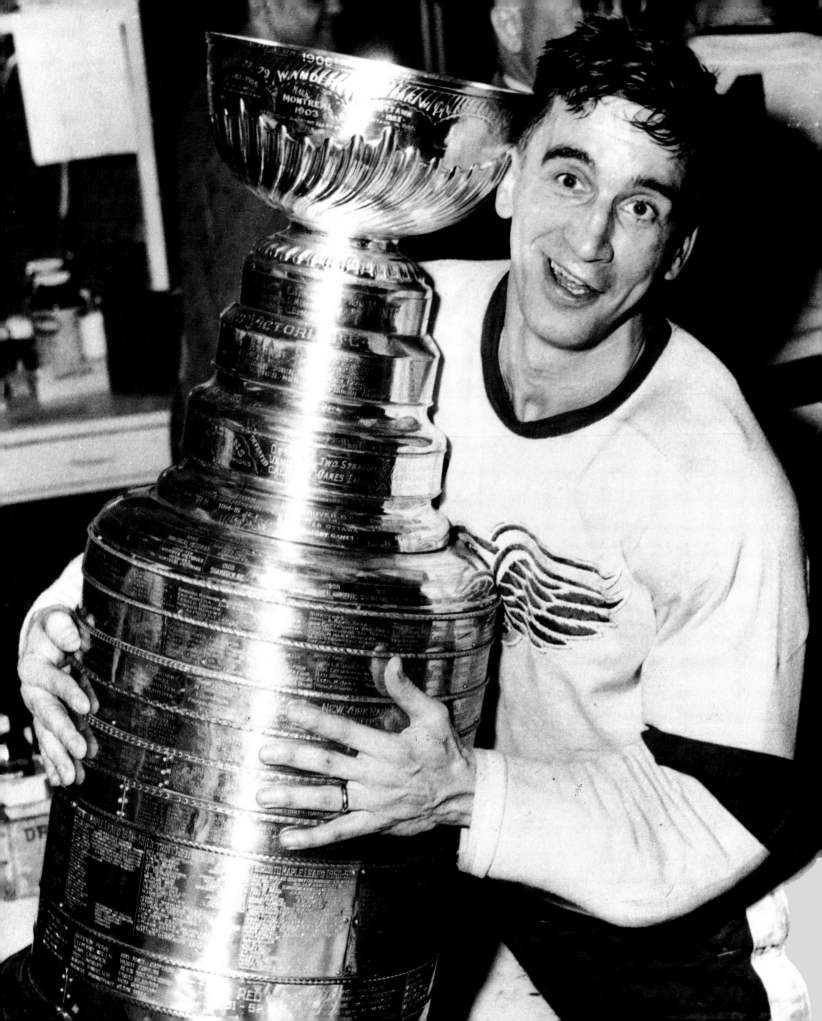

The Golden Age Begins,

1943-1955

BY THE START OF THE 1942-43 SEASON, THE NEW YORK AMERICANS (called the Brooklyn Americans in their last season) had folded, ending a swashbuckling, if unsuccessful, tenure in the NHL. The league now operated with six teams, and would remain in this configuration for the next twenty-five seasons. The regular-season schedule was increased to fifty games from forty-eight, with each team playing its five opponents five times at home and five times on the road. The first four regular-season finishers qualified for the playoffs, with first playing third and second playing fourth in the semi-finals. All series, including the finals, were best-of-seven.

The balance of power belonged to Detroit in the first season of this six-team era, with the Wings bouncing Boston four straight in the 1943 finals. Goaltender Johnny Mowers shut out the Bruins in games three and four.

The following season, the Canadiens, with a bright new star named Joseph Henri Maurice "Rocket" Richard showing signs of greatness, walloped Toronto in five games in the 1944 semi-finals.

Dick Irvin, who had left Toronto to join the Canadiens, had spotted Richard as a junior in 1940, and it wasn't long before experts were mentioning him in the same breath as the great Howie Morenz. If a fault could be found with the fiery, scowling Richard in those early days it was his physical brittleness. He had suffered broken legs in 1941 and 1943. In 1942, his first season in the NHL, he had missed most of the campaign because of a broken wrist.

The rise of the sullen right-winger with the flashing dark eyes was phenomenal in 1943-44. He started slowly, with only nine goals in twenty-eight games, then, in an amazing spurt, Richard rammed in twenty-three more before the season ended.

Toronto fans were prepared to rate him in the same class as Gaye Stewart,

A young Maurice Richard, whose intensity is apparent even in this dressing-room photo, put his stamp on Stanley Cup hockey in the 1944 playoffs, scoring twelve goals in nine games as the Habs won the Stanley Cup.

a high-scoring local newcomer. But any doubts they had as to Richard's superiority were dispelled on the night of March 23 in Montreal, when The Rocket exploded for all five Montreal goals in the second game of the semifinals, won by the Habs by a 5–1 score. Richard's performance equaled a single-game playoff record established by Newsy Lalonde in 1919. It was later matched by Darryl Sittler and Reggie Leach in 1976, and by Mario Lemieux in 1989. Montreal's subsequent 11–0 victory in the final game of the series stands as the most one-sided playoff shutout in NHL history.

The Canadiens advanced to face fourth-place Chicago in the finals. The Hawks entered the series much in the manner of a man going to the gallows. Their fears were well founded, as the Habs swept the Black Hawks, with Richard again the most potent offensive player on the ice. His hat trick accounted for all of Montreal's scoring in a 3–1 win in game two, and the Punch Line of Richard, Elmer Lach, and Toe Blake scored ten of the Canadiens' sixteen goals in the series. The 1944 championship was the Canadiens' first Stanley Cup win since 1931.

In addition to Richard, Blake, and Lach, the Montreal roster included Murph Chamberlain, Emile "Butch" Bouchard, Glen Harmon, Herbert "Buddy" O'Connor, and goalie Bill Durnan, the man who would win the Vezina Trophy six times.

The oddity of this series was the unfair reaction of Montreal fans to Bill Durnan. After the Canadiens had won three games over Chicago, they booed him soundly and rent the air with cries of "fake" when the Habs trailed in game four. Recalling the incident much later, Blake said he was still puzzled but rather thankful that this had happened. "It made us [Richard, Lach, and Blake] so mad," he said, "that we came from three goals behind to win the Cup in overtime." Richard scored twice in the last five minutes of the third period to tie the score 4–4. Blake scored the Cup winner after 9:12 of overtime.

The Canadiens did not appear to run out of gas the following season, 1944-45. They ran away with the league title by a margin of thirteen points over the second-place Red Wings and twenty-eight points over the Maple Leafs, who would go on to upset the Canadiens in a six-game semi-final series, despite losing game five by a lopsided 10–3 score. The Leafs would then capture the Stanley Cup in an exciting seven-game final against the Red Wings.

The 1944-45 regular season was Richard's greatest scoring year. He potted his fiftieth goal in the last game of the fifty-game schedule against Boston. The Canadiens placed five men on the Canadian Press All-Star team: Durnan in goal, Butch Bouchard on defense, and Lach, Richard, and Blake on the forward line. Dick Irvin was selected as the All-Star coach. Defenseman Frank "Flash" Hollett of Detroit was the only intruder.

For the Leafs, Ted Kennedy, a youngster from Port Colborne, Ontario, who had been scouted by Nels Stewart, was coming into his own. Toronto also had Calder Trophy winner Frank "Ulcers" McCool in goal and an assortment of youngsters and veterans, some of them back from the service, in Wally Stanowski, Don Metz, Reg Hamilton, Elwyn Morris, Bob Davidson, Sweeney Schriner, Lorne Carr, Nick Metz, Art Jackson, Mel Hill, and Walter "Babe" Pratt.

The Montreal Canadiens, led by Toe Blake's eighteen playoff points, lost the first game of the 1944 semi-finals to the Toronto Maple Leafs, before reeling off eight straight wins, in which they outscored the Leafs and Chicago by a combined score of 38 to 12.

Jack Adams (center) puts the victory embrace on Harry Lumley (left) and Eddie Bruneteau following Lumley's 1–0 overtime victory in the 1945 finals. Bruneteau scored after fourteen minutes of extra time.

Frank "Ulcers" McCool established an NHL record when he held the Detroit Red Wings off the scoresheet for the first 188 minutes and 35 seconds of the 1945 finals.

The final between Toronto and Detroit was a tame affair in comparison to previous and future meetings between the two clubs. Only seventeen penalties were called, including a major to Lorne Carr.

For a time, though, it appeared as though the Wings were going to avenge their collapse of 1942. This time Toronto went ahead by three straight games, 1–0, 2–0, and 1–0, with McCool recording three straight shutouts.

Detroit won the next three, two of them shutouts, 5–3, 2–0, and 1–0 in overtime, but Toronto's Babe Pratt, perhaps the most flamboyant personality in hockey at that time, deflated the Detroit balloon at 12:14 of the third period in the deciding game when his goal put the Cup in the Leafs' laps with a 2–1 victory.

Toronto's fortunes slid in 1945-46. The Stanley Cup champions finished a miserable fifth, five points out of the last playoff spot held by Detroit and sixteen back of the first-place Canadiens, who went on to win their second Cup in three years.

Montreal romped past Chicago in four straight in the semi-finals, setting up a final-series match-up with the Bruins, who had beaten Detroit in five. Boston's Kraut Line had been reunited and had scored forty-six goals during the regular season. In the finals they were pitted against the Habs' free-wheeling Punch Line, which had scored sixty-nine. Boston had Frank "Mr. Zero" Brimsek in goal, Pat Egan, Johnny Crawford, and the clever Bill Cowley.

The finals went five games, three of which went into overtime, before the Canadiens captured the Cup. The Habs' big line reigned supreme, finishing one-two-three in Stanley Cup scoring, with nineteen goals in the playoffs. The Krauts, in their two series, scored eleven.

The end of World War II marked the start of a rebuilding job in Toronto that, in surprisingly short order, delivered three straight Stanley Cups for the Leafs. Sweeping changes were made, creating a club that manager Conn Smythe, even in his most optimistic moments, felt was still a year or two away from being ready to challenge for the Stanley Cup.

By the 1945-46 season, cherubic Turk Broda had returned from the Canadian Army to tend goal for Toronto. To play in front of him, the Leafs had recruited Jim Thomson and Gus Mortson, two juniors from Toronto's St. Michael's College who worked as a defense pair and later were known as "the Gold Dust Twins."

Garth Boesch, a strong, silent man among boys, had also returned from the army for duty on defense, and later in the year, Bill Barilko, a brash, rollicking rookie from the minor-pro Hollywood Wolves, was paired with him to form another defense tandem. Right-winger Howie Meeker won the Calder Trophy as the NHL's top rookie for 1946-47. The club was further augmented by "Wild Bill" Ezinicki, a right-winger with cast-iron hips who was to be the body-checking specialist on a line with Syl Apps at center and Harry Watson on left wing. As well, Ted Kennedy had become recognized as one of the league's honest workmen and leaders.

The Metz brothers, Don and Nick, were there as well. So were Norman "Bud" Poile, reputed to have one of hockey's hardest shots, Joe Klukay and Bob Goldham, both recently discharged from the navy, as well as Gus Bodnar and Vic Lynn. This was the crew that was to form the nucleus for the Maple Leafs' first great run of success.

The late 1940s saw a renewal of the fierce Detroit–Toronto rivalry that was to last for six years and reached such a fever pitch on one occasion that Detroit captain Sid Abel announced: "They pay us to play the other teams. We'd play the Leafs for nothing."

In their 1947 semi-final series against Detroit, the Leafs had one disastrous setback, a 9–1 defeat in game two, during which Broda seemed to suffer from the shakes. The defeat stirred the Leafs up, for they won two in a row on Detroit ice and then wrapped up the series in Toronto in game five. Apps was the Leafs' scoring leader in the series with four goals.

Montreal, after a driving finish in which they had copped their fourth straight league championship, beat the Bruins in a sluggish five-game semi-final series, highlighted by Bill Reay's four-goal performance for the Habs in the fourth game.

The upstart Leafs were still the underdogs entering the finals against the Canadiens. The odds appeared to be short when the Leafs lost the opener 6–0, causing Montreal goalie Bill Durnan to ask, "How did these guys get in the playoffs anyway?" The Leafs had the answer with a 4–0 shutout in the

Elmer Lach led all scorers with seventeen points in the 1946 playoffs.

Syl Apps cradles a long-and-lean Stanley Cup after the Leafs' victory in 1947. The following season, the Cup was remodeled into a two-part barrel-shaped trophy.

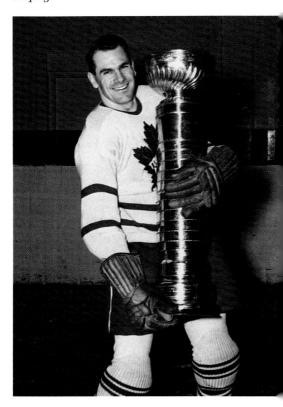

A Toronto forward is surrounded by a trio of Montreal defenders – goaltender Bill Durnan, Butch Bouchard, and Frankie Eddolls – during action in the 1947 Stanley Cup finals.

next game, scoring four power-play goals to tie the series.

Fireworks were expected for game three, but such expectations fizzled out as the Leafs bested the Canadiens 4–2 in a tame encounter back in Toronto. Syl Apps put the Leafs ahead 3–1 in the series in the next game with an overtime goal for a 2–1 win.

Back at the Forum, Rocket Richard potted two goals, as the Canadiens surged back with a 3–1 victory, but the Leafs clinched the Cup on Toronto ice, 2–1, with Ted Kennedy firing the winner at 14:39 of the third period. Despite having missed one game of the finals, Richard led the playoff scoring race with eleven points on six goals and five assists. He also led in penalties, sitting out forty-four minutes.

The Leafs were the youngest club ever to win the Stanley Cup. Each player enjoyed the NHL's upgraded playoff-winner's bonus of $2,500.

(continued on p. 122)

Whistling the Playoffs

by Bill Chadwick

For sixteen years, from 1939 to 1955, I was a National Hockey League official. Except for the very first season, 1939-40, when I served as a linesman, I spent all of that time as referee. They were the best years of my life.

So, when plans were announced to celebrate the centennial of the Stanley Cup, I was hit with a flood of memories – some good, some bad – but all searing reminders of what it meant to be right in the middle of the action when the most famous trophy in professional sport was on the line.

How I came to be a referee, born and raised on the sidewalks of New York, is a story in itself, but it's hardly related to the Stanley Cup.

The Stanley Cup! The very words have a special ring to them. They tug on the emotions and quicken the pulse, especially when you are a referee, with the game riding on the whistles you blow . . . and the ones you don't.

It was Lester Patrick, hockey's famed "Silver Fox," who taught me so much about officiating, and about whistles in particular. "Bill," he said, "You've got all night to blow that thing, but once you do, you can't call it back. A fast whistle often penalizes the wrong team." I found that to be oh so true, especially during the playoffs.

So many of my memories surround the playoffs.

There is the Stanley Cup trophy itself, of course. One year, early in my career, the Cup was under my personal care for so long that I felt like the trophy was part of me. It was like traveling with a relic, a priceless piece of art,

which of course it is.

There are the arenas, basically the homes of the so-called "Original Six" – the Forum in Montreal, Maple Leaf Gardens, Madison Square Garden, Detroit's Olympia, the Chicago Stadium, and Boston Garden. Each had its own personality, separate and distinct from the others, a special feel, special smells, special rink characteristics.

Then there were the players. And my fellow officials. The coaches. The managers. And the fans.

So many memories. So much to tell. But, what the hell, a one hundredth birthday doesn't come along every year, you know. So, here goes . . .

One thing I learned very early in my career was to keep my composure under all circumstances. I learned this from Mickey Ion, a Hall-of-Fame referee like myself. During my first season as a linesman, I worked a game with Mickey at Madison Square Garden. Throughout this particular game, the fans were ranting and raving over almost every call that was made. There were some awful commotions. Somehow, Ion didn't seem the least bit disturbed. After the game, I asked him how he kept so cool.

An NHL referee for fifteen years, Bill Chadwick initiated hand signals for on-ice officials. He worked thirteen Cup-clinching games.

"Bill, when things get like that," Ion said, "I simply remind myself that there are fourteen thousand people in the building and that I'm the only one who is sane." That's a philosophy that has served me well over the years, particularly when I moved on to refereeing.

If ever my composure had been going to crack, it would probably have involved Maurice "Rocket" Richard, the great, great symbol of the Montreal Canadiens – and to this date the fiercest, most intense player I have ever seen.

In particular, one Rocket Richard incident stands out. It happened during the 1947 finals, game two, Montreal Canadiens versus Toronto Maple Leafs. Game one had gone to Montreal handily, 6–0.

Toronto assigned pesky winger Vic Lynn to shadow the Rocket. Lynn was somewhat of an agitator, and he soon got under Richard's skin, and the Rocket cut Lynn with a high stick to the head. I saw the play clearly, and it was a five-minute major for Richard.

Now, Rocket Richard was hardly the most forgiving player in the NHL, and you could almost see steam coming out of his ears as he sat in the penalty box. I knew when I looked over that I had certainly not seen the last of The Rocket that night.

Sure enough, in the second period, Richard became predictably entangled with an old nemesis, Bill Ezinicki of the Leafs. At one point, I separated the two antagonists, but Richard reached over my shoulder and high-sticked Ezinicki even more severely than he had Lynn.

Richard had given me no choice. This was clearly a match penalty for deliberate attempt to injure, which in those days meant the offending team had to serve twenty minutes shorthanded!

Even the powerful Canadiens couldn't skate short-handed that long without being hurt. The Leafs scored two goals during the twenty minutes, and cruised to a 4–0 victory, bringing the series even at one victory apiece.

My boss, Clarence Campbell, the president of the NHL and himself a former official, backed my call completely, and even tagged Richard with an immediate one-game suspension and an additional fine of $250.

Now, you must understand that Maurice Richard at that time could have been elected prime minister of Canada. He was that popular, especially with the French-Canadian fans. When Toronto took the next game, and eventually the series, the anger of the fans only increased. Surprisingly enough, particularly to me, was that the fans' wrath was all directed at Campbell and not towards me. From that day forward, Campbell was never popular in Montreal. Me? Some of my best memories are of that great city.

Three years earlier, in 1944 for instance, it had been Rocket Richard again who had provided what was quite simply the greatest single-man performance in a playoff game that I had ever seen. Certainly, it was the greatest single-man performance of that era, and one of the greatest of all time. The site was the venerable Montreal Forum.

The Rocket was in only his second season. I was in my fifth. It was the second game of a semi-final series, and once again the Canadiens were playing the Leafs. Toronto had won the first game, 3–1.

The job of shadowing The Rocket fell to Bob Davidson of the Leafs, and he held Richard off the scoresheet in the first period of a scoreless game.

Less than two minutes into the second period, The Rocket launched himself and scored twice within seventeen seconds, beating the Leafs' goalie Paul Bibeault. Just before the 17:00 minute mark, Richard connected again – a Stanley Cup hat trick – three goals not only in one game but in one period!

By then, Richard had the Forum fans in a frenzy; they were roaring with every move. Goal number four came at the one-minute mark of the third, and number five followed at 8:54. The final score: Richard, 5, Toronto, 1.

As is still the case in many arenas today, it was usual then to have a writer or a radio broadcaster (television was hardly born at the time) pick the game's three stars. The stars would be announced three-two-one, so the crowd would build a suitable crescendo of applause. As I was leaving the ice, the announcer began:

"Tonight's third star … number nine, Maurice Richard." A silence fell over the crowd. I remember the hush because it stopped me dead in my tracks in the runway.

"Is he kidding?" I remember thinking.

The announcer continued. "Tonight's second star … number nine, Maurice Richard."

With that, the crowd began to understand, and a roar began to spill down from the upper reaches of the Forum. Soon, it encompassed the whole building, and clearly sent chills up the spine of the referee of the evening, yours truly.

"Tonight's first star...number nine, Maurice Richard." I'll never forget it.

The Stanley Cup, as we know it today, stands just under three feet in height, and weighs thirty-two pounds. "My Cup," as I like to call it, was much different, much squatter, about a foot and three-quarters high, with not nearly as many names engraved on it.

I call it "My Cup," because, for eight days in 1942, from April 10 to April 18, when it was finally awarded, it was just that. To be more proper, it belonged to me and my best buddy and fellow referee, Francis Michael "King" Clancy. But, if possession is nine-tenths of the law, then it was mine alone. Clancy had seniority over me (didn't everybody?), so I had to carry the Cup. I remember the brown wooden case, somewhat ragged with wear, a dog-eared handle on the top.

This was the year of "Hockey's Unrivalled Comeback," the miraculous, final-round revival of the Toronto Maple Leafs from a 3–0 deficit in games to defeat the Detroit Red Wings and win the Stanley Cup. It's been fifty years now, and that feat has never been matched in the finals.

With the Wings leading, three games to none, that meant that the Cup could have been awarded after game four, or after game five, after game six, or after game seven.

League president Frank Calder gave us the Cup with only one admonition. "Just don't lose it," he said. By day, it sat in our hotel room, either the King Edward in Toronto or the Cadillac in Detroit. By night, it was in Maple Leaf Gardens or the Olympia, awaiting presentation.

On travel days, there were overnight trips between the two cities, so the Cup stayed in our berth on the Canadian Pacific Railway. One night Clancy and I played cards, and the chips were placed in the Cup. Now, there's one I'll bet you hadn't heard before.

Nowadays, the Cup travels with considerable security, and is met with more of the same whenever it's displayed. Clancy and I didn't have any security, except for our whistles, and that was plenty. We never lost the Cup either.

Maple Leaf Gardens and the Montreal Forum were probably my favorite rinks to work. In my time, there was no question that Toronto and Montreal fans understood the subtleties of the game better than the fans in other NHL cities, and consequently knew whether or not I was doing my job properly.

The Forum, with all its history and its steeply sloped seating areas, always reminded me of a cathedral, although it was a cathedral that could explode (and that *is* the right word) into a frenzy at the drop of a snowshoe.

Maple Leaf Gardens? Oh, I remember the stately portrait of the Queen. The full band at the Wood Street end of the building. The magnificent hallway portraits in later years. And, of course, wonderful Connie Smythe, running the place like the tough major that he was.

Toronto was also the site of what was certainly the most embarrassing – and painful – moment of my officiating career. In those days, there was no protective glass or chicken wire along the sideboards at Maple Leaf Gardens. There was protection at the ends of the rink, in order to shield the fans from errant shots. On the sides of the rink, however, it was wide open.

When players were about to collide at the end of the rink, it was common practice for the officials to grab onto the chicken wire and pull themselves up onto the top of the dasherboards, to avoid the impact. On the sides of the rink, you would simply sit on the boards, literally in the laps of the spectators, to get out of the way.

One night in Toronto, this one fan, sitting right along the sideboards, was giving me an awful verbal beating all through the first period. In the second period, while I was sitting on the boards to avoid a collision, he even held my referee's sweater and prevented me from jumping quickly back into the action.

Later in the period, it happened again. I couldn't get right back on the ice because this moron was tugging on my sweater. Out of sheer frustration, I swung backwards with my hand, the hand that had my whistle in it, and caught my tormentor hard, right in the mouth, with the whistle. There was some blood and a cut, of

course, and the poor guy needed stitches.

What I didn't know at the time, was that the guy I cold-cocked was handicapped and in a wheelchair! Connie Smythe would regularly use the area along the sideboards to place handicapped fans, since their wheelchairs could not fit into the regular seating areas.

You can't imagine how badly I felt when I realized the chap I had belted with my whistle was handicapped. You know, I never saw that guy again, but I still feel badly about that incident.

In all my years in the National Hockey League, I never, not once, wore a striped shirt, the kind today's referees have been wearing for forty years now. I had three different outfits, and none of them were striped.

The first was a woolen, V-necked pullover sweater. It was plain white, with orange and black trim on the neckline and a large NHL crest on the left breast. Underneath, we wore a *collared* shirt and a black tie. Let me tell you, that was one hot outfit. You could easily lose ten pounds working a game in those clothes.

Round about 1950, it got a little better. We discarded

Maple Leaf Gardens in the early 1950s. The Queen's portrait at the north end of the building was later removed to accommodate extra seats (and extra revenue) because, as Leafs owner Harold Ballard put it, "She doesn't buy any tickets, does she?"

the shirts, ties, and woolen sweaters for a lighter-weight sweater that was NHL orange in color, with a crest on the left breast and a zippered neck trimmed in black.

Once, in the mid-1940s, the League experimented with heavy blue sweaters that were even hotter than the shirt-and-tie outfits. They lasted one game only. We all hated them.

It was not until long after my retirement that I wore a striped shirt. I'm pretty sure it was in St. Louis, for an Oldtimers Game, but I then wore it several times after that.

I certainly remember wearing the orange sweater for the closing of the old Madison Square Garden in 1968. I dressed for the game that afternoon between Frank Udvari, who wore a striped shirt, and Cooper Smeaton, who wore the white sweater with a shirt and tie. In fact, a photo of the three of us appeared on the cover of the *1991-92 NHL Rule Book*.

In the other four rinks – Madison Square Garden, the Olympia, Boston Garden, and Chicago Stadium – most fans hadn't grown up with hockey and simply didn't know the game. To many, it was just a bunch of guys on skates gliding around in pretty uniforms. Kind of like an ice show with sticks.

Chicago could get real rough, because they never really controlled the fans there, and they would try anything to get your goat. You were also a sitting duck in Chicago, especially when you went close to the seats to reach the crooked staircase behind the boards that led down to the officials' dressing room. Although the Black Hawks never won the Stanley Cup during my career, still I worked a lot of memorable playoff games at the Stadium.

I'll never forget the noise generated by the powerful Barton organ, which had its pipes built into the Stadium rafters. The organist at the time, Al Melgard, would play "Three Blind Mice" when the officials would take the ice, and repeat it every time he thought a particular call didn't go the Hawks' way. Melgard played "Three Blind Mice" well into the 1960s, before league president Clarence Campbell halted the practice, which was certainly a demeaning one to the officials.

There's one thing I want to get straight about Detroit. It has a long-standing "tradition" of throwing an "octopus" on the ice at various times during playoff games. Now, I was the referee the very first time they threw one of these things, and let me tell you this: they are not throwing an octopus, at least not most of the time. They are throwing a common squid, the kind you can get from any fish market. I know, I have picked a few of these critters up myself, and had quite a few others picked up for me.

Just this year, on television, I saw it again. Twice, in fact, during the Red Wings' opening game against Minnesota at the Joe Louis Arena. I may have only one good eye, but I know the difference between a squid and an octopus!

In fact, from an officials' standpoint, Chicago fans did even Detroit fans one better during a series with the Maple Leafs. This particular game wasn't exactly a

memorable one until about halfway through the second period, when someone tossed a shoebox onto the ice. Lo and behold, out of the shoebox scampered a rabbit. My linesman was Sammy Babcock, and we had the damnedest time cornering the rabbit, I can tell you. Complicating the fact, of course, were twenty thousand howling fans and a dozen or so scampering hockey players.

The rabbit eventually found haven in the Toronto goal net, behind Turk Broda. The rabbit proved to be the only thing Broda didn't stop that night, because he scampered away again, and the merry chase continued. He hippety-hopped right into the Chicago penalty box, where Babcock finally cornered him.

"What did you penalize him for, Bill?" quipped one of the players.

I didn't miss a beat. "Illegal equipment," I said. "He didn't have skates."

By comparison, the squids in Detroit were a piece of cake. They were inert. You just loaded them onto a shovel, and off they went.

Animals weren't all that was thrown on the ice during my career. The items tended to be the usual stuff that fans can buy at or around the arena – soda, cups, peanuts, popcorn, etc. I have also certainly taken my share of beer showers.

But two things – other than octopi and a rabbit –

Three generations of NHL referees – (left to right) Frank Udvari, Chadwick, and Cooper Smeaton – display the three uniforms worn by on-ice officials since 1917. This photo was taken in 1968 at the closing of Madison Square Garden.

stick out as the strangest ever thrown at me. A live string of firecrackers landed on my head during a Cup game in Boston. I thought I had been shot when they went off. There was a lot of smoke, but no damage. Another time, in Chicago, a guy actually threw his false teeth at me. I'll bet they didn't fit too well, because nobody throws away his false teeth.

There actually was a silver lining in being the target for all that stuff. Lots of fans, particularly in Boston, New York, Chicago, and Detroit, would throw coins on the ice. Never any quarters – or even dimes for that matter. But plenty of pennies and the odd nickel. Let's put it this way: my two kids, Barbara and Billy, had two of the fattest piggy banks on Long Island. I had considerable competition in this department, I can tell you. One of my frequent linesmen was a big chap named George Hayes, who eventually made the Hall of Fame. To be sure, George deserves to be in the Hall of Fame, not only for his officiating abilities, but for his skill at being able to spot a penny and retrieve it quickly from a pile of otherwise useless rubbish.

Nowadays, things are usually only thrown on the ice during celebrations, following a hat trick, or whatever. In my time, it wasn't at all uncommon for the fans to litter the ice before a game. It was a regular occurrence, then, for me to signal the ice workers, basically two or three guys with shovels and scrapers, to clean the ice before the game even began. During the playoffs, especially, the ice cleaners were kept awfully busy.

There is nothing like the pressure of the Stanley Cup playoffs, especially the finals. The pressure is there for the players and the officials as well. You work the whole season toward this climax, and when it comes, you try your damnedest to perform up to the standards the playoffs deserve.

The Stanley Cup finals were like nothing else. I should know. I am proud to have worked a record forty-one games in the finals during my fourteen years as a referee, including the deciding game itself on thirteen occasions. The only year I missed was 1946, when Montreal beat Detroit in five games.

With today's large officiating staffs, I'm sure that no other NHL referee will ever work that many. In my day, of course, there were far fewer referees, and it was

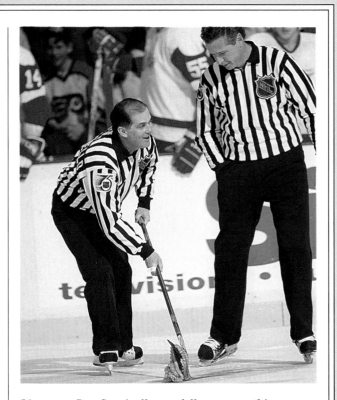

Linesman Ray Scapinello carefully removes this cephalopod from the ice, continuing a Stanley Cup playoff tradition of octopus-tossing that goes back to the Detroit Olympia in 1952.

commonplace for only two of us to work the finals.

Usually, my partner was King Clancy, and we became the best of friends. More on King later.

I am also proud to have developed and implemented the hand signals that are now universally used by hockey officials throughout the world.

I don't remember precisely when this started, but somewhere around 1943 or 1944 would be fairly accurate. It was during the Stanley Cup playoffs, I can tell you that, and it was probably during the finals, because there's so much noise in the building during these games. I never really knew what to do with my hands when I called a penalty, so I started pointing at the man who had committed the foul. That was the beginning. The rest just followed.

I tried to communicate with the penalty timekeeper, using a sign language of sorts. You know, touching my leg for tripping, or my elbow for elbowing, and so on. Rotating clenched fists to indicate charging was my invention. That's better known today for walking in basketball, but the National Basketball Association wasn't even in business when I started to use that signal.

Also, my original sign for cross-checking (crossed arms across the chest) soon gave way to a more accurate signal of two hands supposedly on a stick, indicating a cross-checking motion. The crossed arms across the chest quickly became the indication of an interference penalty.

Not only did the system of hand signals work well for me, but it got the fans more into the game, gave them more information.

For most of my NHL career there were only three referees – me, King Clancy, and George Gravel. We all had our distinct styles, so, from a philosophical standpoint, the games were handled quite differently.

Clancy would let the players go out and play any way they wanted. He'd simply adjust to the tempo, and mostly he called only the basic, most-flagrant violations.

Gravel was just the opposite. He worked strictly by the book, and called just about everything. A real close-to-the-vest kind of referee.

Me? I kind of played it right down the middle. The teams seemed to adjust to each referee's particular style. It worked well, I think, and the games were certainly exciting.

Since Clancy and I were particularly close, we'd often call each other to compare notes and swap stories. Remember, there were only six teams in those days, so King and I were never really too far apart. I would tell King my problems, and he would tell me his. If some players were giving him trouble, I watched for them in the games I handled, and he did the same for me. Eventually, the players came to realize this. They recognized that, once they did something to infuriate Chadwick or Clancy, then they had not one but two referees on the lookout for them.

Personally, I had a pretty good basic instinct, almost a "sixth sense," about when there was going to be trouble in a particular game. And I had a method for dealing with teams that might be coming into a game with more than just hockey on their minds. On that kind of night, as soon as I dropped the puck, the first guy who blinked an eyelash was gone, and I was in control all the way.

King Clancy, who was an NHL official for over a decade, had a simple-yet-effective philosophy: "I can only call what I see. I can't call what happens behind my back."

One other thing about my personal style was a physical one. Having sight in only one eye, I always felt I had to work just a little bit harder to overcome that handicap. It never entered my mind at the time, but as I look back, I was always on top of the play, always closer than the others. I think that made me a better referee.

Lots of people ask me if hockey was better in my day than it is today. The normal, sentimental reaction is to say yes. But the real answer is no.

As I said, we had only six teams back then. Now we've got twenty-two, and we're heading for twenty-four. That's great for the sport, and even greater for the fans.

The athletes themselves are so much bigger now. The equipment is better. Training methods are better. Diets are better. Everything is better. No one, least of all an old referee, should stand in the way of progress.

So, you ask, is today's hockey better? You bet it is. But not when it comes to the memories.

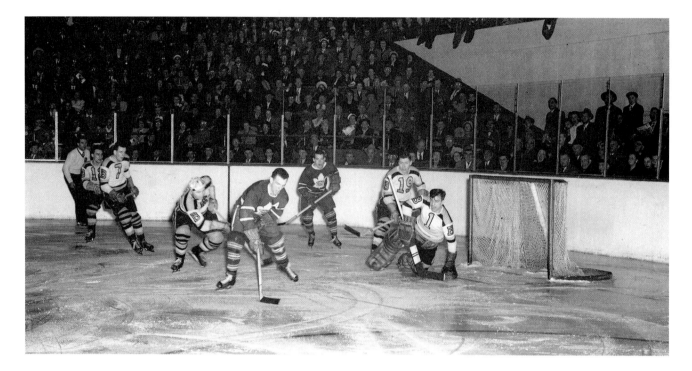

Toronto's Ted Kennedy wheels and fires this Howie Meeker pass behind Boston Bruins' goalie Frankie Brimsek to give Toronto a 3–2 win in the fifth and deciding game of the 1948 semi-finals. Kennedy, who notched four goals in game two of the series, led all post-season scorers with fourteen points in nine games.

Father Knows Best

Les Costello, a member of the 1948 Cup-winning Toronto Maple Leafs, left professional hockey to join the priesthood. He later resurfaced as the organizer of the Flying Fathers, a squad of straight-shooting priests that play charity hockey games throughout the world.

Among the self-fulfilling prophesies that preceded the 1947-48 season was one by Conn Smythe: "If this team wins the Stanley Cup, it is the greatest club the Toronto organization has ever had." Smythe, who was one of hockey's great wheeler-dealers, did not stand pat after winning the Cup in 1947, swinging what was to that time hockey's biggest player-swap, a seven-player deal completed on November 4, 1947. Smythe traded Bob Goldham, Ernie Dickens, Bud Poile, Gaye Stewart, and Gus Bodnar to the Chicago Black Hawks. In return, the Leafs received Max Bentley and Cy Thomas. Smythe wanted the fantastically fast Bentley to augment his theory that strength at center was what a club needed to win championships. With Bentley, Apps, and Kennedy, plus Nick Metz for fill-in duty and penalty killing, the Leafs were extremely strong up the middle.

The Leafs must have read Smythe's comments in the papers, for not only did they win the Stanley Cup, they breezed through the playoffs. Under the coaching of Hap Day, they took the Boston Bruins in a five-game semi-final.

The Red Wings were no match for the Leafs in the final series. Gus Mortson was lost in the first game with a broken leg, and the Leafs spotted the Wings a goal, but Toronto easily won the game 5–3 and then swept the series. Detroit's superb Production Line of Sid Abel, Ted Lindsay, and Gordie Howe could manage only one point, a goal by Lindsay, against the Leafs, whose scoring punch was evenly distributed throughout the line-up.

The Maple Leafs and the Red Wings seemed to be making the Stanley Cup finals their combined company picnic, for the teams met again in 1948-49. To fill the hole left by the retirement of Syl Apps after the 1948 playoffs,

Smythe had swung another deal, this time with the Rangers, getting center Cal Gardner and defenseman Bill Juzda, "the Iron Fireman." Red Wings' manager Jack Adams had made some changes of his own, trading All-Star defenseman Bill Quackenbush and left-winger Pete Horeck to Boston for wingers Jimmy Peters and Pete Babando and defenseman Clare Martin.

In the semi-finals, the Leafs disposed of the Bruins in five games, while the Red Wings needed seven gruelling contests to get past the Canadiens. As a consequence, the Wings entered the finals slightly leg weary and battle fatigued.

The Production Line was in full swing, having scored sixty-six goals during Detroit's march to the NHL title. In the semi-finals against the Canadiens, they had scored twelve of the Wings' seventeen goals, eight of them going to the slope-shouldered, sensational Gordie Howe.

Ray Timgren, never a prolific scorer, broke up the first game of the finals, whipping a goal-mouth pass to Joe Klukay, his right-winger on a line with Max Bentley that sportswriters had dubbed the Feather Line. Klukay's goal came at 17:31 of overtime to give Toronto a 3–2 victory. Then, in the second game, Sid Smith, one of the league's most talented goal scorers, turned on a one-man show, scoring all three goals as the Leafs thumped the Wings 3–1.

The 1948 Toronto Maple Leafs pose with the newly remodeled Stanley Cup after sweeping the Detroit Red Wings in straight games to secure their second consecutive championship. This picture marks the last time that retiring captain, Syl Apps, wore the Maple Leaf jersey.

One of the greatest big-game netminders to ever crouch in the crease, Walter "Turkey Eyes" Broda staged a seven-year battle for goaltending supremacy with Montreal's Bill Durnan. The two combatants, who, between them, won the Vezina Trophy seven times and the Stanley Cup five times from 1944 to 1950, died within two weeks of each other in October 1972.

Back in Toronto, the Leafs rallied behind Turk Broda's great playoff goaltending, as Bill Ezinicki broke out of a long scoring famine to offset a goal by Detroit defenseman Jack Stewart. Ted Kennedy sank the winner, and Gus Mortson salted it away, 3–1, all within five minutes.

In the fourth game, the tired-but-game Red Wings tried whiffs of oxygen on the bench to stimulate their players. Ted Lindsay opened the scoring with the first goal of the series for the Production Line. But Broda again held the Leafs in the game, until Timgren looped home a rebound after a shot by Max Bentley. Cal Gardner put the Leafs ahead with an ankle-high drive that Detroit goalie Harry Lumley couldn't see, and, with five minutes left, Bentley scored to put the game out of reach.

Thus the Leafs became the first NHL club to win three consecutive Stanley Cup championships. Their four-straight victory over the Red Wings marked a second consecutive final-series sweep and ran their unbeaten string in the finals to nine games, stretching back to game six against Montreal in 1947.

The Maple Leafs finished third in 1949-50 and entered the playoffs seeking an unprecedented fourth straight Cup, but the league-champion Red Wings halted them in a bitterly contested seven-game series. It started in the opening game of the semi-finals at Detroit, won by the Leafs, 5–0, when Gordie Howe was sent to hospital, dangerously injured. The Wings vowed revenge on the man they accused of sending him there, Ted Kennedy of the Leafs.

The incident happened so fast that even close observers were unable to say exactly how it occurred. Howe was going full tilt to check Kennedy, who was infiltrating the Detroit zone near the Red Wings' bench. Kennedy drew up abruptly, and Howe plunged face first into the boards, suffering a concussion, a broken nose, a fractured right cheekbone, and a scratched eyeball.

Coach Tommy Ivan of the Wings and several of his players, including Howe's linemate, Ted Lindsay, accused Kennedy of butt-ending the Detroit player. President Clarence Campbell reviewed films of the incident before the second game and exonerated Kennedy of any blame, but the Red Wings didn't take Campbell's ruling as the last word on the subject.

The penalty-filled second game of the series was one of the most hair-raising ever played in the Detroit Olympia. The flash point occurred near the end of the second period when Kennedy was tripped by Lindsay and rapped on the head by a stick. The players on the ice quickly paired off, as the on-ice officials struggled to restore order. At the end of this lengthy contest, the score stood at 3–1 for the Red Wings.

Summarizing the manner in which referee Butch Keeling had conducted himself during the trouble, Conn Smythe announced: "I thought he did all right. The Lord and Twelve Apostles couldn't keep the Wings under control tonight."

Back in Toronto, the Leafs won 2–0 on goals from Max Bentley and Joe Klukay, then lost 2–1 in overtime as a shot by Leo Reise from the blue line ricocheted off several players before getting by Broda.

The Leafs took the next game in Detroit, 2–0, with Kennedy and Bentley doing the honors, and back in Toronto the Wings evened the series at three games apiece with a 4–0 shutout. In the final game in Detroit it was Reise again, scoring his second of the playoffs and his sixth of the year to end Toronto's reign with a 1–0 victory in overtime.

After the drama of the Detroit–Toronto semi-finals, the Stanley Cup finals between the Red Wings and the Rangers might have seemed to everyone except the New Yorkers to be a bit of an anticlimax. But the series would prove to be up to the standard of the first playoff round. It was the Blueshirts' first appearance in the finals in ten years, and they had qualified

The Right Place at the Right Time (Part One)

Doug McKay played one game in his NHL career, but that was during the 1950 Stanley Cup finals as a member of the Detroit Red Wings. McKay is the only player to make his sole NHL appearance with a Cup-winning team in the Stanley Cup finals.

Detroit goaltender Harry Lumley kicks aside this shot by Toronto's Ted Kennedy, while Detroit defenders Ted Lindsay and Red Kelly tie up Howie Meeker during action in the 1949 Stanley Cup finals.

by eliminating the Montreal Canadiens in five games. Toronto fans, not having much left to cheer about, took the Cinderella team coached by Lynn Patrick to their hearts when the Rangers elected to play two of their home games in Maple Leaf Gardens. There was a circus occupying Madison Square Garden, forcing the Rangers onto the road.

The opener in Detroit was a cakewalk for the Wings, who won 4–1. Detroit coach Tommy Ivan rested Ted Lindsay and later Sid Abel as the outcome became obvious. The Rangers evened the series with a 3–1 win in game two. The Wings won 4–0 in the third game, but the Rangers weren't dead yet. Toothpick center Don Raleigh kept them in the fight in the next game, scoring an overtime goal to give New York a 4–3 win. He was their savior again in the fifth game, with another overtime goal for a 2–1 victory, giving the Rangers a lead of three games to two in the series.

New York was only sixteen minutes away from a Stanley Cup when Lindsay scored in the sixth game to tie the score at 4–4. Sid Abel added the game-winning goal for Detroit six minutes later on one of the prettiest plays observers had ever seen.

The gallant Rangers carried the Detroit powerhouse to double overtime in the seventh game before Pete Babando, one of the few American players in the NHL, fired the overtime goal that gave Detroit a 4–3 triumph and the Cup.

Harry Lumley's grimace would soon turn to smiles after he helped lead the Wings past the Rangers in the 1950 Cup finals.

(continued on p. 136)

The 1950 Stanley Cup and the Curse of the Rangers

by Stan Saplin

In April of 1992, I had an overwhelming craving to share a gargantuan chunk of irony with Don "Bones" Raleigh and Chuck Rayner and their 1950 New York Rangers Stanley Cup playoff teammates. Fathers and mothers, with little children in tow, had arrived at the doors of Madison Square Garden on Easter Sunday 1992 to see "The Greatest Show on Earth" – the Ringling Brothers and Barnum and Bailey Circus – only to learn that the performance had been canceled. It had been pre-empted by the needs of the New York Rangers to play a first-round opening Stanley Cup game against the New Jersey Devils. Parents were irate; tickets in many instances had been purchased weeks in advance. Children were crying. The circus cancellation was unexpected. It had been announced hastily in newspapers only two days beforehand, but not too many people saw the story.

To Bones and Chuck and the other Ranger heroes of the 1950 playoffs, perhaps irony is too weak a word to describe the reaction to this tidbit of information, even as it was for this correspondent, who was the team's public-relations director and who lived with them through twenty-one consecutive days on the road during the playoffs. We lived twenty-one days in hotel rooms and railroad cars because we couldn't go home: the elephants and clowns of the Ringling Brothers circus were in New York. In that era, when the elephants arrived, the Rangers (if they still had games

to play) got out of town, pronto!

The suggestion in New York in those days that the circus might have been postponed or canceled because the Rangers needed the arena for a playoff game would have been regarded as absurd. At the outset of the Rangers' homeless trek, Bob Cooke, sports editor of the New York *Herald-Tribune*, the leading hockey enthusiast among New York scribes, wrote sadly, "The greatest show on earth is leaving rather than entering our town."

Despite the handicaps and the inconveniences they endured, these 1950 Blueshirts miraculously got so far as the second overtime period of the seventh-and-deciding game of the Stanley Cup finals before yielding the big, coveted prize to the Detroit Red Wings. What's more, in that seventh game, which climaxed their long, exhausting life on the road, the Broadway Blues were actually leading Detroit, 2–0, at one point. Then they led again, 3–2, but the Wings tied it on a goal by Jimmy McFadden in the sixteenth minute of the second period, and finally came the sorrowful end, at twenty-eight minutes and thirty-one seconds of sudden-death overtime when, at 12:10 a.m. of the next calendar day, Pete Babando sent a thirty-five-foot shot at goaltender Chuck Rayner. A quarter-century later, Chuck remembered it as though it had happened just minutes before. "On a face-off to my left," he said, "they got the puck back to Babando and he put it past my right side, knee high." There went the game and the Cup.

The grim irony of this is that there was, and still is, logical reason to believe the Rangers would have won the Cup, and would not even have permitted the series to go so far as seven games, had they had the physical and psychological benefits of playing their allotment of games in New York. If they had been getting the refreshing opportunity to live normally, if only for a few days, in their own homes and had been sleeping in their own beds and, further, had gained the enormous emotional lift of playing on home ice and having their own fans screaming for them and cheering for them and urging them on, things might have been different. Under those conditions, Rayner says with conviction, "We'd have won the Cup."

Game one was played in Detroit, and the Red Wings

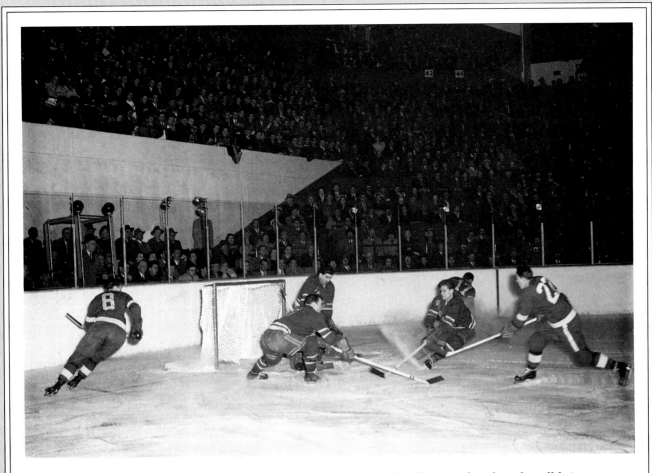

The New York Rangers, forced to play all but one game of their 1950 Stanley Cup final against Detroit on the road, won one of the two games they played on neutral ice in Toronto's Maple Leaf Gardens.

won it easily. Games two and three were designated as Ranger home games for these orphans of the ice, and they played them in Toronto, with the teams swapping victories. Games four and five were played in Detroit (Red Wings home games), but the Rangers were on a roll: they won them both in overtime, both on goals by Bones Raleigh. Now, with the Rangers ahead, three games to two, game six was a New York "home" game, and should have been back in Toronto (it should really have been in New York, but don't forget the elephants), but a strange piece of legislation prevented the use of another club's rink. The rules stipulated that a deciding Stanley Cup game could not be played on a neutral rink. A Ranger triumph would have been a "deciding" result.

Thus Maple Leaf Gardens was out, and Olympia Stadium in Detroit became the "home" site for the Rangers. The Red Wings, with some thirteen thousand of their own fans cheering them lustily, were the visitors(!). "Never mind that we couldn't play in New York," says Raleigh, in recalling the experience. "We probably could have ended it all had we been able to play in Toronto." Ranger players thought the Toronto

fans were on their side; certainly they had cheered enthusiastically for the New Yorkers in games two and three. Ranger manager, Frank Boucher, thought otherwise; he felt that it wasn't that the Torontonians liked the Rangers, they just hated the Red Wings. Nonetheless, they provided something of a lift to the Blueshirts – not the lift that loyal Madison Square Garden fanatics might have supplied, but they were of help.

(Whether Toronto's fans liked the New Yorkers or disliked the Detroiters, they relished the games in Maple Leaf Gardens: the house was sold out forty-five minutes after the box office opened. And the Rangers' lusting for Toronto ice added a curious twist: the Blues hadn't scored a victory there in twenty-two games against the Maple Leafs in more than two seasons.)

So it came to pass that the "visiting" Red Wings came

from behind to win game six, 5–4, scoring twice in the third period, and then got by New York in game seven on the strength of Babando's overtime goal.

After a dismal regular season, in which they scored the fewest goals in the NHL and in which, three times, they ran up losing streaks of seven straight, the Rangers of 1949-50 somehow had earned the fourth and final berth in the Stanley Cup playoffs. Detroit had locked up first place, but Montreal and Toronto were still to settle second and third place in the six-team league standing. The first-place club (Detroit) was to play the third-place team, and the lucky second-place finisher would get New York in the opening round.

How lucky? Hear the words of Pulitzer Prize-winning sports columnist Arthur Daley in the New York *Times*: "All three wanted the Rangers. None was especially anxious to meet the others. Each wanted the Rangers because that was supposed to be the equivalent of drawing a bye, a foolproof guarantee for reaching the final. The Broadway Blues were the soft touch, the patsy, the fall guy."

Well, the Canadiens had been the lucky ones, or so they thought. The Rangers rose from the ashes and demolished Montreal in five games, outscoring them, 15–6. Two games in that playoff round were staged in Madison Square Garden, but then Get lost, Rangers! The circus is a-comin'.

Leading the Canadiens, three games to none, the Rangers left town on April 3 in a New York Central Railroad car designated R-1 and identified as a "12-1 sleeper" accommodating twenty-three persons (obviously in upper and lower berths). Rarely did a sports team fly in that era. That was the last the players saw of their Ranger fans; never again that season would they hear encouraging cheers from the Garden faithful.

New York lost the fourth game in overtime, but shut out the Canadiens in the fifth to clinch the series, whereupon the Rangers waited impatiently in Montreal's Mt. Royal Hotel for Detroit and Toronto to complete their tussle. When the Red Wings finally triumphed, the Rangers went west – to the Leland in Detroit for game one of the Cup finals, to the Royal York in Toronto for the "home" contests at the Maple Leaf Gardens (games two and three), and to the Detroit Leland again for games four and five, and there they

remained for their "home" game (six) and their away game (seven).

For historical purposes, let it also be recorded that there was another car assigned to follow the playoff trail wherever the Rangers went. This, according to the railroad's passenger-traffic directive, was a six-double-bedroom buffet-lounge sleeper, which transported the press. A great honor was bestowed upon this writer by Jack Sweeney, the New York Central executive who oversaw all New York sports movements: he named the car for me – the SS-1. This car housed the eight newspapermen who went the distance with us, throughout the twenty-one-day saga. For the record, aboard the SS-1 were Bill Lauder, Jr., *Herald-Tribune*; Joseph C. Nichols, New York *Times*; Dana Mozley, *Daily News*; Leonard Lewin, *Daily Mirror*; James A. Burchard, *World Telegram & Sun*; Al Jonas, *Journal-American*; Leonard Cohen, *New York Post*; and Ralph Trost, *Brooklyn Eagle*. Carl Grothmann, the club's assistant public-relations man, helped shepherd this congenial, competent group of journalists.

It should also be noted, purely for the record, that Mr. Sweeney's instructions were that these cars, R-1 and SS-1, were to be operated on the rear of trains, with car SS-1 on the extreme rear. What's more, a Mr. J. F. Carroll was given written word that the car designated SS-1 "is to be well stocked." (No, Mr. Sweeney was not talking about milk.)

This same group of New York writers was assembled in the press suite at the Royal York Hotel in Toronto one evening, prior to going to dinner, when an attractive

Railway sleeping-car accommodations were important to any hockey player when the railroad was king. This voucher is from the Rangers–Canadiens semi-final in 1950.

young woman appeared at the door. She was offering her services.

"How much?" she was asked.

"Ten dollars," she said.

"But we're ten men," she was told.

Quicker than you can read this, she replied: "That'll be one hundred dollars."

Now, let's examine "The Curse of the Rangers." To do so, we have to talk about Lester Patrick, father of Lynn and Muzz, grandfather of Craig (general manager of the Pittsburgh Penguins) and David (president of the Washington Capitals). Lester, as a player, coach, manager, and innovator, warrants ranking as the most influential figure the sport has known in shaping the growth of the National Hockey League. His innovations included blue lines, the numbering of players, and the substitution of entire lines on the fly. He introduced the playoffs in hockey, and this led eventually to baseball's playoff system. Lester, known as "the Silver Fox," and his brother Frank built Canada's first artificial ice rinks and they founded the Pacific Coast Hockey Association.

Red Dutton, one-time NHL president, once described Lester Patrick as "the Supreme Head of the Royal Family of Ice Hockey." It is doubtful any other sport has one figure who has stood out so predominantly in shaping its development, reforms, innovations, and conduct.

It was my great fortune that I learned about big-league hockey at the feet of this master. Coach and general manager of the Rangers from 1926 through 1939, he led the Broadway Blues to the Stanley Cup twice. Then in 1939, although remaining as G.M., he relinquished the coaching role to Frank Boucher and saw his beloved team win the Cup again in 1940. At the end of World War II, Lester retired as G.M. and remained on as a consultant.

He was at his Garden desk bright and early every morning and, having just assumed the Rangers' public-relations duties, I took advantage of Lester's presence in the relaxed role of consultant. We talked almost daily. He spoke proudly of his sons, both then coaching Ranger farm clubs, Lynn in New Haven, Muzz in St. Paul. He talked about cherry blossoms back home in Victoria, British Columbia. He loved to tell to whomever would listen one story about a strong-willed player

who just wasn't talented enough to make Lester's team. When informed that he was being given his unconditional release, the rejected stickhandler said, "Why, Lester, I've never been in better condition in my life."

Lester particularly liked to reflect on the boyish, almost innocent, manner in which top management and ownership approached their roles in ice hockey (and now we are closing in on the subject of the "Curse"). Although they were sophisticated and successful in the world of commerce and industry and finance, Lester would shake his head in what I would call affectionate disbelief when he related stories about the corporate heads.

Example: the Chabot/Chabotsky matter. In doing research in 1947 for publication of the first team press guide that the Rangers (or, in fact, any NHL club) ever had, I had detected that, in newspaper accounts of the Rangers' inaugural season in 1926-27, there were three goaltenders on the team. One was Winkler, one was Chabot, and the third Chabotsky. I queried the Silver Fox. Somebody up high in the Garden structure, Lester explained, said that the way to attract people to a sports event in New York City, especially for a new team in town, is to have a Jewish player and an Italian player. The Blueshirts had neither. No problem! They converted Lorne Chabot, a French-Canadian from Montreal, into Lorne Chabotsky. A defenseman of Norwegian descent from Shuswap, British Columbia, Oliver Reinikka, became Ollie Rocco of Yonkers, New York. The Chabotsky tag was foolproof in New York but foolhardy in Canada, where Lorne Chabot was known. Thus, in home games he was Chabotsky, on the road Chabot. I believe it was Patrick who ordered that this bit of nonsense be terminated.

Example: When Col. John S. Hammond was president of Madison Square Garden in the late 1920s, Eddie Shore was establishing a reputation as the sport's most outstanding defenseman; indeed, it is questionable whether his name can be omitted today when one selects an all-time All-Star team. Into the Ranger fold in 1928 came an American, Myles Lane. Lane had become a folk hero in New England because of his prowess as a football star at Dartmouth College and as a hockey player as well. In 1927, he was the nation's top individual scorer in collegiate football ranks. Now, with Lane

Defenseman Eddie Shore – who posed for this photo on the roof of Boston Garden – blended skill, spirit, and toughness into a legacy that still influences Bruins teams more than fifty years after his retirement. Despite trade offers from the Rangers and others, Shore remained a fixture in Boston, and by the end of the 1930s was a four-time league MVP.

on the Rangers, Hammond suggested to Patrick that Lester offer Lane, the New England "superman," to the Boston Bruins in a trade for Eddie Shore. The Boston fans would idolize this native son, Hammond reasoned.

Patrick said he listened in amazement. Wasn't it enough that Boston's Red Sox had given Babe Ruth away to New York? What made Hammond believe Boston's Bruins would give up the Babe Ruth of hockey to New York for an unproved defenseman? When the colonel persisted, Lester persuaded Hammond that, if such a proposal were to be made, he, not Patrick, should make it. A Lane-for-Shore telegram was dispatched by Hammond. A reply came promptly. Memory fails whether this wire was from Charles Adams, the Bruins' president, or, as was more likely, from Art Ross, the club's wily general manager. It read: "Get a life preserver. You are Myles from Shore."

Example: General John Reed Kilpatrick was Col. Hammond's successor as president of the Garden. Extraordinarily successful at anything he undertook, General Kilpatrick had been an All-America end at Yale for two years; years later, in a nationwide poll, he was voted to the All-Time All-America football team. At college, he had also been captain of the track team and a Phi Beta Kappa student. In World War II, he was commanding officer of the Army's Port of Embarkation at Hampton Roads, Virginia, with more than twenty-five officers and enlisted men under his command. But where hockey was concerned, he fit Lester Patrick's mold as a big kid. He reveled in Ranger victories. Autumn weekends, the general attended all Yale football games on Saturday, then Ranger games on Sunday night in the Garden. A special good-luck precaution of the general's: when Yale won on Saturday, Stephanie, his wife, had to wear the same hat on Sunday. That was essential to Ranger fortunes (sometimes it worked).

Example: In 1940 the Rangers won the Stanley Cup, and management had the sacred trophy in its possession. In January of 1941, the Madison Square Garden Corporation paid off the $3,000,000 mortgage on the arena. The officers of the corporation celebrated. In a gleeful ceremony, General Kilpatrick put the mortgage certificate into the Cup and, with the board chairman and other directors of the corporation looking on happily, he lit a match to it.

Lester Patrick shook his head from side to side as he recounted this to me. You drink champagne from the Stanley Cup. You kiss it. You embrace it. You pet it. You fawn over it. With arms raised high, you carry it around the rink proudly. (Years later, I recall reading that Bryan Trottier of the New York Islanders went to sleep one night with it.) But, said Lester Patrick, you don't desecrate it by using it as a furnace. No good would come of this, he said. He didn't use the word "curse," but that, really, was the thrust of his reaction as he told me of the experience. I wish I could now quote him precisely, but it is fair to say that, in effect, he felt the Rangers' punishment was that they never again would have the Stanley Cup in their possession.

Where did the use of the term "curse" come from? It grew upon me in the 1950 playoffs when the blue-shirted stalwarts, ahead three games to two, were leading in the sixth game, 2–0, later by 3–2, then in the last period by 4–3, only to lose, 5–4.

This terrible thought of curse grew stronger in the seventh game, when 2–0 and 3–2 leads went for naught. Rarely is tension as great as it was in the overtime. Here was a team that had once been labeled as pat-sies so close to acquiring the most cherished prize in all hockey, first in the sixth game and now in the seventh, and they couldn't seem to grasp the handle of the Cup and hold on. I had a mental picture of Lester sadly shaking his head. I didn't dare share my nightmarish conviction with anyone, certainly not with my eight newspaper colleagues, nor with Carl Grothmann. Lynn Patrick, our gifted coach, and Frank Boucher, our manager, would have had me courtmartialed. General Kilpatrick would have skipped a legal hearing and had me shot on the spot; he would have ordered a field execution.

After I left the Rangers' public-relations job, except for kittenish, cryptic remarks in 1972 and 1979 when the Blueshirts were Cup finalists, that "they aren't going to win, I assure you," I never voiced a word about a Ranger curse to a soul for at least forty years. I did drop it casually to an old friend one day, who repeated it about a year later to Filip Bondy of the New York *Times*. Bondy sought me out for an interview shortly before the 1992 playoffs began, and wrote about the "Curse of the Rangers."

Legend or myth, take your choice. Many stories written in later years about this most dramatic Ranger–Red Wing series have dwelt on how the New York players repeatedly hit the goal post with the puck, first in the third period of the seventh game when the score was tied, and then in the double overtime.

I never saw a puck hit a Detroit post in these stages of the game. What's more, I recently re-read each of the eight New York byline stories on the game. These were written by crack newspapermen who were reporting the game; certainly their stories would not have omitted such occurrences. Not one wrote of a Ranger-propelled puck hitting a post.

As the legend (or myth) has it, Bones Raleigh was the last player who was supposed to have done so. Bones, whose overtime goals won games four and five for the Blues, would have remembered that he "almost" won this one, too, on yet another overtime goal, but he does not remember hitting a post. However, Raleigh says he did at one point in the overtime take a pass and have Red Wing goalie Harry Lumley beaten, but the

Creating the Rangers' Curse? This cutting from the New York Times *shows General John Reed Kilpatrick and fellow officers of Madison Square Garden Corporation – (left to right) Hamilton Bail, Kilpatrick, Bernard Gimbal, and Jansen Noyles – burning the Garden's $3,000,000 mortgage in the bowl of the Stanley Cup early in 1941.*

Don "Bones" Raleigh became the first player in NHL *history to score an overtime goal in back-to-back games during the Stanley Cup finals. Raleigh, whose timely markers lifted the Rangers to victory in games four and five of the 1950 Detroit–New York final, never scored another playoff goal.*

puck hopped over his stick. "It was like hitting a post," Don says. "It was a sure goal." Nick Mickoski recalls the incident, too. "I was on the ice then," says he. "Don had Lumley beat, but the puck rolled over the top of his stick."

Chuck Rayner, too, says Raleigh had Lumley beaten, but he did not hit a post. "With his tremendous power, the post would have been bent if he had hit it," Chuck says, chuckling at the joke. Explanation for the benefit of those who never had the pleasure of seeing the skilled Raleigh play hockey: Bones might have had trouble denting a toothpick. The *World Telegram*'s rambunctious Jim Burchard described Bones this way: "a toothless frail-looking 150-pounder, who casts no shadow when he stands sideways."

There were many Ranger heroes in defeat, Raleigh and Rayner and defenseman Allan Stanley particularly; Edgar Laprade, in whose honor many still believe the Lady Byng Trophy should be renamed; and his linemate Tony Leswick.

The eight New York sportswriters were unanimous in their choice for the Macbeth Trophy, given to the Rangers MVP in the playoffs. It was Raleigh, and Don's acceptance remarks are worth recalling. "A lot of fellows on this club deserve the award," said Bones, "but since it had to go to someone, it might as well be me."

Lynn Patrick, who brought his team through the playoffs brilliantly, was bombarded by the writers after the third game of the finals in which his club was walloped, 4–0, and fell behind, two games to one. Would he bring in players from his farm teams? Jack Adams, the Detroit G.M., seemed to be hauling in reserves by the carload.

The coach's answer was, in effect, I'm gonna dance with the guys what brung me. "I've had these fellows seventy-eight games now, and I know what they're capable of," Patrick said. He stayed with the guys who "brung him" that far, and their performance, under his leadership, was outstanding, as it was in the semi-final series with Montreal.

Lynn confessed that he failed to play a hunch in the second overtime of the seventh game. "Just before the last face-off," he told Leonard Cohen of the *New York Post*, "I thought [Buddy] O'Connor looked very tired. I was going to put [Fred] Shero in to face off against [George] Gee. But I changed my mind and left Buddy out there, thinking I'd make the switch the next time around." Gee got the face-off, passed to Babando, Babando swiped at the puck, the red light went on, and there was no next time.

A memory of Chuck Rayner, a big-leaguer as a person as well as an athlete, came out of my experience as a lobbyist in Detroit during the final playoffs. Rayner, a standout all season, was an obvious contender for the Hart Trophy as the league's top individual performer, even though a goaltender had won it only once before.

With so many writers and sportscasters in town for the Cup finals, I had a great opportunity to talk up Rayner's candidacy. One morning, I discovered I had sufficient assurance that Chuck would get more than half the necessary votes (at least twenty-eight) to ensure his victory. I was thrilled.

Back at the hotel, I spied Chuck in a group of players in the lobby, rushed over, and said, "Chuck, we've got it!"

"We've got what?" he asked.

He knew what I was talking about, but this cool, talented star was interested only in his team's success and wanted no conversation in front of his teammates about an individual prize for himself. By the way, Rayner won the trophy, breezing, drawing two-thirds of the vote.

April 2 was the date of the last game played in New York that year. It was the third game of the Montreal–Rangers semi-final series. Evidently tickets were still available, inasmuch as the Garden ran an ad in the papers that day. The text of the ad follows, and kindly take note of the price of Stanley Cup playoff tickets four decades ago:

Stanley Cup Playoffs – Tonite 8:30
Rangers vs. Canadiens
General Admission 70¢
Reserved $1.50 to $5 tax included
Madison Square Garden

Although there was no ice available for the Rangers in New York on April 14, when they were in Toronto for their "home" games in the finals against Detroit, there was snow back home that spring day. So much snow, in fact, that an exhibition baseball game between the Yankees and the Dodgers (they were the Brooklyn Dodgers then) at Ebbets Field had to be cancelled. No hockey, no baseball, a dismal day in New York.

I will now reveal a secret that would shake the Rangers free of the Curse and enable them to win the Stanley Cup for the first time since 1940:

Neil Smith, get some brothers on your team! The Rangers never have annexed the Cup without brothers in the line-up. There were the Cooks, Bun and Bill, in 1927 and 1933, the Colvilles, Neil and Mac, and the Patricks, Lynn and Muzz, in 1940.

And, Rangers, when you do win it, remember to tell the Garden brass the Stanley Cup is neither a fireplace nor a furnace.

Maurice Richard, cementing his reputation as one of the greatest playoff players of all time, beat the Red Wings practically single-handed in the semi-final series between Montreal and Detroit in 1951.

The Red Wings and the Canadiens presented an intriguing game-within-a-game in the match-up of their superstar right-wingers, Richard and Howe. In regular-season play, Howe, just then reaching his full maturity as a player, scored 43 goals. Richard had 42. The Red Wings finished the regular season (expanded to 70 games in 1949-50) with a league-record 101 points, six better than the Maple Leafs and a full 36 more than the third-place Canadiens.

The Canadiens were given little chance against the Red Wings, but there was no stopping Richard. Tied 2–2 in the first game in Detroit, the Canadiens battled through sixty-one minutes of overtime before The Rocket stole the puck off the stick of Leo Reise and beat Terry Sawchuk with a rising shot to the far corner of the net.

In the second game, the teams were stalemated 0–0 through regular time and two overtime periods before the explosive Richard scored again, taking a pass from Billy Reay and thumping a backhander past Sawchuk to put the Canadiens in front by two games.

Sawchuk was brilliant in the return match in Montreal, as Howe and Sid Abel scored to rack up a 2–0 win for the Red Wings. Detroit followed up by winning another on Forum ice, 4–1.

The Canadiens, needing another victory at the Olympia to eventually win the series, came through with a 5–2 win in game five. They returned to the Forum, and wrapped up their upset series win by a 3–2 score. Remarkably, it was a penalty-free game, with all the scoring coming in the last period.

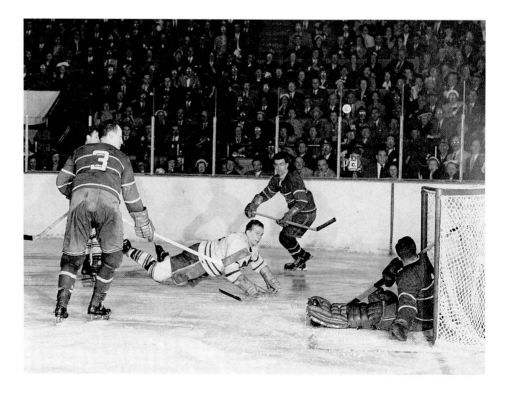

Toronto's Bill Barilko and Montreal's Rocket Richard and Butch Bouchard (3) watch as the Leaf defenseman's backhander eludes goaltender Gerry McNeil to give the Leafs a hard-fought five-game victory in the 1951 Stanley Cup finals.

Both Howe and Richard scored four goals in the series, leaving the "who is greater" argument unresolved.

In the other semi-final series, Toronto defeated Boston. The Maple Leafs won the series four games to one, with one game tied, oddly enough, because sports events were prohibited in Toronto on Sundays. Carrying on with overtime in the second game of the series would have extended play past the city's curfew of midnight on Saturday.

Al Rollins, who had replaced the venerable Broda for much of the season, was injured in the first game, and Broda took over. The Bruins won game one 2–0, and the second was the 1–1 curfew game, but then Toronto took four straight, appearing to grow stronger as the series progressed. They clinched a berth in the finals with a 6–0 win in game six.

The finals between the Canadiens and the Leafs marked the first and only time that every game in a Stanley Cup series went into overtime. In Toronto, on April 11, the Leafs won 3–2 on an overtime goal by Sid Smith. Three nights later, Richard scored his third overtime goal of the playoffs as the Canadiens won, 3–2. The Rocket took a pass from Doug Harvey at the blue line, sidestepped defenseman Gus Mortson, and backhanded a shot into the empty net when Broda came out to try and check him. In Montreal, Ted Kennedy broke up game three with an overtime goal at 4:47 that gave the Leafs a 2–1 win. Harry Watson was the next overtime hero when the Leafs won, 3–2.

But all the drama, all the thrills, of this amazing series were packed into the last few minutes of the fifth and final game in Toronto. Coach Joe

The 1951 Toronto Maple Leafs, the last Toronto team to capture the Stanley Cup until Punch Imlach's troops won the silverware in 1962.

Barnstorming Tours

During the 1950s it wasn't uncommon for teams that missed the post-season to go on "barnstorming tours" of the Maritime provinces or Western Canada, playing exhibition games against regional All-Star teams for extra cash. On one such tour in 1956, Terry Sawchuk, then tending goal for the Boston Bruins, raced the length of the ice and scored a goal in the Bruins' 11–6 victory over the Pictou County All-Stars of Nova Scotia.

Though they are best known for their on-ice flair, this photo proves that Detroit's Production Line of (left to right) Gordie Howe, Sid Abel, and Ted Lindsay formed a dapper trio off the ice as well.

Primeau, down 2–1 with just seconds left to play, pulled his goaltender and sent out Max Bentley as an extra attacker. With only thirty-two seconds left on the clock, Bentley and Kennedy sent Tod Sloan careening in on goalie Gerry McNeil to tie the game and send it into overtime.

It ended with stunning unexpectedness at 2:53 overtime. Bill Barilko, the blond, bustling Leaf defenseman, took a pass from Howie Meeker as he hit the Montreal blue line and, projecting himself full length in the air as he shot, beat McNeil for the goal that won the Cup.

It was Barilko's last goal and last game. A few weeks after he tasted champagne from the Cup in a post-game celebration, Barilko died during a fishing trip in northern Ontario. The plane in which he was traveling with a friend took off in threatening weather and was lost.

Overtime Overdrive

All five games of the 1951 finals between Montreal and Toronto went into overtime, the only time in NHL history that extra time has been required in every game of a final. Four different marksmen — Sid Smith, Ted Kennedy, Harry Watson, and Bill Barilko — scored for the Leafs, the only overtime goals they would score in their careers. Rocket Richard scored for the Canadiens.

In 1951-52 the Red Wings breezed to the Stanley Cup in the minimum eight games, taking Toronto four straight in the semi-finals and the Canadiens four in a row in the finals. The Canadiens had had their troubles in a seven-game semi-final series against a courageous Boston Bruins club that was held together with adhesive tape and playing on guts, before winning four games to three.

Maurice Richard again lifted the Canadiens. He had been dumped hard in the second period of the seventh game by the Bruins' Leo Labine and was knocked cold after cracking his head on the knee of Boston defenseman Bill Quackenbush. Carried to the Forum clinic for repairs, he reappeared on the Canadiens' bench during the third period, with a bandage above his left eye. Still woozy, he told coach Dick Irvin that he was ready to play with four minutes to go in the game and the score tied 1–1.

Richard took a pass beside the Canadiens' net and, gathering speed, cut to

the center of the ice. He bore in on defenseman Bob Armstrong, swung to his left, and passed him. He got by Quackenbush, then cut across in front of the net, tripping over the sticks of Armstrong and goaltender Sugar Jim Henry as he fired the puck into the net. Bill Reay later scored into an open net in the final minute, but this night, like many others, belonged to The Rocket.

The Red Wings team that the Canadiens faced in the finals that year was, according to manager Jack Adams, the greatest Detroit outfit of all time, surpassing the great squads of the mid-1930s that had been built around such stars as Larry Aurie, Marty Barry, Herbie Lewis, Ebbie Goodfellow, and Johnny Sorrell. The Red Wings of 1952 had a superbly balanced attack. In addition to the contribution of the Production Line, the Wings received goal production from Marty Pavelich, Tony Leswick, Glen Skov, Metro Prystai, and Alex Delvecchio. They were backed up by defensemen Leonard "Red" Kelly, Bob Goldham (an excellent shot-blocker), Leo Reise, and Marcel Pronovost. Vezina Trophy winner Terry Sawchuk was in goal.

Detroit swept the final series 3–1, 2–1, 3–0, and 3–0, with Richard, who had knocked the Red Wings out of the playoffs the previous year, held scoreless. Lindsay had three goals in the finals, while Howe, Leswick, and Prystai each had a pair.

The Boston Bruins' strong showing in the 1952 semi-finals served notice that the club, built around the indomitable spirit of Milt Schmidt, was ready to occupy center stage in the Stanley Cup drama of 1953. The Bruins reached the finals for the first time since 1946, and though they didn't win, they tore at the heels of the Canadiens like terriers.

Boston had pulled off an amazing upset by defeating the Red Wings four games to two in the semi-finals. Coach Lynn Patrick asked Woody Dumart,

One of the dominant teams in NHL history, this 1952 version of the Detroit Red Wings compiled 100 points in the regular season and went undefeated in the playoffs, allowing only five goals in eight games.

Octopi on Ice

The first recorded tossing of an octopus onto the Detroit Olympia's ice surface occurred during the second period of the final game of the 1952 finals between Montreal and Detroit. The appearance of the eight-legged creature, meant to represent the eight games it took Detroit to sweep through the playoffs that season, brought this announcement over the PA system: "Octopi shall not occupy the ice. Please refrain from throwing same."

Woody Dumart (left)
and Milt Schmidt (right)
confer with coach Lynn
Patrick before hitting
the ice during the 1953
Stanley Cup finals.

Below: Montreal coach,
Dick Irvin, who guided
three different teams
to a record sixteen
championship finals,
celebrates his club's 1953
Stanley Cup victory over
the Boston Bruins.

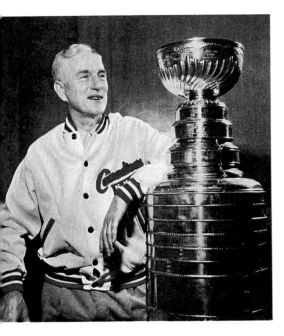

who, along with Schmidt, was celebrating his seventeenth anniversary in the NHL, to cover Gordie Howe. Dumart did his job, as Howe was held to only two goals, one of which was scored when Dumart wasn't on the ice.

The Bruins, set reeling by a 7–0 defeat in the opener, came back with three straight wins, 5–3, 2–1, 6–2, before Detroit managed its last victory, 6–4. The Bruins beat the Stanley Cup champions in the final game, 4–2.

Montreal, meanwhile, wasn't having an easy time with the Chicago Black Hawks, who were making their first playoff appearance since 1946. Adding to their problems was the fact that goalie Gerry McNeil, like his predecessor Bill Durnan, was suffering from an attack of nerves. McNeil asked to be taken out for "the good of the team," and was replaced by Jacques Plante after the fifth game, with Chicago leading the series three games to two. This strategy appeared to work, as Plante played strongly and the Canadiens surged ahead to win the final two games and the series.

In the finals, Boston managed to take only the second game from the Canadiens, by a 4–1 count. A further handicap the Bruins had to overcome was an ill and injured goalkeeper, Sugar Jim Henry, who had to be replaced in the second game by Gordon "Red" Henry from Hershey of the minor-pro American League.

Sugar Jim Henry returned to the Boston nets for game five, but the Bruins' Cup dreams ended in this tense, closely fought affair in the Montreal Forum that was scoreless through regulation time. After just 1:22 of overtime, Elmer Lach, on a pass from Richard, beat Sugar Jim Henry for the Cup, while Schmidt, left sitting on the ice, saw his last chance at a Stanley Cup win as a player float away.

The champion Canadiens grimly attempted to retain their grip on the Cup in 1954, but the Red Wings finished with the silverware. Montreal had finished in second place to Detroit that season and had gained the finals by defeating the Boston Bruins in one semi-final. Meanwhile, the powerhouse Wings were making short work of the Toronto Maple Leafs.

The Leafs opened their semi-final series in Detroit with a dubious distinction. They hadn't won on Detroit ice for eleven games, and they kept the record intact as the Wings walloped them 5–0. With vociferous coaching from King Clancy, who could outshout any coach in the league and who was piloting his first Stanley Cup contender, they managed to win 3–1 in the second game to tie the series. But they lost the next two games on their own ice, 3–1 and 2–1, and were knocked from contention in the next game in Detroit after carrying the Wings into a second overtime period. Ted Lindsay put them out at 21:01 of overtime, as the Red Wings won 4–3. It was a special night for Gordie Howe, who scored twice and established a Stanley Cup record that would stand for more than twenty years by scoring nine seconds from the opening whistle.

In the other series, the Canadiens had defeated Boston 2–0 at Montreal, and then smashed the Bruins, 8–1, in the second game. Left-winger Dickie Moore set an NHL single-game playoff scoring record that stood until 1983, registering six points on two goals and four assists. The Canadiens completed their sweep with 4–3 and 2–0 wins in games three and four.

Detroit's Howe–Lindsay–Delvecchio line was prominent in the opening game of the finals as the Wings won, 3–1. The Canadiens' big guns – Richard, Ken Mosdell, and Bert Olmstead – were in a scoring slump, having gone without a goal for five games.

But they weren't to be held off the scoresheet much longer. In the second game they exploded, with the Red Wings handicapped by penalties. Richard scored twice and Moore completed his impressive total of five goals and eight assists in six games by counting the third, as the Canadiens won, 3–1, to tie the series. Detroit manager Jack Adams, objecting to the penalty calls against his team, engaged in a bit of hyperbole when he announced that he would quit the league.

Back in Montreal, the Canadiens were without big Jean Béliveau, their rising star, and defenseman Doug Harvey, both of whom had been injured in game two. The Wings went on a rampage, winning the third game 5–2, as goalie Jacques Plante fought the puck. Delvecchio, Lindsay, Johnny Wilson, Metro Prystai, and Howe scored for Detroit, while Tom Johnson and Dollard St. Laurent kept the Canadiens from being blanked.

Plante continued to show signs of tenseness as the Wings won the next game, 2–0, with Red Kelly scoring into an empty net. Plante was replaced by Gerry McNeil, called up from the senior Montreal Royals, for the next game. In this contest, Montreal's thirty-one-year-old veteran, Ken Mosdell, netted the game's only goal to keep the Habs' chances alive.

A Birthday Present for Bonny

After the Montreal Canadiens defeated the Boston Bruins in the 1953 Stanley Cup finals, Habs centerman Kenny Mosdell skated around the ice surface hoisting his trophy high. Only in this case, the trophy wasn't the Stanley Cup, it was his four-year-old daughter Bonny, who was celebrating her birthday the following day.

Terry Sawchuk, shown here robbing Montreal's Kenny Mosdell in a rare color action photo from 1954, recorded twelve playoff shutouts in his career, the fourth-highest total in league history.

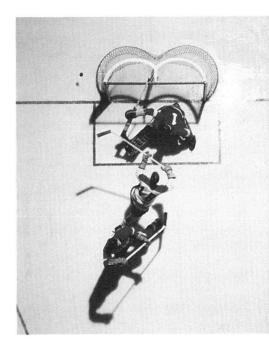

With McNeil again in the nets, the Canadiens swamped the Wings, 4–1, on Forum ice, but the Montreal surge died at the hands of Tony Leswick in the deciding game. Floyd Curry had opened the scoring for the Canadiens, but defenseman Red Kelly tied it up to force the game into overtime. The game ended with dramatic abruptness. Leswick, noted more for his tenacious checking than for his goal-scoring proficiency, had flipped the puck into the Canadiens' end when, at 4:29 of the extra period, All-Star defenseman Doug Harvey reached up with his gloved hand to knock the puck out of the air. Instead, it deflected off of his glove and over goalie Gerry McNeil's shoulder for Leswick's third goal of the post-season and the most auspicious of his NHL career.

Perhaps because of the bitterness stemming from the suddenness of the defeat, the Canadiens conducted themselves in a most irregular manner following the game. It had become the on-ice custom at the end of a playoff series for the losing club to offer congratulations and the winning club to offer condolences. But no such courtesies were exchanged on this occasion. The Canadiens, with the exception of Gaye Stewart, himself a former Wing, left suddenly for their dressing room.

The press and the audience for radio and television broadcasts were outraged at the Canadiens' lack of sportsmanship. Coach Dick Irvin explained in a curt manner: "If I had shaken hands," he commented honestly, "I wouldn't have meant it. I refuse to be a hypocrite." It was only the second time in Stanley Cup history that the finals had stretched into overtime in the seventh and final game of the series.

Detroit won the Cup, but it was the tumultuous Canadiens who made the headlines in 1955. This was also the year of the infamous Richard Riot on St. Patrick's Day in Montreal.

The seeds had been sown in Boston on the night of March 13, 1955, when The Rocket lost his temper, attacked bespectacled Bruin Hal Laycoe with his stick, and jostled linesman Cliff Thompson. The result was that league president Clarence Campbell suspended Richard – regarded as a hero throughout Quebec – for the remainder of the season, including the forthcoming playoffs.

On March 17, the Canadiens played the Detroit Red Wings in the Forum in Montreal. The clubs were tied for first place in the regular-season standings. Tension and a great deal of resentment over Richard's suspension were in the air, but there was no indication of the panic to come.

The trouble started with a few fans pelting Clarence Campbell with peanuts and programs as he sat in his box seat. Then mob psychology took hold. Spectators broke through police lines. A tear-gas bomb, thrown behind one goal, almost started a full-fledged stampede within the building that could have turned into a tragedy. The league president, stoically holding his place, was approached by a thug who offered his hand in a gesture of

Shortly after this smoke bomb exploded in the Montreal Forum, Montreal fire marshal Armand Paré ordered the building evacuated, forcing the Canadiens to forfeit their game to Detroit. It was only the second forfeited game in league history. The first occurred on January 26, 1921, when the Ottawa Senators refused to continue a game against the Montreal Canadiens. Inset photo: Dick Irvin examines the spent smoke bomb.

friendship and then threw a punch at the unsuspecting Campbell.

Outside the building, more trouble was brewing. A mob, incited by a group of teenagers, simmered on the edge of violence. Shots from a small-bore rifle broke a window in the front of the Forum, and the mob, now completely out of hand, moved down Ste-Catherine, the main east-west street in downtown Montreal. Store windows were broken, cars were damaged, and much looting occurred.

The riot left the hockey world on pins and needles. For days afterward, Campbell, who had been spirited from the building, received notes from cranks threatening to do him physical harm. He ignored them. The mayor of Montreal, Jean Drapeau, publicly advised Campbell to stay away from the next Canadiens game. Campbell was determined that his office would not be intimidated, but in the interests of preventing further trouble, he did stay away.

Richard made his own efforts to quell any further violence. He spoke on French-language radio, urging people to "get behind the club so that no further harm will be done."

"I will take my punishment," he said, "and come back next year to help the club and the younger players to win the Cup."

Though most people didn't realize it, he was being prophetic, for the Canadiens did win the Cup the following year, but with Richard out of the line-up, they would fall just short in the playoffs of 1955.

They reached the finals for the fifth consecutive year, by brushing past

Like most great artists, Jack Adams had an discerning eye and a master's stroke. However, in Adams's case, his distinguished touch came with a pen, not a brush. He was responsible for signing much of the talent that brought seven Stanley Cups to Detroit during his tenure as coach and general manager.

Tall Order

Following the Detroit Red Wings' Stanley Cup victory in 1955, the players gathered at center ice for the Cup presentation. With a full house in the Olympia looking on, the microphone to be used by the NHL president Clarence Campbell got tangled on its descent from the rafters. Glen Skov, one of the tallest Wings at 6'1", was hoisted up by a pair of teammates and successfully brought the mike down for Mr. Campbell.

the Bruins four games to one. During the second game of the series against the Bruins, coach Dick Irvin's inventiveness once more came into play. In 1931, as coach of the Black Hawks, he had become the first coach to rotate three complete forward lines in one game. Other teams, which did not use such wholesale substitutions, faltered before the onslaught of fresh Chicago troops, and it did not take long for Irvin's idea to become the norm. In this year, 1955, Irvin rotated goaltenders Jacques Plante and Charlie Hodge during the course of the game, in the belief that frequent changes would counteract the tendency for one goaltender to tire in the late stages of a match.

The Leafs and Detroit had renewed their acquaintance in the other semi-final series. The Wings won four straight, opening with a 7–4 landslide and following with two 2–1 wins before they closed out the Toronto bid, 3–0.

In the opening game of the Montreal–Detroit finals, the Canadiens led 2–1 midway through the third period, but lost, 4–2. Floyd Curry scored both goals for the Canadiens, but Marty Pavelich scored while the Wings were shorthanded late in the game to put Detroit ahead, and Ted Lindsay, with eighteen seconds left, sealed the win.

Lindsay again was the hero in the second game, scoring an amazing four goals as the Red Wings won, 7–1. Marcel Pronovost, Gordie Howe, and Alex Delvecchio also scored for Detroit.

The Canadiens bounced back to win game three, 4–2, with Bernie "Boom-Boom" Geoffrion temporarily making Montreal fans forget the loss of their beloved Rocket by scoring two goals. Rookie Red Wings coach Jimmy Skinner explained Detroit's loss by announcing that his players had lost their heads, and the game.

The Canadiens won game four, 5–3, causing several scribes to comment that it was developing into a "homers' series." Calum MacKay, Jean Béliveau, Tom Johnson, Geoffrion, and Floyd Curry contributed, while Earl "Dutch" Reibel scored twice for the losers. With the series tied at two games apiece, Detroit won game five at home, 5–1, on three goals from Gordie Howe, who thereby boosted his playoff output to a post-season record eight goals and eleven assists.

The "homer" tag held up to the end. The Canadiens tied it up again at the Forum, defeating the Red Wings 6–3 with honest toilers like Curry and MacKay doing the spadework behind Geoffrion and Béliveau. But the Red Wings hadn't lost a game on home ice in almost four months, and they weren't going to break their string in game seven of the finals. They took the Canadiens and the Cup in the payoff game, 3–1, to give Jack Adams his seventh Stanley Cup as a general manager. Alex Delvecchio scored twice, with the indomitable Howe adding another.

It was also a happy victory for Jimmy Skinner, who had taken over from Tommy Ivan as Detroit's coach after leaving the Hamilton Cubs of the Ontario Hockey Association Junior A league.

An intense group of Red Wings, including Johnny Wilson, Red Kelly, and Gordie Howe, concentrate on the on-ice proceedings from the Detroit bench.

The NHL's dominant team for the first half of the 1950s, the Red Wings had reached the top of hockey's ferris wheel with their Cup win in 1955. Their old reliables, with the exception of the durable Howe and the irrepressible Lindsay, were starting to wear down, and a revitalized Montreal team was poised to claim its place atop the NHL.

The Flying Frenchmen,

1956-1967

PROOF OF THE NOT-TO-BE-DENIED CANADIEN SURGE TO POWER AND THE inevitable weakening of the great Detroit machine was evident in the final standings of 1956. The Wings, who had won seven straight NHL regular-season titles, were eased out of contention for their eighth in late February by the Canadiens, who proved their superiority by defeating the Wings 5–1 in Montreal. The Canadiens went on to win their first league championship since 1947.

They added other laurels. Powerful center Jean Béliveau won the Art Ross Trophy as the league's leading scorer with forty-seven goals, and Jacques Plante, their wandering goalie, won the coveted Vezina Trophy as the goaltender for the club allowing the fewest goals-against. Béliveau was joined in the record-setting department (he had the most goals and assists by a center) by left-winger Bert Olmstead, who amassed fifty-six assists.

The Canadiens wound up the season with a twenty-four-point bulge over the Red Wings and the comparatively simple semi-final prospect of defeating the New York Rangers, who, fired up by coach Phil Watson, had finished a respectable third. The Habs needed five games to eliminate the Rangers, including a 7–0 whitewash in the final contest. The Red Wings drew the fourth-place Toronto Maple Leafs, who played aggressive hockey in the playoffs but were defeated in five games. The stage was set again, then, for another Detroit–Montreal final-series clash.

The finals opened in Montreal, and the Canadiens unleashed their full power, beating the Wings 6–4. For two periods it had been all Detroit, with the Canadiens showing a surprising ineptness. But within a space of five minutes of the third period, the illusion had blown up in the Red Wings' faces as Béliveau, Geoffrion, and rookie Claude Provost slammed in three goals. The Canadien avalanche continued unabated in the second game, which they won by an overwhelming 5–1 score.

It began to look like the old pattern. In eleven consecutive Stanley Cup

Opposite: Superstar goaltender Jacques Plante debates diving out to recover his stick in the 1960 Stanley Cup finals.

Below: Montreal captain Butch Bouchard (right) celebrates his last Cup as a player and Toe Blake celebrates his first as a coach after the Habs defeated Detroit in 1956. It was the top portion of this era's two-piece Stanley Cup trophy that was often raised in victory salute.

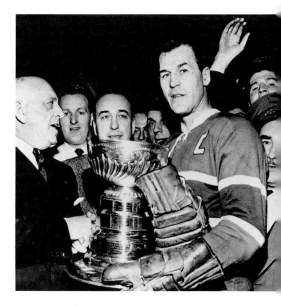

In 1956, Jean Béliveau (left) led the NHL in goals, and Bert Olmstead was the league leader in assists. They combined to give the Canadiens a formidable one-two punch.

Terrible Ted

During the Red Wings—Maple Leafs semi-final encounter in 1956, officials received a threat that Ted Lindsay was going to be shot if he dared take to the ice for the third game of the series. Lindsay not only played that evening, he scored a goal late in the third period that forced overtime, then fired home the winner just 4:22 into the extra session.

final-series games between these two clubs, the team playing in its home rink had won every one. Back at home, Detroit stretched the consecutive home-wins mark to twelve with the big three of Kelly, Lindsay, and Howe doing the damage as the Canadiens were beaten, 3–1. But Montreal broke the home-ice advantage in the fourth game, as Jean Béliveau, who scored twice, proved to be too much for Detroit to handle. Floyd Curry, a dependable playoff performer, added one to make it a 3–0 shutout and, on April 10, back in Montreal, the Habs ended Detroit's two-year Cup tenure with a 3–1 win to capture the series in five games.

Each of the Canadiens' three big scorers had a hand in the final demolition of the Wings, as Béliveau, Geoffrion, and The Rocket scored. Béliveau was the man of the hour, scoring the important first goal of the deciding game, giving him twelve in the playoffs and a combined fifty-nine over the entire season.

The win came in the Habs' sixth year as one of the NHL's best. They had reached the finals in every one of those years, but had won only twice.

This was to mark the end, for a while at least, of the rivalry between the Canadiens and the Red Wings. In 1957, the mighty Wings were missing from the finals, having been eliminated in the semis by a tough, driving Boston Bruins squad.

Detroit had won the NHL title to qualify for the playoffs for the twenty-seventh time in club history. Howe and Lindsay ran away with the regular-season scoring race, amassing 174 points, the highest total recorded in a single season by two players on the same club. Howe had 89 and Lindsay 85. It was Howe's fifth scoring title in eleven seasons.

This was enough to send the experts rushing to the support of the Red Wings and led to predictions of the early demise of the Bruins in the semi-finals. But Jack Adams, the wily Detroit manager, didn't select his own club for the title. "This is the strangest playoff I can recall," he said. "Boston has more hungry players. They're aggressive and they're always digging. Montreal and Detroit have a solid nucleus, but both are going to need extra effort."

The hard-working Bruins eliminated the Red Wings in five games. In game five, the Bruins came from behind with a three-goal final-period splurge to defeat the Wings 4–3 and take the semi-finals. It was the second time in a decade that Boston had reached the Stanley Cup finals. Cal Gardner scored the winning goal for the Bruins.

The Canadiens, meanwhile, disposed of the Rangers, with the turning point of the series occurring in the third game when Geoffrion waged a

The 1956 Montreal Canadiens' line-up featured twelve future Hall-of-Famers, including manager Frank Selke and coach Toe Blake.

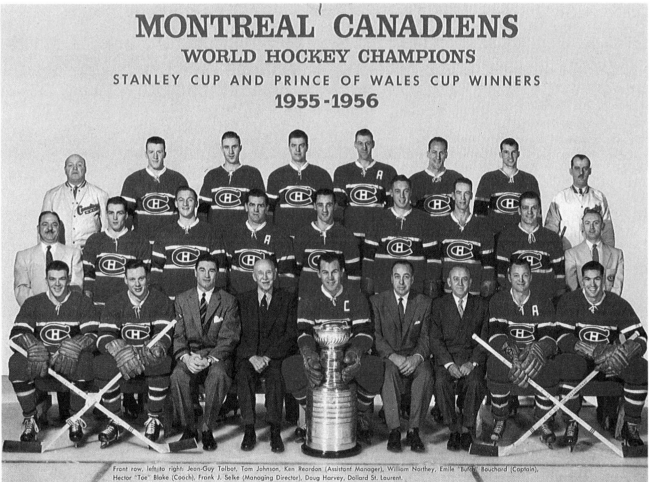

MONTREAL CANADIENS
WORLD HOCKEY CHAMPIONS
STANLEY CUP AND PRINCE OF WALES CUP WINNERS
1955-1956

Front row, left to right: Jean-Guy Talbot, Tom Johnson, Ken Reardon (Assistant Manager), William Northey, Emile "Butch" Bouchard (Captain), Hector "Toe" Blake (Coach), Frank J. Selke (Managing Director), Doug Harvey, Dollard St. Laurent.
Second row: Camil DesRoches (Associate Publicity Director), Henri Richard, Dickie Moore, Maurice Richard, Jacques Plante, Jean Beliveau, Bert Olmstead, Bernie Geoffrion, Frank D. Selke (Associate Publicity Director).
Third row: Gaston Bettez (Assistant Trainer), Claude Provost, Bob Turner, Jackie Leclair, Ken Mosdell, Floyd Curry, Don Marshall, Hector Dubois (Trainer).

Jean Béliveau muscles his way around Bruins' captain Fernie Flaman, only to have his shot bounce off the post, much to the relief of Boston goalie Don Simmons. Simmons and his teammates held the Canadiens off the scoresheet for a 2–0 victory, recording their only win of the 1957 Stanley Cup finals.

one-man war and crumpled the Blueshirts by putting three goals behind Lorne "Gump" Worsley. Jean Béliveau contributed two, and Dickie Moore and Rocket Richard one each, as the Canadiens snowed the Rangers under, 8–3.

The Rangers, rallying desperately, fought to hold a one-goal lead in the fourth game, but finally broke as the Canadiens bombarded them with goals by Henri Richard, Phil Goyette, and Geoffrion to win 3–1. Still battling, the Rangers carried the fifth game to overtime by scoring three in the third period. But at two minutes and eleven seconds of extra time, the old home-run hitter, Rocket Richard, won it for the Habs.

The incomparable Richard also rocked the Bruins back on their heels as the final series opened in Montreal. Richard scored four goals as the Canadiens took the curtain-raiser, 5–1. Both coaches – Toe Blake of the Canadiens and Milt Schmidt of the Bruins – acclaimed Richard's feat. Rookie goalie Don Simmons of the Bruins was not so enthusiastic. "It was humiliating," he told interviewers.

Richard scored three goals in the second period to tie Busher Jackson's modern Stanley Cup playoff record. (This mark was later surpassed by Tim Kerr and Mario Lemieux, both of whom scored four in one period in the 1980s.) The Bruins, leg-weary from their series with the Wings, were peppered with forty-one shots, while they could muster only twenty-one on Jacques Plante.

Boston tightened defensively for the second game. Jean Béliveau scored

The two catalysts of the Montreal Canadiens' Stanley Cup win in 1957, coach Toe Blake and Maurice Richard. Blake's masterful moves behind the bench propelled the Habs to their second straight title, while Richard's overtime goal against the New York Rangers – the fifth extra-session marker of his career – sent the Canadiens to a seventh straight final-series appearance.

the only goal of the contest in the second period, and the Canadiens took a two-game lead by a 1–0 score. Richard, tailed relentlessly by the Bruins' Fleming Mackell, was shut out by Simmons.

The Canadiens' firepower returned in Boston in the third game, as Bernie Geoffrion scored twice in a 4–2 Montreal win that gave the Habs a big three-game edge in the series. Geoffrion's playoff goal output climbed to ten in eight games.

The Bruins pulled out all the stops in the fourth game, and Mackell accounted for both goals as they shut out the Canadiens, 2–0, checking beautifully and getting a stellar performance from rookie Simmons in the nets. Boston, however, would go no further. On April 16, back in the Montreal Forum, the Canadiens wore the Bruins down, defeating them, 5–1, to clinch the Cup in five games.

The Forum was bedlam that night. Richard received the Cup from trustee Cooper Smeaton at center ice as hundreds of fans cheered and milled about. At that moment, he symbolized everything for which the Stanley Cup stands.

(continued on p. 157)

Maurice and Henri Richard

by Réjean Tremblay

Nations have their heroes. Nations have their celebrations. Nations have their great moments, and their people remember great events.

Maurice Richard is more than a hockey player. For the people of Québec he is a hero, in the same way that Muhammad Ali is a hero to black people all over the world.

Historians maintain that the election of Jean Lesage's Liberal Party in 1960 marked the beginning of what is known in Québec as the Quiet Revolution. However, the people of Québec are very well aware that the real revolution started on March 17, 1955, when Montrealers rebelled against a decision by Clarence Campbell, president of the National Hockey League, and took to the streets, smashing department-store windows in the west end of the city.

Nowhere else in Canada – then or now – is there a person like Maurice "Rocket" Richard. And of all the talented pairs of brothers to play in the NHL, none has had a greater impact on Stanley Cup hockey than Maurice and Henri Richard. For it is Maurice's younger brother Henri who played on eleven Stanley Cup winners, captained the Montreal Canadiens, and was single-handedly responsible for the dismissal of coach Al McNeil after the Habs' Stanley Cup win in 1971.

In Québec, hockey, the playoffs, the passion, the true passion, is spelled R–I–C–H–A–R–D. The depth of this feeling is unquestioned by those of us who grew up listening to Michel Normandin's play-by-play of the games late at night – without our parents' knowledge of course. And by those of us who tried unsuccessfully to trade three Gordie Howe cards for one Maurice Richard in the schoolyard. And by those of us, children and adults alike, who sensed the sum total of injustices large and small that Francophone Québeckers were subjected to in their daily lives, the day Clarence Campbell suspended The Rocket.

That day, my mother threw out all the cans of Campbell's soup that we had in the house and replaced them with another brand, even though Clarence Campbell had nothing to do with Campbell's soup and the new products didn't taste as good. And it was then that I decided that the ketchup on my fries would be Heinz.

It is necessary to understand that Québec at that time was still a very Catholic, rural area, and that business and money were reserved for the Anglophones. We listened to the words of our parish priest, who told us again and again that it is easier for a camel to go through the eye of a needle than for a rich man to enter the Kingdom of God. Therefore, we gave away a lot to those who were poorer than we were to guarantee our passage to heaven. But we indulged ourselves with Maurice Richard.

He was the only one. René Lévesque was still a young journalist, Félix Leclerc had not yet become an important national poet, all those Québecois whose songs and dances would later speak for an emerging sense of nationalism were still in school, and the men and women who would become the political elite in Québec were still in their early years of classical education. No doubt their mothers were hoping that they would become priests or nuns.

Rocket Richard was our symbol. When he scored fifty goals in fifty games, "French-Canadians," as we were called at that time, were very proud. Singers trilled: "It's Maurice Richard who scores, who scores. It's Maurice Richard who scores all the time!" And our uncles laughed and slapped their thighs.

And when Maurice twice scored overtime goals in the wee hours of the morning to defeat the Detroit Red Wings in the 1951 semi-finals, he carried all of Québec on his shoulders as he charged, exhausted but lost in his fury of winning, towards Sawchuk's goal. It is important to understand why he made such a difference. The Rocket quickly became a part of Québec's culture.

The novelist Roch Carrier wrote a short story that best depicts the very essence of the relationship between Maurice Richard and Québec. In it, he talks about how his mother had ordered a number-nine sweater from the catalogue issued by Eaton's department store. At the time, the arrival of the winter catalogue was a big event in the rural parishes of Québec. Young boys daydreamed for hours, looking at pictures of Canadiens' sweaters, and of skates, trucks, and other toys. Their dreams were important, because the boys knew very well that the real gifts wouldn't be as numerous or as beautiful. Money was scarce, and looking at the catalogue was a great way to spend the evenings.

Mrs. Carrier felt there was no reason to specify which team sweater she was ordering – number nine, that was The Rocket's sweater. She even added that her son was ten years old and that they must send the right size. But the salesman at Eaton's in Toronto did not know about Mrs. Carrier's great love for The Rocket and the Canadiens, so he sent a vivid blue Toronto Maple Leafs sweater instead. It was too close to Christmas to exchange the gift, and so little Roch had to wear a Maple Leafs sweater to school with his friends. It was a character-building experience for the boy. Johnny Cash, in his song entitled "A Boy Named Sue," tells a similar story. Only he wasn't talking about Mr. Eaton . . .

Claude Clément is one of the Montreal Canadiens' team doctors. He is a man in his fifties, vice-president of the Montreal Metropolitan Opera, cultured, and a great lover of hockey. Maurice Richard had a big impact on his life. Dr. Clément grew up in Côte Saint-Paul, a working-class area of Montreal. His family didn't have much money, so there was no opportunity for him to go to a game at the Forum to cheer on Maurice Richard.

"I used to walk up the hill that separated rich Westmount from the poor St-Henri district. There I would spend hours in front of Hector Dubois's shop. He was the Canadiens' trainer, and he worked where the Forum's souvenir boutique is located today. I kept an eye on the skates that he was sharpening. There were adhesive numbers stuck on the sides of each boot, and I waited for him to sharpen the number-nine skates. My childlike heart beat faster when I saw him

grab one of The Rocket's skates – I no longer dared bat an eyelid. Maurice Richard's skates!" recounts Dr. Clément who today tends to the cuts and bruises of the new generation of Canadiens.

Tom Johnson, now a member of the Hall of Fame and vice-president of the Boston Bruins, played defense for the Canadiens on the night of the famous riot. More than forty years later, Johnson has not forgotten: "The atmosphere in the Forum was explosive. At the end of the first period, the score was 4–1 for the Red Wings. Then the smoke bombs went off. We were told that the game was canceled and awarded to the Red Wings. I had arranged to meet some friends in the lobby of the Forum after the game, so I was a little worried. Finally, I left, accompanied by a police officer from Station 25. He was an impressive giant, the same man who escorted Mr. Campbell and his secretary out of the building. Ste. Catherine Street was swarming with people, but no one bothered us."

Broadcaster Dick Irvin, the son of the Canadiens' coach Dick Irvin, Sr., was also at the game. "In those days, the press box was located at the Ste. Catherine Street end of the Forum, so everything happened right in front of me. There was so much smoke that I couldn't see what was going on. Later that night, my dad told me,

Rocket Richard deftly slips the puck between the pads of Boston goaltender Gordon "Red" Henry. The consummate playoff performer, Richard still holds three individual post-season records, including the mark for most playoff overtime goals (six).

DAVID BIER

and I'll always remember his words: 'Son, I've seen The Rocket fill many arenas. This is the first time that I've seen him empty one.'

"The Rocket was more than a hockey player. It was his fury, his desire, and his intensity that motivated the Canadiens."

That year The Rocket, who had been the top scorer in the playoffs for many years, could not lead the Canadiens in their pursuit of the Stanley Cup. He became a martyr. "I still dream about it at night," he says after all these years. "I am convinced that I did not deserve that suspension. Hal Laycoe was the instigator, and took advantage of the fact that I was being held by the linesman to strike me. I shoved that linesman in order to free myself from his hold. It is interesting that he never again officiated in the NHL. I could have accepted that my suspension be delayed

Maurice Richard uses a radio news conference to broadcast an appeal for calm to the people of Montreal in the aftermath of the "Richard Riot." Note the stitches in his scalp.

until the beginning of the next season, but I didn't feel that it was fair that I could not play in the playoffs. The people felt the same way, too," said Richard.

It is a strange coincidence that the Rocket retired in the spring of 1960 and a few months later Jean Lesage became premier of Québec and launched the Quiet Revolution. In a few years, Québec would take a giant leap into the present and become a society more open to the rest of the world. Years went by. René Lévesque, Pierre Elliott Trudeau, Brian Mulroney, Paul Desmarais, Pierre Peladeau, Jean Chrétien, Lucien Bouchard, Robert Charlebois, Céline Dion, Ginette

Reno, and Jean-Paul Riopelle went on to make their mark in politics, business, and culture. However, there is no doubt that Maurice Richard remains the most popular Québecois, even among the young people who were born after he retired.

Last February, the Canadiens' oldtimers got together with the Maple Leafs' oldtimers for a friendly game at the Forum. All of the players were introduced to the thousands of spectators who filled the building.

Who do you think received the loudest applause?

"And it was deserved," says Brian O'Neill, the former executive vice-president of the National Hockey League.

O'Neill was a student when he first saw The Rocket. And he still remembers the excitement generated by Richard when he crossed the blue line in a furious charge to the net: "The fans would go wild. From the blue line in, Rocket Richard was the most exciting player ever. He could have spoken any language, and still have been an idol to the Canadiens' fans. I don't think there was any political meaning in his huge popularity. It was because he was so good and so exciting."

There was The Rocket and there was The Pocket Rocket. Henri Richard was already a celebrity throughout Québec by the time he was seventeen. Along with Claude Provost and André Vinet, he was part of an amazing forward line for the Montreal Junior Canadiens. I was about ten years old when they came to the Chicoutimi Coliseum to play the Sagueneens of the now-defunct Québec Senior League. At the time Henri was known as "Flash."

The Sagueneens were a good professional club. With Marcel Pelletier in goal, Georges Roy and Gerry Claude on defense, and Sherman White, Ralph "Bucky" Buchanan, and Jimmy Moore up front, they could have beaten the era's lesser NHL clubs like the Chicago Black Hawks or the New York Rangers. At least, this is what we vigorously maintained during recess at Saint-Jean-Baptiste School in North Chicoutimi.

One evening, after watching a wonderful game, I kept seeing this little Richard in my mind's eye. I had not yet seen hockey on television because Radio-Canada did not broadcast to the outlying areas of the province at that time, but I quickly realized that Henri Richard had become my hero.

"Henri and Maurice did not talk to each other a lot," remembers Tom Johnson. "There was quite an age difference between the two brothers and, in any case, neither one of them was a big talker. They both preferred to set an example on the ice."

"Many people thought that Maurice and I were mad at each other because we didn't talk much," says Henri. "But no way. In fifty years, we've never had a disagreement. It's just that the Richards don't talk much."

When Henri was a schoolboy, he had to live in the shadow of a giant: "I was very shy. When I was a child, I didn't want other people to know that I was The Rocket's brother. When the school inspector asked what I wanted to be when I grew up, I never would say that I wanted to be a hockey player. Instead, I'd tell him that I wanted to be a bricklayer, so he wouldn't guess that I was related to The Rocket.

"But in my dreams, I was Maurice Richard and I was playing for the Montreal Canadiens. From the time I was six years old, I didn't miss many games at the Forum. Maurice was my idol. Because of the fifteen-year age difference between us, I never thought I'd get a chance to play with him. But, by the time I reached junior hockey, I realized that it could happen. I think our playing together helped extend Maurice's playing career."

Henri broke in with the Canadiens in 1955-56, and both he and Maurice accomplished a lot during the five years that they played on the same line. Most of the

The Richard brothers combined to score 902 goals and win nineteen Stanley Cup championships in their careers with the Canadiens.

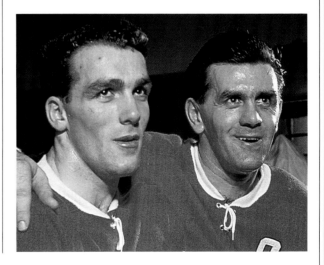

time Dickie Moore played on the left wing. The line was deadly on offense, and together with the forward line of Jean Béliveau, Bernard Geoffrion, and Bert Olmstead, they formed the heart of the great Canadiens' dynasty.

While Maurice was the idol of Québec, for whom people took to the streets – despite his wishes – Henri could demonstrate a lot of moral authority as well. Henri had the same fiery temperament as his older brother, and when The Rocket retired, Henri continued to leave his mark on the history of Stanley Cup hockey in Québec.

Never was this more apparent than in 1971, in the Stanley Cup finals against the Chicago Black Hawks, who were a great team built around Tony Esposito, Stan Mikita, and Bobby Hull. The Canadiens had just lost the fifth game at Chicago Stadium, and Henri had been benched for long stretches by his coach, Al McNeil.

Bertrand Raymond, then a young journalist from the *Journal de Montréal,* in his first season covering the Canadiens, had arrived in the dressing room before any of his colleagues.

"I sat down near Richard, hoping at the very most to get the usual statement. I simply asked him how he felt after this loss. Henri was white with anger. Slowly,

Stealing a page from his brother's playbook, Henri Richard lifts the puck over a sprawling Tony Esposito to give the Habs a 3–2 win over Chicago in game seven of the 1971 Stanley Cup finals.

weighing each word, he lashed out, 'Al McNeil is the worst coach that I have ever known.' Then he continued to vent his anger," recalls Raymond, who has since been honored by the Hockey Hall of Fame for his writing. "Any player who would have dared say anything to Richard at such a time could have been slapped in the face. It was then that I saw how much Jean Béliveau was respected. Coming back from the shower, Jean put his hand on Richard's shoulder and quietly told him to calm down. Henri didn't say another word."

But it was too late. The next day Raymond's story appeared beneath the sensational headline, "Al McNeil is the worst coach that I have ever known!"

When the team arrived at Dorval Airport the next day, the customs officers had left copies of the paper just about everywhere at the checkpoints. McNeil had to fill out his declaration forms under the cold and angry stares of the officers.

The passions of Montreal hockey fans were so incensed that, for the sixth game at the Forum, McNeil was protected by plainclothes police behind the Canadiens' bench. There had been too many death threats to take the situation lightly. Once again, a Richard had stirred passions.

But like The Rocket, Henri Richard did more than just talk. In the seventh game, the Hawks took a 2–0 lead very quickly and appeared to be headed for a Stanley Cup victory. Jacques Lemaire, with a shot from the blue line, beat Tony Esposito. The goal fired up the Canadiens, and a few minutes later Henri Richard tied the game.

And who do you think scored the winning goal?

The Canadiens won another Stanley Cup, and Al McNeil, the winning coach, coached the Canadiens' farm club in Halifax the following season. Today, Henri Richard has changed very little. The silver hair that he sported even during his last seasons as captain of the Canadiens has now turned to white. No longer an NHL star, Richard has become a great tennis player who would rather die than give up a set.

When the Canadiens were eliminated by the Boston Bruins in four straight games in 1992, the two brothers preferred not to say too much.

You see, today they are ordinary Québecois and, unfortunately, there are no new Richards to arouse their anger and their passion!

A pair of Montreal Canadiens' marksmen led all NHL scorers in 1957-58. Dickie Moore unseated Gordie Howe as the league's scoring champion by collecting 84 points, and Maurice Richard's younger brother Henri, "the Pocket Rocket," had his finest professional season, amassing 80 points to finish second to Dickie Moore, who was his linemate. For the third year running, the Canadiens led the NHL in both offense and defense, scoring an NHL record 250 goals over the seventy-game schedule.

In the semi-final round of the playoffs the Habs met their arch rivals, the Detroit Red Wings, who had dropped to third place with a 29–29–12 record. The Habs opened the set with convincing 8–1 and 5–1 victories on Forum ice. The Wings battled back bravely at the Olympia, but an overtime marker by André Pronovost in game three provided the Habs with a 2–1 win. Detroit held a 3–1 lead entering the third period of game four, but Rocket Richard exploded for three goals, including the series winner, to clip the Wings for the season.

The New York Rangers, led by emerging superstar Andy Bathgate, climbed to second place in the standings with seventy-seven points, the highest total in team history. In the semi-finals, however, the Broadway Blues fell victim to the Boston Bruins, who erased the Rangers' regular-season gains in six games. The Bruins' victory assured them of a second consecutive visit to the Cup finals.

The first match of the finals saw fourteen penalties called in the first period alone. The Canadiens' power play quickly converted a bench minor

Rangers' superstar Andy Bathgate clears a rebound from goalie Gump Worsley's crease, while Bill Gadsby and Boston's Leo Labine observe the ensuing play during the Bruins–Rangers' semi-final in 1958. Boston went on win this match, 6–1, and take the series in six games.

Bernie "Boom-Boom" Geoffrion (left) bested all playoff scorers in 1957 with eleven goals and seven assists, while Boston's Fleming Mackell turned in the finest performance of his career during the 1958 playoffs, notching five goals and fourteen assists for a league-leading nineteen points, the second-highest total in NHL post-season history at that time.

against the Bruins into a 1–0 lead. Allan Stanley of the Bruins tied the game early in the second period, but the Habs capitalized on a tripping penalty to Leo Labine to take a 2–1 lead they would never surrender. Only a Herculean effort by Bruins' netminder Don Simmons, who faced forty-four shots, kept the score close. Undaunted, the Bruins bounced back in game two, opening the scoring only twenty seconds after the opening draw. Joseph "Bronco" Horvath was the offensive hero for Boston, slipping a pair of pucks past Jacques Plante as the Bruins tied the set.

The Richard brothers took control of game three, figuring in all the scoring as the Habs tightened their defense and shut out the Bruins, 3–0. In game four, the Bruins rebounded yet again, with Don McKenney's two goals providing the margin of victory in the Bruins' 3–1 series-tying win.

The teams returned to the Montreal Forum for game five, a match that featured another stellar performance by The Rocket. The Bruins took a 1–0 lead into the second period, thanks to Don Simmons, who kicked out eighteen shots, and Fleming Mackell, who fired a power-play marker in the first frame. The Habs countered quickly, with Geoffrion and Béliveau lighting up the scoreboard with a brace of goals only forty-two seconds apart. The Montreal lead held up until midway through the third, when Horvath solved Plante, scoring the tying goal to force the game into an extra session.

In overtime, the focus on the Canadiens' bench fell on Rocket Richard, who once again rose to the occasion. Five minutes in, The Rocket took a pass from Dickie Moore, crossed the blue line, and snapped a screen shot past Simmons to give the Habs a 3–2 lead in games. It was Rocket's sixth – and last – overtime winner of his career. Richard's uncanny ability to manufacture these magic moments led *Boston Globe* scribe Jerry Nason to write: "Richard is an athlete whose production of clutch epics has never known an equal in any sport."

Although the Bruins claimed they weren't deflated by the overtime loss, they appeared lethargic at the onset of game six, and the Habs pounced on their weary adversaries. Geoffrion and The Rocket gave the Canadiens a quick 2–0 lead before the match was two minutes old. Although the Bruins managed to pull within a goal, the Habs fired twenty shots at Simmons in the second period and salted away the series with a 5–3 win. With the victory, the Canadiens became only the second NHL team to capture three consecutive Stanley Cups. Simmons received numerous accolades for his post-season heroics, but most of the attention was focused on The Rocket, whose eleven post-season goals led all playoff performers.

The decade ended with the Montreal Canadiens once again dominating the standings, the All-Star team, and the scoring ladder. Dickie Moore's reign as Art Ross Trophy winner continued, as the smooth right-winger set an NHL record with ninety-six points. Detroit general manager Jack Adams, who predicted that a good hockey team usually disintegrates after five years, watched the Wings fall into the league basement for the first time in twenty-one seasons.

The surprise of the campaign was the play of the Toronto Maple Leafs, who rebounded from a sixth-place finish in 1958 to earn a playoff berth. The Leafs, with George "Punch" Imlach calling the shots behind the bench and in the front office, edged out the Rangers for the final playoff spot by winning six of their last eight games. Imlach, who had brashly predicted the Leafs' turn of fortune, boldly insisted that the Leafs would dispose of the second-place Bruins in six games in the semi-finals. The bald prognosticator was a game off, but the Leafs still reached the finals for the first time since 1951, with a seven-game series win over Boston. The Leafs won three games by a single goal, including back-to-back 3–2 overtime victories in games three and four.

The Montreal Canadiens survived a six-game battle with the Chicago Black Hawks to earn their ninth straight visit to the finals. The Leafs battled gamely in game one, holding the Habs to a 3–3 tie at the start of the third period. The Canadiens took advantage of some sloppy Leaf work in their own zone to score a pair of goals in a four-minute stretch and come away with a 5–3 opening-game triumph. Game two was a mirror image of the first contest, with the Leafs once again entering the third stanza tied with the

defending champions. The Canadiens' firepower, however, broke down the Leafs' resolve, as the Habs, propelled by a two-goal effort by Claude Provost, took a two-game series lead with a 3–1 home-ice win.

The Maple Leaf Gardens faithful, who hadn't seen Stanley Cup final-series action since Bill Barilko's dramatic overtime goal in 1951, witnessed a brave Leaf effort in the third game. The teams see-sawed through regulation before Dick Duff broke through the Habs' defense at the 10:06 mark of overtime to put the Leafs back in the series. The teams were tentative through two periods of the fourth game, but then the Habs notched a trio of goals in a six-minute span to earn a 3–2 victory. Bernie "Boom-Boom" Geoffrion set up two and scored the winner himself, as the Canadiens pulled to within one game of their fourth straight title.

The Habs burst from the starting gate in the fifth game, firing three pucks past Johnny Bower in the first sixteen minutes. Once again, Geoffrion was the catalyst, drawing an assist on the first tally and blasting home the second. Although the Leafs fought back in the third, Montreal held on to deliver a 5–3 verdict to the Forum jury and hand their fans an NHL-record fourth consecutive Cup victory. Rocket Richard, who played in only four post-season games, was held scoreless in the playoffs for the first time in his career. Amid the euphoria of the Canadiens' celebration, there was guarded talk of The Rocket ending his remarkable career.

The 1959-60 season featured the closest scoring race since 1954-55, as Chicago's Bobby Hull edged out Boston winger Bronco Horvath by a single point to win the Art Ross Trophy. The Montreal Canadiens, 40–18–12, held down first place throughout the season, while the Leafs slipped into second with a 35–26–9 mark, their best finish since 1951.

The Habs again met the improved Black Hawks in the semi-finals, and although the games were fairly close, the Canadiens ousted the Hawks in four straight. Goaltender Jacques Plante, who had donned a protective face mask after suffering a serious facial injury in November, allowed only six goals in the series and registered back-to-back shutouts in the final two games of the Habs' sweep.

In the other semi-final round, the Toronto Maple Leafs won a hard-fought six-game tussle with Detroit. The series featured a marathon overtime match in game three, won by the Leafs, 5–4, on Frank Mahovlich's goal after forty-three minutes of extra time. The Leafs' series win qualified them for a rematch with the Canadiens in the finals.

For the Canadiens, the objective was clear: a fifth straight Stanley Cup. Toronto coach and manager Punch Imlach, aware of the Habs' strength and playoff savvy, wasn't making any bold predictions. Montreal started quickly

Habs' blueliner Doug Harvey, closely pursued by Toronto's Dick Duff, begins a patented zone-clearing rush during the 1959 finals. Harvey, a six-time Norris Trophy-winner with Montreal, became the first defenseman in NHL history to record more than forty assists in a season when he set up forty-three goals in 1954-55.

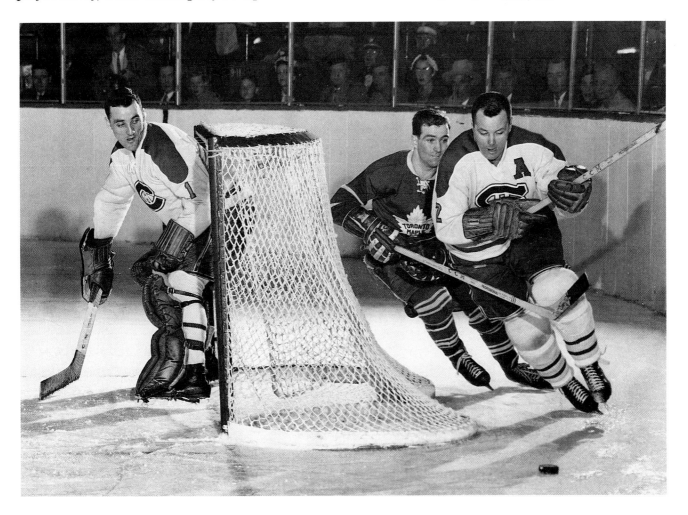

A Little Fresh Air

During their semi-final series with Toronto in 1960, the Detroit Red Wings used oxygen to give them an extra lift during the third game, which went into a third overtime period. Leafs' coach Punch Imlach dismissed the idea as a "gimmick," and the Leafs won the set in six games.

Consistency was the key to Montreal's incredible success in the second half of the 1950s. Eleven players – Geoffrion, Talbot, Provost, Plante, Béliveau, Moore, Harvey, Johnson, Marshall, and the Richard brothers – were members of all five Cup-winning teams.

in game one, throwing an offensive barrage at the Leafs that resulted in three goals before the game was twelve minutes old. Henri Richard collected assists on all three goals. The Leafs cut the margin to 3–2 with a pair of their own in the second period, but the Pocket Rocket capped off a great post-season performance with a goal only a minute and a half into the third period and the Habs left the ice with a 4–2 opening-game win.

The Canadiens continued to knock the Leafs off the puck in the early stages of game two, with predictable results. Dickie Moore scored early, and Jean Béliveau added another to give the Habs a 2–0 lead before the Leafs found their skating legs. A Larry Regan goal in the dying seconds brought the Leafs to within one at 2–1, but that's as close as they would come. Johnny Bower held the fort the rest of the way, stopping the Habs' final twenty-six shots, but the Leafs couldn't put the puck past Jacques Plante, and Toronto returned to Maple Leaf Gardens down two games to none.

Prior to game three, Leafs' president Stafford Smythe observed, "You can't give [the Canadiens] a two-goal lead and expect to beat them." The Leafs, who had surrendered such a margin to the Canadiens in each of the first two games, obviously weren't listening to their boss, as the Habs had a three-goal bulge on the board by the midway point of the second period. Johnny Wilson put the Leafs on the scoresheet late in the period, but the Canadiens

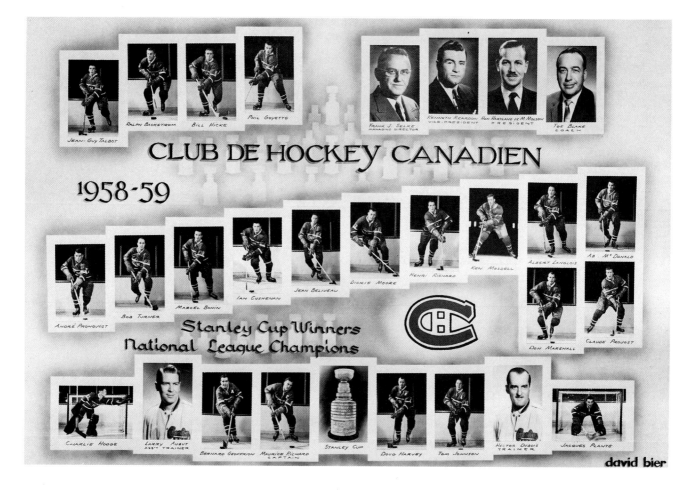

CLUB DE HOCKEY CANADIEN

1958-59

Stanley Cup Winners
National League Champions

david bier

scored two more in a two-minute span in the third to put the game away by a 5–2 score. The Canadiens' fifth goal was notched by Maurice Richard, his thirty-fourth goal in the Stanley Cup finals. Richard reached into the net and retrieved the puck as a souvenir, fueling speculation that he was going to retire after the series.

Game four was dominated completely by the Canadiens and Jacques Plante. Jean Béliveau and Doug Harvey scored twenty-eight seconds apart in the first period, and the Canadiens closed the door from there, shutting out the Leafs 4–0 to win their fifth straight Stanley Cup. Over that five-year span, the Canadiens won twenty of twenty-five games they played in the finals.

Hot-shot Leafs' winger Frank Mahovlich rides shotgun on Canadiens' rear guard Jean-Guy Talbot's shoulders during the 1960 Stanley Cup finals.

(continued on p. 171)

The Titans– Shapers of the NHL in the 1940s and 1950s

by Milt Dunnell

It was almost as if the battling governors of the National Hockey League knew that unprecedented prosperity – as well as unprecedented problems – were at hand as they convened for their final semi-annual meeting of the Dirty Thirties and geared up for what were to be a couple of tempestuous decades in pursuit of hockey's most coveted prize, the Stanley Cup.

The Montreal Maroons were gone. That meant the league was reduced to seven clubs, and the rumor was already out that Madison Square Garden would be denying a new lease to the New York Americans. So there no longer was need for a two-division schedule. The era of the fondly remembered six-team league, with no town farther away than an overnight train ride, was approaching.

Less apparent to observers was that the twilight of the titans was setting in. Men who were pioneers of modern pro hockey, who had played the game, promoted the game, and fought for the game, were growing old in the game. Within the next two decades, many of them would be gone – some retired, some fired, some, including Frank Calder, the league's first president, dead.

These were the men who would battle each other at the drop of an adjective or a puck. But, when consensus was reached and they spoke as a group, they always felt they were right.

It was Leafs manager Conn Smythe's arch-enemy, Art Ross, crusty general manager of the Boston Bruins, who seemed to be most aware of tougher and rougher competition coming up. Ross, who hadn't spoken to Smythe socially in a number of years (he always referred to Smythe as "the Big Wind Off Lake Ontario"), was annoyed with his own club, an easy winner of the American Division in the previous season, but a patsy in the battle for the Stanley Cup.

So Ross startled the hockey community when he sold famed goalie Cecil "Tiny" Thompson to Jack Adams, who ran the Detroit Red Wings for the elder James Norris, whose ample bankroll and love of the game had kept the NHL alive in some of its hungry years.

Ross took a lot of flack for dumping Tiny Thompson. Some of his own colleagues even hinted he was losing his grip. What they didn't know was that Ross had spotted a young goalie named Frank Brimsek, and that the era of "Mister Zero" was about to begin at Boston Garden. It wouldn't be long before Jack Adams discovered that Tiny Thompson wasn't the answer to his problems, either.

Because they didn't like each other much, Smythe and Ross got special satisfaction out of outwitting each other in a deal. Frequently it was this business of barter that fueled feuds. Smythe, for example, thought Ross had slickered him when he sold the Leafs a player named Jimmy "Sailor" Herberts, for whom Smythe had paid what was then the substantial sum of $12,500 in 1927. Feeling he had been taken by a supposed colleague who had sold him a player whose best days were behind him, Smythe deemed himself justified in using any means to obtain adequate compensation.

"We were having an exhibition game in Detroit," Smythe would reveal, much later, "and we got our players together. I told them frankly we were in danger of going broke, and we had to sell Sailor Herberts. Just about everybody who got hold of the puck that night made a pass to Sailor Herberts. He seemed to have the puck all the time. After the game, we sold Herberts to Detroit for $15,000."

That was before Jack Adams became complete boss in Detroit, of course. Otherwise, Smythe might not have got away with it. Although Adams and Smythe were not exactly palsy, either, they did business with each other in this build-up for the battles of the 1940s. In 1938-39, Adams traded Bucko McDonald, a lacrosse player to whom Smythe had taken a fancy, to the Leafs.

Smythe's smartest move, though, was at the expense of the long-suffering New York Americans, whose days in the league were numbered. For quantity, Smythe got quality. Before the start of the 1939-40 season, he traded Harvey "Busher" Jackson, one-time member of the famous Kid Line, along with Jimmy Fowler and Buzz Boll, both popular with Toronto fans, for Sweeney Schriner, who was recovering from surgery. Although he got bad press for the deal, Smythe, as usual, had it right. With the Leafs, Schriner became a Hall-of-Famer.

The 1939-40 season was to become a favorite with trivia buffs. Which team was out of the playoffs? The Canadiens. Even the orphan Americans finished ahead of them. And who beat the Toronto Maple Leafs in the finals? Why, it was the New York Rangers. That made it a season to remember. A footnote worthy of mention, too, was a sporting gesture by Smythe. He agreed to play the first two games of the finals on successive nights in New York, because Madison Square Garden had reserved dates for Barnum and Bailey's circus. Thus, New York's faithful fans were denied the opportunity of seeing a Stanley Cup presentation ceremony for what was to be more than half a century. All remaining games of the series were played in Toronto, so the Rangers clinched the Cup in Maple Leaf Gardens.

One post-game picture every photographer had to get, if he favored his job, was that of manager Lester Patrick, with sons, Lynn and Muzz, both of whom were in the line-up. Smythe, earlier, had done a personal scouting job on Lynn, and had offered Lester $20,000 for Lynn's contract. Lester, who knew a few things about publicity gigs, too, said he would give the offer his earnest consideration. He probably did.

Having shown the Rangers what a sportsman he could be, Smythe promptly got in their hair, early in the next season. At least, Bill Stewart, the long-time National League baseball umpire, hockey referee, and coach, who had taken the Chicago Black Hawks to the Stanley Cup by defeating the Leafs in the spring of 1938, thought Smythe was harassing the Rangers by parading up and down behind their bench during a game at Maple Leaf Gardens. Stewart, who was the referee in this game, threatened to have Smythe ejected from his own building.

Of course, there was a definite lack of cordiality between Smythe and "Bald Bill." For one thing, Smythe had nice things to say about Major Frederic McLaughlin, owner of the Black Hawks. (At that time, they hadn't changed to the one-word spelling.) McLaughlin had fired Stewart while Bill was still making speeches on his Stanley Cup victory.

Furthermore, Stewart and Smythe had almost gotten into a fistfight before the first game of the 1938 Stanley Cup finals as a result of a dispute over Chicago's use of a substitute goaltender.

That was the background of Stewart's possible malice toward Smythe. As it turned out, Stewart was vindicated in his belief that Smythe was looking for trouble. The very next night, after the incident at the Rangers' bench, Smythe hopped over the boards at Madison Square Garden, during a fight between Wally Stanowski of the Leafs and the Rangers' fiery Phil Watson. Photographs next day plainly showed Smythe's trademark spats (who else wore them?) protruding from beneath a tangle of bodies that included the referee, Mickey Ion. Told that he had been fined the standard fee of $100, Smythe said he wouldn't pay it.

By September of 1942, with both Canada and the United States fighting in World War II, the question had arisen: Could the league continue operations? Many players were already in military service and others were sure

Former Bruins' standout Cooney Weiland (left), who made a successful transition from on-ice leader to bench boss by guiding the Bruins to a Stanley Cup triumph in 1941, discusses strategy with Boston general manager Art Ross.

Toronto general manager Conn Smythe offers congratulations to Leafs' coach Hap Day, another outstanding player who achieved considerable success behind the bench. Day, who coached the team for ten years, won five Cup titles, the most of any Leaf coach.

to follow. Smythe, himself, was one of the first to go. This was his second world war. He had been shot down and captured in the first one.

Frank Calder finally issued a statement, which read, in part:

> The league, now approaching its fourth wartime season, is confronted with more difficulties of operation than have been present in the three preceding years. With the institution of selective national service, it, at first, was feared that suspension of operations for 1943-44 must follow. However, the authorities have recognized the place which the operation of the league holds in public interest and have agreed the league should carry on.

Irony is not exactly new to hockey, but who could have guessed that a rowdy Stanley Cup final the previous spring might have contributed greatly to the government's decision?

That was the series, between the Leafs and the Red Wings, in which the Leafs came back from the dead. At least they had been declared deceased by anyone who claimed to know the difference between a puck and a frozen potato. Having lost the first three games of the set, the Leafs were supposedly ready for burial,

and Detroit's Jack Adams, a non-drinker himself, had the ceremonial champagne on ice for those who were not averse to a sip of the bubbly.

The Leafs – as has been widely retold – made a miracle comeback to win four consecutive emotion-packed games. When the Leafs finally captured the Cup, with a 3–1 victory on home ice, the audience was described as the biggest crowd ever to see a hockey game in Canada. The government undoubtedly took notice.

For much of the 1940s, clubs based in U.S. cities endured the paradox of increased demand for their product, accompanied by their inability to keep up the quality. They had no trouble selling tickets. Their problem was finding qualified people to fill the uniforms. Even the Black Hawks, perennially talent-starved, established an attendance record of 20,004 in February of 1946, while losing a game to the Bruins.

These were things that were not lost on the league's new president, Clarence Campbell, a Rhodes Scholar, a lawyer, and a former referee, who had returned from overseas to accept the job. Red Dutton had occupied it, strictly as a caretaker, since the death of Frank Calder, who had suffered a heart attack while chairing a league meeting in January of 1943.

As the 1940s wound down, new talent appeared that would produce some of the finest games in Stanley Cup history during the next decade. Newsy Lalonde, himself a member of the Hockey Hall of Fame, had spotted Maurice Richard when he came up to the Canadiens in 1942. Newsy predicted The Rocket would be one of the game's greatest stars – an understatement, as it turned out.

Doug Harvey arrived, as a raw rookie, five years later. In Detroit, Jack Adams was proclaiming that a slope-shouldered, shy kid from the Canadian West named Gordie Howe was already the best young player in the league.

Jim Norris, Jr., and his associate, Arthur Wirtz, had taken over the Chicago club from the estate of Frederic McLaughlin, but Norris had made their position clear. He said: "We're willing to spend money, as long as we can get some players to make this club respectable until we can develop some players of our own." It was too soon for Norris to know that players such as Bobby Hull and Stan Mikita were on the way. But players were made available to the Black Hawks in one of the best moves ever made by old horse-traders such as Smythe and Frank Selke – Smythe's former assistant, who moved on to become general manager of the Canadiens when Smythe returned from overseas in 1946.

Sensing that Syl Apps, the Leafs' great center, was nearing retirement, Smythe made one of the most unusual deals in hockey history with Bill Tobin, who was operating the Chicago club between the death of Major McLaughlin and the take-over by Jim Norris. To acquire Max Bentley, Smythe gave up five players – a full team, minus a goalie. Bob Goldham, Ernie Dickens, Bud Poile, Gus Bodnar, and Gaye Stewart. Bentley, one of the game's great stick-handlers, played an important role in the Leaf Stanley Cup victories of 1947-48 and 1948-49.

The Leafs dominated Stanley Cup competition during the 1940s, winning the Cup five times, including three straight, starting in 1946-47, the first time that this feat had been accomplished since the inception of the NHL in 1917.

The rivalry between the Bruins and the Maple Leafs continued unabated through the 1940s as well. In the 1948 semi-finals, Leaf coach Hap Day and player Garth Boesch were roughed up by fans as they proceeded to their dressing room in the Boston Garden. Even King Clancy, a standby referee, who was famous for never having won a hockey fight, was charged with assault, though these charges were later dismissed. Bruins' club owner Weston Adams went to the Leaf dressing room, possibly to express regrets. Smythe ordered him out.

Entering the 1950s, the Stanley Cup had never enjoyed such esteem. Never had so many millions been aware of its annual spring rites. Never had so many people paid to see the league's star attractions in action.

With the situation in Chicago stabilized, the league now had six solid clubs. The old titans, advised by their new president, realized the importance of defending the tremendous gains that had been made, despite the difficulties imposed by a world war.

Some of the players who had returned to their clubs after military service were getting long in the tooth, but the system that brought fresh talent to the NHL

had been revamped and was about to pay dividends. Scouting staffs had been expanded. No longer would a player like the great Howie Morenz be discovered by a referee who was officiating in a railway-league game. (Morenz had been playing for the Stratford, Ontario, railway-shop apprentices at a game in Montreal in the early 1920s when he was first noticed.)

Junior amateur teams, many now sponsored by NHL clubs, played more games. Players who came from those teams had been coached by people who knew the systems of the parent clubs. At the NHL level, players were much better conditioned and were required to play longer schedules. This raised salaries, making professional hockey a desirable career.

What no one could foresee, entering the 1950s, was how completely two teams – the Montreal Canadiens and the Detroit Red Wings – would command possession of the Stanley Cup. The Canadiens and the Wings monopolized Lord Stanley's rose bowl for the entire decade–with one notable exception. In 1951, the Maple Leafs, with rookie coach Joe Primeau behind the bench, beat the Canadiens in the tightest final series up to that time. The Leafs won four games to one and every game went to overtime.

Jack Adams, whose off-ice feuds with Conn Smythe were legendary, watches from the safety of the Detroit bench at Maple Leaf Gardens.

Comparing the fabulous Montreal and Detroit clubs that kept the Stanley Cup practically to themselves in the 1950s became a national obsession, and is likely to be the subject of irresolvable debate as long as the game is played.

The rise of the Canadiens began with the hiring of Frank Selke, who, during the Depression, had played an important role in the construction of Maple Leaf Gardens by persuading union members to accept part of their pay in Gardens stock. Selke immediately began the exacting job of establishing a farm system and rebuilding the team. By the mid-1950s, his finished product was one of the finest teams the sport had seen. It just happened that, in the same period, Selke's old rival, Jack Adams, was doing a similar rebuilding job with the Red Wings.

Until he went to Chicago, prior to the 1955-56 season, Dick Irvin was Selke's coach. Irvin was a taciturn, dedicated career hockey man, who recalled how his first playing contract with Portland of the PCHA paid $700. The top salary in the league at the time was $1,250. Irvin had come to the NHL in 1926, when the Portland club moved to Chicago, lock, stock, and goal stick. As a coach, Irvin was a stickler for conditioning.

Frank Selke helped build both the Maple Leafs and the Canadiens into perennial Stanley Cup contenders. The "elephant's leg" trophy shown here was the first version of the Cup with space for the names of future winners, but it was soon filled and was replaced in 1947-48.

He used to say he could look at his outstanding center-ice ace, Elmer Lach, and tell him: "You're one pound over 165. Take it off."

Adams's coach, until he also took off to participate in the rehabilitation job at Chicago, was Tommy Ivan. He left a sparkling record of three Stanley Cup winners in five seasons behind the bench.

When the Red Wings won the Cup in 1951-52, without losing a game – and without having a goal scored against them on home ice – Adams promptly called his club the best he had seen in the league. Selke, while giving full credit to the Red Wings, quietly told those who would listen: "From what I see in our farm system, we may have a team that will force Jack to revise his ratings before long." Inasmuch as the Canadiens hadn't won the Stanley Cup since 1946, this sounded like a brash prediction, especially from an executive who was not renowned for running off at the mouth, as they say at the racetrack.

But Selke had made an accurate appraisal of the talent which "Sad Sam" Pollack, later to become a legend in the league, had accumulated for the Montreal Canadiens juniors and for the Montreal Royals, who played in the Quebec Senior Hockey League.

He didn't bother to remind Jack Adams that Jean Béliveau had scored forty-five goals that same season of 1951-52 for the Quebec Aces, and that he would be joining the Habs as soon as the idea appealed to him. Within five years, he would win the Art Ross Trophy as scoring champion of the NHL, along with the Hart Trophy as the league's most valuable player. In the playoffs of 1956, he would score twelve goals, to tie the existing record.

Bernard Geoffrion, another of Pollack's pupils, had just arrived with the Habs. He already was known as Boom-Boom, and he justified the handle by winning the Calder Trophy as the league's leading rookie. In addition, Dickie Moore, up for a trial from the senior Royals, had scored eighteen goals in thirty-three games – quite a trial.

Still with the junior Canadiens were Henri Richard, who was to become renowned as "the Pocket Rocket" and would finally retire with eleven Stanley Cup rings. Then there was a lanky forward named Bert Olmstead, whom Selke had stolen from Chicago.

Selke's prediction that a surprise might be in

store for Adams came true sooner than expected, but the Canadiens couldn't take credit for it. The overconfident Red Wings were upset by the Boston Bruins in the first round of the 1952-53 Stanley Cup playoffs. It was a shocking defeat for the proud defending champions.

They had finished twenty-one points ahead of the Bruins in the regular season, winning ten of the fourteen meetings between the two clubs. They played up to that form in the first game of the playoffs, beating the Bruins, 7–0. Then, they flattened out and lost the series in six games. Lynn Patrick, who was coaching the Bruins, credited his veteran, Woody Dumart, with making the difference. Tommy Ivan, Detroit's coach, differed. He said Boston goalie Sugar Jim Henry killed the Red Wings.

In the Stanley Cup finals, the Bruins were no match for the Habs, losing the series, 4–1. A crowd of 14,450 gave Montreal captain Butch Bouchard a tremendous ovation as he accepted the old basin from Clarence Campbell. Montreal fans hadn't seen the Stanley Cup in seven years. To Montrealers, that seemed like a generation.

The upset was obviously good for the Red Wings. With practically the same roster – new acquisitions were Bill Dineen and Earl Reibel – they regained the Stanley Cup twelve months later, beating the Canadiens in seven games. Two aspects of the final game provided ammunition for future trivia buffs. The crowd of 15,791 was the biggest in Detroit history and, for the first time in the history of Stanley Cup play, the recipient of the trophy was a woman, Marguerite Norris, president of the Red Wings.

That was Ivan's last Stanley Cup winner as coach. In the spring of 1955, Jimmy Skinner would coach the Red Wings to their fourth Cup in six seasons, again beating the Canadiens. No one was willing to predict it then, but that victory ended an historic era in Stanley Cup play. Decades would pass – the number is still undetermined – before Detroit would again win the trophy which, for so long, it had taken for granted.

This was one of Adams's greatest teams. Since it was his last great one, the line-up that is inscribed on the Stanley Cup deserves posting, if only to stimulate debate in the parsonages and the pubs: Terry Sawchuk, Red Kelly, Bob Goldham, Marcel Pronovost,

Benny Woit, Jim Hay, Larry Hillman, Ted Lindsay, Tony Leswick, Gordie Howe, Alex Delvecchio, Marty Pavelich, Glen Skov, Earl Reibel, Johnny Wilson, Bill Dineen, Vic Stasiuk, and Marcel Bonin. Six members of that roster are in the Hockey Hall of Fame.

In the wake of the departures of both Ivan and Irvin to Chicago, there had been hopes, in rival cities, that competition for the Stanley Cup would open up to include clubs outside of the Detroit–Montreal axis. This didn't happen. An even more frustrating period for those towns was to begin.

Toe Blake, who had been a member of the Montreal Maroons, Stanley Cup champions of 1934-35, and of two Canadiens winners in the mid-forties, succeeded Irvin as coach for the 1955-56 season. There were the usual predictions that Blake would get away to a shaky season. The game had changed, it was argued, since his days as "the Old Lamplighter" on the Punch Line with Rocket Richard and Elmer Lach.

Indeed the game had changed, but Toe had gone right along with the parade. The Canadiens had changed, too. They were loaded with talent and youth. Blake showed he knew how to utilize those skills. The Canadiens finished the season with a hundred points – twenty-four more than Detroit and fifty more than the rebuilding Hawks.

The playoffs proved to be a repeat of what the season had been – the Canadiens in a breeze. They swept by the New York Rangers and the Red Wings, losing only two games. When they did it again in Blake's second season as coach, the players shouldered him and lugged him to center ice for the Cup presentation. Toe Blake, the coach, was for real – just as Toe Blake, the player, had been.

Now, the question was being asked: Who will stop the Blake bulldozer – and when? Adams, now admittedly impressed, said a club on a roll – as the Canadiens had been, and as his own club had been – could be expected to run out of gas in three years. But the astute Lynn Patrick got it right. The Canadiens, he said, somewhat wistfully, might keep right on going for five years.

In 1960, the Canadiens won their fifth straight Stanley Cup – something no other NHL club had accomplished – roaring through the playoffs undefeated, duplicating what the Red Wings had done in 1951-52. The members of this team include eight Hall-of-

Fame players, but all deserve acclaim: Jacques Plante, Charlie Hodge, Doug Harvey, Tom Johnson, Bob Turner, Jean-Guy Talbot, Albert Langlois, Ralph Backstrom, Jean Béliveau, Marcel Bonin, Bernie Geoffrion, Phil Goyette, Bill Hicke, Don Marshall, Ab McDonald, Dickie Moore, André Pronovost, Claude Provost, Henri Richard, Rocket Richard. The manager, of course, was Frank Selke, who had seen his forecast come true.

Heading into the 1960s, it was the Chicago Black Hawks, now coached by Rudy Pilous, who had developed several of his top stars in junior hockey, who were destined to derail the Montreal express. They served notice during a torrid 1959 semi-final with the Habs, which ended with a wild demonstration in the sixth game at Chicago, and led to the loss of the league's most colorful referee, Red Storey.

More than 18,000 fans – the second-largest crowd in Chicago history – showered the ice with beer cans, fruit, programs, and other garbage because Storey failed to call penalties for what they thought were tripping infractions against Chicago's Eddie Litzenberger and Bobby Hull. Several fans invaded the ice, and one caught a crease in his scalp from Doug Harvey's stick.

Toe Blake, whose scoring touch earned him the nickname of "the Old Lamplighter" during his playing days, guided the Montreal Canadiens to eight Stanley Cup victories in thirteen seasons as the Habs' coach.

League president Campbell, who was at the game, was quoted by Ottawa sports columnist Bill Westwick as saying that he felt Storey "froze" on one of the calls. Storey, who thought he had called a good game under most difficult conditions, promptly announced his resignation when Campbell's comment became public. He vowed he would never officiate in another game as long as Campbell was president. And he never did.

Campbell, who took a lot of flak for this comment – some of it from Red Dutton, his predecessor – did not claim to have been misquoted. He did say he had considered his remarks off the record, but he knew who Westwick was and what he did for a living. So he had no excuse and claimed none, although he did urge Storey to continue. The league governors, at their next meeting, decided to take no action.

And so the decades of the 1940s and 1950s ended as the titans probably figured they would. There always would be controversy. There always would be name-calling. There always would be vendettas. It had been that way since the day Lord Stanley of Preston donated that rose bowl. But more people knew about it now, because of increased media attention. First radio, then television, had created millions of new fans.

By 1960, many of those hard-nosed pioneers who had helped to make it happen were gone. McLaughlin, Calder, Norris, Sr., and Irvin were dead. Ross had announced his retirement from the Bruins, and his bitterest foe, Smythe, had moved the motion of happy retirement at the next meeting of the governors. Dutton, the caretaker president, had returned to Calgary, where he was making money in his construction business. Adams was in his last few seasons with Detroit.

Smythe, himself, would sell his controlling interest in Maple Leaf Gardens to his son, Stafford, Harold Ballard, and John Bassett in November of 1961. Hap Day had gone earlier. In Montreal, Selke would hand over the reins of general manager to Sam Pollack in 1964.

Those tumultuous twenty years had indeed been the twilight of the titans. It had never been dull. Nor would it ever be dull. That's the secret of the success of Lord Stanley's rose bowl. Every show is new. There are no reruns.

Most of the attention in the 1960-61 season was centered on a pair of hard-shooting wingers. Toronto's Frank Mahovlich and Montreal's Bernie Geoffrion battled to match Rocket Richard's mark of fifty goals in a single season. Mahovlich stalled at forty-eight goals, but Geoffrion hit the magic plateau in his last game of the season to become only the second player to score fifty goals in a single campaign.

A dramatic year-long struggle for first place between the Canadiens – without Rocket Richard, who had retired midway through training camp – and the Leafs resulted in the Habs edging out Toronto for the regular-season crown by two points. In the semi-finals, the Canadiens were sidelined by Chicago in six games, depriving them of an eleventh consecutive trip to the finals. The Hawks, behind the goaltending of Glenn Hall, shut out the

Rocket Richard receives the Stanley Cup from NHL president Clarence Campbell for the last time on April 14, 1960, following the Habs' sweep of the Leafs in the Stanley Cup finals. Richard retired during training camp in September of 1960.

Bobby Hull, whose blond locks and chiseled features made him a popular cover boy during the 1960s, shares the spotlight here with "Mr. Goalie," Glenn Hall, during the Hawks' Stanley Cup-winning season in 1960-61.

Shutout Shutout

Since the establishment of the NHL in 1917, there has been at least one shutout recorded in every playoff year except 1959, when every team hit the scoreboard in the eighteen games played.

Canadiens by identical 3–0 scores in the final two games to earn their first trip to the Cup finals in seventeen seasons. The other semi-final featured a return duel between the Leafs and the Red Wings. Toronto opened the series with a 3–2 win in double overtime, but the Wings rebounded to capture the next four games and set up the first all-American Stanley Cup final since 1950.

The finals opened in Chicago Stadium on April 6, and with the noisy Chicago crowd urging them on, the Hawks quickly took control of the game. Ken Wharram's goal was bracketed by a pair off the stick of Bobby Hull to send the Hawks to the dressing room with a 3–0 lead. Detroit's Terry Sawchuk injured his shoulder in the first period and was replaced by Hank Bassen when the teams took to the ice to start the second period. The Wings battled back on goals by Len Lunde and Al Johnson, but couldn't force the tying marker past Hall, as the Hawks opened the series with a 3–2 victory. Sawchuk remained on the shelf in game two, forcing the Wings to tighten up their defense to protect Bassen. The offense chipped in with a pair of goals by Howie Young and Alex Delvecchio and the defense limited the Hawks to two harmless shots on goal, enabling the Red Wings to take a 2–0 lead into the dressing room after twenty minutes of play. Pierre Pilote put Chicago on the board early in the second period, but Bassen closed the door from there. Delvecchio's goal in the final minute ended the Hawks' hopes, and the Wings tied the best-of-seven battle with a 3–1 win. Chicago used a three-goal second period in game three to take a 3–1 decision, but Detroit replied in game four by squeezing out a 2–1 victory on Bruce McGregor's first NHL goal with six minutes remaining in the contest.

Game five was a terrific see-saw battle that saw the Black Hawks and the Red Wings combine for eighty shots on goal. The teams traded goals in the first period, with Leo Labine and Howie Glover scoring for Detroit, and Murray Balfour and Ron Murphy replying for the home-side Hawks. Balfour's goal gave the Hawks the lead again at the 16:23 mark of the second, but Vic Stasiuk tied the game for the Red Wings heading into the final period of regulation time, which was completely dominated by the Black Hawks, who peppered Sawchuk with twenty-four shots. Stan Mikita slipped a pair of pucks past Sawchuk and assisted on another to leave Chicago a single win away from its third Stanley Cup.

Hank Bassen returned to the Wings' net in game six, but he couldn't ground the Hawks' flight toward the Stanley Cup title. Chicago spotted Detroit an early 1–0 lead on a Parker MacDonald power-play goal, then stormed back to score five unanswered goals by five different players to capture the Cup. The key goal was a shorthanded, unassisted marker by Reggie Fleming, who stole the puck from Len Lunde and blasted one past Bassen. Bobby Hull commented, "Reg put us even. That gave everybody a big lift and we just took over from there." Pierre Pilote, with twelve assists and fifteen points, was the top scorer for the Hawks, while Gordie Howe, also with fifteen post-season points, topped all Detroit scorers.

For the second time in three seasons, a player made a run at a fifty-goal season. In 1961-62, it was the scoring catalyst for the Chicago Black Hawks, "the Golden Jet," Bobby Hull. Hull scored thirty-four goals in the last thirty games of the schedule to hit the fifty-goal plateau. Despite Hull's goal-scoring heroics, however, he couldn't outdistance the Rangers' Andy Bathgate, who tied Hull for the scoring lead.

The Canadiens won their fifth consecutive points title, registering a league-high forty-two wins. The Habs met the defending champion Black Hawks in the semi-finals, and for the second straight year they bowed to the Hawks in six games. Montreal opened impressively, winning the first two

In 1961, the Chicago Black Hawks won their third Stanley Cup – the franchise's first since 1938, with a solid line-up that combined veterans Ed Litzenberger, Tod Sloan, Jack Evans, and Al Arbour with some of the league's finest young talent in Bobby Hull, Stan Mikita, Pierre Pilote, and Kenny Wharram.

matches on home ice by 2–1 and 4–3 scores. The Hawks took over from there, sweeping the next four games, including a 2–0 shutout in the decisive sixth contest.

The New York Rangers returned to the playoff picture, and although they finished twenty-one points behind the second-place Leafs, they gave Toronto all they could handle in the semi-finals. The teams traded home-ice victories in the first four games, before the Leafs took a stranglehold on the series with a 3–2 win on Red Kelly's goal in double overtime in game five. The teams then returned to Toronto, where the Rangers had been held winless in sixteen straight games, and the Leafs wrapped things up with a resounding 7–1 victory over the Broadway Blues.

Toronto and Chicago met in the finals for the first time since the Hawks shocked the Leafs in 1938. The Leafs had now gone eleven years without a Cup victory, the longest drought in club history to that time. In game one, Chicago opened the scoring on Bobby Hull's power-play goal, with a pair of Leafs in the penalty box. However, Toronto held the Hawks off the board for the remainder of the game while scoring four goals themselves. George Armstrong scored one and assisted on a pair as the Leafs captured the first game, 4–1.

The second game was a closely fought contest that saw the Leafs survive a brace of third-period goals by Stan Mikita to take a commanding 2–0 lead in games with a 3–2 win. George Armstrong was again the catalyst, scoring the winning goal with less than four minutes remaining in regulation time.

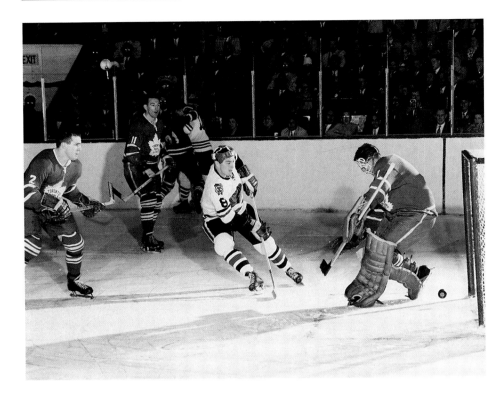

Leaf defenders Bob Nevin (11) and Carl Brewer (2) can only watch as Chicago's Murray Balfour (8) finds an opening between the pads of Leafs' goalie Don Simmons during first-period action in game five of the 1962 Stanley Cup championship round. The Leafs went on to batter the Hawks 8–4 in this match, before wrapping up the franchise's eighth Cup title three days later.

Chicago threw a defensive blanket over the Leafs in games three and four, limiting Toronto to a single goal in the two games, tying the best-of-seven series with 3–0 and 4–1 victories.

Finding a way to solve the Hawks' stubborn defense was just one of the problems confronting the Leafs as they prepared to take the ice for game five. Johnny Bower, who had pulled a thigh muscle in game four, was unable to suit up, forcing the Leafs to use backup Don Simmons. Although Simmons was very impressive in Boston's two trips to the Cup finals in the 1950s, he had appeared in only nine games during the season. Instead of sitting back and protecting Simmons, the Leafs put on their most formidable post-season offensive display since a nine-goal effort against Detroit in 1942. Toronto fired eight goals past Glenn Hall to move within one victory of the Stanley Cup in an 8–4 trouncing of the Hawks.

As expected, the sixth game lacked the offensive pyrotechnics of the fifth match. The teams appeared tentative through the first two periods, and although the Leafs outshot the Hawks by a 27–12 margin, Glenn Hall held them off the board. The Hawks broke the stalemate at the 8:56 mark of the third period when Bobby Hull took a pass from Balfour and eased the puck past Simmons. Hull's goal was met by a barrage of debris from the fans, and a lengthy delay was needed to clear the ice. This unscheduled time-out helped the Leafs regain their composure, and less than two minutes after the resumption of play, Bob Nevin notched the equalizer for Toronto.

Slowly, confidently, the Leafs took control of the play. With just over six minutes remaining, Dick Duff secured a pass from Tim Horton and, with Dave Keon running interference in front of the Chicago net, drilled a wrist-

Different Teams, Same Result

Ed Litzenberger and Al Arbour were teammates in 1961 when the Chicago Black Hawks won their first Stanley Cup since 1938. The following season, they were teammates again, this time with the Toronto Maple Leafs, Cup winners in 1962. They are the last two players to win back-to-back Cups with different teams.

Dave Keon, seen here entangled with Black Hawks' policeman Reg Fleming and goaltender Glenn Hall, glances over his shoulder to see Dick Duff's shot give Toronto a 2–1 lead in game six of the 1962 finals. Duff's marker held up, giving the Maple Leafs their first championship in eleven years.

shot past Glenn Hall. In the remaining minutes, the Hawks stormed the Leafs' cage, but Simmons was equal to the challenge, and when the Chicago Stadium foghorn blew at the end of regulation time, the Leafs had won their first Stanley Cup championship since 1951 with the 2–1 victory. Stan Mikita set a new NHL record for assists (15) and points (21) in the post-season, breaking Gordie Howe's mark of twenty set in 1955. Tim Horton set a new mark for defensemen, with twelve assists in thirteen playoff games.

The 1962-63 season featured a season-long struggle for first place, the league's closest race since the NHL had adopted its single-division format in 1938. Only five points separated the first four clubs. The defending Cup-champion Toronto Maple Leafs won their first regular-season crown in fifteen years with a 35–23–12 mark, finishing a single point ahead of the runner-up Black Hawks. Gordie Howe returned to the top of the scoring ladder for the first time in six seasons, capturing his sixth Art Ross Trophy.

The Leafs began the defense of their Stanley Cup title in a semi-final match-up with the Montreal Canadiens. Johnny Bower shut down the league's most potent offense, registering a pair of shutouts as the Leafs convincingly downed the Habs in five games. Perhaps the key moment of the series came during game three, when Montreal had a one-man advantage for five minutes but couldn't manage a single scoring chance. In the other semi-final, Detroit lost the first two games to Chicago, then reeled off four victories to give Sid Abel his second trip to the Stanley Cup finals as a coach.

In game one of the finals, the Leafs wasted little time in serving notice that they weren't about to surrender their throne easily. Dick Duff established an NHL record that still stands by scoring two goals only sixty-eight seconds from the opening face-off, and the Leafs cruised from there, taking the opener by a 4–2 score. The second game followed a similar blueprint, with Toronto getting goals from Eddie Litzenberger, Ron Stewart, and Bob Nevin before the Wings hit the scoresheet. Howe scored a pair for Detroit, and Stewart added another for Toronto to give the Leafs another 4–2 win and a two-game series lead. Back at the Olympia, the Wings finally played up to their capabilities, moving back into contention with a 3–2 win. Vic Stasiuk scored in the first minute of the game, and Alex Faulkner added a pair in the second frame to take care of the offense. Terry Sawchuk stopped thirty Leaf shots to keep the Red Wings in the hunt.

Detroit opened strongly in the fourth match as well, using a Gordie Howe marker early in the first period to take a 1–0 lead. A pair of Leaf goals by Armstrong and Kelly surrounded a single Detroit marker by Eddie Joyal, to leave the affair tied 2–2 heading into the final stanza. Although the Wings

Thirteen members of this 1962 Cup-winning Toronto Maple Leafs team would still be on the Leafs' roster two years later when the squad made its third consecutive trip to the Stanley Cup winners' circle.

had clearly outplayed the Leafs, they couldn't breach the "China Wall," Toronto's venerable goaltender Johnny Bower, who made seventeen saves in the second period alone and kicked out another nine in the third. The outcome was still very much in question until midway through the period, when Dave Keon picked up a bad clearing pass and rifled an unassisted goal past Sawchuk. Red Kelly added another to give the Leafs their third win by an identical 4–2 score, leaving them one victory shy of repeating as Cup champions.

Game five began with Toronto adopting a defensive posture, allowing the Wings only five shots on goal in the first period. Dave Keon opened the scoring for the Leafs late in the frame when he beat Sawchuk with a nifty move while his team was a man short. Alex Delvecchio tied the game early in the second, but the Wings couldn't break through the Leafs' defense for the go-ahead goal. With a little over seven minutes remaining in the game, Eddie Shack scored for the Leafs, forcing the Wings to press all-out for the equalizer. A golden opportunity was handed to them when Bob Pulford took a holding penalty with two minutes to go. Sawchuk was yanked for an extra attacker, but Keon coolly took a pass from George Armstrong and hit the empty net to close the door on Detroit and seal a 3–1 Cup-winning victory for the Leafs. Keon became the first player to score two shorthanded goals in a Stanley Cup final game. Five different Leafs had multiple-goal games in the series, prompting Gordie Howe to say, "There's not a bad apple in the barrel."

Johnny Bower prepares to challenge the Red Wings' great Gordie Howe with his patented poke check during the 1963 Stanley Cup finals. Howe's three goals and three assists in the series were not enough, as the Leafs defeated the Red Wings in five games.

NATHAN PHILLIPS, Q.C.
MAYOR

Leafs captain George Armstrong shares a handshake and a smile with Toronto mayor, Nathan Phillips, after a City Hall celebration for the reigning NHL champions.

Dave Keon's hat-trick in game seven of the Toronto–Montreal semi-final propelled the Leafs into their fifth Stanley Cup final in six years.

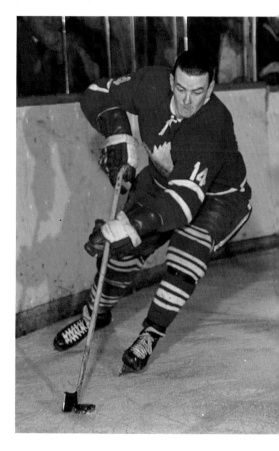

A rousing two-team battle for the NHL's regular-season crown highlighted 1963-64, with Montreal edging out Chicago by a single point. Resigned to a third-place finish, the Leafs bolstered their post-season line-up by sending five players to the Rangers for Andy Bathgate. The swap marked only the seventh time in league history that a top-ten scorer changed teams in mid-season.

For the first time since the six-team league had been established in 1943, both semi-final showdowns went seven games. The Leafs–Canadiens series was a fiercely played affair. The first game, won by the Habs 2–0, set a playoff record for penalties, with referee Frank Udvari whistling down thirty-one separate infractions. The teams traded victories in the next four matches, to give the Canadiens a 3–2 edge in the series entering game six. The Leafs rose to the occasion, shutting out the Habs 3–0 to even the series. In game seven, Dave Keon scored all three Leaf goals in a 3–1 win – one shorthanded, one even strength, and one into the empty net – as the Leafs rolled into their fifth Stanley Cup final in six years.

The series between the Red Wings and Black Hawks unfolded in similar fashion. Detroit won games six and game seven to qualify for a final-series rematch with the Maple Leafs.

The 1964 final was the first championship series to go seven games since the Habs and Wings met in 1955. Detroit carried a 2–1 lead into the third period of game one, but George Armstrong tied the game early in the frame. The teams appeared headed for overtime when Bob Pulford intercepted Norm Ullman's cross-ice pass and broke in all alone on Sawchuk. Pulford's wrist-shot found the net behind the Wings' goaltender, with only two seconds remaining on the clock.

In 1964, Terry Sawchuk came out of the hospital, where he was receiving treatment for a pinched nerve in his shoulder, to lead the Red Wings into their second consecutive championship final by defeating the Black Hawks in a hard-fought seven-game semi-final series.

A similar scenario played itself out in game two. The Wings, on goals by Ullman, Joyal, and Floyd Smith, entered the third period up 3–1. However, Red Kelly put the Leafs back in the game, and Gerry Ehman's last-minute goal, just two seconds after a Detroit penalty had expired, sent the game into overtime. The Red Wings, who had outshot Imlach's troops 41–28 in regulation time, regrouped and poured it on in the extra session. Ullman made up for his lapse in the series opener by dodging a pair of Leaf defenders at the blue line and drilling a pass to Gordie Howe near the Leaf net. As Horton and Stanley converged on him, Howe slipped a cross-crease feed to Larry Jeffrey, who calmly flipped the puck into the net to tie the series.

Two nights later in Detroit, the Wings dominated early, opening up a 3–0 first-period lead. However, as was the case in the previous games, the Leafs fought back to tie the contest, the equalizer coming off the stick of Don McKenny with seventy-three seconds remaining. But with merely seventeen seconds left, Gordie Howe played magician again, stealing the puck from Frank Mahovlich and feathering a pass to Alex Delvecchio, who was parked on the Leafs' doorstep. The Wings' captain neatly deflected the pass past Bower to give Detroit the series lead. Game four featured more third-period heroics by the Leafs, as Bathgate and Mahovlich found the mark in the final twenty minutes for a 4–2 series-tying triumph.

Sawchuk was in top form for game five, stopping thirty-three Leaf shots. With a 2–1 victory safely tucked away, the Wings came home a single win away from their first Cup celebration since 1955.

One of hockey's oft-repeated tales of heroism occurred in the sixth game. With the teams tied 3–3 in the third period, Leaf defenseman Bob Baun was felled by a slapshot on the ankle and was removed from the ice on a stretcher. It appeared likely that he was gone for the game and would presumably be out for the series. The match went into overtime, and, just over a minute in, Baun appeared on the ice, taking a regular shift. Following a face-off in the Wings' zone, Bob Pulford fired the puck along the boards to

The Birth of Pay-Per-View

During the Minnesota North Stars' phenomenal playoff run in 1991, pay-per-view television coverage of their games was a financial success for the club. However, the first pay-per-view coverage of the playoffs had occurred in Detroit, when a pair of local theaters showed both rounds of the 1964 playoffs that featured the Red Wings.

A contented group of Toronto Maple Leafs, including (left to right) Harris, Stewart, Bower, Stanley, Bathgate, Shack, Pulford, and Baun, surround the Stanley Cup after shutting out the Red Wings, 4–0, in game seven of the 1964 showdown.

Black Hawk forwards Bobby Hull and Phil Esposito scramble for a loose puck, while Terry Harper and Claude Provost attempt to impede their progress, during action in the 1965 Montreal–Chicago title bout. The Canadiens won the battle, but the fight went the distance.

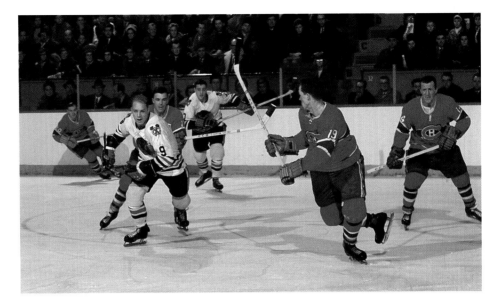

In 1965, Jean Béliveau was named the first winner of the Conn Smythe Trophy, awarded to the NHL's playoff MVP.

the point, where Baun let go a drifting shot that deflected off Bill Gadsby's stick and past a bewildered Sawchuk. It wasn't until after the series' seventh game that it was disclosed that Baun was playing on a tightly taped but fractured ankle.

With the emotional high of this decisive victory propelling them, the Leafs easily disposed of the Red Wings in the seventh game of the series. Andy Bathgate opened the scoring for Toronto on a wrist-shot to the top corner in the fourth minute of play, and Johnny Bower slammed the door from there, leading the Leafs to their third consecutive Stanley Cup victory with a 4–0 shutout of the Red Wings.

Amid the euphoria of the Leafs' dressing-room celebration, Punch Imlach took time to reflect on the efforts of his troops. "They showed all the signs of true champions tonight. Baun, Brewer, and Kelly all took needles to deaden the pain in their legs ... boy were they up for it tonight." Andy Bathgate sat back, contented just to see the Cup up close. "Not only is this the first time I've won the Cup, this is the first time I've even been in the finals."

The Detroit Red Wings climbed from fourth place to first in 1964-65, winning ten more games than they had the previous season. Despite their lofty finish, the Red Wings were dismissed from the post-season by Chicago in an exciting seven-game semi-final series. The other semi-final featured a return bout between the Leafs and the Canadiens. This time the Habs were victorious, winning the set on Claude Provost's overtime winner in the sixth game.

The first Montreal–Chicago final in twenty-one years opened on April 17 in Montreal, the latest start in league history. Gump Worsley got the nod to start in goal for the Habs, his first Stanley Cup final-series appearance since he came to the league twelve years earlier. The Hawks entered game one without Pilote and Wharram, two key ingredients in their attack, both

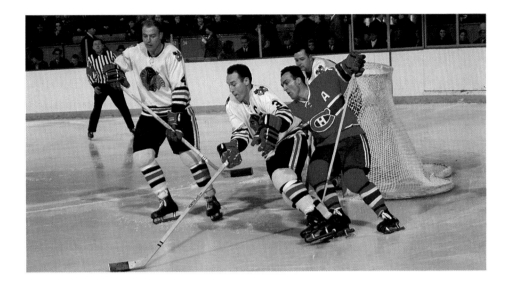

Pierre Pilote attempts to corral a loose puck, while warding off a check from Montreal's Henri Richard.

of whom were sidelined by injuries that would keep them out of the line-up until game three. The teams traded goals through the first forty-five minutes, before Yvan Cournoyer scored the first playoff goal of his career to boost Montreal to a 3–2 triumph.

Defense and special teams were the keys in Montreal's 2–0 shutout of the Hawks in game two of the final. The Habs limited Chicago to eighteen shots over sixty minutes, while Jean Béliveau and Dick Duff each scored when the Canadiens enjoyed a man advantage, to take a commanding two-game lead in the series.

Game three was played cautiously. John Ferguson gave Montreal the lead in the second period, but Phil Esposito countered for Chicago less than a minute later. Ken Wharram, who had returned to the Hawks' line-up despite a twisted right knee, contributed the winning tally on a feed from Stan Mikita. An empty-net goal by Chico Maki sealed the 3–1 win for Chicago.

Charlie Hodge replaced Worsley in goal for Montreal, but the move backfired on Toe Blake, as the Hawks scored four goals on only eight shots in the third period for a 5–1 triumph. Bobby Hull led the Hawks' attack, scoring a pair, including the game winner on a seventy-foot slapshot that caught Hodge napping, to bring the Hawks and the Canadiens back to even terms in the series.

The Canadiens rebounded convincingly in the fifth contest, sending Glenn Hall to the showers in a 6–0 drubbing. Toe Blake stayed with Hodge, and the thirty-two-year-old veteran rewarded his coach with twenty-three saves in recording the second playoff shutout of his career. Jean Béliveau collected four points on two goals and two assists, while J. C. Tremblay chipped in with a three-point effort. Denis DeJordy replaced Hall for the third period, but the Canadiens fired three pucks past him to pull within one game of the title. Back on home ice for game six, the Hawks needed a pair of third-period goals two minutes apart by Elmer Vasko and Doug Mohns for a 2–1 victory that sent the series to its limit.

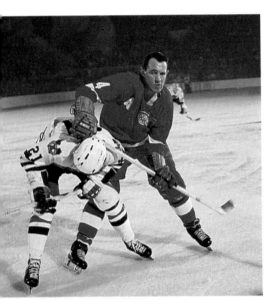

Bill Gadsby (right) checks Chicago's Stan Mikita in the 1966 semi-finals. Mikita was the NHL's second-leading scorer in 1965-66, but was held to just three points in the playoffs.

Long Careers; No Cups

Three Hall-of-Fame defensemen hold the record for the longest tenure without a Stanley Cup win. Bill Gadsby played twenty seasons without playing on a winner, while Harry Howell played 1,411 games without even reaching the Cup finals. Brad Park, who made the playoffs in each of his seventeen NHL campaigns, never played on a championship team.

Although Chicago had won it all in 1961, this was the first seventh-game final in franchise history. The Canadiens, perhaps sensing this, opened the game with an offensive flurry that resulted in Jean Béliveau scoring only fourteen seconds into the match. The Habs scored three more in the opening frame, and held on from there for a 4–0 win and their twelfth Stanley Cup victory. Béliveau, who scored three game winners and set up the fourth, was the first recipient of the Conn Smythe Trophy, a new piece of silverware awarded to the most valuable player in the post-season.

The eyes of the hockey world were focused on Bobby Hull throughout 1965-66, charting the Golden Jet's bid to become the first player to score more than fifty goals in a season. Hull ended the campaign with a record fifty-four goals, earning the Art Ross Trophy with ninety-seven points, also an NHL record.

The semi-finals featured return match-ups between the Leafs and the Canadiens and the Red Wings and the Black Hawks. Montreal swept Toronto, while Detroit won its last three contests against Chicago to take its series in six games.

The Red Wings, who finished sixteen points behind the Canadiens in regular-season play, were considered longshots to wrest the Cup from the Habs. However, the Wings confounded the oddsmakers by playing a picture-perfect opening game, using goals by Andy Bathgate, now with Detroit, Paul Henderson, and thirty-seven-year-old Bill Gadsby to squeeze out a 3–2 win. Detroit continued to amaze its followers in the second contest, receiving goals from five different marksmen – four of which came in the third period – to open up a two-game edge with a 5–2 victory on the Forum ice. Following the victory, much of the credit for the Wings' Forum sweep was given to goaltender Roger Crozier, who thwarted numerous Montreal scoring chances with a series of dazzling saves.

It was a determined group of Montreal Canadiens who took to the ice at the Olympia for the start of game three. Although they allowed a goal to Norm Ullman in the early going, the Habs rebounded to take a 2–1 lead into the second period. After a scoreless second frame, Gilles Tremblay lifted the Habs to victory with a pair of goals less than two minutes apart to put the wrap on a tidy 4–2 victory.

The fortunes of the Detroit faithful took a downturn early in the first period of game four. Crozier wrenched his leg against the left post and was forced to leave the game. While his replacement, veteran Hank Bassen, couldn't be faulted on the two shots that eluded him, the Wings appeared to lose confidence after Crozier's injury, managing only twenty-three shots on the Montreal net. Bassen kept the Wings in the game until Ralph Backstrom scored the winner for the Habs late in the third period to tie the series.

Crozier returned to the net for game five, but wasn't sharp in a 5–1 defeat. Sid Abel refused to blame his goaltender for the Wings' loss, emphasizing

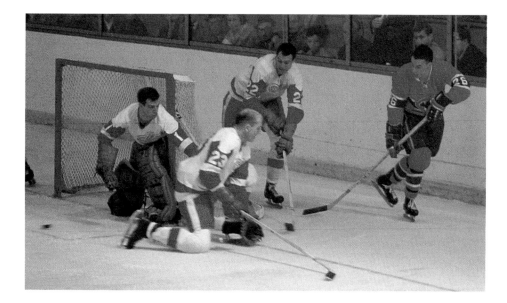

Jimmy Roberts feathers a backhand feed past Detroit's Gary Bergman (23) and Ab McDonald.

that "we didn't give the little guy any protection. With his heavily taped knee, he just couldn't move out there."

As the teams returned to the Olympia for game six, much of the media's attention was focused on Crozier, who was adamant that he would be able to suit up for the match. Goals by Béliveau and Léon Rochefort staked the Habs to a 2–0 lead after thirty minutes, but the Wings fought back with a shorthanded effort by Ullman and entered the third period down by one. Midway through the frame, Floyd Smith converted a pass from Ab McDonald to force overtime.

Two minutes into the extra period, Henri Richard, closely pursued by Gary Bergman, drove toward the Wings' goal. Dave Balon fired a pass toward Richard, who was now sliding along the ice. Somehow the Pocket Rocket directed the puck behind Crozier for the Cup-winning goal. Following the game, Crozier was presented with the Conn Smythe Trophy as the playoff MVP. The Canadiens' win denied Bill Gadsby his last chance to see his name inscribed on the Stanley Cup. After twenty seasons in the league, the seven-time All-Star announced he had played his final game.

Detroit's Roger Crozier was the first member of a losing team, and the first goaltender, to win the Conn Smythe Trophy.

Canada celebrated its centennial in 1967, a year that also marked the end of an era in NHL history. The league announced plans to double in size for the 1967-68 campaign, making the 1967 season the last of the six-team "Golden Age." It was appropriate that the finals should come down to a series between the Canadiens and the Leafs, the two NHL clubs based in Canada and winners of the Stanley Cup in eighteen of the past twenty-four seasons.

The Chicago Black Hawks were the dominant team in hockey during the regular season, leading the league in defense and offense. However, in their semi-finals against the Leafs, the Hawks met a determined group of veterans who realized that this was probably their last opportunity to savor a Stanley Cup victory.

A backhander by Chicago's Pierre Pilote finds the top corner behind Terry Sawchuk in Chicago's 4–3 win over the Leafs in game four of the 1967 semi-finals. Ellis (8), Horton (7), and Kelly (4) are the helpless Leaf defenders.

With Terry Sawchuk, who was now a Leaf, providing the dramatics, including a forty-nine-save effort over forty minutes after replacing an injured Bower in game five, the Leafs bucked the odds and defeated the league-champion Black Hawks in six games. The Montreal Canadiens easily swept past the Rangers in four games to set up a made-in-Canada Stanley Cup final.

The Canadiens entered the series on a fifteen-game unbeaten streak with rookie Rogatien Vachon in goal. Veteran Terry Sawchuk started in goal for the Leafs in game one, but he couldn't stop the Habs and retired for the evening after forty minutes, thirty shots, and four goals. The Canadiens pumped six goals into the Leaf net while cruising to a 6–2 opening-game victory. Imlach elected to go with Bower in the second game, and the forty-two-year-old veteran responded by stopping all thirty-one shots he faced. The Leafs, on power-play goals from Pete Stemkowski and Mike Walton and an insurance marker from Tim Horton, evened the series with a 3–0 shutout.

Game three was an eighty-eight-minute marathon, highlighted by outstanding performances by both Vachon and Bower. Bower faced sixty-three shots but allowed only two pucks to elude him as the Leafs won in double overtime on a tap-in goal by Bob Pulford. Prior to game four, Bower pulled a leg muscle, forcing Imlach to go with Sawchuk. The Canadiens greeted

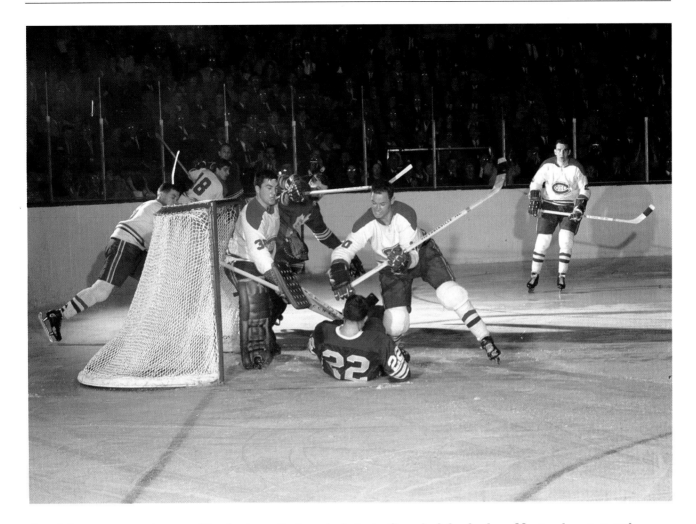

the eighteen-year veteran with nineteen first-period shots. Sawchuk looked tentative most of the evening, allowing six goals as the Habs tied the series with an easy 6–2 win over Punch Imlach's troops.

Any doubts the Leafs and their fans had about Sawchuk were erased in the pivotal fifth game. He was sensational in the first two periods, robbing Béliveau and Cournoyer with superb saves. The teams traded markers in the first period, but the Leafs broke loose in the second with a three-goal effort. A shorthanded breakaway goal by Marcel Pronovost, who had thwarted a Canadiens' rush, marked the turning point of the game. In the third period, the Leafs' defense closed off the Canadiens' passing lanes, forcing the Habs to dump and chase, a style that played right into the Leafs' hands. Sawchuk shut the door the rest of the way for a 4–1 win.

Montreal coach Toe Blake replaced Vachon with Gump Worsley for the sixth game, but the veteran couldn't hold back the Leafs. The Habs fired seventeen shots at Sawchuk in the first period, but he was equal to the task, keeping the Canadiens off the board until the Leafs hit the scoresheet in the second frame. Ron Ellis gave Toronto the lead, and Jim Pappin added to it when his cross-ice pass deflected off the skate of Habs' rear guard Terry Harper and skidded past Gump Worsley.

Montreal rear guard Ted Harris decks Brian Conacher in the Habs' crease, while Savard and Pappin battle for position in the Leafs–Habs final series of 1967. While much of the attention in the Leafs' Centennial Year Cup victory focused on the club's veterans, newcomers like Stemkowski, Pappin, and Conacher were important contributors in Toronto's six-game triumph.

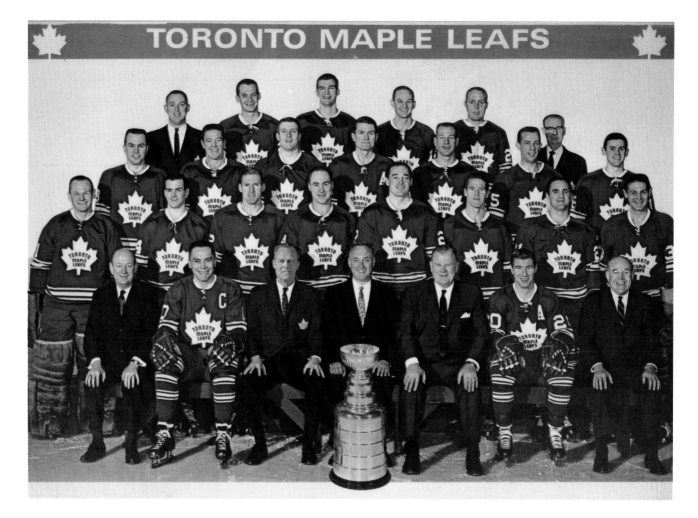

TORONTO MAPLE LEAFS

"A bunch of old pappies and some young blood" is how coach Punch Imlach described the 1966-67 Toronto Maple Leafs.

The Right Place at the Right Time (Part Two)

Milan Marcetta and Aut Erickson were both members of the Maple Leafs' Cup-winning team in 1967, although they never played a regular-season game with the team. Erickson appeared in one game with the Leafs during the 1967 finals. Marcetta, who later played with Minnesota, suited up for three matches in the 1967 playoffs.

Dick Duff brought the Canadiens to within one with a marvelous individual effort early in the third period, breaking away from Allan Stanley to put the Habs on the board. The score remained 2–1 until the final minute, when Montreal forced a face-off in the Leaf zone and pulled Worsley for an extra attacker. In a dramatic move, Imlach sent out an all-veteran line-up for the final minute. The Leafs won the draw and worked the puck to George Armstrong, who stepped over center and drifted the puck into the unguarded Canadiens' net to seal the Leafs' thirteenth Stanley Cup victory. "It's nice to win this time," Imlach said. "Everybody wrote us off as being just a bunch of old guys." They were old, but they were also winners.

(continued on p. 195)

The 1967 Finals

by George Gross

Every Stanley Cup is viewed as a national treasure by the club that has it in its possession in that particular year.

But, nostalgically, the 1967 Stanley Cup has a special value, for it was the last Cup fought for by the teams of the inaccurately named "Original Six." This last pre-expansion Stanley Cup final was accorded no special nickname, but, perhaps, the almost-shocking triumph of a collection of aging Toronto Maple Leafs over a highly favored, smooth, talented group of Montreal Canadiens could be referred to as "the Over-the-Hill Gang's Cup."

With justification, I might add.

The Leafs, winners of the 1967 Stanley Cup in six games, paraded an array of distinguished-looking players, some of them qualifying as hockey "senior citizens."

It also might have been called "the Junior B Goaltender's Cup." Again, with some justification, since that's what George "Punch" Imlach called the Montreal Canadiens' rookie goalie, Rogatien Vachon, who was called up to replace the injured Gump Worsley.

And, finally, it could have been called "the Triumph of the Veteran Netminders," a reference to the phenomenal goaltending displayed by Toronto's seasoned goaltending twosome of Terry Sawchuk and Johnny Bower.

The Toronto Maple Leafs, who struggled to make the playoffs before finishing in third place in the regular schedule, nineteen points behind Chicago, had been given little hope of even reaching the Stanley Cup finals.

In the first round of the playoffs, the Leafs had to face the potent offense of the Black Hawks, whose two scoring stars, Stan Mikita and Bobby Hull, had finished

first and second in the NHL scoring race. The Leafs countered with players such as Brian Conacher, who had never scored against the Chicago powerhouse.

But that was before, and 1967 was then. Indeed, the much-maligned Conacher helped propel the Leafs into the finals by scoring two goals in one semi-final game against the Hawks. He had to pinch himself to believe it had really happened.

Going up against the Montreal Canadiens at the Montreal Forum in the mid-1960s seemed a daunting task. Winners of the Stanley Cup in each of the two previous seasons, the Habs had the champagne bottles in the cooler at the Forum even before the series began. And after all, the Canadiens had no lesser players in their star-studded line-up than Jean Béliveau, Henri Richard, Yvan Cournoyer, Jean-Claude Tremblay, Serge Savard, Jacques Laperriere, John Ferguson, Dick Duff, and many others. "Awesome" would have been an apt description of this team's talent.

"The Old Guard," Terry Sawchuk (left), and "the China Wall," Johnny Bower, following the Leafs' Stanley Cup victory in 1967.

GAME ONE
April 20, 1967 – Toronto, 2 – Montreal, 6

The Canadiens kicked off the series the way everyone expected – by humiliating the Maple Leafs on three goals by Henri Richard, a pair by Yvan Cournoyer, and a single by Jean Béliveau, while Jim Pappin and Larry Hillman replied for the Maple Leafs.

Punch Imlach, then *generalissimo* of the Maple Leafs, a top motivator of his players and a detractor of the opposition, had pulled off a few stunts during his illustrious career, most of which worked to his advantage: like when he started a game with five defensemen, throwing the opposition completely off balance.

He knew he had to come up with a new gimmick in the 1967 finals against Montreal, something that would lift his team and adversely affect the opposition. And that's when he gave birth to a still-famous line by telling a few media observers in the stands at the Forum: "There's no way the Habs can win this series with a Junior B goaltender."

This was a reference to rookie goalie Rogatien Vachon, who was called up by the Habs and tossed into the fray against the Leafs – and who played reasonably well in the opening game.

Even twenty-five years later, Rogie Vachon, now an executive with the Los Angeles Kings, recalls the event with some trepidation.

"You know, that line stuck with me for the rest of my career," admitted Rogie. "Punch didn't tell me, personally, but I found out from reporters who were talking to him. You see, I was a kid of twenty-one, and nothing bothered me then. I felt no pressure. The fact that I was part of a team in the Stanley Cup finals was a bonus."

As the finals progressed, Imlach's comment became a focal point for media coverage of the series. Vachon admitted, "It was embarrassing. Everybody began needling me about Punch's statement. His words were echoed all around the league. Even today, when I come to Canada, people remind me of Punch's words.

"It was a good series for the Leafs. They had two great goaltenders in Sawchuk and Bower, and an older team that played a certain style. They were hooking and grabbing to slow us down. We couldn't play our own game and we were frustrated. They played it smart and won."

GAME TWO
April 22, 1967 – Toronto, 3 – Montreal, 0

It was the first of many spectacular performances by Leaf goaltender Johnny Bower, who drove Montreal's superstars to frustration. Pete Stemkowski tallied for the Leafs in the first period, Tim Horton and Mike Walton in the second. After that, the game belonged to Bower. Allan Stanley, the senior citizen of the 1967 Maple Leafs, has fond memories of the series, and still pays tribute to Terry Sawchuk and the evergreen Johnny Bower.

There's no doubt the two netminders had a sensational series, but "Ol' Sam," as Stanley was referred to by his friends, stood out with his intelligent play as a stay-at-home blue-liner.

"You don't win Stanley Cups without good goaltending," said Stanley. "And we had, in Sawchuk and Bower, the two best goalies in hockey. But our whole team played well as a unit.

"Punch was a good leader, and told us what to do. But we took it a step further. Even in the semi-finals, the players called a meeting and discussed strategy against the Black Hawks. We knew that Mikita and Hull were their big guns, and we said to each other that the guy closest to them will make sure the puck doesn't reach them. It's a time of the year when players have to be honest with each other. I mean the forwards and the defensemen. It worked well, and we knocked off Chicago.

"Prior to the final against Montreal, we had another meeting. We realized that if we let them into our end, we were going to lose. Davey Keon said that the defense has to stand up on the blue line, but that they can only do it if the wingers come back. Most of the series was played at center ice, because we kept them out of our end. In my view, that was the best team effort you'd want to see anywhere."

GAME THREE
April 25, 1967 – Montreal, 2 – Toronto, 3

It was a goaltenders' battle. Vachon was called on to handle sixty-two shots, while Bower's assignment included fifty-four. Despite the high shot totals, it was a true, close-checking playoff game. Béliveau and Stemkowski scored in the first period, with Pappin and John Ferguson evening the score at 2–2 after forty minutes of play. Bobby Pulford scored the winner at 8:26 of the second overtime period.

Bobby Baun was one of the Maple Leafs' most solid defenseman. He certainly was the hardest hitter, and his pain threshold didn't seem to exist. His performance in the Leafs' 1964 Stanley Cup win, when he scored an overtime winner and then played the seventh game of the series on a broken ankle, remains one of the NHL's most-repeated stories of athletic heroism. But three years later, he had had a misunderstanding with Punch Imlach and was used sparingly in the 1967 finals. Still, he remembers the series with fondness.

"There's no doubt about it that Montreal should have beaten us," he said. "We had older guys, who played way over their heads. Red Kelly also had an inspiring series, although it wasn't expected of him, since he was busy as a Member of Parliament in Ottawa. As for myself, I used to brag that I knew every inch of the Forum ice, which was true. But after my tiff with Punch, I learned everything about every inch of wood on the players' bench."

Bob Pulford taps in Pete Stemkowski's cross-crease pass to give the Leafs a 3–2 overtime win in game three of the 1967 finals.

GAME FOUR
April 27, 1967 – Montreal, 6 – Toronto, 2

Montreal's "Junior B" goaltender was in splendid form. So were the Habs' sharpshooters: particularly Jean Béliveau and Ralph Backstrom, each of whom contributed a pair of goals, the others going to Henri Richard and Jimmy Roberts. Johnny Bower hurt himself in the pre-game warm-up and was replaced by Sawchuk.

"Le Gros Bill," as Jean Béliveau was often called in the French-Canadian media, shudders even today when he thinks of Toronto's goaltending duo, whose heroics in the Leafs' crease could have resulted in charges of grand larceny, for all of the sure goals they stole from the Habs' sharpshooters.

Béliveau scored four goals in the six games, but against other netminders he may have doubled that output. He remembers one particular save by Sawchuk that almost made him cry.

"It was in the first period of the game that I walked in on Sawchuk," recalled Béliveau. "I lifted the puck, when, suddenly, his glove came out of nowhere, and gone was the glorious scoring chance. Sawchuk and Bower kept doing it to us throughout the series."

Every member of the Leafs stressed defensive hockey. "As the games went on," continued Béliveau, "I had the feeling that each of their players was responsible for an opponent. The checking was so close we felt like we each had a twin for a shadow. Nonetheless, it was a great series."

GAME FIVE
April 29, 1967 – Toronto, 4 – Montreal, 1

Punch Imlach assembled his players before the game and told them that this was the game they had to win. His rationale was simple: if the series went seven games, there would be little hope of beating the Canadiens in the deciding game at the Forum. By Imlach's logic, if the Leafs were to win, they would have to clinch the series in six games at home. And to win in six, they would have to take a 3–2 lead in the series by winning game five. The team, with Sawchuk in goal, responded, as Jimmy Pappin, Brian Conacher, Dave Keon, and Marcel Pronovost more than offset

Léon Rochefort's first goal of the game.

Superstition is usually part of a championship final, but when Punch Imlach was involved, it played a bigger role than usual. Bobby Haggert, who was the trainer of the Leafs in those years, was forced to assist Punch with his idiosyncrasies.

That year, towards the end of the regular schedule, Punch bought a new suit in Chicago, but didn't have a tie to go with it. He asked Haggert to go out and buy one. "I didn't want to waste too much time, so I just popped into the nearest shop and bought a tie," recalled Haggy. "It was my undoing, because we won that night and, being superstitious, Punch then asked me before each road game to go and buy him a tie.

"In the Montreal series Punch wore a brown suit. So when he sent me out to buy him a tie, I bought him one with seven hundred colors. It clashed so badly with his suit that he wore a scarf around his neck to hide the tie and told everyone he had a cold. We lost the game in Montreal, and he never asked me to buy a tie for him again. 'You dummy, I look like a neon sign,' he told me in no uncertain terms."

Montreals' speedy "Roadrunner," Yvan Cournoyer, is slowed down by a trio of Leafs – Hillman, Pronovost, and Sawchuk – as he attempts to pry the puck loose in the Leafs' crease.

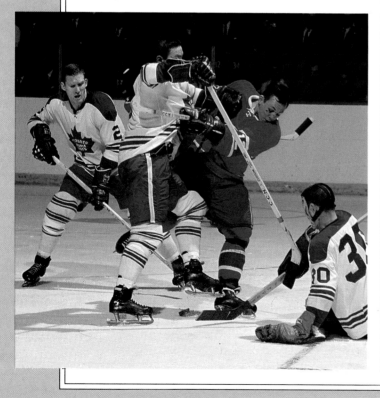

GAME SIX
May 2, 1967 – Montreal, 1 – Toronto, 3

Imlach's vision of how the series could unfold in the Leafs' favor came true in game six. Gump Worsley returned to the nets for the Canadiens, in what proved to be the deciding game of the finals. He and Sawchuk were brilliant in the first period, which ended in a goal-less tie. The Toronto crowd went wild in the second period, as the Leafs scored twice. Ron Ellis's goal opened the scoring before Jim Pappin's shot from the corner deflected off Montreal defenseman Terry Harper and past Worsley to give the Leafs a 2–0 lead. Former Leaf Dick Duff narrowed the margin with a goal for the Canadiens. With a minute to go in regulation time and the Canadiens trailing by a goal, Montreal coach Toe Blake yanked Worsley in favor of an extra attacker.

"Boy, those were thrilling moments," said Allan Stanley. "I remember that sixth and last game. Punch was walking up and down behind the bench, thinking. Then he sent out [Bob] Pulford, [George] Armstrong, [Red] Kelly, [Tim] Horton, and myself. I was the last guy over the boards when Punch called me back.

"He looked me in the eyes and said, 'You take the face-off.' I gave him a second look, and he said it again for the bench to hear: 'You take the face-off.' I hadn't taken a face-off for six or seven years. I skated out to the face-off circle and found Béliveau waiting for me. I kept thinking what to do. Then I decided to do what our guys always did – take a swipe at the puck and then take a run at the opposing center.

"I knew it would be face-off interference, but we had to gamble. I pulled the puck back to Kelly, slapped Béliveau's stick, and shoved my stick between his legs. Kelly passed the puck to Pulford, and he relayed it to Armstrong, who slid it into the empty net, while Béliveau was chasing after the referee calling for a face-off interference penalty, which the ref refused to call."

The Leafs were Cup champions.

Toronto's win was laced with a bit of sweet irony. That year, the city of Montreal was the site of the successful world's fair, Expo '67, and, as a gesture of thanks, the Czechoslovakian government presented the Montreal Canadiens with a crystal version of the

Stanley Cup. The Leafs hadn't even been invited to the presentation ceremony, let alone presented with a crystal trophy.

When it was all over, insiders began to talk about the immense rivalry that existed not only between Toronto and Montreal players and executives, but also between members of the media in the two cities. This rivalry was never more apparent than during the 1967 Stanley Cup finals.

Ralph Mellanby, Canada's most-often-honored television sports executive, had just been made executive producer of *Hockey Night in Canada* that year, and he found out how intense the rivalry was.

"It started with Punch, who told me that, 'The Leafs have to be on in the first three minutes of the first intermission.' Seconds later, Sammy Pollock approached me and demanded exactly the same time slot for the Canadiens. It was bizarre." The general managers of the two most successful hockey teams of the post-war era were competing over everything – even top billing on between-periods television interviews.

"Among the announcers, the Montreal games were called by Danny Gallivan, Dick Irvin, Jr., and Frank Selke, Jr. Toronto games were done by Brian McFarlane, Jack Dennett, and Ward Cornell. It was impossible to interchange them."

In some ways, the 1967 finals felt like a private family squabble. No American television coverage was offered, so games were broadcast only in Canada by the Canadian Broadcasting Corporation and by *Société Radio-Canada* in French. The cost to obtain the right to broadcast a game in the 1967 finals was just $5,000 – less than the cost of the airtime for one commercial during the 1992 Stanley Cup playoffs.

With NHL expansion and new color TV technology beckoning, 1966-67 saw some significant changes in *Hockey Night in Canada* broadcasts. For the first time, Foster Hewitt put on a HNIC jacket and tie and sat through a make-up session before going on the air to announce the game's three stars. Dick Irvin also made his television debut on HNIC that season, and it was during an interview with Irvin that Imlach repeated for the television audience what he thought of Rogatien Vachon.

Red Kelly, one of the heroes of Toronto's Over-the-Hill Gang, said: "There was an underlying knowledge for some of the guys that there won't be many more for us to win. For some of us, indeed, it was sort of a last shot."

It was, indeed. The Maple Leafs haven't appeared in the finals or won a Stanley Cup in the ensuing twenty-five years. But in the spring of 1967, no Hollywood scriptwriter could have stitched together a better thriller than one in which a bunch of old guys played their best hockey to win the game's most coveted trophy in the last year of the six-team NHL.

The 1967 Toronto Maple Leafs' honor role is proudly inscribed on the barrel of the Stanley Cup.

The Great Expansion,
1968-1979

O N JUNE 5, 1967, THE NHL OFFICIALLY ADDED NEW FRANCHISES IN Minnesota, Philadelphia, Oakland, Los Angeles, Pittsburgh, and St. Louis. The six new teams would comprise a new division – the West – and although there would be interdivisional play during the regular season, there would be no crossover in the playoffs until the finals, when the East Division champion would meet the West Division champion for the Stanley Cup.

For only the third time in NHL history the defending Stanley Cup champions missed the post-season, as the Leafs fell to fifth place. In the East Division playoffs, the Montreal Canadiens defeated the Bruins and the Black Hawks, losing only one game in the process. The first West Division title holders were the St. Louis Blues, who needed all fourteen games, including four overtime victories, to dispose of Philadelphia and Minnesota.

Although they were a new team, the St. Louis Blues had a number of future Hall-of-Famers in their line-up, many of them from the Montreal Canadiens' organization. Coach Scotty Bowman had spent nearly two decades coaching in the Habs' system, while Dickie Moore and Doug Harvey had been mainstays of the Habs' five consecutive Stanley Cup wins in the 1950s. Other Montreal alumni included Red Berenson, the first college player to move directly into the NHL when he joined the Habs in 1962, defensive specialist Jim Roberts, and defenseman Jean-Guy Talbot. Add Glenn Hall, Al Arbour, and brothers Barclay and Bob Plager to the line-up, and the Blues presented a formidable challenge to the Canadiens.

Any illusions the Canadiens may have had that this would be an easy series were quickly put to rest in the first game. St. Louis battled the Habs goal for goal through three periods, before Jacques Lemaire won it for the Canadiens after only 1:41 of overtime. In game two, Glenn Hall kept the game scoreless with a series of brilliant saves. Early in the third period, the Blues got their opportunity to take the lead when Dick Duff was called for

Opposite: Fog from the ice delayed play in the NHL's first all-expansion final series between the Philadelphia Flyers and the Buffalo Sabres in 1975. Here Jim Watson checks Buffalo's Jim Schoenfeld to the right of Conn Smythe Trophy-winning goaltender Bernie Parent.

elbowing by referee John Ashley. However, only twenty-two seconds later, Habs defenseman Serge Savard forced a St. Louis turnover and fired the puck through a maze of legs past a screened Glenn Hall. The Canadiens' defense smothered the Blues the rest of the way, allowing only three shots on goal for the 1–0 victory.

The third game featured another outstanding effort from Hall, who faced forty-six Montreal drives in the game. The Canadiens beat the St. Louis goaltender three times, while the Blues, who managed only fifteen shots at Worsley in the Canadiens' net, received a pair of goals from Berenson and a power-play marker from Frank St. Marseille to force the game into overtime. Montreal dominated the extra session, reeling off four quick shots as the Habs' Bobby Rousseau ended it only a minute into the extra period.

St. Louis took a 2–1 lead into the third period of game four, but the Canadiens got goals from Tremblay and Richard to earn a 3–2 victory and their fifteenth Stanley Cup. Glenn Hall was awarded the Conn Smythe Trophy, only the second player from a losing team to be so honored. While the Canadiens were still celebrating in the dressing room, Toe Blake announced that he was retiring after thirteen years as the coach of the Canadiens.

The Montreal Canadiens, with Claude Ruel replacing Blake behind the bench, finished atop the Eastern Division standings in 1968-69, compiling an NHL-record 103 points over the seventy-six-game schedule. However, much of the media's attention during the season was centered on the Boston Bruins, who, after a decade of mediocrity, fashioned the league's second-best record with a franchise-high forty-two wins and a hundred points. The rebirth of the Boston franchise that had begun with the addition of Bobby Orr, the most highly touted prospect in hockey, was completed when the Bruins obtained Ken Hodge, Phil Esposito, and Fred Stanfield prior to the 1967-68 season. The St. Louis Blues became the first expansion team to finish with a winning record, registering eighty-eight points on thirty-seven wins

Dick Duff deposits Jacques Lemaire's perfect pass behind Glenn Hall to give Montreal a 1–0 lead in game four of the 1968 finals.

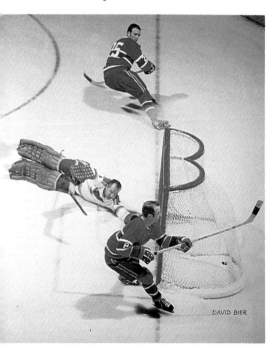

DAVID BIER

Dick Duff, Claude Provost, and coach Toe Blake gather around the Cup after Montreal's sweep of the St. Louis Blues in 1968. This was Blake's last victory as a coach and the last game played in the Montreal Forum before the facility underwent major renovations to increase seating capacity and eliminate the pillars that are visible in this photo.

and fourteen ties. Phil Esposito, the offensive leader of the Bruins, became the first player to break the hundred-point plateau. He was later joined by Bobby Hull and Gordie Howe in reaching the century mark for points that season.

In the East Division playoffs, the Canadiens swept the Rangers four straight, then captured a hard-fought six-game set against a determined Boston Bruins squad. The Habs needed three overtime victories, including a double-overtime clincher in game six, to advance to the finals. St. Louis had a much easier route, sweeping past both the Flyers and the Kings to earn a return bout with the Canadiens.

The Blues added another ex-Canadien to the fold in 1969. Jacques Plante came out of retirement and immediately paid handsome dividends for St. Louis, combining with Glenn Hall to win the Vezina Trophy. The Canadiens opened the finals by registering power-play and shorthanded goals in the first five minutes of game one to take a quick 2–0 lead. Despite Frank St. Marseille narrowing the gap near the end of the first period, the St. Louis offense couldn't get untracked, and the Blues dropped the opener, 3–1.

For the second consecutive outing, the Canadiens limited the Blues to five shots on goal in the opening period of game two, while mounting a three-goal offensive effort of their own. A power-play goal by Dick Duff proved to be the winner in a 3–1 Montreal triumph. The Blues mounted a more balanced attack back on home ice in game three, but they were continually frustrated by Rogie Vachon, who turned away all twenty-nine shots he faced to earn his first career post-season shutout in a contest that finished 4–0.

The fourth game saw referee Vern Buffey call twenty penalties in the first two periods alone. The aggressive Blues' attack paid early dividends, and they nursed a 1–0 lead through two periods. However, only forty-three

Going Out a Winner

Toe Blake, who won three Cups as a player, holds the record for most Cup wins as a coach, leading the Montreal Canadiens to eight championships. Blake won the Cup in his first year behind the bench in 1955 and his last in 1968.

Gerry Cheevers, whose mask has not yet been adorned with its trademark stitches, stages an in-crease battle with Montreal tough guy John Ferguson during the 1969 semi-finals.

Playoff Postponements

The assassination of Dr. Martin Luther King, Jr., forced the postponement of three series games during the quarter-final round of the 1968 Stanley Cup playoffs. Match-ups between the Rangers and Chicago, St. Louis and Philadelphia, and Minnesota and Los Angeles were delayed by a minimum of two days.

Serge Savard was the first defenseman to win the Conn Smythe Trophy.

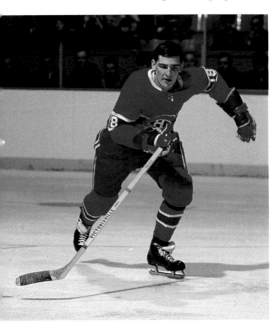

seconds after the opening face-off in the third period, Ted Harris fooled Glenn Hall with a shot from the point to swing the momentum back in the Habs' favor. Montreal left-winger John Ferguson scored the game – and Cup – winner two minutes later on a feed from Ralph Backstrom, and the Canadiens had captured their ninth Stanley Cup in fourteen seasons.

Serge Savard, whose dependable work along the Habs' blue line helped to limit the opposition to twenty-eight goals in fourteen post-season games, became the first defenseman to win the Conn Smythe Trophy.

The 1969-70 season featured a dramatic playoff battle in the East Division. Only seven points separated first from fifth in the East, with Montreal missing the playoffs, despite compiling ninety-two points. Toronto joined Montreal on the sidelines, marking the first time in NHL history that Canada was not represented in the playoffs. Bobby Orr became the first defenseman to win the league scoring title, registering 120 points, including an NHL record eighty-seven assists. The St. Louis Blues continued to be the toast of the West, outdistancing their nearest rival by eighteen points. In the early playoff rounds, the Bruins scrambled to defeat the Rangers in six games, then easily swept the Black Hawks in four games. The Blues earned their third consecutive trip to the Cup finals by eliminating both the North Stars and the Penguins, using victories in the fifth and sixth games in each series to earn the berth.

The Blues were no match for the Bruins in the opener, allowing a four-goal third period by a quartet of marksmen for Boston's 6–1 victory. John Bucyk, appearing in his first Stanley Cup final since 1958, paced the Bruins' attack with a goal in each period to record his first post-season three-goal game. In the second game, Eddie Westfall was the offensive hero, firing a pair of goals in the first period, including the eventual game-winner, as Boston rolled to a convincing 6–2 victory over St. Louis.

In game three, Frank St. Marseille gave the Blues an early lead, while Boston rear guard Don Awrey served a boarding infraction, but the Bruins quickly responded on tallies off the sticks of Bucyk and John McKenzie to take a 2–1 lead into the third period. Wayne Cashman sealed the Bruins' win with two goals in the final stanza to pull Boston to within a single victory of their first Stanley Cup in twenty-nine years.

If the Bruins felt the Blues were going to hand the championship to them meekly, those thoughts were quickly dispelled in the early moments of the

The 1968-69 Montreal Canadiens lost only two games en route to their fifth Cup win of the decade.

Gagnants de la coupe Stanley et du trophée Prince de Galles
Stanley Cup and Prince of Wales Trophy winners

1ère rangée—1st row: Sam Pollock, vice-président & gérant général—Vice-President & General Manager; Jean Béliveau, capitaine—Captain; Peter Molson, vice-président—Vice-President; J. David Molson, président—President; William Molson, vice-président—Vice-President; Henri Richard, Claude Ruel, instructeur—Coach. 2ème rangée—2nd row: Lorne Worsley, Jacques Lemaire, Dick Duff, Ralph Backstrom, Robert Rousseau, Yvan Cournoyer, Gilles Tremblay, Rogatien Vachon. 3ème rangée—3rd row: Larry Aubut, entraîneur—Trainer; Ted Harris, Christian Bordeleau, Claude Provost, Mickey Redmond, Jean-Claude Tremblay, Eddy Palchak. 4ème rangée—4th row: Serge Savard, Larry Hillman, John Ferguson, Jacques Laperrière, Terry Harper.

Gerry Cheevers makes a nifty toe save as Bruins' rear guards Dallas Smith (20) and Rick Smith (10) defend against St. Louis forwards Tim Ecclestone (14) and Larry Keenan.

Stanley Cup Bookends

Claude Provost, a fifteen-year veteran of the Montreal Canadiens, and Cooney Weiland, who played eleven years for Boston, Detroit, and Ottawa, are the only players to spend at least a decade in the NHL and win the Stanley Cup in both their first and last seasons in the league.

fourth game. The Blues played a rugged game, body-checking the Bruins from whistle to whistle, but Boston got on the board first, when defenseman Rick Smith neatly beat Glenn Hall on a cross-ice feed from Derek Sanderson. However, a last-minute, first-period goal by Red Berenson and an early second-period marker by Gary Sabourin gave St. Louis what was only their second lead of the series. Esposito evened the affair for Boston, but Larry Keenan countered at the nineteen-second mark of the third period to once again give the Blues the lead. The Bruins turned on the offensive heat, and the resulting pressure earned them the tying goal with just over six minutes remaining in the contest. The teams remained deadlocked through the rest of regulation time, setting up the first overtime drama in the series.

The Bruins controlled the tempo of the extra period from the opening draw, quickly moving the puck into the offensive zone. Bobby Orr, who had had yet to score in the finals, slid the puck to Derek Sanderson, who was stationed behind the Blues net. Orr, on the receiving end of the give-and-go, took Sanderson's pass and flipped the puck behind a sprawling Glenn Hall to give the Bruins the title and Boston the championship denied them for three decades. Just as the puck entered the net, Blues defenseman Noel Picard pulled Orr's skates out from under him, sending him sailing through the air. The photo of the Bruins' defenseman, in mid-air but already celebrating his goal, is one of the enduring images in Stanley Cup history.

Two new teams entered the NHL fold in 1970-71. The Vancouver Canucks and the Buffalo Sabres both joined the East Division, while Chicago was shifted to the West. The playoff format was modified so that the league's two divisions crossed over in the second round of the playoffs.

The Hawks easily took control of their new division, finishing with 107 points, the third-best record in the league. However, the NHL's dominant team was the "Big Bad Bruins." In the fifty-three-year history of the NHL, no team had ever scored more than 303 goals in a single season. The Bruins came within a single goal of scoring 400, settling for 399 for the campaign. The Bruins roster featured the top four scorers in the league and six of the top eight, led by Phil Esposito, who established NHL records for goals (76) and points (152) in a single season. Boston's 57 wins and 121 points were also new NHL marks, making the Bruins heavy favorites to repeat as Stanley Cup champions. However, the favorites would soon be victims of a first-round playoff upset.

In one of the most dramatic playoff series of all time, the Montreal Canadiens defeated the powerhouse Bruins in seven incredible games. Much of the credit for the Canadiens' stunning upset went to goaltender Ken Dryden, a lanky graduate of Cornell University and the Canadian National Team, whom the Habs promoted from their Nova Scotia farm team towards the end of the regular season. Dryden stymied the Bruins with a series of

One of the most famous images in the history of Stanley Cup competition, Bobby Orr's Cup-winning goal in the 1970 finals. Orr's defensive partner Dallas Smith, who observed number four's bold dash into the Blues' zone, was particularly pleased with Orr's efforts. If Orr's gamble had failed, the Blues would have had a four-on-one break, and, as Smith points out, "I would have been the one."

The Chief, Johnny Bucyk, accepts the first Stanley Cup to be awarded to a Boston Bruin since Dit Clapper received the prize in 1941.

remarkable saves, and the Canadiens, buoyed by the upset, moved past Minnesota in the semi-finals to reach the Stanley Cup finals for the sixteenth time in twenty-one seasons. The Chicago Black Hawks emerged as the West Division's representative in the finals by sweeping the Philadelphia Flyers and edging the New York Rangers in a tight seven-game series.

With a full house at Chicago Stadium cheering them on, the Hawks mounted an overwhelming offensive barrage at the young Dryden and his Canadiens' teammates in game one of the finals. The Hawks fired forty-six shots at the Habs' net in regulation, but needed a third-period goal by Bobby

Ken Dryden, whose outstanding performance during the 1971 playoffs was rewarded with the Conn Smythe Trophy, is the only player to win a major NHL award before earning rookie-of-the-year honors.

Hull to gain a 1–1 draw going into overtime. The first stanza of extra time was also scoreless, necessitating the first double overtime in the finals since 1967. Two minutes into the second overtime period, Jim Pappin propelled a pass from Bill White past Dryden to give the Hawks the early series lead.

Chicago continued to force the play in the second contest, using a pair of third-period goals by Lou Angotti to edge the Canadiens, 5–3. The tables were turned in game three at the Montreal Forum, as the Habs outshot the Black Hawks, 40–18, and pulled to within a game of Chicago with a 4–2 victory. Frank Mahovlich, playing perhaps the finest hockey of his distinguished career, led the attack with a pair of goals. Montreal completed the home-ice sweep in the fourth game, as Yvan Cournoyer scored a pair of goals in the Habs' 5–2 triumph.

Defense was the key in game five, as the Hawks capitalized on Tony Esposito's thirty-one saves to shut out the Habs, 2–0. Dennis Hull's power-play marker, midway through the first period, stood up as the winning goal to put Chicago within a win of its first Stanley Cup championship in ten seasons. However, the Mahovlich brothers, Frank and Peter, put the Chicago celebration on ice in game six, figuring in all four of the Canadiens' goals in a 4–3 victory. The key goal of the game, and perhaps of the series, was Peter Mahovlich's shorthanded winning tally, scored only ten seconds after Réjean Houle went into the box.

There was an overriding air of tension in Chicago Stadium as the teams prepared for the finale of the first final series to go seven games since 1965. Henri Richard, who had been benched early in the series, was in the line-up

Stanley Before Calder

Tony Esposito and Danny Grant both won the Stanley Cup one year and the Calder Trophy the next with different teams. Grant was a member of the 1968 Cup-winning Montreal Canadiens before winning the Calder as the NHL's top rookie in 1969 with Minnesota. Tony Esposito won the Cup with the Canadiens in 1969 and the Calder Trophy the following season with the Chicago Black Hawks. A player remains eligible for the Calder if he has played twenty-five or fewer NHL regular-season games.

Frank Mahovlich, who was often criticized for his previous post-season performances, played the most consistent hockey of his career during the 1971 playoffs.

The Oldest Goalie

When Johnny Bower appeared in his last playoff game on April 6, 1969, at the age of 44 years, 4 months, and 28 days, he became the oldest goalie to don the pads for a playoff game in NHL history. Lester Patrick at 44 years, 3 months, and 8 days and Jacques Plante at 44 years, 2 months, and 19 days are more-than-honorable mentions.

for the deciding game and, in typical Richardian fashion, was the catalyst in Montreal's 3–2 Stanley Cup-winning victory. Chicago, on goals by Danny O'Shea and Dennis Hull, carried a 2–0 lead in the late stages of the second period, but Jacques Lemaire and Richard scored four minutes apart to send the teams to the dressing room tied at two. Richard emerged heroic in the third period, scoring the eventual Cup-winning goal at the 2:34 mark, then helping his teammates kill a pair of penalties to make the slim margin hold up. Frank Mahovlich set a new playoff record for goals (14) and points (27), and goaltender Ken Dryden won the Conn Smythe Trophy, becoming the first rookie to receive the award.

The Boston Bruins returned to the top of the NHL heap in 1972, losing only thirteen games over a seventy-eight-game schedule. Phil Esposito captured his second consecutive Art Ross Trophy, while teammate Bobby Orr compiled his third straight 100-point campaign. The New York Rangers finished second in the league, compiling a franchise-high 109 points, while allowing only 192 goals, the third-lowest total in the NHL. The stars of the Rangers' run on Broadway were the members of the Goal-A-Game Line, Rod Gilbert, Jean Ratelle, and Vic Hadfield, who finished third, fourth, and fifth in the scoring race.

Shouldering the responsibility. Henri Richard hoists the Stanley Cup and prepares to give the trophy a stately tour of the Chicago Stadium ice surface following the Habs' seven-game victory over the Hawks in 1971.

The Bruins carried grim memories of their shocking playoff exit in 1971 and easily disposed of the Toronto Maple Leafs in five games, then eliminated St. Louis, outscoring the Blues 28–8 in a four-game sweep. The New York Rangers, who surprised many experts with a six-game series victory over Montreal, sidelined the Black Hawks in four straight games to earn a berth in the finals for the first time since 1950.

The Rangers fell victim to Boston's offensive power in the first game of the finals. After Dale Rolfe had given New York an early 1–0 lead, the Bruins countered with four unanswered goals, including a final-series record of two shorthanded goals scored during the same penalty. After the squads traded goals in the second period, the Rangers started fast in the third, firing a trio of goals to tie the game 5–5, with ten minutes remaining. The match appeared to be headed into overtime when Garnet Bailey scored the second, and last, playoff goal of his career to give the Bruins a 6–5 triumph in the opener.

Bobby Orr and Brad Park were the league's dominant defensemen in the early 1970s, sharing the blueliners' spots on the First All-Star Team on three occasions.

Bobby Rousseau, who once scored five goals in a game for Montreal, led the New York Rangers into the 1972 finals with seventeen points in the playoffs.

The second game was a tight-checking affair that was undecided until Ken Hodge, on assists from Mike Walton and Phil Esposito, beat Ed Giacomin low to the stick side on a third-period power play. Hodge's goal stood up for a 2–1 Boston win.

Many of the Madison Square Garden faithful were still shuffling into the arena when Brad Park tallied a power-play goal to give the Rangers an early lead in game three. By the thirteen-minute mark of the opening period, the Rangers had added another pair of power-play markers to increase their lead to 3–0. Although the Bruins fought back on goals by Orr and Walton to close the gap to one, Rod Gilbert and Pete Stemkowski delivered insurance markers to secure the Rangers' 5–2 win.

The two teams checked each other closely in the first period of game four, but Bobby Orr managed to slip two of Boston's five first-period shots past Ed Giacomin to give the Bruins a lead they would never surrender. Don Marcotte upped the ante to three, with a shorthanded goal in the second stanza, before Ted Irvine finally got the Rangers on the board near the conclusion of the second period. Rod Seiling brought the Rangers close with a power-play goal in the dying minutes, but the Bruins' defense held the fort, and Boston stood perched on the Stanley Cup threshold with a 3–2 win.

For the first forty-three minutes of the fifth game, it appeared that the Boston Garden faithful would be treated to their second on-ice Stanley Cup victory celebration in three years, but the Rangers rebounded from a 2–1 third-period deficit to stave off elimination. Two goals by Bobby Rousseau, coupled with a thirty-six-save performance from Ed Giacomin, sent the Rangers back to Madison Square Garden, trailing 3–2 in games.

The Big Bad Bruins were at their opportunistic best in the early going of game six. With Walt Tkaczuk off for hooking, Bobby Orr scored what turned out to be the Cup-winning goal. A pair of third-period goals by Wayne Cashman sealed the victory, as the Bruins rode the shutout goaltending of Gerry Cheevers to a 3–0 Cup-clinching win. Bobby Orr became the first two-time winner of the Conn Smythe Trophy, earning the post-season MVP award with twenty-four playoff points.

A rival league appeared on the hockey horizon in 1972, with the emergence of the World Hockey Association. The WHA convinced a number of established stars, including Bobby Hull, Derek Sanderson, Gerry Cheevers, Bernie Parent, and J. C. Tremblay, to leave the NHL and sign on with the fledgling league.

The 1971-72 Boston Bruins were the last team to capture the Cup before the advent of the WHA. In 1973, the Bruins lost starters Derek Sanderson, Johnny McKenzie, Gerry Cheevers, Wayne Carleton, and Ted Green to the rival league and were unable to defend their Stanley Cup title.

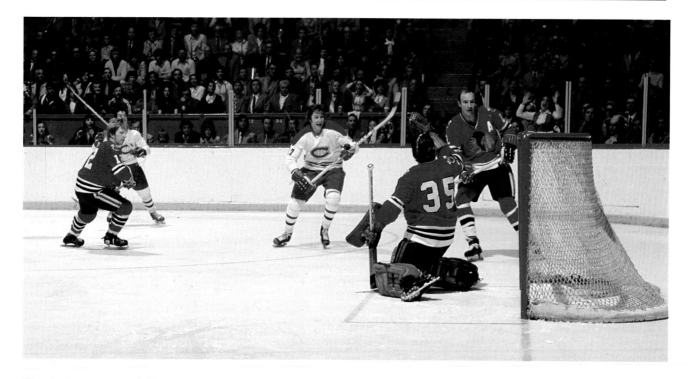

Claude Larose, partially obscured in this photo by Chicago's Pat Stapleton, scored two goals in the first five minutes of the second period of game five of the 1979 finals. Larose's markers opened the floodgates, as both teams combined to score a final-series record eight goals in the period. Montreal rookie Murray Wilson and Chicago rear guard Bill White look on.

The NHL expanded once again for 1972-73, adding franchises in Long Island (the New York Islanders) and Atlanta (the Flames). At the conclusion of the regular season, Montreal, Boston, Chicago, and New York once again finished at the top of the standings.

Another change in the playoff setup affected match-ups in the first round. Under the new system, the first-place club would play the fourth-place finisher, while second would play third. The old setup, in effect since 1943, had seen first play third and second play fourth.

In the playoffs, the Canadiens fought off a determined Buffalo squad in six games, then met an equally resolute Philadelphia team. Although Montreal ousted the Flyers in five games, all the matches were decided by slim margins. Led by Hart Trophy-winner Bobby Clarke, the Flyers gave evidence they were on the verge of post-season success.

The defending Cup champion Boston Bruins entered the post-season crippled by injuries that limited the effectiveness of Phil Esposito and Bobby Orr. Boston fell to the Rangers in five games. The Broadway Blues, however, were quickly dispatched from the post-season by Chicago, setting up a rematch battle between the league's best netminders, Tony Esposito and Ken Dryden.

Although the series was promoted as a goaltenders' duel, it turned out to be a goal-scorers' feast, establishing numerous offensive records. The stage was set in the first game, which featured five first-period goals on only eighteen shots. Chicago escaped the first twenty minutes with a 3–2 advantage, but the Habs responded with six unanswered tallies, to pull away with an easy 8–3 win. Chuck Lefley, held scoreless in thirty-one career playoff games, fired a pair of goals for the Canadiens.

Defense prevailed in the second game. Montreal took control of the match midway through the second period, scoring three straight goals, two by Yvan Cournoyer, to take a two-game lead in the series with a 4–1 win. The Black Hawks received a well-needed boost from their special teams in game three at the Chicago Stadium. Scoring early and often in the first period, the Hawks built a 4–0 advantage on pairs of power-play and shorthanded goals. After John Marks made it 5–0 for Chicago, the Canadiens responded with four goals of their own, but the Hawks were able to weather the storm, adding two empty-net markers for a 7–4 final.

As was the case in the second contest, the Canadiens' defense once again stood firm in game four, allowing the Hawks only nineteen shots, as Dryden shut out Chicago 4–0. Marc Tardif had the winning goal and added an assist to lead the Habs' attack. The defensive lessons of the previous match were quickly forgotten in the fifth game, as the teams did very little checking – only two minor penalties were called in the entire game – and settled in for a good old-fashioned game of shinny. The finalists combined for twelve goals on forty-five shots through the first forty minutes of play. Eight goals were scored in the second period alone, five of them by Chicago, as the Hawks built a 7–5 margin. The Habs pulled to within one early in the third period, but Lou Angotti scored the eventual game-winner in this 8–7 shootout.

Game six opened with a similar display of firepower, thanks to a pair of goals by Chicago's Pit Martin. The Hawks seemed sure bets to carry that advantage into the dressing room, but Henri Richard converted a Frank Mahovlich pass, with only seconds left on the clock, to make it 2–1. The Habs poured it on in the second stanza, finally pulling into the lead on a power-play goal by Frank Mahovlich. However, Pit Martin put the finishing touches on his hat trick to pull the teams even after two periods. In the third, Montreal threw a defensive blanket over the Hawks, limiting them to four shots. Fittingly, the Habs got the last goal they would need in the 1972-73 season from Yvan Cournoyer, whose fifteenth tally set a playoff record and gave the Canadiens a lead they would never surrender. Marc Tardif potted an insurance goal, as the Habs won their eighteenth Stanley Cup championship with the 6–4 victory. Cournoyer was awarded the Conn Smythe Trophy for leading all post-season snipers, with fifteen goals and twenty-five points.

The 1973-74 campaign featured the arrival of a new NHL powerhouse. The Philadelphia Flyers, who had reached the .500 level only once since joining the league in 1968, became the first expansion team to reach the 100-point plateau, finishing the season with 112 points, the second-best total in the NHL. Known as "the Broad Street Bullies" because of their willingness to do whatever was necessary to win, the Flyers were well coached by Fred Shero, using strong defense and opportunistic offense to win fifty games in the regular season. Continuing their impressive play throughout the playoffs, the Flyers easily dispatched the Atlanta Flames in straight games,

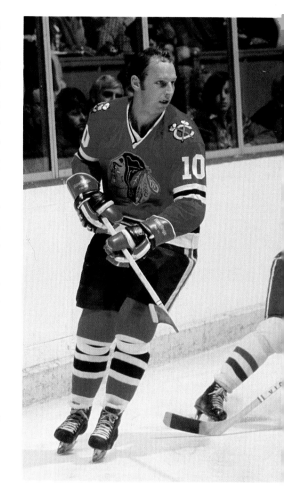

Although he played much of his career in the shadow of his famous brother, Dennis Hull's abilities were finally recognized after the Golden Jet left Chicago. In the 1973 playoffs, the younger Hull compiled twenty-four points, three shy of the single-playoff-year record held jointly at that time by Phil Esposito and Frank Mahovlich.

then emerged victorious from a seven-game marathon with the New York Rangers. The outcome of that series was in doubt until the final moments, when the Rangers were penalized for having too many men on the ice as they attempted to replace their goaltender with an extra attacker, and the Flyers iced the set with a 4–3 win.

On the other side of the playoff slate, the Boston Bruins returned to the finals with convincing series wins over Toronto and Chicago, setting up a final series match-up between the Bruins and the Flyers. As expected, Boston was a heavy favorite to win the Cup, having never lost a playoff game to an expansion opponent.

The series opened at the Boston Garden, where the Flyers had not tasted victory since their first visit in 1968. Tentative in the early going, the Flyers just seemed to be gaining confidence when the Bruins erupted for a pair of goals less than a minute apart. Wayne Cashman banged in Carol Vadnais's rebound on a power play, and Gregg Sheppard scored on the next shift to give the Bruins a 2–0 advantage. To their credit, however, the Flyers didn't

Although the predicted goaltenders' battle between Chicago's "Tony O" and Montreal's Ken Dryden in the 1973 finals never materialized, both made a number of outstanding saves, including this showstopper by Esposito off the playoff's leading scorer, Yvan Cournoyer.

fold. Taking advantage of the opportunites presented them, the Flyers fought back on tallies from Orest Kindrachuk and Bobby Clarke to tie the game. However, with overtime looming, Bobby Orr converted a Wayne Cashman feed past Parent at the 19:38 mark to give the Bruins the series lead.

Early in the second contest, the Flyers still appeared to be reeling from Orr's late goal in game one, as the Bruins built up another two-goal first-period advantage. Undaunted, the Flyers kept pressing, finally tying the match with some late-game magic of their own. With only fifty-two seconds left on the clock, and Parent on the bench for an extra attacker, Philadelphia forced overtime when Andre "Moose" Dupont pounced on a loose puck in a goal-mouth scramble. The Flyers knew that, if they were to have any chance of winning this series, they had to win one of the first two games in Boston Garden. They accomplished this feat when Bobby Clarke tapped home a rebound at the twelve-minute mark of the first overtime period to send the teams to the Spectrum tied at a game apiece.

As the home team for games three and four, the Flyers had the advantage

Thanks to the efforts of Bernie Parent and Ed Van Impe, the Philadelphia Flyers survived a seven-game marathon with the New York Rangers to enter their first-ever championship final. The Rangers introduced the practice of stitching players' names on the backs of their jerseys in this playoff year.

The spiritual and offensive leader of the Flyers, Bobby Clarke wasn't intimidated by the physical game, taking every opportunity to practice what he preached.

Kate Smith delivers the knockout punch to the Bruins with a rousing rendition of "God Bless America" prior to game six.

of being able to make the last player change whenever there was a stoppage in play. This enabled Shero's players to execute their game plan of neutralizing Bobby Orr and shutting down the Bruins' big three of Esposito, Hodge, and Cashman. In game three, the Broad Streeters allowed an early goal by John Bucyk, then stormed back with four straight of their own in a 4–1 win. In game four, the Bruins unwisely attempted to match the Flyers' physical style. Although Boston held on through forty minutes, the Flyers had the staying power, converting a pair of scoring chances in the final period to grab a 4–2 victory and a 3–1 lead in games. The Flyers stood one win away from their first championship.

The fifth game of the series saw twenty roughing and fighting infractions called. The resulting four-on-four and three-on-three situations opened up the ice for Bobby Orr, who responded with two goals and an assist in Boston's 5–1 victory. Returning to Philadelphia, the Flyers tried to gain an inspirational edge by having Kate Smith appear before game six to sing "God Bless America." The club had frequently used a taped version of Miss Smith's rousing rendition of the patriotic anthem and had had an incredible run of success when it was played. It was their hope that her appearance in person would give the team an added boost. As it turned out, the only lift the Flyers needed was provided by the glove hand of goaltender Bernie Parent, who stopped all thirty shots fired his way. Rick MacLeish's deflection of Moose Dupont's point drive in the first period was all the offense the Flyers required, and Parent did the rest. A late third-period penalty to Bobby Orr stalled the Bruins' attack, and, when the final siren sounded, the Flyers had become the first expansion team to win the Stanley Cup. Bernie Parent, whose expertise between the pipes prompted a placard reading "Only God saves more than Parent," was awarded the Conn Smythe Trophy.

Another expansion added the Kansas City Scouts and the Washington Capitals to the NHL for 1974-75 and prompted the league to realign its eighteen teams into two conferences – the Wales and the Campbell – and four divisions – the Norris, Smythe, Patrick, and Adams. This new divisional structure brought with it a revamped playoff format. Under the new system, twelve teams qualified for post-season play. The four division winners received a bye to the quarter-final round. The second- and third-place finishers in each division were required to play a best-of-three preliminary round series. Clubs participating in this round were ranked from one to eight, based on points in the regular-season standings. The team ranked first would play the team ranked eighth; second would play seventh; third would play sixth; and fourth would play fifth. The four preliminary-round winners and the four division winners would then be grouped and ranked in the same manner for a best-of-seven quarter-final round. The four quarter-final winners would be similarly ranked for semi-final play.

Philadelphia, Buffalo, and Montreal tied for the league lead with 113 points, with the Flyers earning first place by virtue of having won the greatest number of games. The Flyers earned their second consecutive trip to the finals, but not without some anxious moments. After disposing of the Leafs in four straight games, they collided with the New York Islanders, who, at the expense of the Pittsburgh Penguins, had become only the second team in NHL history to rebound from a 3–0 series deficit and win. After winning the first three matches, the Flyers watched as the Islanders rallied to tie their series at three games apiece. Lightning did not strike twice, however, as Philadelphia ended the Islanders' Cinderella story with a 4–1 verdict in the seventh game.

Meanwhile, the Buffalo Sabres earned their first berth in the Stanley Cup finals by downing Chicago and Montreal to set up the first all-expansion final in league history. Built on offensive speed and defensive stability, the Sabres, with their French Connection Line of Gilbert Perreault, Rick Martin,

The 1973-74 Philadelphia Flyers, the first modern-era expansion franchise to have its name inscribed on the Stanley Cup.

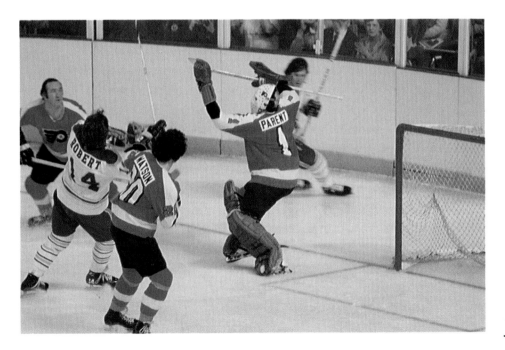

Bernie Parent and teammates Jimmy Watson and Ed Van Impe join Buffalo's René Robert in corralling an airborne puck during the 1975 finals.

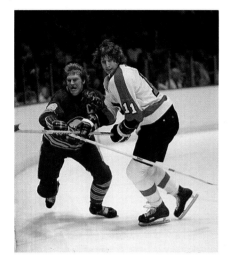

Jim Schoenfeld and Don Saleski battle along the boards during the NHL's first all-expansion final.

Penalty Shot Drought

A total of six penalty shots have been awarded in the Stanley Cup finals, but none of them have resulted in goals. Alex Shibicky, Virgil Johnson, Frank Mahovlich, Ron Sutter, Dave Poulin, and Petr Klima were the unlucky shooters. Earl Robertson, Bill Durnan, Tony Esposito, Grant Fuhr (twice), and Réjean Lemelin were in goal.

and René Robert, reminded many of a youthful Canadiens team. In goal, the Sabres' tandem of Gerry Desjardins and Roger Crozier was matched against the Flyers' Bernie Parent, who proved difficult to beat in the opening game of the series. Although Buffalo matched the Flyers shift for shift through two periods, outshooting the defending champs 22–10 at the Spectrum, they couldn't beat Parent. In the third period, the Flyers erupted with four goals on only twelve shots to grab the early series advantage with a 4–1 win.

Both teams played cautious hockey in the second game. After a scoreless first period, Reggie "the Rifle" Leach opened the scoring for the Flyers, but an early third-period goal by Gerry Korab evened the score. Only twenty seconds after Don Luce of the Sabres was penalized for hooking, however, Bobby Clarke potted the game-winner for Philadelphia. The Flyers allowed the Sabres only one shot after Clarke's goal and took a commanding two-game lead in the series.

As the series shifted to Buffalo, the Sabres were confident that the smaller ice surface of Buffalo's Memorial Auditorium would provide them with an advantage. And they were right. Buffalo withstood an early two-goal barrage from the Flyers to mount a forty-six-shot attack of their own. René Robert's overtime goal gave the Sabres new life, while a determined effort in the fourth match earned Buffalo a hard-fought 4–2 decision. A key to both games was the ability of Buffalo coach Floyd Smith to get the Perreault line away from Fred Shero's relentless checkers. As a result, Perreault recorded his first points in the finals to help the Sabres tie the series.

Back in Philadelphia, the Flyers exhibited resolve and poise, taking only four minor penalties in game five. The Sabres were unable to mount much of an attack and lost, 5–1. The Flyers' five goals were scored on only twenty-six shots. In the sixth game, Buffalo fired twenty-six shots at Parent in the first two periods, but the future Hall-of-Famer got a toe or a glove on all of them. With Parent performing magic in the nets, the Flyers could afford to wait patiently for their opportunities. Philadelphia received all the offense it needed from "Hound Dog" Bob Kelly, who shook off a Sabre defender and steamed in from the corner to beat Crozier only eleven seconds into the third period. Bill Clement added an insurance goal, as the Flyers clinched the Cup with a 2–0 shutout victory. Bernie Parent became the first back-to-back Conn Smythe Trophy recipient, with four shutouts and a post-season goals-against average of 1.89.

The Montreal Canadiens returned to the summit of the NHL in 1975-76. With Art Ross Trophy-winner Guy Lafleur providing the offense, and Vezina Trophy recipient Ken Dryden stabilizing the defense, the Habs collected an NHL record 58 wins and 127 points. The Flyers, Sabres, Bruins, and Islanders also broke the 100-point barrier, with the Flyers reaching the finals. The Flyers survived a grueling seven-game series with the Leafs that saw both Toronto's Darryl Sittler and Philadelphia's Reggie Leach tie Newsy Lalonde's

and Maurice Richard's NHL post-season record with five goals in a single game. The Flyers dropped the first game of their semi-final to the Bruins before rolling off four consecutive wins to reach the finals for the third year running. The Canadiens had an easier route, sweeping the Hawks in straight games and downing the Islanders in five.

In what many considered a dream match-up, the Flyers and the Canadiens faced off for the Stanley Cup in the Montreal Forum on May 9. The Flyers may have been older and wiser, but the Habs were younger, faster, and more skilled. Perhaps the most impressive aspect of the Canadiens' attack was the mobility of their defensemen. With Larry Robinson, Guy Lapointe, and Serge Savard continually cruising through the offensive zone, the Habs persistently frustrated their opponents' defensive strategies. Another important ingredient was missing in the Flyers' attack. Bernie Parent, injured for most of the season, was fighting the puck, forcing Shero to go with back-up Wayne Stephenson.

The Philadelphia Flyers pose proudly with silverware earned from a successful 1974-75 season. Left to right: the Conn Smythe Trophy, the Hart Trophy, the Stanley Cup, the Clarence Campbell Bowl, and the Vezina Trophy.

Larry "Big Bird" Robinson flies past Philadelphia's Joe Watson during the 1976 Stanley Cup finals.

Reggie "the Rifle" Leach fired a record nineteen goals during the 1976 playoffs, a mark equaled by Edmonton's Jari Kurri in 1985.

The Flyers started strongly in the series opener, scoring a goal only twenty-one seconds after the initial face-off. After Montreal fought back to tie, a third-period power-play tally by Larry Goodenough gave the Flyers a 3–2 lead. Jacques Lemaire quickly got that one back, and when Guy Lapointe beat Stephenson with less than two minutes remaining, the Habs had posted a 4–3 come-from-behind victory. Montreal continued to frustrate the Flyers with close checking in the second match, using a pair of unassisted goals by Lemaire and Lafleur to seal a 2–1 win and give them a commanding two-game series margin.

After surrendering a power-play goal to Steve Shutt early in the third game, the Flyers rebounded to take a 2–1 lead on a pair of goals by Reggie Leach. However, Gary Dornhoefer took an elbowing penalty at the expiration of the period, and the Canadiens used the resulting man advantage to tie the score, Shutt registering his second power-play goal of the game in the first minute of the second stanza. The teams battled through another twenty-eight minutes of scoreless hockey before Pierre Bouchard tallied the winning goal to put Montreal a single win away from the Stanley Cup.

Game four was played in a sweltering Spectrum, conditions that clearly favored Scotty Bowman's strategy of short shifts for the Canadiens. Reggie Leach scored the Flyers' first goal for the third time in the series, converting a feed from rookie Mel Bridgman at the forty-one-second mark of the first period. The two teams went on to score five consecutive power-play goals, leaving the score knotted at 3–3 after two periods of play. With under six minutes remaining in regulation time, Guy Lafleur scored what proved to be the Cup-winning goal. Peter Mahovlich added another goal fifty-eight

Philadelphia's Terry Crisp, who would later add a Stanley Cup ring to his collection as the coach of the Calgary Flames, heads up-ice with Montreal's Rick Chartraw in pursuit.

seconds later, and the Montreal Canadiens had ended the Flyers' reign as Stanley Cup champions. "They have the biggest, most mobile defense in the world," Fred Shero admitted. "All of them skate and shoot like forwards." Reggie Leach, who set an NHL record with nineteen playoff goals, became the first non-goalie from a losing team to be awarded the Conn Smythe Trophy.

Never in the history of the NHL has a team dominated a season like the Montreal Canadiens in 1976-77. The Habs lost only once on home ice and dropped only eight games in total, while racking up 132 points on sixty wins and twelve ties. In addition, the Habs outscored their nearest opponent by fifty-four goals and allowed only 171 goals against, the fewest by any team since the eighty-game schedule was introduced in 1973-74. The Montreal machine kept rolling in the playoffs, allowing only twenty goals while sweeping St. Louis and defeating the Islanders. The reconstructed Boston Bruins, with Jean Ratelle and Brad Park replacing Orr and Esposito, had an equally easy time reaching the finals, needing only ten games to get past the Los Angeles Kings and the Philadelphia Flyers.

Boston's Jean Ratelle, who joined the Bruins midway through the 1975-76 season in the decade's biggest trade, looks for an opportunity to shift and score against Montreal's Larry Robinson and Ken Dryden.

In game one of the finals, the Canadiens set the tone of the series with a two-goal burst in the first five minutes of the game. The Habs had only twenty-four shots in the game but made the most of their opportunities by piling seven pucks behind Gerry Cheevers in a convincing 7–3 decision. Yvon Lambert and Mario Tremblay paced the Habs' attack, each contributing a two-goal effort to the opening-game win.

Montreal was limited to only nineteen shots in the second match, but three of them found their way past Cheevers to ensure a 3–0 verdict. Steve Shutt, with a goal and two assists, was the offensive hero, while Ken Dryden

Engraving Names on the Cup

To have his name engraved on the Cup, a player from the winning team must have appeared in a minimum of forty regular-season games and be with the team after the trading deadline, or have participated in the finals. The current rules were introduced after Don Awrey's name was omitted from the Cup in 1976. Awrey played seventy-two games with Montreal during the regular season but didn't appear in the playoffs.

Guy Lafleur added the Conn Smythe Trophy to his overcrowded mantelpiece in 1977, leading all playoff scorers with 26 post-season points.

kicked away twenty-two shots to earn the shutout. In game three, Montreal collected three first-period, power-play goals on only six shots en route to an easy 4–2 victory. Guy Lafleur, with a goal and three assists, led the Habs' attack.

With their backs to the wall, the Bruins played their finest hockey of the series in the fourth game. Bobby Schmautz gave Boston its first lead of the series, but Jacques Lemaire's second-period tally tied the game at 1–1. The score remained deadlocked through sixty minutes of regulation and four minutes of overtime, until Lemaire broke free for the Cup-winning goal. Despite controlling the tempo of play during overtime, the Canadiens did not have a good scoring chance until the 4:32 mark. And just as they had done throughout the series, they capitalized on the opportunity. Lafleur moved into the Bruins' zone, forcing rear guard Gary Doak to pull away from Lemaire, who was stationed near the crease. Lafleur feathered a pass that the now-unprotected Lemaire redirected behind Cheevers to give the Canadiens their twentieth Stanley Cup victory. Lafleur, the NHL's leading playoff scorer with twenty-six points, was awarded the Conn Smythe Trophy.

In 1977-78, for the third consecutive season, the Montreal Canadiens dominated the standings and the scoring race. The Habs racked up fifty-nine victories against only ten defeats, while Guy Lafleur reached the sixty-goal plateau for the first time in his career.

Montreal continued to steamroll past its opposition in the playoffs, knocking Detroit to the sidelines in five games and sweeping the Leafs in four. The Montreal–Toronto series, made possible by the Leafs' seven-game upset win over the favored Islanders, was the first playoff meeting of the teams since the 1967 finals. The Boston Bruins, who finished as runners-up to Montreal in the regular-season standings, needed a total of only nine games to dispatch Chicago and Philadelphia in the first two rounds of the playoffs.

Although the Bruins were determined to avoid the mistakes that had caused their downfall in the 1977 finals, they found themselves having to hook and hold the speedy Habs in an attempt to contain the Montreal attack. The Canadiens quickly responded, notching a couple of early power-play goals by Lafleur and Yvon Lambert to take a lead they would never surrender. Boston successfully stayed out of the penalty box for the rest of the match but could muster only sixteen shots at Dryden and dropped the first game 4–1. For the most part, the second match was a well-disciplined, entertaining game. Brad Park's second-period goal was matched by Steve Shutt's, while Bob Gainey's go-ahead marker in the third was equaled by Rick Smith, sending the game to overtime.

With three overtime victories to their credit in the preliminary rounds, the Bruins were confident their streak could continue. However, the Habs

Brad Park, who appeared in the playoffs in each of his seventeen NHL seasons but never played on a Cup winner, sends Jacques Lemaire tumbling during the 1978 finals.

Lemaire, whose pinpoint accuracy made him one of the NHL's most-consistent shooters, scored the overtime winner to seal the Habs' Cup victory in 1977.

dominated the extra session, firing fifteen shots at Cheevers before Lafleur ended the game at the 13:09 mark.

The Bruins worked their game plan to perfection in the third game, using a patient, disciplined attack to carve out a convincing 4–0 verdict. Gary Doak's goal, just fifty-nine seconds into the encounter, proved to be the winner, as the Bruins allowed the Canadiens only sixteen shots on net. Boston got on the board even faster in game four, with Gregg Sheppard scoring on Dryden after only twenty-five seconds of play. The Canadiens, on goals by Robinson and Doug Risebrough, rebounded to take a 2–1 advantage into the third period, but Boston regained its momentum – and the lead – on goals by Park and Peter McNab. Boston clung to the lead until the last minute, when the Habs, with Dryden on the bench for an extra attacker, tied the game on Guy Lafleur's shot through a maze of arms and legs in front of Cheevers. Although the Canadiens seemed to control the overtime, it was Bobby Schmautz who took a feed from Sheppard and Park and blasted it past Dryden to give Boston a 4–3 decision and a tie in the series.

Bobby Schmautz, who led all marksmen with eleven goals in the 1977 playoffs, followed up with an impressive seven-goal, eight-assist effort in the 1978 post-season.

Bob Gainey breaks free from the tight checking of Walt Tkachuk and Ron Duguay on his way to winning the 1979 Conn Smythe Trophy.

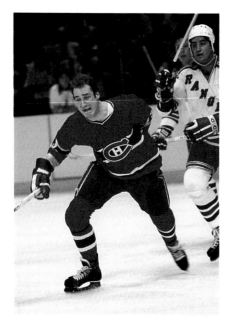

Returning to the Forum for game five, the Canadiens' superior speed created power-play opportunities for the Habs, as the Bruins were forced to pull down their faster opponents. The Canadiens used a pair of power-play goals by Pierre Mondou and Pierre Larouche in the first forty minutes to move within a game of the Cup after a 4–1 win. Game six featured an impressive display by Montreal's largely underrated pluggers and grinders. Réjean Houle, Doug Jarvis, and Brian Engblom combined to limit the Bruins to only eight shots through two periods, while playing prominent roles in two of the Habs' four goals. With the defensive blanket securely in place, the Canadiens shut down the Bruins for the last twenty minutes to carve out a Cup-winning 4–1 victory. Larry Robinson, who tied for the post-season scoring lead with Guy Lafleur, was named winner of the Conn Smythe Trophy.

A new team topped the NHL charts in the last season of the decade. The New York Islanders, a well-coached collection of youth and offensive talent, compiled 116 points to win the league's overall crown. Led by Hart Trophy-winner Bryan Trottier and two-time Norris recipient Denis Potvin, the Islanders had been gathering momentum since their spectacular playoff comeback against the Penguins in 1975. Ironically, rallying from three games to none against Pittsburgh was their first, and last, post-season highlight. After a bitter loss to Toronto in 1978, the Islanders were shunted from the 1979 playoffs by their crosstown rivals, the New York Rangers, who made their second visit to the finals in six seasons. While the Rangers' presence in the championship round may have been a surprise, it was business as usual for the Montreal Canadiens, who survived a thrilling seven-game series with Boston to arrive in the finals for the fourth consecutive year.

The finals began on May 13 in Montreal, just three nights after the Canadiens eliminated the Bruins in a contest that turned on one of the most talked-about penalties in Stanley Cup history. Boston was holding a 4–3 lead in the game's dying minutes, when a bench minor penalty was called against the Bruins for having too many men on the ice. Taking advantage of this last-chance power play, Guy Lafleur, skating at top speed, unleashed a brilliant shot from right wing that tied the game. In overtime, Yvon Lambert jammed in a centering pass from Doug Risebrough to put the Canadiens into the finals for the fourth consecutive season.

The Rangers took full advantage of the weary Canadiens with an impressive 4–1 decision in the opening game of the finals. Phil Esposito, obtained by New York in 1976, and Anders Hedberg, a flashy acquisition from the WHA, led the Rangers' attack. Michel Larocque, Dryden's back-up since 1974, saw his first post-season action in five seasons, replacing a shaky Dryden at the start of the third period.

Things didn't start any better for the Canadiens in game two. Larocque was chosen to start the contest, but was felled by an injury in the pre-game

The 1977-78 Montreal Canadiens led the league in wins, points, goals-for, goals-against, and power-play efficiency on their way to a third straight Stanley Cup title.

warm-up, and coach Scotty Bowman was forced to return an inconsistent Dryden to the nets. Goals by Hedberg and Ron Duguay on the Rangers' first two shots may have left the Forum faithful stunned, but it served as a wake-up call for the Canadiens, who stormed back with half a dozen unanswered goals by six different marksman to win going away, 6–2. Although there was still a lot of hockey to be played, the momentum in the series had shifted to the Habs. Except for a brief portion of game four, the Rangers would never lead in a game again. "When you get to the finals as many times as they have, you get experience," Ranger forward Pat Hickey remarked, "and with experience comes confidence and with confidence comes victory."

Dryden returned to form in game three, holding the fort in a 4–1 Montreal victory. In game four, New York played its best game since the opener, forcing overtime, but the Canadiens prevailed on a goal by Serge Savard to send the Habs home one win away from their fourth consecutive title. After winning three straight Cups on the road, the Canadiens were eager to salute their fans with a Cup victory at home. The Habs' defensive specialists, so vital to the team's reign of success, neutralized the Rangers in dramatic

Phil Esposito, traded to the New York Rangers in 1975-76, had a starring role as the Broadway Blues surprised the experts by landing a spot in the 1979 finals.

fashion by limiting the Broadway Blues to fifteen shots at Dryden. For the fourth straight game, the Canadiens received goals from at least four different marksmen, to close out the decade as Stanley Cup champions with a convincing 4–1 win.

In winning four consecutive Stanley Cup championships from 1976 to 1979, the Canadiens won sixteen out of nineteen games played in the finals. In the 1979 final, they never allowed the Rangers more than twenty-five shots on goal in any single game, and completely shut down New York's power-

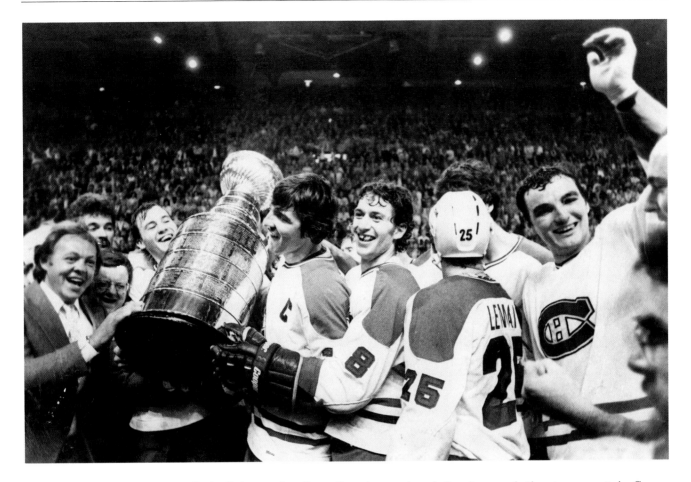

play unit after game one. Bob Gainey, the Canadiens' premier defensive forward, received well-deserved recognition as the recipient of the Conn Smythe Trophy.

It was the end of an era for both the NHL and the Canadiens, as the 1970s came to a close. The WHA had ceased operations and the NHL added four former WHA clubs to become a twenty-one-team league. The Canadiens announced they were losing four cornerstones of their dynasty. When the 1979-80 season opened, Ken Dryden, Jacques Lemaire, Yvan Cournoyer, and Scotty Bowman would not be back with the team.

Acting team captain Serge Savard, replacing an injured Yvan Cournoyer, cradles the Stanley Cup with teammates Cournoyer (not in uniform), Doug Risebrough (8), Jacques Lemaire, and Mario Tremblay, following the Canadiens' fourth consecutive Cup championship.

The Time
of the Great One,

1980-1992

THE NHL ENTERED THE 1980s WITH FOUR NEW TEAMS – THE EDMONTON Oilers, the Quebec Nordiques, the Hartford Whalers, and the Winnipeg Jets – and a budding superstar named Wayne Gretzky, who finished with fifty-one goals and eighty-six assists, tying Marcel Dionne of the Los Angeles Kings for the league's scoring lead. (Dionne, who had fifty-three goals, was awarded the Art Ross Trophy as the NHL's top scorer.)

The top story of the 1979-80 season was the Philadelphia Flyers' thirty-five-game unbeaten streak. With a new post-season format that saw all sixteen playoff qualifiers engage in a best-of-five preliminary round, upsets seemed likely, but the favorites all emerged unscathed. In the quarter-finals, however, the Montreal Canadiens were eliminated in seven games by Minnesota, ensuring a new Cup champion. The North Stars then fell victim to the Flyers, who had a relatively easy time marching to the finals, winning eleven games while losing only two. Their opponents in the finals were the New York Islanders, who eliminated Los Angeles, Boston, and Buffalo to reach the finals for the first time in their eight-year history.

In the finals, the Flyers and the Islanders traded goals in each period of game one, forcing overtime. Two minutes into the extra session, Flyer defenseman Jimmy Watson was called for holding, giving the Islanders a rare overtime power play. The Islanders, who had also scored with a man advantage to tie the game late in the third period, were quick to capitalize in extra time, as John Tonelli spotted Denis Potvin moving into the slot and sent him a perfect feed. Potvin shoveled the puck past Pete Peeters in the Flyers' net to put the Islanders ahead in the series. For only the third time in NHL history, an overtime game in the Cup finals was decided on a power-play goal.

In game two, the Flyers scored three power-play goals and drove Isles goaltender Billy Smith to the bench in an 8–3 win. Philadelphia's Paul

Opposite: Supercenters Bryan Trottier and Wayne Gretzky.

Below: Denis Potvin, the first draft selection of the New York Islanders to earn a berth in the Hockey Hall of Fame, anchored the Isles' blue line through four consecutive Stanley Cup triumphs.

Paul Holmgren was the quintessential Philadelphia Flyer, a fearless plugger and an opportunistic offensive contributor. In the 1980 playoffs, he fired ten goals and added ten assists as the Flyers made the finals for the fourth time in franchise history.

Holmgren became the first American-born player to score three goals in a final-series game, hitting the scoresheet in each period to record a hat trick. The Flyers were frequently penalized in game three, losing 6–2. The Islanders' power-play and penalty-killing units figured in all six goals, including five on the power play. Denis Potvin, hero of game one, was the offensive star with four points.

The Islanders' offense continued to click in the pivotal fourth match, building 2–0 and 3–1 leads. The Flyers pulled to within one on a Ken Linseman backhander, but the Islanders pulled away when Bob Bourne blocked a shot off the stick of Bob Dailey and fed Bob Nystrom, who made no mistake in beating Peeters. Clark Gillies, who set up the first two New York goals, finished the scoring in the Islanders' 5–2 romp.

The Flyers fought for their playoff lives in game five at the Spectrum, and emerged with a 6–3 victory. A pair of familiar names, Rick MacLeish and Bobby Clarke, were the catalysts, with gutsy performances that evoked the glory days of the 1970s. Game six was a seesaw battle that saw the teams split four goals in the first period. The Islanders broke out in front with two in the second period, only to have the Flyers match with a pair of their own in the third. The Flyers pressed, outshooting New York 11–5, but couldn't score the tie-breaker, sending the game into overtime.

Seven minutes into extra time, John Tonelli spotted Bob Nystrom behind Flyer defenseman Bob Dailey. Tonelli laid a perfect pass on Nystrom's stick, and Nystrom deftly placed the puck past Peeters for a 5–4 Cup-clinching win and the fourth, and last, overtime goal of his career. Bryan Trottier, with a post-season record twenty-nine points, took home the Conn Smythe Trophy as the playoff MVP.

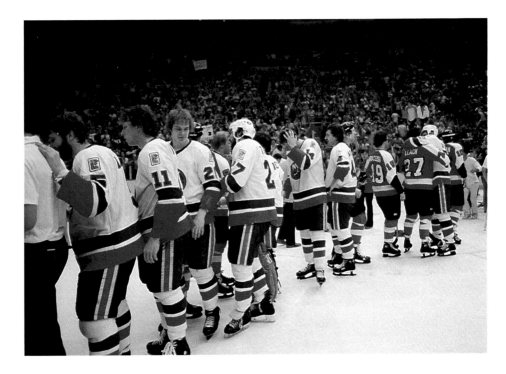

After only eight seasons in the NHL, the New York Islanders joined the list of Stanley Cup champions, defeating the Philadelphia Flyers in six games.

The New York Islanders remained at the top of the class of 1981, with the surprising St. Louis Blues a close second. The Montreal Canadiens, winners of forty-five games during the regular season, were eliminated in a shocking three-game sweep by the Edmonton Oilers in the preliminary round. The Oilers then gave the Islanders all they could handle before succumbing to the defending Cup champions in six entertaining matches.

The Islanders then swept past the Rangers to advance to the finals for the second consecutive time. Their opponent turned out to be the Minnesota North Stars, who had parlayed their success in the 1980 post-season into a berth in the 1981 finals. Led by Bobby Smith and Steve Payne, the Stars were boosted in the playoffs by rookie Dino Ciccarelli, who had joined the team early in the second half of the season.

Bobby Nystrom, whose four career overtime goals ranks him second on the NHL's all-time list, fires the puck past Philadelphia's Pete Peeters to secure the Islanders' first Cup championship.

Minnesota's Dino Ciccarelli set an NHL rookie scoring record with twenty-one points in the 1981 playoffs.

It appeared that the Stars were victims of their own nervousness in the opening game of the finals. After Anders Kallur gave New York a quick 1–0 advantage, the Stars had a chance to get back into the game when Bob Bourne was assessed a major penalty for spearing. However, Kallur and Trottier scored shorthanded goals for the Islanders during the five-minute disadvantage, and the Stars were never able to regain their composure. A pair of third-period Islander goals on only three shots sealed New York's 6–3 win. Minnesota managed to break out on top in the second encounter, using a Dino Ciccarelli power-play goal to gain a brief 1–0 lead. Exactly one minute later, however, Mike Bossy tied things up for the Islanders, opening the flood gates for goals by Potvin and Nystrom. The Stars slowly gained confidence, battling back to tie the game at 3–3 on a second-period goal by Brad Palmer and a nice effort by Steve Payne at the thirty-second mark of the third, but this was as close as the Stars could come. Potvin, Ken Morrow, and Bossy each scored in a span of eight minutes to mirror the result of the series opener in a 6–3 Islander victory.

The Stars appeared headed for a better fate in game three, securing a 3–1 lead after twenty minutes. Butch Goring, the pepperpot forechecker and relentless worker, whose acquisition in 1980 helped carry the Islanders to the title, scored twice in the second period, allowing the Islanders to take a 4–3 lead into the final twenty minutes. Again, the Stars fought back, tying the game at the 1:11 mark of the third, only to see the defending champions regain the lead less than a minute later. Goring completed his hat trick with the eventual game-winner at the six-minute mark, and the Islanders stood sixty minutes away from the Cup with a 7–5 decision.

Minnesota delayed the Islanders' celebration for at least another day with

Butch Goring, whom the New York Islanders obtained from Los Angeles in 1980, proved to be the missing piece that completed the Islanders' Stanley Cup puzzle.

their best effort of the series in game four. After trading goals through two periods, Minnesota took a 3–2 lead on Steve Payne's goal at the 12:26 mark of the third. This time the Minnesota defense held firm, thanks to an excellent effort from goalie Don Beaupre. Bobby Smith put the finishing touches on the 4–2 win with a late-period power-play marker to send the teams back to the Islanders' home rink in Uniondale, Long Island.

In game five, the Islanders quickly made up for their poor performance in the previous match, and once again Butch Goring provided the dramatics. Goring opened the scoring and added insurance, all in the first ten minutes, as the Islanders rode to a 5–1 Cup-clinching victory. To no one's surprise, Goring won well-deserved accolades as the Conn Smythe Trophy winner.

In 1981-82, after only three seasons in the NHL, the Edmonton Oilers emerged as a powerhouse squad, finishing second to the Islanders in the league's overall standings and capturing their first Smythe Division flag. Led by Wayne Gretzky, who rewrote the record book with a 92-goal, 212-point season, the Oilers became the first – and only – team in NHL history to score 400 goals in a single season.

The league's playoff system was revised to emphasize divisional play. The

Olympic Gold and Stanley Silver

In 1980, defenseman Ken Morrow became the only player to win an Olympic gold medal and a Stanley Cup championship in the same year. Morrow was a member of the U.S. Olympic team that captured gold at Lake Placid, and then joined the New York Islanders and helped them win their first Stanley Cup.

Staying power: Sixteen New York Islanders played on all four Cup-winners from 1980 to 1984.

THE NEW YORK ISLANDERS

Tonelli's Timely Tallies

The New York Islanders were minutes away from suffering one of the greatest upsets in playoff history in 1982. The defending champion Islanders were down 3–2 to Pittsburgh in the decisive fifth game of the opening round when John Tonelli tied the score with only two minutes left. He later fired the winner in overtime only seconds after Pittsburgh's Mike Bullard hit the post. The Islanders went on to win their third straight Cup.

first two rounds would match clubs in the same division. In each division's best-of-five semi-finals, the team finishing first would play the fourth-place club, while second would play third. The winners would then meet in a best-of-seven division final. The two divisional winners in each conference would then meet in a best-of-seven conference final to determine the Wales and Campbell conference champions and the Stanley Cup finalists.

Despite their unprecedented success during the regular schedule, the Oilers were upset in the first round of this new playoff structure, losing to the Los Angeles Kings in the best-of-five Smythe Division semi-final. Two other first-place finishers – Montreal and Minnesota – were also eliminated in their division semi-finals. The only division-winner to get past its first playoff match-up was the New York Islanders, who won the first two games of their series with Pittsburgh, dropped games three and four, and needed an overtime goal by John Tonelli in the decisive fifth game of the series to advance. Once they rid themselves of the Penguins, the Islanders rolled over the Rangers and the Quebec Nordiques to secure their third straight trip to the championship showdown.

The Campbell Conference yielded a surprise champion. The Vancouver Canucks, who finished three games under .500 during the regular season, knocked off the Kings and the Black Hawks to become the first team with fewer than eighty points to reach the finals since the expansion-era St. Louis Blues in 1967-68.

The Islanders were heavily favored against the Canucks. But the Vancouver squad, with goaltender "King" Richard Brodeur playing strongly and feisty Dave "Tiger" Williams supplying leadership, gave the Islanders all they could handle in the series opener, fighting back from 2–1 and 4–2 deficits to

Pittsburgh Penguins' defenseman Randy Carlyle battles Butch Goring in the 1982 Patrick Division semi-finals.

lead 5–4 with only seven minutes to play. The Canucks' lead was short-lived, however, as Mike Bossy tied the game with less than five minutes showing on the clock. In overtime, it was Bossy again who emerged as the hero. With only two seconds left in the overtime period, he pounced on an errant clearing attempt in the Canucks' zone and whipped a wrist-shot past Brodeur to give the Islanders the series lead.

Vancouver played very well through two periods in the second game as well, using goals from Thomas Gradin, Ivan Boldirev, and Lars Lindgren to build a 3–2 lead. Nevertheless, the Islanders were confident, and before the third period was a minute and a half old, New York had re-established a one-goal lead. By the end of the period, the Islanders had beaten Brodeur twice more to skate away with a 6–4 decision.

The Canucks tightened up defensively back at the Pacific Coliseum, where they were met by an arena full of noisy, towel-waving fans. In an earlier playoff round, coach Roger Neilson, upset at an official's call, had raised the "white flag" of surrender, using a towel on the end of a hockey stick. Vancouver fans made this an instant craze, waving thousands of small white "terrible towels" throughout the Canucks' remaining post-season games. This demonstrative fan support didn't translate into success on the ice for the Canucks, who were constantly thwarted by Billy Smith, who allowed only one goal during the rest of the series. Clark Gillies, Bob Nystrom, and Mike Bossy supplied the offensive punch in a 3–0 shutout that iced game three, and Bossy again provided the heroics in the fourth game with a pair of goals in the Islanders' Cup-clinching 3–1 victory. Bossy, whose seventeen post-season goals led all scorers, was a unanimous choice as the winner of the Conn Smythe Trophy.

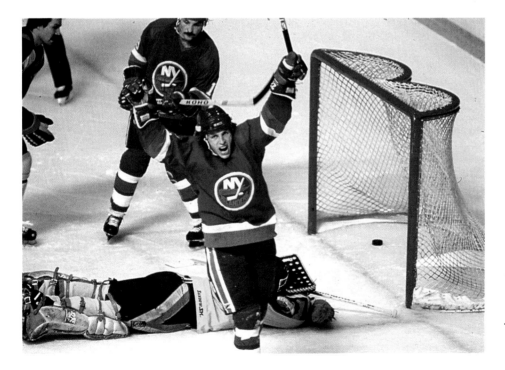

Mike Bossy celebrates his Cup-winning goal in game four of the 1982 finals. Bossy also scored the overtime winner in game one of this series.

Defenseman Denis Potvin, who scored twenty-or-more goals in seven of his first nine NHL seasons, hoists the Stanley Cup for the third time, May 16, 1982.

Billy Smith, whose willingness to clear space in and around his goal crease frustrated the Edmonton Oilers in the 1983 finals, won the Conn Smythe Trophy as playoff MVP.

The Islanders relinquished their overall-points crown to the Boston Bruins in 1983, finishing with ninety-six points, good enough for second spot behind Philadelphia in the Patrick Division. Following series wins over Washington and the Rangers, the Islanders faced the regular-season champion Bruins, defeating them in six games to earn their fourth consecutive journey to the finals. The Edmonton Oilers, who set another NHL mark with 424 goals during the season, were the dominant team in the Campbell Conference, losing only one game on their way to the Cup finals.

The championship showdown between Edmonton and the Islanders was a much-anticipated series. The Oilers were blessed with hockey's most prolific scorer in Wayne Gretzky, and a supporting cast that included top-ten scorers Jari Kurri, Glenn Anderson, and Mark Messier. It was unclear whether the Oilers' offense could break through the close-checking style that had characterized the Islanders' post-season success. That style was very much in evidence in the first game of the series. Although the Oilers managed thirty-five shots on Billy Smith, few were quality chances, and those that were threatening were turned away by the savvy veteran. Duane Sutter opened the scoring in the first period, and that was all the offense that Smith and company would require. An empty-netter off the stick of Ken Morrow rounded out the scoring at 2–0.

The Oilers outshot New York again in game two, but the opportunistic Islanders made the most of their twenty-five shots, putting six past Oiler goaltender Andy Moog. Three goals in less than five minutes in the first period and another pair thirty-eight seconds apart in the second provided the Islanders with a 6–3 win and a two-game lead in the series.

In game three, Edmonton played its finest hockey of the finals in the first forty minutes, but could only score once. With the game tied 1–1 entering the third period, the Islanders exploded, scoring four goals without an Oiler reply. The Sutter brothers, Brent and Duane, were major factors in the victory with a goal and an assist each. With a 5–1 victory in hand, the Islanders stood one game away from their fourth straight Stanley Cup.

The mature, experienced Islanders made quick work of the Oilers in game four, scoring three goals in ninety seconds to take control of the match. Three men who were instrumental in the Islanders' first Cup win – Trottier, Tonelli, and Bossy – were the first-period marksmen. The Oilers fought bravely, pulling to within a goal, but couldn't beat goaltender Billy Smith to tie the score.

In addition to holding the Oilers to only six goals in the series, the Islanders kept Gretzky off the scoresheet, the only time all season he had gone four games without scoring a goal. Oilers' coach Glen Sather summed it up best, admitting that "the Islanders just didn't make any mistakes. They didn't fold when the pressure was on." Billy Smith capped his finest performance with the Conn Smythe Trophy as playoff MVP.

As the clock was winding down on the Edmonton Oilers' unsuccessful Stanley Cup challenge in 1982-83, Glen Sather boasted to anyone who would listen that the Oilers would be back in 1984 to "register a hundred points, win our division, and win the Stanley Cup." By the end of their eighty-game, regular-season schedule, two-thirds of that prophecy had been accomplished. Not only did the Oilers win the Smythe Division, they vaulted into top spot in the league with one of the strongest teams in NHL history. They won 57 games, scored 446 goals, and, in Gretzky, Jari Kurri, and Glenn Anderson, had three 50-goal scorers. Edmonton moved to within sight of their ultimate goal by eliminating Winnipeg in straight games, surviving a tough seven-game series with Calgary, and sweeping Minnesota to reach the finals for the second straight year.

The New York Islanders, of course, hoped to match the Montreal Canadiens' record of five consecutive wins. The Islanders gave themselves the opportunity to share space with Montreal in the *NHL Official Guide &*

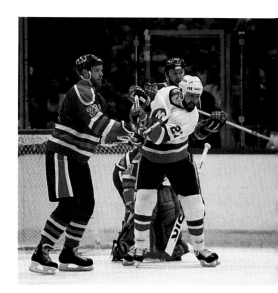

John Tonelli causes havoc for Edmonton's Grant Fuhr and Randy Gregg during the 1983 finals.

The Current Cup

The Stanley Cup trophy was extensively modified in 1958 with the addition of a new barrel made up of five wide silver bands that provide space to inscribe the names of each year's Cup winners. The Pittsburgh Penguins used the last available space when they captured the trophy in 1991. To accommodate the names of future champions, the top band, containing the names of the winners from 1928 to 1940, has been removed and retired to the Hockey Hall of Fame, and a new blank band will be added to the bottom of the trophy.

Record Book by defeating the Rangers, the Capitals, and the Habs themselves on their way to the championship round.

From the onset of the final series, it was evident that the Oilers were prepared to play defensive hockey. In the series opener, the teams battled through two periods of scoreless play, with Grant Fuhr in the Oilers' net and Smith in the Islanders' goal, sharing the spotlight with excellent work in the crease. The third period was almost two minutes old when Dave Hunter of the Oilers pounced on a loose puck in the Islanders' zone and relayed it to Pat Hughes, who passed off to Kevin McClelland. Though never noted as a scorer, McClelland connected on a sharp-angled shot to give the Oilers the lead. From there, Edmonton's defense took over, allowing the Islanders only eight shots on goal the rest of the way. When the final siren sounded, the Oilers had shut down, and shut out, the Islanders by the slimmest margin possible, 1–0.

New York displayed its resilience, bouncing back quickly in game two. Clark Gillies's hat trick was all the Islanders needed as they beat the Oilers

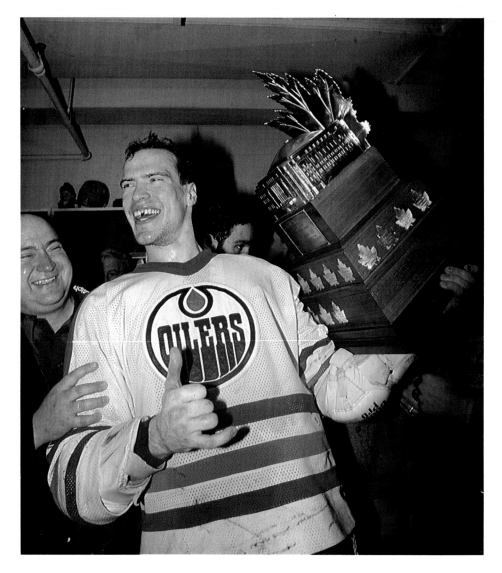

Vindication! Mark "Moose" Messier, whose determination and tenacity helped the Oilers to a second final-series appearance and their first Cup championship in 1984, poses with the Conn Smythe Trophy.

6–1 for a series-tying win. Edmonton turned the tables on the Isles in game three, finally breaking through New York's defensive barrier to slide six goals past Billy Smith and banish him to the Islanders' bench. The outcome of this game was still in doubt, until Glenn Anderson and Paul Coffey scored seventeen seconds apart in the last minute of the second period. But from there, it was all Edmonton. The Oilers added three more in the third to skate home with an easy 7–2 decision.

With the Oilers' offense finally clicking, and their confidence soaring, Edmonton dominated the Islanders again in game four. Wayne Gretzky, who hadn't scored against New York in twelve post-season games, dating back to 1981, finally broke through with a two-goal effort in Edmonton's second consecutive 7–2 romp over the defending champions. Gretzky continued to shine in game five, taking passes from Jari Kurri to score the first two goals of the game. With Billy Smith out of the game after the first period, Gretzky set up Ken Linseman for a power-play marker, then Jari Kurri scored to put Edmonton up 4–0 and give the Oilers a lead they would never relinquish. Despite two goals by Islander rookie Pat LaFontaine in the first thirty-five seconds of the third period, at the end of regulation time the Oilers led 5–2 and found themselves the NHL's new Stanley Cup champions.

Wayne Gretzky has often said that one of his proudest moments as a player was watching Mark Messier receive the Conn Smythe Trophy as the playoff MVP. Messier, an Edmonton native, was the heart and soul of the Oiler team, and his contribution to the Oilers' 1984 Stanley Cup drive was appropriately recognized.

(continued on p. 243)

EDMONTON OILERS 1983–84
PETER POCKLINGTON OWNER
~~BASIL POCKLINGTON~~
GLEN SATHER G. M. & COACH
BRUCE MACGREGOR ASST. G. M.
JOHN MUCKLER TED GREEN ASST. COACHES
BARRY FRASER DIR. P. P. & C. SCOUT

W. GRETZKY CAPT. G. ANDERSON P. COFFEY
P. CONACHER L. FOGOLIN G. FUHR R. GREGG
C. HUDDY P. HUGHES D. HUNTER D. JACKSON
J. KURRI W. LINDSTROM K. LINSEMAN K. LOWE
D. LUMLEY K. MCCLELLAND M. MESSIER A. MOOG
J. POUZAR D. SEMENKO
P. MILLAR ATHLETIC THERAPIST B. STAFFORD TR.
L. KULCHISKY ASST. TR.

The Edmonton Oilers' first Cup-winning team, as inscribed on the Stanley Cup. The crossed-out name is that of Basil Pocklington, father of the club's owner.

The Islanders and The Oilers

by Pat Calabria

The torch was not simply passed from one generation to the next on the evening of May 19, 1984. Instead, it was tugged, yanked, and finally loosened in an epic match-up between two dynasties – one ending and one beginning – in a thrilling and momentous Stanley Cup final. On the night the New York Islanders surrendered the Stanley Cup to the Edmonton Oilers, it marked more than just a change in champions. It was a departure in style and substance, too.

While no one could be sure at the time, expectations ran rampant that the Oilers would match, or surpass, the Islanders' resounding achievements, and that what the sixteen-thousand fans in Edmonton's Northlands Coliseum were witnessing was the orderly and anticipated succession from one powerful ruler to the next. As when the Islanders inherited the crown from the Montreal Canadiens four years earlier, the Oilers were a worthy replacement whose time had come, after a series of bitter disappointments. But in other ways, this changing of the guard was unlike any that had come before.

First, the Islanders had not defeated the Montreal dynasty in the 1980 final; the Canadiens had been eliminated in the quarter-finals, so they never actually got the opportunity to defend their championship head-to-head. In retrospect, the meeting between the Islanders and the Oilers was a monumental pivot-point in NHL history, with two great hockey clubs battling like a pair of champion thoroughbreds charging wire-to-wire.

In fact, you have to go back to the Detroit Red Wings and the Montreal Canadiens of the mid-1950s to find rival dynasty teams that faced each other one-on-one in the final round two years in a row. The Islanders swept the Oilers in four games in 1983, but Edmonton reversed the decision the following year in five games. From 1980 to 1990, the Islanders and the Oilers accounted for nine of the eleven Stanley Cups contested. Not since Montreal and the Toronto Maple Leafs captured thirteen Cups in fourteen years, from 1956 to 1969, had two great franchises been so dominant – and so distinctive.

But the clash between New York and Edmonton also came when the sport itself was in a period of transition. The older, conservative Islanders were a hard-hitting, defensive-minded, counter-punching team, whose goal-scoring was built on the foundation of sound fore-checking. On the other hand, the brash Oilers – led by the incomparable Wayne Gretzky – represented the new move toward speedier and more unpredictable offenses, piling up goals not in bunches but in bushels. The Oilers' best defensive efforts were usually reserved for fending off attacks on their flamboyant lifestyles.

The franchises were built differently, came from different backgrounds, and employed vastly different strategies. The Islanders, although not NHL bluebloods, had nevertheless been born in a conventional fashion: Long Island was granted an expansion franchise, which began toiling in futility in 1972-73. Although the team went through two coaches in its first two seasons, winning a total of only twenty-three games, Al Arbour took over in the third season and quickly steered it to respectability. And, despite several years of falling short of the Stanley Cup with a star-laden line-up, general manager Bill Torrey continued to build patiently through the amateur draft.

Edmonton, however, was largely regarded as a team of bandits, as much for its outlaw past as for its new-fangled, thunderbolt offense. The franchise had not started in the NHL. Indeed, it began operating in the old rival World Hockey Association. It became a part of the established league when the NHL expanded, adding four former WHA franchises in 1979-80, at a time when many of its players were unheralded or even unknown. There was even suspicion that the great Gretzky would not be able to take the nightly pounding in his new league that he had been able to avoid in the more goal-oriented WHA.

But the Islanders and the Oilers did have something in common.

New York had made a shocking leap to contender in only its third year of existence, twice rallying from 0–3 deficits in playoff series and coming within one game of reaching the Stanley Cup finals in 1975. Edmonton was eliminated in the preliminary playoff round its first year in the NHL, but, after ranking only fourteenth in the 1980-81 regular season, it knocked off heavily favored and third-ranked Montreal before being ousted – by the champion Islanders – in the quarter-finals. Two years later, the Oilers would reach the finals. Three years later, they would win their first Cup.

So the rise of both teams was quick and surprising. And it was against this backdrop that New York met Edmonton in the 1983 finals, a meeting filled with soap-opera theatrics, gamesmanship, and outward animosity between the clubs. In many ways, this landmark series of the 1980s was a throwback to the time of goalies with no masks, players without helmets, and chicken-wire mesh around the rink instead of glass – not because of the style of play, but because of the intensity which characterized this heated, riveting, remarkable series.

The Islanders were virtually unchanged from the club that had swept Quebec and then Vancouver in the last two playoff rounds the year before. But, thinned by injuries and fighting complacency, the team dropped to second-place in the Patrick Division (behind Philadelphia) with a 42–26–12 record, only good enough for sixth overall in the league. Until 1986 when the seventh-place Canadiens won, this was the lowest finish ever recorded by a team that would go on to capture the Cup.

Durable center Bryan Trottier suffered through ten games without a goal during one stretch in the regular season. Sixty-goal scorer Mike Bossy went seven games without scoring. Bill Smith, the fearless goalie, played

The Edmonton Oilers' first taste of playoff success came here, in the preliminary round of the 1981 playoffs, when they swept the Montreal Canadiens out of post-season competition in three straight games.

from November 30 to January 18 without recording a victory. Rookie defenseman Paul Boutilier, bewildered by the turmoil disrupting the three-time champions he had just joined, asked: "Is this what it's like every year?"

Nevertheless, the Islanders eliminated the pesky Washington Capitals in four games in the first round of the playoffs, before battling the Rangers, their resilient and dangerous rivals from Manhattan, in the next round. They won this series in six games, then ousted the Boston Bruins in a six-game Wales Conference final. Even then the Islanders were thought to be vulnerable, especially against the young, fresh Oilers and their powerhouse offense.

"It's them, the big city guys, against us, the small-town guys," Oilers coach Glen Sather warned, forgetting that his opponents were located in the leafy Long Island suburbs, twenty-five miles from the city skyline. "We're the new kids on the block, and we're ready to take their marbles."

Edmonton was led by Gretzky, whose 71 goals and 125 assists both topped the league. Three other players – Mark Messier, Jari Kurri, and Glenn Anderson – scored at least 45 goals. The offense set a league record with 424 goals, and the team's 47–21–12 record for 106 points was the NHL's second best, bettering the Islanders' finish by ten points. Although the Islanders convincingly won all four regular-season meetings between the clubs, the Oilers had charged into the playoffs, anxious to rebound from their stunning first-round loss to Los Angeles the year before.

Edmonton, in fact, compiled an 11–1 record over the first three rounds, needing just three games to sideline the Winnipeg Jets in the best-of-five preliminary round, eliminating the Calgary Flames in five games, and sweeping Chicago in four games in the Campbell Conference finals – outscoring the overmatched Blackhawks 23–11. Edmonton's whopping ten shorthanded goals had already set a Stanley Cup record. The Oilers' speed and daring seemed to be matched only by their abundant confidence – many would say cockiness – a characteristic that infuriated the defending champions.

"We want to beat them more than anything," Islander left wing Clark Gillies said. "You know why? Because they think they're the greatest thing since sliced bread."

Said teammate Bob Bourne: "They think they're so hot. They're so damn cocky. The thing that really bugs me is, they don't respect us. They're not the Stanley Cup champions. We are."

As if the series didn't already have enough ingredients, game one in Edmonton featured two events that fueled the drama. First, Bossy was a surprise scratch because of a sudden, mysterious illness, later described as tonsillitis. Then, after some verbal sparring, Glenn Anderson and Bill Smith exchanged slashes, with Smith's clubbing of the Oiler forward inciting the hometown fans, not to mention Glen Sather. But Smith kept his composure and protected the tender 1–0 lead Duane Sutter had provided with a first-period goal. Ken Morrow's empty-net goal in the final seconds cemented the shutout of the astonished Oilers.

But game two was no less shocking, with the Oilers' top guns again held in check and the Islanders scoring three times in the first period, en route to a 6–3 victory. The game marked the return of Bossy, whose goal gave the Islanders a 3–1 lead, but the biggest news continued to be the Islanders' handling of Gretzky. He again failed to score and was credited with only two assists in the game, far from the explosion that the Oilers and their followers anticipated.

"You don't expect to win the first two games of the finals when you're on the road," said Islander Brent Sutter, Duane's younger brother. "But then a lot of things have happened that we didn't expect."

With the series moving to Nassau Coliseum on Long Island for the next two games, the Oilers vowed they would turn the series around with the display of firepower for which they had become famous. But with only nineteen seconds left in the first period, Islander Anders Kallur scored for a 1–0 lead. Kurri evened the score in the second period, but third-period goals by Bourne, Morrow, and both of the Sutter brothers propelled the Islanders to a 5–1 victory and the threshold of a fourth straight title.

The team's careful, defensive style and opportune goal-scoring confounded the Oilers early in game four, too. The Islanders scored three times in the first period, the Oilers replied with two goals in the second, and Smith acrobatically preserved the lead, until Morrow added another empty-net goal for a 4–2 victory. Gretzky was held without a goal – and to just four assists –

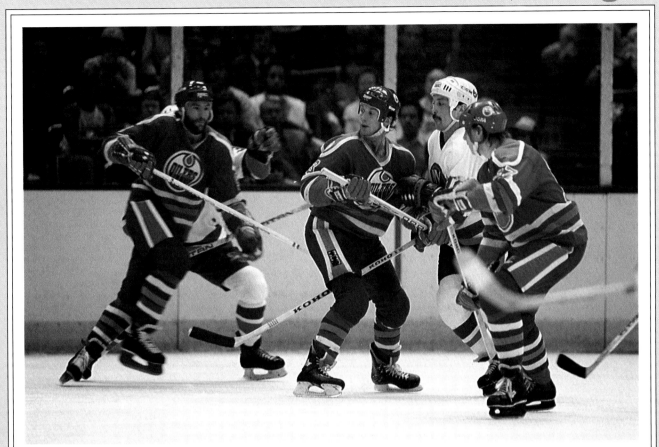

in the series, and Smith was voted the Conn Smythe Trophy-winner.

The Islanders allowed the mighty Oilers just six goals in the four games. They trailed for only six minutes during the whole series. They extended their streak in the Stanley Cup finals to nine straight victories and their record in the finals to a remarkable 16–3. They became only the second franchise in history to win as many as four straight Cups, joining the Montreal teams that won four, from 1976 to 1979, and five, from 1956 to 1960.

"They dominated us completely," Edmonton defenseman Kevin Lowe said. "They were always ahead, and it's virtually impossible to try to play catch-up with them."

"The Oilers are a great hockey team," said Bourne, conciliatory after helping his team clinch the victory. "They're going to win the Stanley Cup some day, but right now, we're still the best team. Why? Because we're scared of losing. We know the feeling. We remember it, and that's what keeps us going. We like being champions too much. Tell 'em, we'll see 'em again next year."

A trio of Oilers – Glenn Anderson, Jari Kurri, and Ken "Rat" Linseman – surround a deserted Bryan Trottier. Linseman played two seasons for Edmonton – 1982-83 and 1983-84 – and reached the finals in both campaigns.

Bourne's words turned out to be prophetic. The Islanders rose back into first place in the Patrick Division in 1983-84 with an impressive 50–26–4 record, their 104 points lagging only behind the Oilers' resounding 57–18–5 mark for 119 points. Edmonton also set another record with 446 goals, Gretzky pacing the club with 87 goals and 118 assists for 205 points. But while Edmonton faced only one big obstacle in its march back to the finals – winning the seventh game of the division final against Calgary – the Islanders struggled much of the way.

They needed overtime to eliminate the Rangers in the conclusive fifth game of the division semi-finals, lost the first game against Washington before rallying to win four straight games in the next round, and lost the first two games against the inspired Canadiens, who were hoping to keep the Islanders from matching their record of five straight Cups, before winning the last four games of the conference finals.

The barrel of the Cup records the roster of 1982-83 New York Islanders who eliminated the Capitals, Rangers, Bruins, and Oilers en route to their fourth consecutive championship.

That victory extended the Islanders' playoff winning streak to an eye-popping record of nineteen straight series wins. But their offense was slumping, their team was among the oldest in the league, and several of their key players were injured, including Pat LaFontaine, the speedy center who had joined the Islanders after the 1984 Winter Olympics and given them a much-needed jolt. And they no longer had much of an edge in experience over the Oilers, who no longer seemed awed by the opportunity to compete for the Cup.

The Oilers proved they were ready with a 1–0 victory in the opener on Long Island, turning the tables on the Islanders' strategy with a sound defensive performance of their own. That ended Edmonton's ten-game losing streak to the Islanders, which extended back to 1981, and, more importantly, it shattered the Islanders' aura of invincibility. The Islanders once again smothered Gretzky, and tangled the Oilers in checks, but still the Oilers showed their patience and maturity in finding a way to win.

The turning point came after two scoreless periods, thanks not to one of the stars in the Edmonton galaxy, but to Kevin McClelland and Pat Hughes. The journeymen forwards teamed up on the play that deposited the puck past Smith, Hughes passing from

the corner and McClelland directing the puck inside the far post 1:55 into the third period. At the other end of the ice, Edmonton goalie Grant Fuhr held on to the lead, despite a flurry of Islander shots in the final seconds.

"Aah," Fuhr said, "it was a piece of cake."

Behind a hat trick by Gillies, the Islanders rebounded to win game two by a score of 6–1, a victory that appeared to get the four-time champions back on track. They had, after all, played two games, permitted only two goals, and had blanked Gretzky on the scoresheet – only the seventh time all season that the Oilers' famed number 99 had not recorded a point. But now the series was moving to Edmonton, not for two games, as had long been the practice in the playoffs – but for three.

It was the only time in history that the playoffs were scheduled this way, in an effort to reduce travel costs, and it worked to the Oilers' advantage. Fuhr responded with an outstanding effort in the pivotal third game, stopping Bossy and Kallur on breakaways in the first period to keep his team in the contest. Edmonton's dangerous Mark Messier scored a picturesque goal to tie the score, 2–2, in the second period, feinting past defenseman Gord Dineen and slapping a shot past Smith. Then Edmonton got goals from Anderson and Coffey, only seventeen seconds apart, within the final minute of the period. That outburst sparked the Oilers to a rousing 7–2 victory and injected them with another dose of confidence.

They had dealt the Islanders one of the worst playoff losses in their history, and they knew it. "They had done it to us before," Gretzky said. "I always wondered what it would be like to do it to them."

"This is not the same team we beat last year," Islander defenseman Stefan Persson moaned. "They are better – much better."

During the Stanley Cup luncheon the next afternoon, the teams traded barbs, and a controversy arose over the early nine a.m. practice time the Oilers had assigned to the Islanders that morning. Sather, the fast-talking Edmonton coach, revealed that he had "discovered" that Smith was vulnerable on low shots. Smith, noting Sather's journeyman career as a player, replied: "I never knew Glen Sather to be much of a goal scorer."

But the Oilers' vast improvement became even more

evident in game four. Led by Messier, they checked the Islanders hard without sacrificing any of their offense. And, although a soft backhand shot by Gretzky, just 1:53 into the game, barely slid across the goal line, it had the effect of a lightning bolt. Even with Fuhr sidelined with a bruised shoulder, back-up goalie Andy Moog needed little help in keeping Edmonton in front. Just eighty-nine seconds after the opening goal, Glenn Anderson curled around the Islander net, lost control of the puck, and then brushed Smith as the Islander goalie reached to cover it.

But Oiler Willy Lindstrom beat Smith to the puck and poked a shot into the net for a 2–0 lead. Lindstrom's second goal of the game in the second period pushed the Edmonton lead to 4–1 and, behind another solid performance by Moog, the Oilers moved to within one game of their first Cup with another 7–2 victory. Said Messier: "I can't sleep just thinking about it."

When the teams appeared for game five, Northlands Coliseum was a cauldron of emotion. There were cheers and jeers and wild ovations, as the crowd sensed that the Oilers' time finally had arrived. If there was any doubt, it disintegrated, along with the Islanders' famous poise, when Edmonton soared to a 4–0 lead after two periods. Two breakaway goals by Gretzky started Edmonton rolling, and Smith was yanked in the second period and replaced by Rollie Melanson in the Islander net. Gretzky assisted on Ken Linsemen's goal, just thirty-eight seconds into the second period, and Kurri added another, carrying the Oilers to a 5–2 victory and their first Stanley Cup championship.

Mike Bossy (22) motors past Dave Hunter (12) on one of the rare occasions when he was able to break free from the Oilers' tight checking system in the 1984 finals.

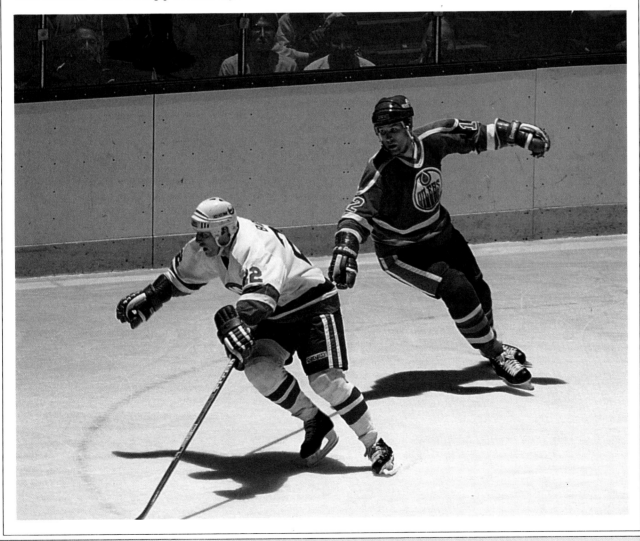

"We got the Islanders in the position of having to come from behind," Edmonton defenseman Kevin Lowe said. "We never allowed them to get ahead. We forced them to play a wide-open game with us."

That was the undoing of the Islanders' dynasty, and the beginning of the one assembled by the Oilers. Edmonton enjoyed unprecedented success with their dizzying "free-flow" offense. Wings were no longer tethered to flanks of the ice, but were encouraged to weave and wander. Defensemen, such as the dangerous Paul Coffey, became part of the offense. Indeed, Coffey would rank among the NHL's top scorers for years. Messier, who was awarded the Conn Smythe Trophy, was the prototype of the next generation of forwards — not only fast, but strong and powerful, a forceful and intimidating leader.

The beginning of the dynasty that would dominate the NHL for the rest of the decade: The 1984 Edmonton Oilers. By the end of the 1980s, four players from this squad – Gretzky, Messier, Kurri, and Anderson – would rank among the top six on the NHL's all-time playoff point-scoring list.

Unlike previous champions, who stuck to a plan of trying to win a game by a score of 3–1, the Oilers were happy to win 7–5. They were exciting, flashy, and entertaining, and their victory over the Islanders in 1984 was a promise of things to come. And while the Oilers expressed their utmost admiration for the Islanders and for New York's record nineteen series wins, they had admiration for themselves, too. "There have been a lot of great teams," Messier said, "but I don't think there's ever been a team quite like us."

For 1984-85, the Edmonton Oilers retained their Smythe Division crown and again led the NHL in offensive output with 401 goals. With a second consecutive two-hundred-point season under his belt, Gretzky was assured his fifth straight Art Ross Trophy as the league's leading scorer, though he had to share the spotlight with defenseman Paul Coffey, who became only the third rear guard in NHL history to record a second hundred-point campaign. The surprise story of the year was written by the Philadelphia Flyers, who won a league-high fifty-three games and led all teams by registering 113 points.

From the time the playoffs began, the Oilers' offense was in high gear. They easily swept past the Jets and the Kings before burying Chicago in a record-breaking offensive barrage. Edmonton scored forty-four goals against Chicago, setting an NHL mark for goals in a six-game series. Gretzky was superb against the Black Hawks, compiling eighteen points in the half-dozen games. The Oilers' opponents in the Cup finals were the Philadelphia Flyers, who parlayed their regular-season accomplishments into post-season success. Although the familiar names of the past, such as Parent, Clarke, Barber, and MacLeish, were gone, they were replaced by a new Flyer family of Pelle Lindbergh, Tim Kerr, Mark Howe, and Brian Propp.

If the Oilers entered the series taking the Flyers lightly, they were promptly shaken from their lethargy. Using air-tight defense, the Flyers grabbed the series lead with a 4–1 victory in the opener. A power-play goal by Ilkka Sinisalo, even-strength markers by Ron Sutter and Tim Kerr, and an empty-net goal by Dave Poulin, accounted for the Flyers' scoring. The Flyers continued to impress in game two, allowing a goal by Wayne Gretzky in the first period before tying the contest on Tim Kerr's shot from the slot in the second. Still, the Oilers were able to slow down the Flyers' buzzing forwards and slowly take control of the game. Edmonton's line of Mike Krushelnyski, Willy Lindstrom, and Kevin McClelland combined to give the Oilers the lead late in the second period, allowing Edmonton's defense to take over and secure a 3–1 series-tying triumph.

Wayne Gretzky took control of the third game, chalking up a natural hat trick in the first period as the Oilers blasted Philadelphia goaltenders Pelle Lindbergh and Bob Froese with twenty shots in the first twenty minutes. Although the Flyers would allow the Oilers only six shots in the remaining two periods, the damage had been done, and Edmonton took the series lead with a 4–3 win. Four power-play goals, two of them off the stick of Gretzky, spelled the difference in game four, as the Oilers came back from a 3–1 deficit to win 5–3 and take a secure lead in the series, three games to one.

The final game of the 1985 finals belonged to the Oilers' offense. Playing in front of their home crowd in Northlands Coliseum, Gretzky and Coffey combined for eight points as the Oilers built a 7–1 lead after forty minutes and cruised from there to capture their second consecutive title with a

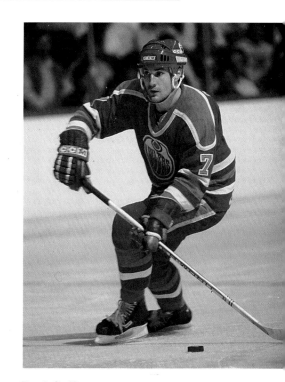

Paul Coffey set an NHL record for defensemen with 37 points in the 1985 playoffs.

Charlie Huddy pins the Flyers' Rich Sutter along the glass during the 1985 finals.

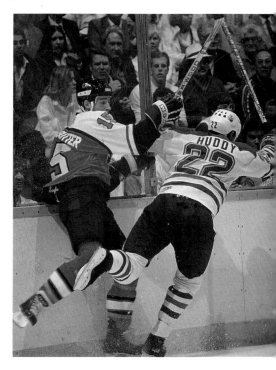

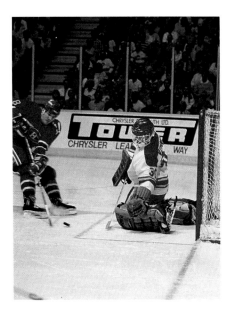

Montreal's David Maley eases the puck past Calgary's Mike Vernon to even game two of the 1986 finals at 2–2.

Mike Lalor checks Lanny McDonald near Patrick Roy's crease, 1986.

lopsided 8–3 decision over the Flyers. The Great One, who established a new NHL record for post-season points with forty-seven, was the clear choice to win his first Conn Smythe Trophy.

Edmonton remained atop the Smythe Division standings in 1985-86, registering a league-best 56 victories and 119 points. It was a season of accomplishments for Wayne Gretzky, who established a new NHL single-season record with 215 points. Paul Coffey became the first defenseman to score forty-eight goals in a single season, and three Oilers – Anderson, Kurri, and Gretzky – broke through the fifty-goal barrier. Yet, as was the case in Gretzky's record-breaking season of 1982, the Oilers couldn't translate regular-season success into post-season prosperity. The Calgary Flames, themselves an emerging NHL power, ended Edmonton's hopes of a third consecutive Cup win by eliminating the defending champs in a thrilling seven-game series, Calgary's winning goal coming when Oiler rear guard Steve Smith's clearing attempt bounced off goaltender Grant Fuhr into the Edmonton net. The Flames, who finished thirty points behind the Oilers, continued into the finals by downing the stubborn St. Louis Blues in another seven-game marathon.

Calgary's Wales Conference opponents were the Montreal Canadiens, who used a rookie-laden roster to defeat the Whalers, Bruins, and Rangers to reach the finals. Many of these first-year players had been promoted from the Canadiens' farm club in Sherbrooke, Quebec, where they had been part of an American Hockey League Calder Cup championship in 1985. Two of these newcomers, goaltender Patrick Roy and right winger Claude Lemieux, were major contributors to the Habs' resurgence. Despite never having appeared in the NHL playoffs before, Roy played superbly, posting a goals-against average of 1.92, while Lemieux scored ten goals in post-season play.

In the first period of game one of the finals, Calgary took a 2–1 lead on goals by Jim Peplinski and former Islander standout John Tonelli. After a scoreless second period, the Flames' Dan Quinn and Lanny McDonald scored power-play goals to increase Calgary's lead to 4–1. Game one ended 5–2 for the Flames. Calgary started quickly in the second game as well, opening a 2–0 advantage by the fifteen-second mark of period two. The Canadiens, who had been outplaying the Flames, refused to fold, and tied the game on goals by Gaston Gingras and rookie David Maley. The teams remained deadlocked through regulation time, setting up the first overtime of the series. Brian Skrudland scored the winner for Montreal just nine seconds after the start of the extra session, the quickest overtime clincher in NHL history.

Both teams played hard-checking hockey in the crucial third game of the series. Calgary secured an early edge, using the goal Joel Otto scored with two minutes left in the first period to go up 2–1, but the Canadiens scored three goals in the next ninety-three seconds to erase the deficit and build a two-goal lead. The Habs held on from there for a 5–3 victory. Patrick Roy

Rookie Claude Lemieux and the magic of the Stanley Cup, 1986.

provided the dramatics in the fourth game, becoming the first rookie goalie since Harry Lumley in 1945 to register a shutout in the finals. Roy faced only fifteen shots, but every save was crucial, since the margin of victory was 1–0. Claude Lemieux tallied the only goal when he intercepted Doug Risebrough's clearing attempt at the blue line and blasted the puck past Flames' goalie Mike Vernon for the game-winner.

The Habs ended the Flames' title hopes in game five, building a 4–1 lead, then holding on for a 4–3 championship-clinching win. The Flames, who had already scored once with their net empty, just missed tying the game when Roy made a difficult pad save on a shot by Jamie Macoun. The win marked the twenty-third time the Canadiens had won the championship, eclipsing the all-pro-sports total of twenty-two titles they had shared with baseball's New York Yankees. Patrick Roy joined fellow Montreal goaltender Ken Dryden as the only rookie to win the Conn Smythe Trophy.

The 1986-87 season saw increased parity in the NHL. The top team in the league, the Edmonton Oilers, collected only 106 points, the lowest total for a league-leader since 1970. For the first time in five seasons, the Oilers didn't

The City of Champions

Six teams representing the city of Montreal have captured the Stanley Cup: the Montreal AAA, the Montreal Wanderers, the Montreal Victorias, the Montreal Shamrocks, the Montreal Maroons, and, of course, the Montreal Canadiens.

reach the four-hundred-goal mark, but, with 372 goals scored, they led the NHL for the sixth consecutive season.

The playoff structure was fine-tuned for 1987, with the division semi-finals increased from a best-of-five to a best-of-seven series. The Patrick Division semi-finals between the Washington Capitals and the New York Islanders took the new format to its limit and beyond, as game seven went into quadruple overtime before an exhausted Pat LaFontaine scored the winner on a rising shot from just inside the Caps' blue line.

After losing out in 1986, Edmonton approached the post-season with a single purpose and, upon eliminating Los Angeles, Winnipeg, and Detroit, reached the Stanley Cup finals for the fourth time in the team's eight-year history. The Oilers' opponents were the only other team to register a hundred points in the regular season, the Philadelphia Flyers. The Flyers' place in the finals was achieved with great effort, as they survived a pair of tough six-game series with the Rangers and the Canadiens and a marathon seven-game set with the Islanders. With rookie Ron Hextall in goal and solid two-way performers like Rick Tocchet and Scott Mellanby, the Flyers had proven themselves to be stubborn opponents.

Edmonton used a familiar blueprint to establish a one-game lead in the

Wayne Gretzky, who finished with 34 playoff points in 1987, takes the outside track to elude the Flyers' Mark Howe.

series, erupting for three third-period goals by Anderson, Kurri, and Coffey to win 4–2. The Oilers increased their series lead with an overtime victory in game two, erasing a 2–1 deficit on a pretty goal by Glenn Anderson before winning the game on Jari Kurri's goal at 3:16 of the first overtime period.

The Flyers proved they had a little late-game magic of their own, scoring five unanswered goals in the final stages of game three to pull themselves back into the series. A pair of goals by Scott Mellanby and Brad McCrimmon, only seventeen seconds apart, helped reverse a 3–0 disadvantage in a game the Flyers would win 5–3. However, in game four, the Oilers, on a shorthanded goal by Kevin Lowe and a power-play marker by Randy Gregg – both set up by Gretzky – moved to within a game of their third championship with a well-played 4–1 win.

Down 3–1 in games, the Flyers played superbly to tie the series. Although they fell into early 2–0 holes in both games five and six, the Flyers refused to quit, constantly digging themselves out of trouble. In game five, down 3–1, Philadelphia struck back, allowing Hextall to stymie the Oilers' sharpshooters, while the Flyer forwards, led by Brian Propp with three assists, struck for a trio of goals in a 4–3 win. In game six, Kevin Lowe scored another shorthanded goal for Edmonton, as the Oilers scored twice in the first twenty minutes. Yet Philadelphia stormed back again, shocking Edmonton with three straight goals – by Lindsay Carson, Brian Propp and J. J. Daigneault – to tie the series with a 3–2 victory. It's worth noting that the only time in the series that the Flyers had the lead was when they scored the eventual winning goal in each of their victories. Every win featured a comeback effort of courage and determination.

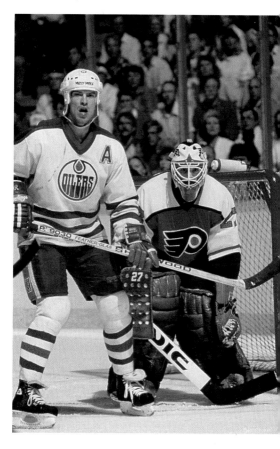

Mark Messier stands guard over Philadelphia's Ron Hextall during the 1987 finals. Hextall's heroics couldn't halt the Oilers' express, but it did earn him the Conn Smythe Trophy as playoff MVP.

Unfortunately for the Flyers, the Oilers fashioned the most important comeback of the series in the game that mattered most. After allowing Philadelphia a power-play goal in the first two minutes of game seven, the Oilers regrouped. Mark Messier shed his checkers to tie the game, and Jari Kurri took a cross-ice feed from Wayne Gretzky to win it, but it was the Oilers' defense that won the game, allowing the Flyers only two third-period shots in the 3–1 decision. As the players gathered around the Cup, Gretzky sought out Steve Smith and gave the trophy to the young defenseman whose errant pass had deflected off goaltender Fuhr into his own net, leading to the elimination of the Oilers in 1986.

Ron Hextall, who led all playoff goalies in games, minutes, and shutouts, was awarded the Conn Smythe Trophy.

After the series concluded, a new piece of Stanley Cup lore emerged. With his club trailing 3–1 in games, Philadelphia coach Mike Keenan had inspired his players by wheeling the Stanley Cup into the Philadelphia dressing room before games five and six, both of which were won by the Flyers. When Keenan wanted to continue this instant tradition before game seven, the Cup was nowhere to be found. The Flyers were forced to play the deciding game of the series without the benefit of communing with the trophy before taking

Oilers' captain Wayne Gretzky gets a little help from his friends in raising the Stanley Cup in a victorious salute to the Edmonton fans in the Northlands Coliseum after the Oilers downed the Flyers in seven games.

to the ice. Shortly after the game began, the missing Cup was located. Years later, the true story emerged. The Oilers, wanting to disrupt the Flyers' pre-game ritual, had locked the Cup in the trunk of a car belonging to one of their trainers.

The 1987-88 NHL season saw Mario Lemieux unseat Wayne Gretzky as the league's top scorer and the Calgary Flames vault into first place in the Smythe Division and the league. The tightest playoff race of the year took place in the Patrick Division, where eight points separated six clubs. It took the last goal of the regular season – an overtime marker by John MacLean of the New Jersey Devils in a game against Chicago – to determine the last playoff spot in the Patrick. With the win, the Devils eliminated the Rangers and earned their first berth in the playoffs since moving to New Jersey in 1982.

The long-awaited rematch between the two Alberta powerhouses finally occurred when the Oilers and the Flames met in the Smythe Division semi-finals. The end was anticlimactic, as the Oilers swept the Flames in four straight, the key goal being a shorthanded overtime counter by Wayne Gretzky in the second game. Edmonton then eliminated Detroit in five games to qualify for the finals. Their Wales Conference opponents were the Boston Bruins, who defeated Montreal in a playoff round for the first time since 1929 and then eliminated the New Jersey Devils in seven games to advance to the championship.

In the defensive struggle that opened the finals, the teams combined for only thirty-six shots on goal. Gretzky got the Edmonton express rolling, capitalizing on a Boston bench minor penalty for too many men on the ice only 1:56 into the second period. Cam Neely evened the score before the end of the period, but Keith Acton won it for the Oilers in the opening seconds of the third. Boston, constantly frustrated by the fine play of the Oilers' defense corps, was held to fourteen shots on goal, and dropped the series opener, 2–1. The "Big Four" figured strongly in game two for the Oilers. Messier, Gretzky, Anderson, and Kurri all scored for Edmonton, who limited the Bruins to only twelve shots while firing thirty-two at Boston goaltender Reggie Lemelin. Despite the disparity in shots on goal, the Bruins were in an excellent position to steal a win in this game. After giving up a pair of power-play goals in the first period, Boston battled back to tie the match on goals by Bob Joyce and Ken Linseman in the opening moments of the third. But that was as close as the Bruins would come, since Gretzky and Kurri both scored in the second half of the period to secure a 4–2 Edmonton victory.

The Bruins responded with a solid offensive effort in game three, but by opening up their play in an attempt to create scoring chances, they allowed

Grant Fuhr, who established a new NHL record by appearing in seventy-five games during the 1987-88 regular season, became the first goalie to win sixteen playoff games in a single season, leading the Oilers to their fourth Cup in five years in 1988.

*Esa Tikkanen, the Oilers'
designated harrier,
receives a taste of his
own medicine as he gets
hijacked by the Bruins'
equally feisty Willi Plett in
the 1988 finals.*

the Oilers' forwards too much room to maneuver, and in the end they paid
the price. Esa Tikkanen scored three times, and Gretzky added four assists,
as the Oilers moved to within a game of their fourth Stanley Cup with a
convincing 6–3 triumph at Boston Garden.

The Oilers' march to the Cup was delayed when, for only the second time in modern history, a Stanley Cup playoff game was halted before a final decision was reached. The fourth game of the series was scheduled for May 24, which turned out to be an exceedingly hot and humid day. In a sweltering Boston Garden, the game was delayed numerous times because of fog rising from the ice. In their best effort of the series, the Bruins reversed an early 2–0 deficit to score three consecutive goals, two by rear guard Glen Wesley, to take a 3–2 second-period lead. However, just moments after Craig Simpson tied the game for Edmonton, the lights went out in the Garden when an overloaded transformer sent the arena into darkness, the fans into the streets, and the players back to Edmonton. It was decided that the game, if necessary, would be replayed at the end of the series, but the Oilers ensured this wouldn't happen, easily dispatching the Bruins with a 6–3 series-capping win. Wayne Gretzky, who compiled a record thirteen points in the four-game series, was awarded the Conn Smythe Trophy.

The on-ice winners' celebration at the end of the game saw the spawning of a new Stanley Cup tradition. After the Oilers had circled the ice with the Cup, Gretzky gathered all the players, trainers, coaches, and executives onto the ice, where they posed for a celebratory group photo, surrounding the Cup. Since 1988, similar on-ice portraits have been taken of each winning team.

The off-season trade of Wayne Gretzky to the Los Angeles Kings overshadowed most of the on-ice activities of the 1988-89 season. Calgary captured the regular-season pennant, winning a franchise-high fifty-four games to finish with 117 points, two more than the Montreal Canadiens. In the natural progression of the playoffs, the NHL's top two teams made it to the finals, but not without a few exciting moments along the way. Philadelphia goaltender Ron Hextall shot the puck the length of the ice to score an empty-net goal against Washington in the Patrick Division semi-finals. Calgary needed a seventh-game overtime goal to advance past Vancouver, while

The Edmonton Oilers' family portrait, 1988. Less than three months later, Wayne Gretzky was traded to Los Angeles. By 1992, the core players of the team that dominated the game in the second half of the 1980s had moved on to other clubs.

Mario's Magic

Mario Lemieux tied a pair of NHL records on April 25, 1989, in a game against the Philadelphia Flyers. Lemieux's eight-point evening tied a record for most points in a post-season game, and his four goals in the opening stanza tied a record for most goals in a single period.

Calgary's Jamie Macoun rides Mike Keane into the boards as the Flames singe the Canadiens in the 1989 finals.

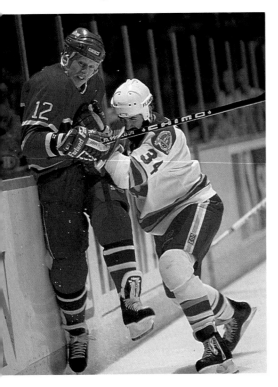

the defending-champion Oilers were eliminated in a tension-filled, seven-game marathon at the hands of the Los Angeles Kings. The Kings proved easy pickings for the Flames, however, who swept Los Angeles in four one-sided games. Calgary then ousted Chicago to reach the NHL's pinnacle series for the second time in franchise history. The Canadiens, looking for a record twenty-fourth championship banner, had a smooth ride to the finals, dropping Hartford, Boston, and Philadelphia to the sidelines by winning twelve games while losing only three.

It was expected that the Calgary–Montreal series would be a tight, low-scoring affair, but by the ten-minute mark of the opening period of game one, the teams had already scored four goals. The game remained tied at 2–2 until its mid-point, when Theoren Fleury broke through to score the winner for Calgary on a pretty solo effort. In game two, the Habs surrendered a 2–0 lead, but third-period markers scored ninety seconds apart by Chris Chelios and Russ Courtnall gave the Habs a 4–2 win and a split in the series.

Back at the Montreal Forum for game three, the Canadiens started quickly, using Mike McPhee's unassisted goal, only ninety-two seconds after the opening face-off, to take a 1–0 lead. Joey Mullen brought the Flames back, tying the match in the first period and sending Calgary into the lead with a power-play goal in the second stanza. Bobby Smith quickly knotted things in the third, but Doug Gilmour put the Flames back in the lead with only seven minutes remaining. With Patrick Roy on the bench for an extra attacker, Mats Naslund tied the game for the Habs, sending the match into overtime. The first overtime period was scoreless, and it appeared the second would be as well, until defensive specialist Ryan Walter banged the winner home from the edge of the crease to give the Canadiens a 4–3 victory and what would prove to be their last lead in the series.

In game four, Calgary limited Montreal to nineteen shots, as Doug Gilmour and Joe Mullen provided the offense in a 4–2 Flames win. Calgary's air-tight defense continued to stymie the Habs in the pivotal fifth game. After Joel Otto, Al MacInnis, and Mullen staked the Flames to a 3–1 first-period advantage, the Flames' defense held the fort in a 3–2 victory, with defenseman MacInnis and goaltender Mike Vernon earning most of the accolades.

The teams returned for game six to the Montreal Forum, where the Flames had an historical obstacle to overcome before hoisting the Cup. In their long history, the Canadiens had never allowed an opponent to win the Stanley Cup on Forum ice. This was about to change. The key moment of the game came with the score knotted at one goal apiece. Lanny McDonald, Calgary's team captain and a much-respected veteran player, came out of the penalty box in time to snare a pass from Joe Nieuwendyk and burst in on Patrick Roy in the Montreal net. McDonald's wrist-shot found the top corner, giving the Flames a lead they never relinquished. Doug Gilmour added a pair of third-period markers to give Calgary its first Stanley Cup title with

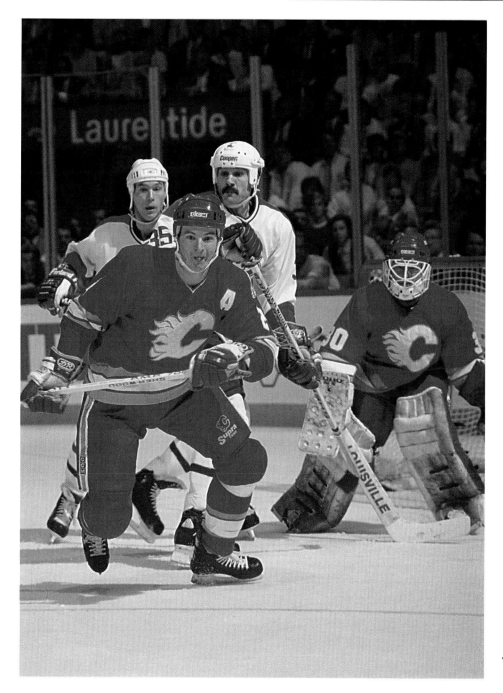

In 1990-91, Calgary's Al MacInnis became the third rear guard to record 100 points in a season. Here he skates away from Brian Skrudland and Mike McPhee in the 1989 finals. Goaltender Mike Vernon looks on.

Lanny McDonald, savoring champagne at last, reflects on his sixteen-year NHL career. McDonald's last season brought him into milestone territory: he finished with 500 goals, 1,006 points, and his first Cup championship.

a 4–2 victory. Al MacInnis, who became the first defenseman to lead the post-season scoring parade, won the Conn Smythe Trophy.

The Boston Bruins were the NHL's top club in regular-season play in 1989–90, winning home-ice advantage throughout the playoffs with a 46–25–9 record. After surviving a seven-game series with Hartford in the opening round of the playoffs, the Bruins cruised past Montreal and Washington to reach the finals for the second time in three years.

Once again, the Bruins' opponents were the Edmonton Oilers, who, despite having traded Paul Coffey and Wayne Gretzky, and having lost

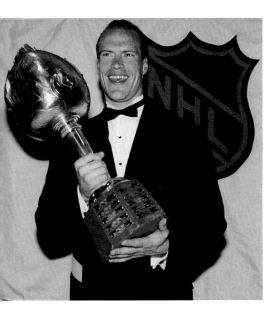

Mark Messier, who expanded his leadership role with the Oilers after the departure of Wayne Gretzky, cradles the Hart Trophy he received as the NHL's MVP in 1989-90.

An all-star in each of his thirteen seasons, Ray Bourque scored twice to force overtime in game one of the 1990 finals. In 1992, Bourque joined Denis Potvin and Paul Coffey as the third NHL defenseman to reach the 1,000-point milestone.

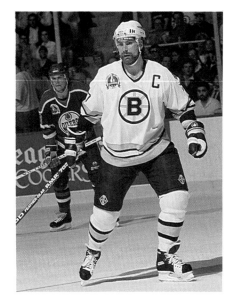

goaltender Grant Fuhr to injury, appeared to be as strong and competitive as ever, thanks in large part to team captain Mark Messier, who had been awarded the Hart Trophy as league MVP. Messier's combination of skill, power, and leadership sparked the Oilers' comeback after being down three games to one against Winnipeg in the Smythe Division semi-finals. Edmonton then swept Los Angeles to reach the Campbell Conference championship against Chicago. In this series, Messier dominated a must-win game four for the Oilers. With Chicago leading the series two games to one and playing at home, Messier had two goals and two assists in a 4–2 victory that tied the series. Edmonton went on to eliminate Chicago in six games.

The opening match of the finals was one of the most exciting in recent Cup competition. Edmonton, on goals by Adam Graves and Glenn Anderson, carried a 2–0 lead into the third period, only to see Ray Bourque, the Bruins' consummate All-Star rear guard, score twice to tie the game and send it into overtime. The two squads battled through fifty-five minutes of extra time before Edmonton's Petr Klima, on the ice for his only overtime shift of the evening, fired the puck through Andy Moog's pads to end the longest final-series overtime game ever played. Klima shared the spotlight with Oilers' goaltender Bill Ranford, who faced fifty-two shots in the game.

The loss seemed to drain the Bruins, who came up with a lackluster performance in game two, allowing seven goals on only twenty-two shots in a 7–2 thumping. Adam Graves, Joe Murphy, and Craig Simpson each scored a goal to pace the Oilers' attack. The Bruins received a solid night's work from Moog in game three, as the former Oiler stopped twenty-eight shots in Boston's 2–1 victory. A goal just ten seconds after the opening draw by John Byce had put the Bruins into the lead, and they pulled back into contention with the win. One of the Oilers' veteran offensive stars took charge in game four. Glenn Anderson scored two and set up a pair of goals for a four-point night en route to a 5–1 Edmonton win. He played a pivotal role in the Oilers' Cup-clinching victory in game five as well. Following a scoreless first period, Anderson put the Oilers on the board with an unassisted goal, then set up Craig Simpson for the eventual Cup-winner at the 9:31 mark of the second frame. Steve Smith and Joe Murphy added third-period tallies, before Lyndon Byers ruined Ranford's shutout with less than four minutes remaining.

Only two seasons after trading the greatest scorer in the history of the game, the Oilers' depth of talent and character enabled club president Glen Sather to engineer a revamped team that captured the franchise's fifth Stanley Cup title in seven years. Bill Ranford, who won a record-tying sixteen games in the post-season, was a popular choice as the Conn Smythe Trophy-winner.

The Norris Division featured the top two teams in the league during the 1990-91 campaign, as Chicago and St. Louis fought a year-long battle for the regular-season crown. The Blackhawks, whose team name had been officially changed from two words to one in 1986 to conform to the wording on the club's original charter of league membership, were one-point winners of the Presidents' Trophy, which is awarded to the club with the best regular-season record in the NHL. In the playoffs, however, both St. Louis and Chicago fell victim to the Minnesota North Stars, who later added a third upset, eliminating the defending champion Edmonton Oilers to win the Campbell Conference championship. The Stars, who finished the regular season in fourth place in the Norris Division with a record of 27–38–14, qualified for the Stanley Cup finals for the second time in franchise history.

The finalist from the Wales Conference proved to be the Pittsburgh Penguins, who were making only their second playoff appearance since two-time Art Ross Trophy-winner Mario Lemieux joined the club in 1984. The 1990-91 edition of the Penguins featured Tom Barrasso in goal and an explosive offense, ignited by Lemieux, Kevin Stevens, Mark Recchi, and Jaromir Jagr. Stanley Cup veterans Paul Coffey, Bryan Trottier, and Joe Mullen added skill and character as the Penguins seemed poised to give coach Bob "Badger" Johnson his first NHL championship.

The series marked the first time since Detroit and Chicago met in 1934, that both finalists had never won a Stanley Cup. The Stars–Penguins series also represented the first time two teams who had missed the playoffs the previous year had come back to reach the finals. It also was the first final-series meeting of two teams that had joined the NHL during the league's 1967 expansion.

Minnesota had arrived on the Stanley Cup doorstep largely because of its power play, which had registered thirty-one goals in the first three rounds of the playoffs. Led by Mark Tinordi, Bobby Smith, who had returned to his original team from Montreal, Neal Broten, and Brian Bellows, Minnesota continued to play well, winning the opening game, 5–4. The Penguins, staked to a lead by Bob Errey and Kevin Stevens, evened the series with a 4–1 home-ice triumph in game two.

Back at Minnesota's home rink, the North Stars were greeted by a full house after playing to small crowds for most of the year. Bobby Smith fired his second straight game-winner for Minnesota, as the Stars took a lead in the series with a 3–1 victory. Back spasms forced Mario Lemieux out of the line-up for this game.

Pittsburgh coach Bob Johnson had his club play all-out from the opening face-off in game four, hoping to knock Minnesota off its game, forcing mistakes and unnecessary penalties. This proved to be a master stroke. Before three minutes had elapsed in game four, the Penguins had a 3–0 lead. The Stars fought back to 4–3 by the end of the second period, but an empty-net goal by Phil Bourque iced a 5–3 series-tying win by Pittsburgh.

Game five had an identical plotline. By the time Mark Recchi scored his second goal of the game at the 13:41 mark of the first period, Pittsburgh had

Ladies of the Cup

Three women have had their names engraved on the Stanley Cup: Marguerite Norris (1955) was president of the Detroit Red Wings; Sonia Scurfield (1989) is a co-owner of the Calgary Flames; and Marie-Denise DeBartolo York (1991) was president of the Pittsburgh Penguins.

The 1990 finals featured a match-up between two goaltenders – Bill Ranford and Andy Moog – who had previously been traded for one another. In this photo, Ranford juggles the puck, as Craig Simpson, Mark Messier, and Boston's Dave Christian look on.

Pittsburgh's Phil Bourque was shifted to left wing by coach Bob Johnson, despite being named the outstanding defenseman in the minor pro International Hockey League in 1988. Here he challenges Minnesota's Gaetan Duchesne for possession of the puck.

Minnesota's Shawn Chambers rocks and blocks Pittsburgh left-winger Kevin Stevens during the Penguins–North Stars' worst-to-first Stanley Cup final.

a 4–0 lead. Again, Minnesota fought back to make it close, but the Penguins' Troy Loney scored the game-winner while perched in the crease during a wild goal-mouth scramble, and the persistent North Stars ended up on the short end of a 6–4 score. Minnesota ran out of miracles in game six, when, once again, the Penguins scored early and often on their way to an 8–0 shutout of the Campbell Conference finalists.

The Penguins' Stanley Cup triumph was a tribute to their firepower and their ability to regroup. Despite trailing in every playoff series – indeed, they lost game one of each round – they were decisive winners in every deciding game, outscoring their opponents by a combined score of 23–4 in these contests.

Mario Lemieux, who picked up four points in the final game of the series, was named the winner of the Conn Smythe Trophy. Despite persistent back problems, Lemieux scored forty-four points in post-season play, the second-highest total in playoff history.

The 1991-92 regular season saw the New York Rangers win a franchise-high fifty games to finish as the league's top club for the first time since 1942. Ranger winger Mike Gartner joined Hall-of-Famers Phil Esposito, Bobby Hull, and Wayne Gretzky as the only players to record at least thirty goals in thirteen consecutive seasons and became the first player to reach the milestone totals of five hundred goals, five hundred assists, one thousand points, and one thousand games played in the same season.

The playoffs began on a later date than in any previous year because an eleven-day strike by members of the NHL Players' Association delayed the conclusion of the regular season. The division semi-finals proved to be one of the most exciting playoff rounds in league history, with a record six of eight series requiring seven games to determine a winner. Four teams – Boston, Vancouver, Pittsburgh, and Detroit – all rebounded from deficits of three games to one to win their opening round match-ups. All four divisional winners (Montreal, the New York Rangers, Detroit, and Vancouver) advanced to the second round for the first time since 1980, but each lost its respective division final, as Boston, Pittsburgh, Chicago, and Edmonton reached the NHL's final four.

The Chicago Blackhawks blazed an early trail through the post-season, winning eleven consecutive playoff games en route to the finals. Chicago's

Seventh Heaven

In the opening round of the 1992 playoffs, all four of the Wales Conference series went to a seventh and deciding game. In total, six of the eight opening rounds needed all seven games to determine a winner, the most in post-season history.

The Magnificent Mario basks in the Stanley Cup spotlight after the Penguins brought their first Stanley Cup to Steel Town. Lemieux's game-breaking scoring skills also earned the big center the Conn Smythe Trophy for 1991.

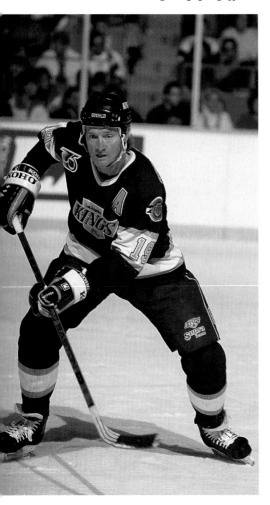

Larry Robinson, who scored at least ten goals in twelve of his first fourteen NHL seasons, bowed out in 1992 after an NHL record twenty straight years in the Stanley Cup playoffs.

string eclipsed the Boston Bruins' record of ten straight wins, established in 1970. Guided by Mike Keenan behind the bench, the Hawks featured a well-balanced attack that included Steve Smith and Chris Chelios on the blue lines and emerging superstar Jeremy Roenick at center. After sweeping Edmonton in the Campbell Conference finals, the Hawks earned a visit to the championship round for the first time since 1973.

Chicago's opponents in the finals were the defending Cup-champion Pittsburgh Penguins. The Pens' regular-season performance had been overshadowed by off-ice developments. The franchise aquired new ownership and withstood the death of coach Bob Johnson, who was lost to the club before the start of the campaign and passed away on November 26, 1991. Scotty Bowman was named interim head coach, and Pittsburgh finished third in the Patrick Division with eighty-seven points, the third-highest total in franchise history. The Penguins prepared for their Cup defense by adding hard-nosed winger Rick Tocchet and steady defender Kjell Samuelsson at the trading deadline. Pittsburgh reached the finals by defeating Washington, the New York Rangers, and Boston. Despite post-season injuries to Mario Lemieux, Joe Mullen, and Bob Errey, the Penguins gathered strength in each successive playoff round, arriving at the finals riding a seven-game winning streak of their own.

Game one of the 1992 Stanley Cup finals opened with the Hawks jumping to a quick 3–0 lead, before Phil Bourque got one back for the Penguins late in the first period. Brent Sutter re-established the Hawks' three-goal margin at the 11:36 mark of period two, but Pittsburgh closed the gap to one with a pair of markers late in the frame by Tocchet and by Lemieux, who banked a shot off Chicago goaltender Ed Belfour from a seemingly impossible angle. However, the goal of the game, and perhaps the series, was scored by Jaromir Jagr with less than five minutes remaining in the third period. Jagr, who had dazzled fans throughout the playoffs with his on-ice wizardry, picked up a loose puck near the Hawks' net and sidestepped a trio of Chicago defenders before sliding a backhand past Ed Belfour in the Hawks' net to tie the game at 4–4. The game appeared headed for overtime, but Mario Lemieux supplied the Penguins with a last-minute victory, snapping home a power-play goal off a cleanly won face-off with only thirteen seconds left in regulation time.

Chicago started strongly in game two, forcing Pittsburgh goaltender Tom Barrasso to make a number of difficult saves to keep the game scoreless. At the mid-point of the opening frame, Bob Errey broke free during a Blackhawks' power-play and slipped a backhand shot past a sprawling Belfour to score shorthanded and give the Penguins the lead. Shortly after this, Chicago's Bryan Marchment tied the game at the 10:24 mark of period two. Mario Lemieux restored, then increased, the Penguins' advantage with a pair of goals, the first on a cross-crease feed from Tocchet and the second on a wrist shot through Belfour's pads from the circle. The Pittsburgh defense took over, limiting Chicago to four third-period shots in the 3–1 win that

enabled the Penguins to carry a two-game advantage into Chicago Stadium.

As they had done in game two, the Blackhawks stormed the Penguins' net, but Barrasso turned away all thirteen first-period shots he faced. The Penguins received the only goal they would need, when a first-period shot by Jim Paek struck Kevin Stevens and deflected into the Chicago net. Barrasso was flawless, kicking aside fourteen shots over the final forty minutes to record the first 1–0 shutout in the Stanley Cup finals since Patrick Roy blanked Calgary in 1986.

Game four featured a wide-open offensive display, in which the teams erupted for six goals in the first period, including a final-series record three in a thirty-second span. Chicago captain Dirk Graham kept the Hawks' hopes alive with a first-period hat trick, each time erasing a Pittsburgh lead. The teams entered the third period tied at 4–4, but the Penguins took the lead again on Stevens's goal only twenty-five seconds into the final frame. Ron Francis added a sixth Pittsburgh counter, but Jeremy Roenick, with his second goal of the game, brought the Hawks to within one with four minutes remaining. Chicago mounted a final barrage, but the Pittsburgh defense held firm, giving the Penguins their second consecutive title while tying the Blackhawks' record of eleven consecutive playoff wins.

Despite the sweep, the Penguins had outscored the Blackhawks by only

Chicago's Steve Smith upends Mario Lemieux, setting up a last-minute power play that led to the Penguins' winning goal in game one of the 1992 finals.

The Eye in the Sky

For the first time in NHL history, a playoff result was determined by a video replay during the 1992 division semi-finals between Detroit and Minnesota. In overtime Sergei Fedorov's shot appeared to hit the crossbar. After a stop in play, referee Rob Shick consulted the supervisor of officials and video-replay official Wally Harris, who determined that the puck had entered the net, giving the Wings a 1—0 win.

Bryan Trottier (center), seen here celebrating his second Cup with the Penguins, joined Frank Mahovlich, Dick Duff, and Red Kelly as the only players to win two-or-more Stanley Cups with two different teams.

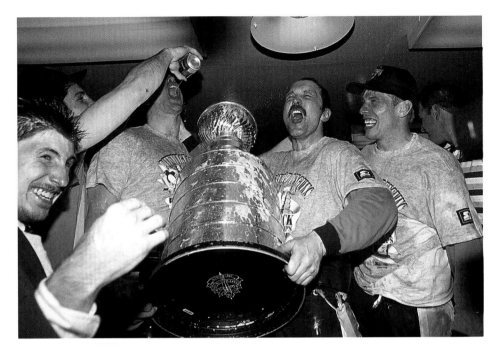

Jaromir Jagr, a magician on skates, breaks free from Chicago's Frantisek Kucera.

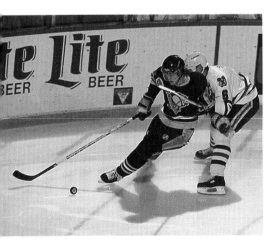

five goals over the four games, the lowest differential between the two clubs in the Stanley Cup finals in twenty-four years. Mario Lemieux joined Hall-of-Fame goaltender Bernie Parent as the only players to win the Conn Smythe Trophy in consecutive playoff years. Lemieux, despite missing six games due to an injured hand, finished with thirty-four points in post-season play.

The Penguins' Cup wins of 1991 and 1992 have a direct connection to the earliest days of Stanley Cup competition. Lester Patrick, grandfather of Pittsburgh general manager, Craig Patrick, was a player on Cup-winning teams for the Montreal Wanderers in 1906 and 1907. Frank Patrick, Craig's great-uncle, was part of the Vancouver Millionaires, winners in 1915. Lynn and Muzz Patrick, Craig's father and uncle respectively, were members of the New York Rangers' 1940 Cup-winning team.

One hundred years of Stanley Cup competition came to a close with the Penguins' 1992 championship. For a century, the passion and spectacle that is hockey – from the seven-man, no-substitution game of the 1890s, to the lightning-fast international spectacle of today – has flowed through the game's glittering touchstone, the Stanley Cup. The trophy, like hockey, has always grown and adapted to suit the times. Today, every surface of the Cup – even the inside of its bowl – is inscribed with the names of a century of great champions, and, in a larger sense, is inscribed with the dreams of countless fans and players.

Notes on Contributors

Pat Calabria, formerly of *Newsday*, reported on the New York Islanders from 1975 to 1986. He is now vice-president and director of communications for the club. He lives in Seaford, New York.

Bill Chadwick is a New York City native who officiated in the NHL for seventeen seasons. He is a member of the Hockey Hall of Fame and a recipient of the Lester Patrick Trophy for service to hockey in the United States.

Antonia Chambers is a graduate of Notre Dame University Law School. She maintains a private law practice in Delaware and works as an athletes' agent.

Dan Diamond has been the NHL's consulting publisher since 1984. He produces all of the NHL's annual statistical publications and edited *The Official NHL 75th Anniversary Commemorative Book*, published in 1991.

Ralph Dinger has done extensive research in hockey archival photo collections. He was photo editor of the 1991 bestseller, *The Official NHL 75th Anniversary Commemorative Book* and is managing editor of *The NHL Official Guide & Record Book*,

Phil Drackett edits the hockey magazine *Ice Hockey World*, published in Norfolk, England. He played professional hockey in Britain and is the author of several sports books, including *Flashing Blades*, a history of British ice hockey.

Milt Dunnell is a member of the Hockey Hall of Fame Player Selection Committee. He is a recipient of the Elmer Ferguson Memorial Award for journalistic excellence and is a veteran sports editor and writer, covering hockey for the Toronto *Star* for more than half a century.

James Duplacey is the former curator of the Hockey Hall of Fame and Museum. He is the author of several books about hockey and baseball, including a recently published children's book about the Stanley Cup.

Stan Fischler has authored some sixty-five books about the game of hockey. Based in New York, he operates the Fischler Hockey Service in partnership with his wife, Shirley Walton Fischler. He also works as a commentator on telecasts of New York Islanders' and New Jersey Devils' games.

George Gross is the Corporate Sports Editor of the Toronto *Sun*. He is a recipient of the Elmer Ferguson Memorial Award for journalistic excellence and worked for the Toronto *Telegram* at the time of the Toronto Maple Leafs' 1967 Stanley Cup win.

Bob Hesketh covered the Toronto Maple Leafs for the Toronto *Telegram* during the Pullman-car era of the 1940s and 1950s. He won a National Newspaper Award in 1957. He joined CFRB Radio in 1959.

Roy MacGregor is co-writer of the 1989 television mini-series and bestselling book *Home Game*. He also wrote *The Last Season*, a novel set in the hockey world. He is a general columnist for the Ottawa *Citizen* with a special assignment to cover the new Ottawa Senators in 1992-93.

Stan Saplin is a noted journalist and public-relations executive with specific expertise in hockey and in track and field. He is a former New York Rangers' publicity man who, in 1947, published the first team press guide in NHL history.

Myer Siemiatycki is Professor of Politics at Ryerson Polytechnical Institute in Toronto, and hosts a weekly radio program on labor issues. He is a recipient of the Distinguished Educator award of the Ontario Institute for Studies in Education in recognition of his contribution to labor education.

Jack Sullivan joined Canadian Press in 1929 and was appointed CP's first sports editor in 1948. He retired in 1976 and was inducted into Canada's Sports Hall of Fame in 1983. He passed away in 1992.

Réjean Tremblay is a columnist and feature writer for *La Presse* in Montreal. He also wrote the successful dramatic television series, *He Shoots, He Scores!*, which was produced in both French and English.

Photo Credits

Stanley Cup Champions
and Finalists

YEAR	WINNING TEAM	COACH	FINALIST	COACH
1992	Pittsburgh Penguins	Scotty Bowman	Chicago Black Hawks	Mike Keenan
1991	Pittsburgh Penguins	Bob Johnson	Minnesota North Stars	Bob Gainey
1990	Edmonton Oilers	John Muckler	Boston Bruins	Mike Milbury
1989	Calgary Flames	Terry Crisp	Montreal Canadiens	Pat Burns
1988	Edmonton Oilers	Glen Sather	Boston Bruins	Terry O'Reilly
1987	Edmonton Oilers	Glen Sather	Philadelphia Flyers	Mike Keenan
1986	Montreal Canadiens	Jean Perron	Calgary Flames	Bob Johnson
1985	Edmonton Oilers	Glen Sather	Philadelphia Flyers	Mike Keenan
1984	Edmonton Oilers	Glen Sather	New York Islanders	Al Arbour
1983	New York Islanders	Al Arbour	Edmonton Oilers	Glen Sather
1982	New York Islanders	Al Arbour	Vancouver Canucks	Roger Neilson
1981	New York Islanders	Al Arbour	Minnesota North Stars	Glen Sonmor
1980	New York Islanders	Al Arbour	Philadelphia Flyers	Pat Quinn
1979	Montreal Canadiens	Scotty Bowman	New York Rangers	Fred Shero
1978	Montreal Canadiens	Scotty Bowman	Boston Bruins	Don Cherry
1977	Montreal Canadiens	Scotty Bowman	Boston Bruins	Don Cherry
1976	Montreal Canadiens	Scotty Bowman	Philadelphia Flyers	Fred Shero
1975	Philadelphia Flyers	Fred Shero	Buffalo Sabres	Floyd Smith
1974	Philadelphia Flyers	Fred Shero	Boston Bruins	Bep Guidolin
1973	Montreal Canadiens	Scotty Bowman	Chicago Black Hawks	Billy Reay
1972	Boston Bruins	Tom Johnson	New York Rangers	Emile Francis
1971	Montreal Canadiens	Al MacNeil	Chicago Black Hawks	Billy Reay
1970	Boston Bruins	Harry Sinden	St. Louis Blues	Scotty Bowman
1969	Montreal Canadiens	Claude Ruel	St. Louis Blues	Scotty Bowman
1968	Montreal Canadiens	Toe Blake	St. Louis Blues	Scotty Bowman
1967	Toronto Maple Leafs	Punch Imlach	Montreal Canadiens	Toe Blake
1966	Montreal Canadiens	Toe Blake	Detroit Red Wings	Sid Abel
1965	Montreal Canadiens	Toe Blake	Chicago Black Hawks	Billy Reay
1964	Toronto Maple Leafs	Punch Imlach	Detroit Red Wings	Sid Abel
1963	Toronto Maple Leafs	Punch Imlach	Detroit Red Wings	Sid Abel
1962	Toronto Maple Leafs	Punch Imlach	Chicago Black Hawks	Rudy Pilous
1961	Chicago Black Hawks	Rudy Pilous	Detroit Red Wings	Sid Abel
1960	Montreal Canadiens	Toe Blake	Toronto Maple Leafs	Punch Imlach
1959	Montreal Canadiens	Toe Blake	Toronto Maple Leafs	Punch Imlach
1958	Montreal Canadiens	Toe Blake	Boston Bruins	Milt Schmidt
1957	Montreal Canadiens	Toe Blake	Boston Bruins	Milt Schmidt
1956	Montreal Canadiens	Toe Blake	Detroit Red Wings	Jimmy Skinner
1955	Detroit Red Wings	Jimmy Skinner	Montreal Canadiens	Dick Irvin
1954	Detroit Red Wings	Tommy Ivan	Montreal Canadiens	Dick Irvin
1953	Montreal Canadiens	Dick Irvin	Boston Bruins	Lynn Patrick
1952	Detroit Red Wings	Tommy Ivan	Montreal Canadiens	Dick Irvin
1951	Toronto Maple Leafs	Joe Primeau	Montreal Canadiens	Dick Irvin
1950	Detroit Red Wings	Tommy Ivan	New York Rangers	Lynn Patrick
1949	Toronto Maple Leafs	Hap Day	Detroit Red Wings	Tommy Ivan
1948	Toronto Maple Leafs	Hap Day	Detroit Red Wings	Tommy Ivan
1947	Toronto Maple Leafs	Hap Day	Montreal Canadiens	Dick Irvin
1946	Montreal Canadiens	Dick Irvin	Boston Bruins	Dit Clapper
1945	Toronto Maple Leafs	Hap Day	Detroit Red Wings	Jack Adams
1944	Montreal Canadiens	Dick Irvin	Chicago Black Hawks	Paul Thompson
1943	Detroit Red Wings	Jack Adams	Boston Bruins	Art Ross

YEAR	WINNING TEAM	COACH	FINALIST	COACH
1942	Toronto Maple Leafs	Hap Day	Detroit Red Wings	Jack Adams
1941	Boston Bruins	Cooney Weiland	Detroit Red Wings	Ebbie Goodfellow
1940	New York Rangers	Frank Boucher	Toronto Maple Leafs	Dick Irvin
1939	Boston Bruins	Art Ross	Toronto Maple Leafs	Dick Irvin
1938	Chicago Black Hawks	Bill Stewart	Toronto Maple Leafs	Dick Irvin
1937	Detroit Red Wings	Jack Adams	New York Rangers	Lester Patrick
1936	Detroit Red Wings	Jack Adams	Toronto Maple Leafs	Dick Irvin
1935	Montreal Maroons	Tommy Gorman	Toronto Maple Leafs	Dick Irvin
1934	Chicago Black Hawks	Tommy Gorman	Detroit Red Wings	Jack Adams
1933	New York Rangers	Lester Patrick	Toronto Maple Leafs	Dick Irvin
1932	Toronto Maple Leafs	Dick Irvin	New York Rangers	Lester Patrick
1931	Montreal Canadiens	Cecil Hart	Chicago Black Hawks	Dick Irvin
1930	Montreal Canadiens	Cecil Hart	Boston Bruins	Art Ross
1929	Boston Bruins	Cy Denneny	New York Rangers	Lester Patrick
1928	New York Rangers	Lester Patrick	Montreal Maroons	Eddie Gerard
1927	Ottawa Senators	Dave Gill	Boston Bruins	Art Ross

(The National Hockey League took over sole control of Stanley Cup competition after 1926)

YEAR	WINNING TEAM	COACH	FINALIST	COACH
1926	Montreal Maroons	Eddie Gerard	Victoria Cougars	Lester Patrick
1925	Victoria Cougars	Lester Patrick	Montreal Canadiens	Léo Dandurand
1924	Montreal Canadiens	Léo Dandurand	Calgary Tigers	-
			Vancouver Maroons	-
1923	Ottawa Senators	Pete Green	Edmonton Eskimos	-
			Vancouver Maroons	-
1922	Toronto St. Pats	Eddie Powers	Vancouver Millionaires	Frank Patrick
1921	Ottawa Senators	Pete Green	Vancouver Millionaires	Frank Patrick
1920	Ottawa Senators	Pete Green	Seattle Metropolitans	-
1919	No decision (series between Montreal and Seattle called off due to influenza epidemic)			
1918	Toronto Arenas	Dick Carroll	Vancouver Millionaires	Frank Partick
1917	Seattle Metropolitans	Pete Muldoon	Montreal Canadiens	George Kennedy
1916	Montreal Canadiens	George Kennedy	Portland Rosebuds	-
1915	Vancouver Millionaires	Frank Patrick	Ottawa Senators	-
1914	Toronto Blueshirts	Scotty Davidson	Victoria Cougars	-
			Montreal Canadiens	George Kennedy
1913	Quebec Bulldogs	Joe Malone	Sydney Miners	-
1912	Quebec Bulldogs	C. Nolan	Moncton Victories	-
1911	Ottawa Senators	Bruce Stuart	Port Arthur Bearcats	-
			Galt	-
1910	Montreal Wanderers	Pud Glass	Berlin Union Jacks	-
1910	Ottawa Senators	Bruce Stuart	Edmonton Eskimos	-
			Galt	-
1909	Ottawa Senators	Bruce Stuart	(no challengers)	
1908	Montreal Wanderers	Cecil Blachford	Edmonton Eskimos	-
			Toronto OPHL	-
			Winnipeg Maple Leafs	-
			Ottawa Victorias	-
1907	Montreal Wanderers	Cecil Blachford	Kenora Thistles	Tommy Phillips
	Kenora Thistles	Tommy Phillips	Montreal Wanderers	Cecil Blachford
1906	Montreal Wanderers	Cecil Blachford	New Glasgow Cubs	-
			Ottawa Silver Seven	Alf Smith
	Ottawa Silver Seven	Alf Smith	Smiths Falls	-
			Queen's University	-
1905	Ottawa Silver Seven	Alf Smith	Rat Portage Thistles	-
			Dawson City	-
1904	Ottawa Silver Seven	Alf Smith	Brandon Wheat Kings	-
			Montreal Wanderers	-
			Toronto Marlboros	-
			Winnipeg Rowing Club	-
1903	Ottawa Silver Seven	Alf Smith	Rat Portage Thistles	-
			Montreal Victorias	-
	Montreal AAA	C. McKerrow	Winnipeg Victorias	-
1902	Montreal AAA	C. McKerrow	Winnipeg Victorias	Dan Bain
	Winnipeg Victorias	Dan Bain	Toronto Wellingtons	-
1901	Winnipeg Victorias	Dan Bain	Montreal Shamrocks	Harry Trihey
1900	Montreal Shamrocks	Harry Trihey	Halifax Crescents	-
			Winnipeg Victorias	Dan Bain
1899	Montreal Shamrocks	Harry Trihey	Queen's University	-
	Montreal Victorias	Frank Richardson	Winnipeg Victorias	Jack Armitage
1898	Montreal Victorias	Frank Richardson	(no challengers)	
1897	Montreal Victorias	Mike Grant	Ottawa Capitals	-
1896	Montreal Victorias	Mike Grant	Winnipeg Victorias	Jack Armitage
	Winnipeg Victorias	Jack Armitage	Montreal Victorias	Mike Grant
1895	Montreal Victorias	Mike Grant	(no challengers)	
1894	Montreal AAA	-	Ottawa Capitals	-
1893	Montreal AAA	-	(no challengers)	

Stanley Cup Winners: Rosters and Final Series Scores

1991-92 – Pittsburgh Penguins – Mario Lemieux (Captain), Ron Francis, Bryan Trottier, Kevin Stevens, Bob Errey, Phil Bourque, Troy Loney, Rick Tocchet, Joe Mullen, Jaromir Jagr, Jiri Hrdina, Shawn McEachern, Ulf Samuelsson, Kjell Samuelsson, Larry Murphy, Gord Roberts, Jim Paek, Paul Stanton, Tom Barrasso, Ken Wregget, Jay Caufield, Jamie Leach, Wendell Young, Grant Jennings, Peter Taglianetti, Jock Callander, Dave Michayluk, Mike Needham, Jeff Chychrun, Ken Priestlay, Jeff Daniels, Howard Baldwin (Owner and President), Morris Belzberg (Owner), Thomas Ruta (Owner), Donn Patton (Executive Vice President and Chief Financial Officer), Paul Martha (Executive Vice President and General Counsel), Craig Patrick (Executive Vice President and General Manager), Bob Johnson (Coach), Scott Bowman (Director of Player Development and Coach), Barry Smith, Rick Kehoe, Pierre McGuire, Gilles Meloche, Rick Paterson (Assistant Coaches), Steve Latin (Equipment Manager), Skip Thayer (Trainer), John Welday (Strength and Conditioning Coach), Greg Malone, Les Binkley, Charlie Hodge, John Gill, Ralph Cox (Scouts).
Scores: May 26 at Pittsburgh – Pittsburgh 5, Chicago 4; May 28 at Pittsburgh – Pittsburgh 3, Chicago 1; May 30 at Chicago – Pittsburgh 1, Chicago 0; June 1 at Chicago – Pittsburgh 6, Chicago 5.

1990-91 – Pittsburgh Penguins – Mario Lemieux (Captain), Paul Coffey, Randy Hillier, Bob Errey, Tom Barrasso, Phil Bourque, Jay Caufield, Ron Francis, Randy Gilhen, Jiri Hrdina, Jaromir Jagr, Grant Jennings, Troy Loney, Joe Mullen, Larry Murphy, Jim Paek, Frank Pietrangelo, Barry Pederson, Mark Recchi, Gordie Roberts, Ulf Samuelsson, Paul Stanton, Kevin Stevens, Peter Taglianetti, Bryan Trottier, Scott Young, Wendell Young, Edward J. DeBartolo, Sr. (Owner), Marie D. DeBartolo York (President), Paul Martha (Vice-President & General Counsel), Craig Patrick (General Manager), Scotty Bowman (Director of Player Development & Recruitment), Bob Johnson (Coach), Rick Kehoe (Assistant Coach), Gilles Meloche (Goaltending Coach & Scout), Rick Paterson (Assistant Coach), Barry Smith (Assistant Coach), Steve Latin (Equipment Manager), Skip Thayer (Trainer), John Welday (Strength & Conditioning Coach), Greg Malone (Scout).
Scores: May 15 at Pittsburgh – Minnesota 5, Pittsburgh 4; May 17 at Pittsburgh – Pittsburgh 4, Minnesota 1; May 19 at Minnesota – Minnesota 3, Pittsburgh 1; May 21 at Minnesota – Pittsburgh 5, Minnesota 3; May 23 at Pittsburgh – Pittsburgh 6, Minnesota 4; May 25 at Minnesota – Pittsburgh 8, Minnesota 0.

1989-90 – Edmonton Oilers – Kevin Lowe, Steve Smith, Jeff Beukeboom, Mark Lamb, Joe Murphy, Glenn Anderson, Mark Messier, Adam Graves, Craig MacTavish, Kelly Buchberger, Jari Kurri, Craig Simpson, Martin Gélinas, Randy Gregg, Charlie Huddy, Geoff Smith, Reijo Ruotsalainen, Craig Muni, Bill Ranford, Dave Brown, Eldon Reddick, Petr Klima, Esa Tikkanen, Grant Fuhr, Peter Pocklington (Owner), Glen Sather (President/General Manager), John Muckler (Coach), Ted Green (Co-Coach), Ron Low (Ass't Coach), Bruce MacGregor (Ass't General Manager), Barry Fraser (Director of Player Personnel), John Blackwell (Director of Operations, AHL), Ace Bailey, Ed Chadwick, Lorne Davis, Harry Howell, Matti Vaisanen and Albert Reeves (Scouts), Bill Tuele (Director of Public Relations), Werner Baum (Controller), Dr. Gordon Cameron (Medical Chief of Staff), Dr. David Reid (Team Physician), Barrie Stafford (Athletic Trainer), Ken Lowe (Athletic Therapist), Stuart Poirier (Massage Therapist), Lyle Kulchisky (Ass't Trainer).
Scores: May 15 at Boston – Edmonton 3, Boston 2; May 18 at Boston – Edmonton 7, Boston 2; May 20 at Edmonton – Boston 2, Edmonton 1; May 22 at Edmonton – Edmonton 5, Boston 1; May 24 at Boston – Edmonton 4, Boston 1.

1988-89 – Calgary Flames – Mike Vernon, Rick Wamsley, Al MacInnis, Brad McCrimmon, Dana Murzyn, Ric Nattress, Joe Mullen, Lanny McDonald (Co-captain), Gary Roberts, Colin Patterson, Hakan Loob, Theoren Fleury, Jiri Hrdina, Tim Hunter (Ass't. captain), Gary Suter, Mark Hunter, Jim Peplinski (Co-captain), Joe Nieuwendyk, Brian MacLellan, Joel Otto, Jamie Macon, Doug Gilmour, Rob Ramage. Norman Green, Harley Hotchkiss, Norman Kwong, Sonia Scurfield, B.J. Seaman, D.K. Seaman (Owners), Cliff Fletcher (President and General Manager), Al MacNeil (Ass't General Manager), Al Coates (Ass't to the President), Terry Crisp (Head Coach), Doug Risebrough, Tom Watt (Ass't Coaches), Glenn Hall (Goaltending Consultant), Jim Murray (Trainer), Bob Stewart (Equipment Manager), Al Murray (Ass't Trainer).
Scores: May 14 at Calgary – Calgary 3, Montreal 2; May 17 at Calgary – Montreal 4, Calgary 2; May 19 at Montreal – Montreal 4, Calgary 3; May 21 at Montreal – Calgary 4, Montreal 2; May 23 at Calgary – Calgary 3, Montreal 2; May 25 at Montreal – Calgary 4, Montreal 2.

1987-88 – Edmonton Oilers – Keith Acton, Glenn Anderson, Jeff Beukeboom, Geoff Courtnall, Grant Fuhr, Randy Gregg, Wayne Gretzky, Dave Hannan, Charlie Huddy, Mike Krushelnyski, Jari Kurri, Normand Lacombe, Kevin Lowe, Craig MacTavish, Kevin McClelland, Marty McSorley, Mark Messier, Craig Muni, Bill Ranford, Craig Simpson, Steve Smith, Esa Tikkanen, Peter Pocklington (Owner), Glen Sather (General Manager/Coach), John Muckler (Co-Coach), Ted Green (Ass't Coach), Barry Fraser (Director of Player Personnel), Bill Tuele (Director of Public Relations), Dr. Gordon Cameron (Team Physician), Peter Millar (Athletic Therapist), Barrie Stafford (Trainer), Juergen Mers (Massage Therapist), Lyle Kulchisky (Ass't Trainer).
Scores: May 18 at Edmonton – Edmonton 2, Boston 1; May 20 at Edmonton – Edmonton 4, Boston 2; May 22 at Boston – Edmonton 6, Boston 3; May 24 at Boston – Boston 3, Edmonton 3 (suspended due to power failure); May 26 at Edmonton – Edmonton 6, Boston 3.

1986-87 – Edmonton Oilers – Glenn Anderson, Jeff Beukeboom, Kelly Buchberger, Paul Coffey, Grant Fuhr, Randy Gregg, Wayne Gretzky, Charlie Huddy, Dave Hunter, Mike Krushelnyski, Jari Kurri, Moe Lemay, Kevin Lowe, Craig MacTavish, Kevin McClelland, Marty McSorley, Mark Messier, Andy Moog, Craig Muni, Kent Nilsson, Jaroslav Pouzar, Reijo Ruotsalainen, Steve Smith, Esa Tikkanen, Peter Pocklington (Owner), Glen Sather (General Manager/Coach), John Muckler (Co-Coach), Ted Green (Ass't. Coach), Ron Low (Ass't. Coach), Bruce MacGregor (Ass't. General Manager), Barry Fraser (Director of Player Personnel), Peter Millar (Athletic Therapist), Barrie Stafford (Trainer), Lyle Kulchisky (Ass't Trainer).
Scores: May 17 at Edmonton – Edmonton 4, Philadelphia 3; May 20 at Edmonton – Edmonton 3, Philadelphia 2; May 22 at Philadelpia – Philadelphia 5, Edmonton 3; May 24 at Philadelphia – Philadelphia 4, Edmonton 1; May 26 at Edmonton – Philadelphia 4, Edmonton 3; May 28 at Philadelphia – Philadelphia 3, Edmonton 2; May 31 at Edmonton – Edmonton 3, Philadelphia 1.

1985-86 – Montreal Canadiens – Bob Gainey, Doug Soetaert, Patrick Roy, Rick Green, David Maley, Ryan Walter, Serge Boisvert, Mario Tremblay, Bobby Smith, Craig Ludwig, Tom Kurvers, Kjell Dahlin, Larry Robinson, Guy Carbonneau, Chris Chelios, Petr Svoboda, Mats Naslund, Lucien DeBlois, Steve Rooney, Gaston Gingras, Mike Lalor, John Kordic, Claude Lemieux, Mike McPhee, Brian Skrudland, Stephane Richer, Ronald Corey (President), Serge Savard (General Manager), Jean Perron (Coach), Jacques Laperrière (Ass't. Coach), Jean Béliveau (Vice President), Francois-Xavier Seigneur (Vice President), Fred Steer (Vice President), Jacques Lemaire (Ass't. General Manager), André Boudrias (Ass't. General Manager), Claude Ruel, Yves Belanger (Athletic Therapist), Gaetan Lefebvre (Ass't. Athletic Therapist), Eddy Palchek (Trainer), Sylvain Toupin (Ass't. Trainer).
Scores: May 16 at Calgary – Calgary 5, Montreal 3; May 18 at Calgary – Montreal 3, Calgary 2; May 20 at Montreal – Montreal 5, Calgary 3; May 22 at Montreal – Montreal 1, Calgary 0; May 24 at Calgary – Montreal 4, Calgary 3.

1984-85 – Edmonton Oilers – Glenn Anderson, Bill Carroll, Paul Coffey, Lee Fogolin, Grant Fuhr, Randy Gregg, Wayne Gretzky, Charlie Huddy, Pat Hughes, Dave Hunter, Don Jackson, Mike Krushelnyski, Jari Kurri, Willy Lindstrom, Kevin Lowe, Dave Lumley, Kevin McClelland, Larry Melnyk, Mark Messier, Andy Moog, Mark Napier, Jaroslav Pouzar, Dave Semenko, Esa Tikkanen, Peter Pocklington (Owner), Glen Sather (General Manager/Coach), John Muckler (Ass't. Coach), Ted Green (Ass't. Coach), Bruce MacGregor (Ass't. General Manager), Barry Fraser (Director of Player Personnel/Chief Scout), Peter Millar (Athletic Therapist), Barrie Stafford, Lyle Kulchisky (Trainers)
Scores: May 21 at Philadelphia – Philadelphia 4, Edmonton 1; May 23 at Philadelphia – Edmonton 3, Philadelphia 1; May 25 at Edmonton – Edmonton 4, Philadelphia 3; May 28 at Edmonton – Edmonton 5, Philadelphia 3; May 30 at Edmonton – Edmonton 8, Philadelphia 3.

1983-84 – Edmonton Oilers – Glenn Anderson, Paul Coffey, Pat Conacher, Lee Fogolin, Grant Fuhr, Randy Gregg, Wayne Gretzky, Charlie Huddy, Pat Hughes, Dave Hunter, Don Jackson, Jari Kurri, Willy Lindstrom, Ken Linseman, Kevin Lowe, Dave Lumley, Kevin McClelland, Mark Messier, Andy Moog, Jaroslav Pouzar, Dave Semenko, Peter Pocklington (Owner), Glen Sather (General Manager/Coach), John Muckler (Ass't. Coach), Ted Green (Ass't. General Manager), Barry Fraser (Director of Player Personnel/Chief Scout), Peter Millar (Athletic Therapist), Barrie Stafford (Trainer)
Scores: May 10 at New York – Edmonton 1, NY Islanders 0; May 12 at New York – NY Islanders 6, Edmonton 1; May 15 at Edmonton – Edmonton 7, NY Islanders 2; May 17 at Edmonton – Edmonton 7, NY Islanders 2; May 19 at Edmonton – Edmonton 5, NY Islanders 2.

1982-83 – New York Islanders – Mike Bossy, Bob Bourne, Paul Boutilier, Bill Carroll, Greg Gilbert, Clark Gillies, Butch Goring, Mats Hallin, Tomas Jonsson, Anders Kallur, Gord Lane, Dave Langevin, Mike McEwen, Roland Melanson, Wayne Merrick, Ken Morrow, Bob Nystrom, Stefan Persson, Denis Potvin, Bill Smith, Brent Sutter, Duane Sutter, John Tonelli, Bryan Trottier, Al Arbour (coch), Lorne Henning (ass't coach), Bill Torrey (general manager), Ron Waske, Jim Pickard (trainers)
Scores: May 10 at Edmonton – NY Islanders 2, Edmonton 0; May 12 at Edmonton – NY Islanders 6, Edmonton 3; May 14 at New York – NY Islanders 5, Edmonton 1; May 17 at New York – NY Islanders 4, Edmonton 2

1981-82 – New York Islanders – Mike Bossy, Bob Bourne, Bill Carroll, Butch Goring, Greg Gilbert, Clark Gillies, Tomas Jonsson, Anders Kallur, Gord Lane, Dave Langevin, Hector Marini, Mike McEwen, Roland Melanson, Wayne Merrick, Ken Morrow, Bob Nystrom, Stefan Persson, Denis Potvin, Bill Smith, Brent Sutter, Duane Sutter, John Tonelli, Bryan Trottier, Al Arbour (coach), Lorne Henning (ass't coach), Bill Torrey (general manager), Ron Waske, Jim Pickard (trainers)
Scores: May 8 at New York – NY Islanders 6, Vancouver 5; May 11 at New York – NY Islanders 6, Vancouver 4; May 13 at Vancouver – NY Islanders 3, Vancouver 0; May 16 at Vancouver – NY Islanders 3, Vancouver 1

1980-81 – New York Islanders – Denis Potvin, Mike McEwen, Ken Morrow, Gord Lane, Bob Lorimer, Stefan Persson, Dave Langevin, Mike Bossy, Bryan Trottier, Butch Goring, Wayne Merrick, Clark Gillies, John Tonelli, Bob Nystrom, Bill Carroll, Bob Bourne, Hector Marini, Anders Kallur, Duane Sutter, Garry Howatt, Lorne Henning, Bill Smith, Roland Melanson, Al Arbour (coach), Bill Torrey (general manager), Ron Waske, Jim Pickard (trainers).
Scores: May 12 at New York – NY Islanders 6, Minnesota 3; May 14 at New York – NY Islanders 6, Minnesota 3; May 17 at Minnesota – NY Islanders 7, Minnesota 5; May 19 at Minnesota – Minnesota 4, NY Islanders 2; May 21 at New York – NY Islanders 5, Minnesota 1.

1979-80 – New York Islanders – Gord Lane, Jean Potvin, Bob Lorimer, Denis Potvin, Stefan Persson, Ken Morrow, Dave Langevin, Duane Sutter, Garry Howatt, Clark Gillies, Lorne Henning, Wayne Merrick, Bob Bourne, Steve Tambellini, Bryan Trottier, Mike Bossy, Bob Nystrom, John Tonelli, Anders Kallur, Butch Goring, Alex McKendry, Glenn Resch, Billy Smith, Al Arbour (coach), Bill Torrey (general manager), Ron Waske, Jim Pickard (trainers).
Scores: May 13 at Philadelphia – NY Islanders 4, Philadelphia 3; May 15 at Philadelphia – Philadelphia 8, NY Islanders 3; May 17 at New York – NY Islanders 6, Philadelphia 2; May 19 at New York – NY Islanders 5, Philadelphia 2; May 22 at Philadelphia – Philadelphia 6, NY Islanders 3; May 24 at New York – NY Islanders 5, Philadelphia 4.

1978-79 – Montreal Canadiens – Ken Dryden, Larry Robinson, Serge Savard, Guy Lapointe, Brian Engblom, Gilles Lupien, Rick Chartraw, Guy Lafleur, Steve Shutt, Jacques Lemaire, Yvan Cournoyer, Réjean Houle, Pierre Mondou, Bob Gainey, Doug Jarvis, Yvon Lambert, Doug Risebrough, Pierre Larouche, Mario Tremblay, Cam Connor, Pat Hughes, Rod Langway, Mark Napier, Michel Larocque, Richard Sévigny, Scotty Bowman (coach), Irving Grundman (managing director), Eddy Palchak, Piere Meilleur (trainers).
Scores: May 13 at Montreal – NY Rangers 4, Montreal 1; May 15 at Montreal – Montreal 6, NY Rangers 2; May 17 at New York – Montreal 4, NY Rangers 1; May 19 at New York – Montreal 4, NY Rangers 3; May 21 at Montreal – Montreal 4, NY Rangers 1.

1977-78 – Montreal Canadiens – Ken Dryden, Larry Robinson, Serge Savard, Guy Lapointe, Bill Nyrop, Pierre Bouchard, Brian Engblom, Gilles Lupien, Rick Chartraw, Guy Lafleur, Steve Shutt, Jacques Lemaire, Yvan Cournoyer, Réjean Houle, Pierre Mondou, Bob Gainey, Doug Jarvis, Yvon Lambert, Doug Risebrough, Pierre Larouche, Mario Tremblay, Michel Larocque, Scotty Bowman (coach), Sam Pollock (general manager), Eddy Palchak, Pierre Meilleur (trainers).
Scores: May 13 at Montreal – Montreal 4, Boston 1; May 16 at Montreal – Montreal 3, Boston 2; May 18 at Boston – Boston 4, Montreal 0; May 21 at Boston – Boston 4, Montreal 3; May 23 at Montreal – Montreal 4, Boston 1; May 25 at Boston – Montreal 4, Boston 1.

1976-77 – Montreal Canadiens – Ken Dryden, Guy Lapointe, Larry Robinson, Serge Savard, Jimmy Roberts, Rick Chartraw, Bill Nyrop, Pierre Bouchard, Brian Engblom, Yvan Cournoyer, Guy Lafleur, Jacques Lemaire, Steve Shutt, Pete Mahovlich, Murray Wilson, Doug Jarvis, Yvon Lambert, Bob Gainey, Doug Risebrough, Mario Tremblay, Réjean Houle, Pierre Mondou, Mike Polich, Michel Larocque, Scotty Bowman (coach), Sam Pollock (general manager), Eddy Palchak, Pierre Meilleur (trainers).
Scores: May 7 at Montreal – Montreal 7, Boston 3; May 10 at Montreal – Montreal 3, Boston 0; May 12 at Boston – Montreal 4, Boston 2; May 14 at Boston – Montreal 2, Boston 1.

1975-76 – Montreal Canadiens – Ken Dryden, Serge Savard, Guy Lapointe, Larry Robinson, Bill Nyrop, Pierre Bouchard, Jim Roberts, Guy Lafleur, Steve Shutt, Pete Mahovlich, Yvan Cournoyer, Jacques Lemaire, Yvon Lambert, Bob Gainey, Doug Jarvis, Doug Risebrough, Murray Wilson, Mario Tremblay, Rick Chartraw, Michel Larocque, Scotty Bowman (coach), Sam Pollock (general manager), Eddy Palchak, Pierre Meilleur (trainers).
Scores: May 9 at Montreal – Montreal 4, Philadelphia 3; May 11 at Montreal – Montreal 2, Philadelphia 1; May 13 at Philadelphia – Montreal 3, Philadelphia 2; May 16 at Philadelphia – Montreal 5, Philadelphia 3.

1974-75 – Philadelphia Flyers – Bernie Parent, Wayne Stephenson, Ed Van Impe, Tom Bladon, André Dupont, Joe Watson, Jim Watson, Ted Harris, Larry Goodenough, Rick MacLeish, Bobby Clarke, Bill Barber, Reggie Leach, Gary Dornhoefer, Ross Lonsberry, Bob Kelly, Terry Crisp, Don Saleski, Dave Schultz, Orest Kindrachuk, Bill Clement, Fred Shero (coach), Keith Allen (general manager), Frank Lewis, Jim McKenzie (trainers).
Scores: May 15 at Philadelphia – Philadelphia 4, Buffalo 1; May 18 at Philadelphia – Philadelphia 2, Buffalo 1; May 20 at Buffalo – Buffalo 5, Philadelphia 4; May 22 at Buffalo – Buffalo 4, Philadelphia 2; May 25 at Philadelphia – Philadelphia 5, Buffalo 1; May 27 at Buffalo – Philadelphia 2, Buffalo 0.

1973-74 – Philadelphia Flyers – Bernie Parent, Ed Van Impe, Tom Bladon, André Dupont, Joe Watson, Jim Watson, Barry Ashbee, Bill Barber, Dave Schultz, Don Saleski, Gary Dornhoefer, Terry Crisp, Bobby Clarke, Simon Nolet, Ross Lonsberry, Rick MacLeish, Bill Flett, Orest Kindrachuk, Bill Clement, Bob Kelly, Bruce Cowick, Al MacAdam, Bobby Taylor, Fred Shero (coach), Keith Allen (general manager), Frank Lewis, Jim McKenzie (trainers).
Scores: May 7 at Boston – Boston 3, Philadelphia 2; May 9 at Boston – Philadelphia 3, Boston 2; May 12 at Philadelphia – Philadelphia 4, Boston 1; May 14 at Philadelphia – Philadelphia 4, Boston 2; May 16 at Boston – Boston 5, Philadelphia 1; May 19 at Philadelphia – Philadelphia 1, Boston 0.

1972-73 – Montreal Canadiens – Ken Dryden, Guy Lapointe, Serge Savard, Larry Robinson, Jacques Laperrière, Bob Murdoch, Pierre Bouchard, Jim Roberts, Yvan Cournoyer, Frank Mahovlich, Jacques Lemaire, Pete Mahovlich, Marc Tardif, Henri Richard, Réjean Houle, Guy Lafleur, Chuck Lefley, Claude Larose, Murray Wilson, Steve Shutt, Michel Plasse, Scotty Bowman (coach), Sam Pollock (general manager), Ed Palchak, Bob Williams (trainers).
Scores: April 29 at Montreal – Montreal 8, Chicago 3; May 1 at Montreal – Montreal 4, Chicago 1; May 3 at Chicago – Chicago 7, Montreal 4; May 6 at Chicago – Montreal 4, Chicago 0; May 8 at Montreal – Chicago 8, Montreal 7; May 10 at Chicago – Montreal 6, Chicago 4.

1971-72 – Boston Bruins – Gerry Cheevers, Ed Johnston, Bobby Orr, Ted Green, Carol Vadnais, Dallas Smith, Don Awrey, Phil Esposito, Ken Hodge, John Bucyk, Mike Walton, Wayne Cashman, Garnet Bailey, Derek Sanderson, Fred Stanfield, Ed Westfall, John McKenzie, Don Marcotte, Garry Peters, Chris Hayes, Tom Johnson (coach), Milt Schmidt (general manager), Dan Canney, John Forristall (trainers).
Scores: April 30 at Boston – Boston 6, NY Rangers 5; May 2 at Boston – Boston 2, NY Rangers 1; May 4 at New York – NY Rangers 5, Boston 2; May 7 at New York – Boston 3, NY Rangers 2; May 9 at Boston – NY Rangers 3, Boston 2; May 11 at New York – Boston 3, NY Rangers 0.

1970-71 – Montreal Canadiens – Ken Dryden, Rogatien Vachon, Jacques Laperrière, Jean-Claude Tremblay, Guy Lapointe, Terry Harper, Pierre Bouchard, Jean Béliveau, Marc Tardif, Yvan Cournoyer, Réjean Houle, Claude Larose, Henri Richard, Phil Roberto Pete Mahovlich, Leon Rochefort, John Ferguson, Bobby Sheehan, Jacques Lemaire, Frank Mahovlich, Bob Murdoch, Chuck Lefley, Al MacNeil (coach), Sam Pollock (general manager), Yvon Belanger, Ed Palchak (trainers).
Scores: May 4 at Chicago – Chicago 2, Montreal 1; May 6 at Chicago – Chicago 5, Montreal 3; May 9 at Montreal – Montreal 4, Chicago 2; May 11 at Montreal – Montreal 5, Chicago 2; May 13 at Chicago – Chicago 2, Montreal 0; May 16 at Montreal – Montreal 4, Chicago 3; May 18 at Chicago – Montreal 3, Chicago 2.

1969-70 – Boston Bruins – Gerry Cheevers, Ed Johnston, Bobby Orr, Rick Smith, Dallas Smith, Bill Speer, Gary Doak, Don Awrey, Phil Esposito, Ken Hodge, John Bucyk, Wayne Carleton, Wayne Cashman, Derek Sanderson, Fred Stanfield, Ed Westfall, John McKenzie, Jim Lorentz, Don Marcotte, Bill Lesuk, Dan Schock, Harry Sinden (coach), Milt Schmidt (general manager), Dan Canney, John Forristall (trainers).
Scores: May 3 at St. Louis – Boston 6, St. Louis 1; May 5 at St. Louis – Boston 6, St. Louis 2; May 7 at Boston – Boston 4, St. Louis 1; May 10 at Boston – Boston 4, St. Louis 3.

1968-69 – Montreal Canadiens – Lorne Worsley, Rogatien Vachon, Jacques Laperrière, Jean-Claude Tremblay, Ted Harris, Serge Savard, Terry Harper, Larry Hillman, Jean Béliveau, Ralph Backstrom, Dick Duff, Yvan Cournoyer, Claude Provost, Bobby Rousseau, Henri Richard, John Ferguson, Christian Bordeleau, Mickey Redmond, Jacques Lemaire, Lucien Grenier, Tony Esposito, Claude Ruel (coach), Sam Pollock (general manager), Larry Aubut, Eddy Palchak (trainers).
Scores: April 27 at Montreal – Montreal 3, St. Louis 1; April 29 at Montreal – Montreal 3, St. Louis 1; May 1 at St. Louis – Montreal 4, St. Louis 0; May 4 at St. Louis – Montreal 2, St. Louis 1.

1967-68 – Montreal Canadiens – Lorne Worsley, Rogatien Vachon, Jacques Laperrière, Jean-Claude Tremblay, Ted Harris, Serge Savard, Terry Harper, Carol Vadnais, Jean Béliveau, Gilles Tremblay, Ralph Backstrom, Dick Duff, Claude Larose, Yvan Cournoyer, Claude Provost, Bobby Rousseau, Henri Richard, John Ferguson, Danny Grant, Jacques Lemaire, Mickey Redmond, Toe Blake (coach), Sam Pollock (general manager), Larry Aubut, Eddy Palchak (trainers).
Scores: May 5 at St. Louis – Montreal 3, St. Louis 2; May 7 at St. Louis – Montreal 1, St. Louis 0; May 9 at Montreal – Montreal 4, St. Louis 3; May 11 at Montreal – Montreal 3, St. Louis 2.

1966-67 – Toronto Maple Leafs – Johnny Bower, Terry Sawchuk, Larry Hillman, Marcel Pronovost, Tim Horton, Bob Baun, Aut Erickson, Allan Stanley, Red Kelly, Ron Ellis, George Armstrong, Pete Stemkowski, Dave Keon, Mike Walton, Jim Pappin, Bob Pulford, Brian Conacher, Eddie Shack, Frank Mahovlich, Milan Marcetta, Larry Jeffrey, Bruce Gamble, Punch Imlach (manager-coach), Bob Haggart (trainer).
Scores: April 20 at Montreal – Toronto 2, Montreal 6; April 22 at Montreal – Toronto 3, Montreal 0; April 25 at Toronto – Toronto 3, Montreal 2; Apil 27 at Toronto – Toronto 2, Montreal 6; April 29 at Montreal – Toronto 4, Montreal 1; May 2 at Toronto – Toronto 3, Montreal 1.

1965-66 – Montreal Canadiens – Lorne Worsley, Charlie Hodge, Jean-Claude Tremblay, Ted Harris, Jean-Guy Talbot, Terry Harper, Jacques Laperrière, Noel Price, Jean Béliveau, Ralph Backstrom, Dick Duff, Gilles Tremblay, Claude Larose, Yvan Cournoyer, Claude Provost, Bobby Rousseau, Henri Richard, Dave Balon, John Ferguson, Léon Rochefort, Jim Roberts, Toe Blake (coch), Sam Pollock (general manager), Larry Aubut, Andy Galley (trainers).
Scores: April 24 at Montreal – Detroit 3, Montreal 2; April 26 at Montreal – Detroit 5, Montreal 2; April 28 at Detroit – Montreal 4, Detroit 2; May 1 at Detroit – Montreal 2, Detroit 1; May 3 at Montreal – Montreal 5, Detroit 1; May 5 at Detroit – Montreal 3, Detroit 2.

1964-65 – Montreal Canadiens – Lorne Worsley, Charlie Hodge, Jean-Claude Tremblay, Ted Harris, Jean-Guy Talbot, Terry Harper, Jacques Laperrière, Jean Gauthier, Noel Picard, Jean Béliveau, Ralph Backstrom, Dick Duff, Claude Larose, Yvan Cournoyer, Claude Provost, Bobby Rousseau, Henri Richard, Dave Balon, John Ferguson, Red Berenson, Jim Roberts, Toe Blake (coach), Sam Pollock (general manager), Larry Aubut, Andy Galley (trainers).
Scores: April 17 at Montreal – Montreal 3, Chicago 2; April 20 at Montreal – Montreal 2, Chicago 0; April 22 at Chicago – Montreal 1, Chicago 3; April 25 at Chicago – Montreal 1, Chicago 5; April 7 at Montreal – Montreal 6, Chicago 0; April 29 at Chicago – Montreal 1, Chicago 2; May 1 at Montreal – Montreal 4, Chicago 0.

1963-64 – Toronto Maple Leafs – Johnny Bower, Carl Brewer, Tim Horton, Bob Baun, Allan Stanley, Larry Hillman, Al Arbour, Red Kelly, Gerry Ehman, Andy Bathgate, George Armstrong, Ron Stewart, Dave Keon, Billy Harris, Don McKenney, Jim Pappin, Bob Pulford, Eddie Shack, Frank Mahovlich, Eddie Litzenberger, Punch Imlach (manager-coach), Bob Haggert (trainer).
Scores: April 11 at Toronto – Toronto 3, Detroit 2; April 14 at Toronto – Toronto 3, Detroit 4; April 16 at Detroit – Toronto 3, Detroit 4; April 18 at Detroit – Toronto 4, Detroit 2; April 21 at Toronto – Toronto 1, Detroit 2; April 23 at Detroit – Toronto 4, Detroit 3; April 25 at Toronto – Toronto 4, Detroit 0.

1962-63 – Toronto Maple Leafs – Johnny Bower, Don Simmons, Carl Brewer, Tim Horton, Kent Douglas, Allan Stanley, Bob Baun, Larry Hillman, Red Kelly, Dick Duff, George Armstrong, Bob Nevin, Ron Stewart, Dave Keon, Billy Harris, Bob Pulford, Eddie Shack, Ed Litzenberger, Frank Mahovlich, John MacMillan, Punch Imlach (manager-coach), Bob Haggert (trainer).
Scores: April 9 at Toronto – Toronto 4, Detroit 2; April 11 at Toronto – Toronto 4, Detroit 2; April 14 at Detroit – Toronto 2, Detroit 3; April 16 at Detroit – Toronto 4, Detroit 2; April 18 at Toronto – Toronto 3, Detroit 1.

1961-62 – Toronto Maple Leafs – Johnny Bower, Don Simmons, Carl Brewer, Tim Horton, Bob Baun, Allan Stanley, Al Arbour, Larry Hillman, Red Kelly, Dick Duff, George Armstrong, Frank Mahovlich, Bob Nevin, Ron Stewart, Bill Harris, Bert Olmstead, Bob Pulford, Eddie Shack, Dave Keon, Ed Litzenberger, John MacMillan, Punch Imlach (manager-coach), Bob Haggert (trainer).
Scores: April 10 at Toronto – Toronto 4, Chicago 1; April 12 at Toronto – Toronto 3, Chicago 2; April 15 at Chicago – Toronto 0, Chicago 3; April 17 at Chicago – Toronto 1, Chicago 4; April 19 at Toronto – Toronto 8, Chicago 4; April 22 at Chicago – Toronto 2, Chicago 1.

1960-61 – Chicago Black Hawks – Glenn Hall, Al Arbour, Pierre Pilote, Elmer Vasko, Jack Evans, Dollard St. Laurent, Reg Fleming, Tod Sloan, Ron Murphy, Eddie Litzenberger, Bill Hay, Bobby Hull, Ab McDonald, Eric Nesterenko, Ken Wharram, Earl Balfour, Stan Mikita, Murray Balfour, Chico Maki, Wayne Hicks, Tommy Ivan (manager), Rudy Pilous (coach), Nick Garen (trainer).
Scores: April 6 at Chicago – Chicago 3, Detroit 2; Aprl 8 at Detroit – Detroit 3, Chicago 1; April 10 at Chicago – Chicago 3, Detroit 1; April 12 at Detroit – Detroit 2, Chicago 1; April 14 at Chicago – Chicago 6, Detroit 3; April 16 at Detroit – Chicago 5, Detroit 1.

1959-60 – Montreal Canadiens – Jacques Plante, Charlie Hodge, Doug Harvey, Tom Johnson, Bob Turner, Jean-Guy Talbot, Albert Langlois, Ralph Backstrom, Jean Béliveau, Marcel Bonin, Bernie Geoffrion, Phil Goyette, Bill Hicke, Don Marshall, Ab McDonald, Dickie Moore, André Pronovost, Claude Provost, Henri Richard, Maurice Richard, Frank Selke (manager), Toe Blake (coach), Hector Dubois, Larry Aubut (trainers).
Scores: April 7 at Montreal – Montreal 4, Toronto 2; April 9 at Montreal – Montreal 2, Toronto 1; April 12 at Toronto – Montreal 5, Toronto 2; April 14 at Toronto – Montreal 4, Toronto 0.

1958-59 – Montreal Canadiens – Jacques Plante, Charlie Hodge, Doug Harvey, Tom Johnson, Bob Turner, Jean-Guy Talbot, Albert Langlois, Bernie Geoffrion, Ralph Backstrom, Bill Hicke, Maurice Richard, Dickie Moore, Claude Provost, Ab McDonald, Henri Richard, Marcel Bonin, Phil Goyette, Don Marshall, André Pronovost, Jean Béliveau, Frank Selke (manager), Toe Blake (coach), Hector Dubois, Larry Aubut (trainers).
Scores: April 9 at Montreal – Montreal 5, Toronto 3; April 11 at Montreal – Montreal 3, Toronto 1; April 14 at Toronto – Toronto 3, Montreal 2; April 16 at Toronto – Montreal 3, Toronto 2; April 18 at Montreal – Montreal 5, Toronto 3.

1957-58 – Montreal Canadiens – Jacques Plante, Gerry McNeil, Doug Harvey, Tom Johnson, Bob Turner, Dollard St-Laurent, Jean-Guy Talbot, Albert Langlois, Jean Béliveau, Bernie Geoffrion, Maurice Richard, Dickie Moore, Claude Provost, Floyd Curry, Bert Olmstead, Henri Richard, Marcel Bonin, Phil Goyette, Don Marshall, André Pronovost, Connie Broden, Frank Selke (manager), Toe Blake (coach), Hector Dubois, Larry Aubut (trainers).
Scores: April 8 at Montreal – Montreal 2, Boston 1; April 10 at Montreal – Boston 5, Montreal 2; April 13 at Boston – Montreal 3, Boston 0; April 15 at Boston – Boston 3, Montreal 1; April 17 at Montreal – Montreal 3, Boston 2; April 20 at Boston – Montreal 5, Boston 3.

1956-57 – Montreal Canadiens – Jacques Plante, Gerry McNeil, Doug Harvey, Tom Johnson, Bob Turner, Dollard St. Laurent, Jean-Guy Talbot, Jean Béliveau, Bernie Geoffrion, Floyd Curry, Dickie Moore, Maurice Richard, Claude Provost, Bert Olmstead, Henri Richard, Phil Goyette, Don Marshall, André Pronovost, Connie Broden, Frank Selke (manager), Toe Blake (coach), Hector Dubois, Larry Aubut (trainers).
Scores: April 6, at Montreal – Montreal 5, Boston 1; April 9, at Montreal – Montreal 1, Boston 0; April 11, at Boston – Montreal 4, Boston 2; April 14, at Boston – Boston 2, Montreal 0; April 16, at Montreal – Montreal 5, Boston 1.

1955-56 – Montreal Canadiens – Jacques Plante, Doug Harvey, Emile Bouchard, Bob Turner, Tom Johnson, Jean-Guy Talbot, Dollard St. Laurent, Jean Béliveau, Bernie Geoffrion, Bert Olmstead, Floyd Curry, Jackie Leclair, Maurice Richard, Dickie Moore, Henri Richard, Ken Mosdell, Don Marshall, Claude Provost, Frank Selke (manager), Toe Blake (coach), Hector Dubois (trainer).
Scores: March 31, at Montreal – Montreal 6, Detroit 4; April 3, at Montreal – Montreal 5, Detroit 1; April 5, at Detroit – Detroit 3, Montreal 1; April 8, at Detroit – Montreal 3, Detroit 0; April 10, at Montreal – Montreal 3, Detroit 1.

1954-55 – Detroit Red Wings – Terry Sawchuk, Red Kelly, Bob Goldham, Marcel Pronovost, Ben Woit, Jim Hay, Larry Hillman, Ted Lindsay, Tony Leswick, Gordie Howe, Alex Delvecchio, Marty Pavelich, Glen Skov, Earl Reibel, John Wilson, Bill Dineen, Vic Stasiuk, Marcel Bonin, Jack Adams (manager), Jimmy Skinner (coach), Carl Mattson (trainer).
Scores: April 3, at Detroit – Detroit 4, Montreal 2; April 5, at Detroit – Detroit 7, Montreal 1, April 7 at Monreal – Montreal 4, Detroit 2; April 9, at Montreal – Montreal 5, Detroit 3; April 10, at Detroit – Detroit 5, Montreal 1; April 12, at Montreal – Montreal 6, Detroit 3; April 14, at Detroit – Detroit 3, Montreal 1

1953-54 – Detroit Red Wings – Terry Sawchuk, Red Kelly, Bob Goldham, Ben Woit, Marcel Pronovost, Al Arbour, Keith Allen, Ted Lindsay, Tony Leswick, Gordie Howe, Marty Pavelich, Alex Delvecchio, Metro Prystai, Glen Skov, John Wilson, Bill Dineen, Jim Peters, Earl Reibel, Vic Stasiu, Jack Adams (manager), Tommy Ivan (coach), Carl Mattson (trainer).
Scores: April 4, at Detroit – Detroit 3, Montreal 1; April 6, at Detroit – Montreal 3, Detroit 1; April 8, at Montreal – Detroit 5, Montreal 2; April 10, at Montreal – Detroit 2, Montreal 0; April 11, at Detroit – Montreal 1, Detroit 0; April 13, at Montreal – Montreal 4, Detroit 1; April 16, at Detroit – Detroit 2, Montreal 1.

1952-53 – Montreal Canadiens – Gerry McNeil, Jacques Plante, Doug Harvey, Emile Bouchard, Tom Johnson, Dollard St. Laurent, Bud MacPherson, Maurice Richard, Elmer Lach, Bert Olmstead, Bernie Geoffrion, Floyd Curry, Paul Masnick, Billy Reay, Dickie Moore, Ken Mosdell, Dick Gamble, Johnny McCormack, Lorne Davis, Calum McKay, Eddie Mazur, Frank Selke (manager), Dick Irvin (coach), Hector Dubois (trainer).
Scores: April 9, at Montreal – Montreal 4, Boston 2; April 11, at Montreal – Boston 4, Montreal 1; April 12, at Boston – Montreal 3, Boston 0; April 14, at Boston – Montreal 7, Boston 3; April 16, at Montreal – Montreal 1, Boston 0.

1951-52 – Detroit Red Wings – Terry Sawchuk, Bob Goldham, Ben Woit, Red Kelly, Leo Reise, Marcel Pronovost, Ted Lindsay, Tony Leswick, Gordie Howe, Metro Prystai, Marty Pavelich, Sid Abel, Glen Skov, Alex Delvecchio, John Wilson, Vic Stasiuk, Larry Zeidel, Jack Adams (manager) Tommy Ivan (coach), Carl Mattson (trainer).
Scores: April 10, at Montreal – Detroit 3, Montreal 1; April 12 at Montreal – Detroit 2, Montreal 1; April 13, at Detroit – Detroit 3, Montreal 0; April 15, at Detroit – Detroit 3, Montreal 0.

1950-51 – Toronto Maple Leafs – Turk Broda, Al Rollins, Jim Thomson, Gus Mortson, Bill Barilko, Bill Juzda, Fern Flaman, Hugh Bolton, Ted Kennedy, Sid Smith, Tod Sloan, Cal Gardner, Howie Meeker, Harry Watson, Max Bentley, Joe Klukay, Danny Lewicki, Ray Timgren, Fleming Mackell, Johnny McCormack, Bob Hassard, Conn Smythe (manager), Joe Primeau (coach), Tim Daly (trainer).
Scores: April 11, at Toronto – Toronto 3, Montreal 2; April 14, at Toronto – Montreal 3, Toronto 2; April 17, at Montreal – Toronto 2, Montreal 1; April 19, at Montreal – Toronto 3, Montreal 2; April 21, at Toronto – Toronto 3, Montreal 2.

1949-50 – Detroit Red Wings – Harry Lumley, Jack Stewart, Leo Reise, Clare Martin, Al Dewsbury, Lee Fogolin, Marcel Pronovost, Red Kelly, Ted Lindsay, Sid Abel, Gordie Howe, George Gee, Jimmy Peters, Marty Pavelich, Jim McFadden, Pete Babando, Max McNab, Gerry Coutur, Joe Carveth, Steve Black, John Wilson, Larry Wilson, Jack Adams (manager), Tommy Ivan (coach), Carl Mattson (trainer).
Scores: April 11, at Detroit – Detroit 4, NY Rangers 1; April 13, at Toronto* – NY Rangers 3, Detroit 1; April 15, at Toronto – Detroit 4, NY Rangers 0; April 18, at Detroit – NY Rangers 4, Detroit 3; April 20, at Detroit – NY Rangers 2, Detroit 1; April 22, at Detroit – Detroit 5, NY Rangers 4; April 23, at Detroit – Detroit 4, NY Rangers 3.

*Ice was unavailable in Madison Square Garden and Rangers elected to play second and third games on Toronto ice.

1948-49 – Toronto Maple Leafs – Turk Broda, Jim Thomson, Gus Mortson, Bill Barilko, Garth Boesch, Bill Juzda, Ted Kennedy, Howie Meeker, Vic Lynn, Harry Watson, Bill Ezinicki, Cal Gardner, Max Bentley, Joe Klukay, Sid Smith, Don Metz, Ray Timgren, Fleming Mackell, Harry Taylor, Bob Dawes, Tod Sloan, Conn Smythe (manager), Hap Day (coach), Tim Daly (trainer).
Scores: April 8, at Detroit – Toronto 3, Detroit 2; April 10, at Detroit – Toronto 3, Detroit 1; April 13, at Toronto – Toronto 3, Detroit 1; April 16, at Toronto – Toronto 3, Detroit 1.

1947-48 – Toronto Maple Leafs – Turk Broda, Jim Thomson, Wally Stanowski, Garth Boesch, Bill Barilko. Gus Mortson, Phil Samis, Syl Apps, Bill Ezinicki, Harry Watson, Ted Kennedy, Howie Meeker, Vic Lynn, Nick Metz, Max Bentley, Joe Klukay, Les Costello, Don Metz, Sid Smith, Conn Smythe (manager), Hap Day (coach), Tim Daly (trainer).
Scores: April 7, at Toronto – Toronto 5, Detroit 3; April 10, at Toronto – Toronto 4, Detroit 2; April 11, at Detroit – Toronto 2, Detroit 0; April 14, at Detroit – Toronto 7, Detroit 2.

1946-47 – Toronto Maple Leafs – Turk Broda, Garth Boesch, Gus Mortson, Jim Thomson, Wally Stanowski, Bill Barilko, Harry Watson, Bud Poile, Ted Kennedy, Syl Apps, Don Metz, Nick Metz, Bill Ezinicki, Vic Lynn, Howie Meeker, Gaye Stewart, Joe Klukay, Gus Bodnar, Bob Goldham, Conn Smythe (manager), Hap Day (coach), Tim Daly (trainer).
Scores: April 8, at Montreal – Montreal 6, Toronto 0; April 10, at Montreal – Toronto 4, Montreal 0; April 12, at Toronto – Toronto 4, Montreal 2; April 15, at Toronto – Toronto 2, Montreal 1; April 17, at Montreal – Montreal 3, Toronto 1; April 19, at Toronto – Toronto 2, Montreal 1.

1945-46 – Montreal Canadiens – Elmer Lach, Toe Blake, Maurice Richard, Bob Fillion, Dutch Hiller, Murph Chamberlain, Ken Mosdell, Buddy O'Connor, Glen Harmon, Jim Peters, Emile Bouchard, Bill Reay, Ken Reardon, Leo Lamoureux, Frank Eddolls, Gerry Plamondon, Bill Durnan, Tommy Gorman (manager), Dick Irvin (coach), Ernie Cook (trainer).
Scores: March 30, at Montreal – Montreal 4, Boston 3; April 2, at Montreal – Montreal 3, Boston 2; April 4, at Boston – Montreal 4, Boston 2; April 7, at Boston – Boston 3, Montreal 2; April 9, at Montreal – Montreal 6, Boston 3.

1944-45 – Toronto Maple Leafs – Don Metz, Frank McCool, Wally Stanowski, Reg Hamilton, Elwyn Morris, Johnny McCreedy, Tommy O'Neill, Ted Kennedy, Babe Pratt, Gus Bodnar, Art Jackson, Jack McLean, Mel Hill, Nick Metz, Bob Davidson, Dave Schriner, Lorne Carr, Conn Smythe (manager), Frank Selke (business manager), Hap Day (coach), Tim Daly (trainer).
Scores: April 6, at Detroit – Toronto 1, Detroit 0; April 8, at Detroit – Toronto 2, Detroit 0; April 12, at Toronto – Toronto 1, Detroit 0; April 14, at Toronto – Detroit 5, Toronto 3; April 19, at Detroit – Detroit 2, Toronto 0; April 21, at Toronto – Detroit 1, Toronto 0; April 22, at Detroit – Toronto 2, Detroit 1.

1943-44 – Montreal Canadiens – Toe Blake, Maurice Richard, Elmer Lach, Ray Getliffe, Murph Chamberlain, Phil Watson, Emile Bouchard, Glen Harmon, Buddy O'Connor, Jerry Heffernan, Mike McMahon, Leo Lamoureux, Fernand Majeau, Bob Fillion, Bill Durnan, Tommy Gorman (manager), Dick Irvin (coach), Ernie Cook (trainer).
Scores: April 4, at Montreal – Montreal 5, Chicago 1; April 6, at Chicago – Montreal 3, Chicago 1; April 9, at Chicago – Montreal 3, Chicago 2; April 13, at Montreal – Montreal 5, Chicago 4.

1942-43 – Detroit Red Wings – Jack Stewart, Jimmy Orlando, Sid Abel, Alex Motter, Harry Watson, Joe Carveth, Mud Bruneteau, Eddie Wares, Johnny Mowers, Cully Simon, Don Grosso, Carl Liscombe, Connie Brown, Syd Howe, Les Douglas, Hal Jackson, Joe Fisher, Jack Adams (manager), Ebbie Goodfellow (playing-coach), Honey Walker (trainer).
Scores: April 1, at Detroit – Detroit 6, Boston 2; April 4, at Detroit – Detroit 4, Boston 3; April 7, at Boston – Detroit 4, Boston 0; April 8, at Boston – Detroit 2, Boston 0.

1941-42 – Toronto Maple Leafs – Wally Stanowski, Syl Apps, Bob Goldham, Gord Drillon, Hank Goldup, Ernie Dickens, Dave Schriner, Bucko McDonald, Bob Davidson, Nick Metz, Bingo Kampman, Don Metz, Gaye Stewart, Turk Broda, Johnny McCreedy, Lorne Carr, Pete Langelle, Billy Taylor, Conn Smyte (manager), Hap Day (coach), Frank Selke (business manager), Tim Daly (trainer).
Scores: April 4, at Toronto – Detroit 3, Toronto 2; April 7, at Toronto – Detroit 4, Toronto 2; April 9, at Detroit – Detroit 5, Toronto 2; April 12, at Detroit – Toronto 4, Detroit 3; April 14, at Toronto – Toronto 9, Detroit 3; April 16, at Detroit – Toronto 3, Detroit 0; April 18, at Toronto – Toronto 3, Detroit 1.

1940-41 – Boston Bruins – Bill Cowley, Des Smith, Dit Clapper, Frank Brimsek, Flash Hollett, John Crawford, Bobby Bauer, Pat McCreavy, Herb Cain, Mel Hill, Milt Schmidt, Woody Dumart, Roy Conacher, Terry Reardon, Art Jackson, Eddie Wiseman, Art Ross (manager), Cooney Weiland (coach), Win Green (trainer).
Scores: April 6, at Boston – Detroit 2, Boston 3; April 8, at Boston – Detroit 1, Boston 2; April 10, at Detroit – Boston 4, Detroit 2; April 12, at Detroit – Boston 3, Detroit 1.

1939-40 – New York Rangers – Dave Kerr, Art Coulter, Ott Heller, Alex Shibicky, Mac Colville, Neil Colville, Phil Watson, Lynn Patrick, Clint Smith, Muzz Patrick, Babe Pratt, Bryan Hextall, Kilby Macdonald, Dutch Hiller, Alf Pike, Sanford Smith, Lester Patrick (manager), Frank Boucher (coach), Harry Westerby (trainer).
Scores: April 2, at New York – NY Rangers 2, Toronto 1; April 3, at New York – NY Rangers 6, Toronto 2; April 6, at Toronto – NY Rangers 1, Toronto 2; April 9, at Toronto – NY Rangers 0, Toronto 3; April 11, at Toronto – NY Rangers 2, Toronto 1; April 13, at Toronto – NY Rangers 3, Toronto 2.

1938-39 – Boston Bruins – Bobby Bauer, Mel Hill, Flash Hollett, Roy Conacher, Gord Pettinger, Milt Schmidt, Woody Dumart, Jack Crawford, Ray Getliffe, Frank Brimsek, Eddie Shore, Dit Clapper, Bill Cowley, Jack Portland, Red Hamill, Cooney Weiland, Art Ross (manager-coach), Win Green (trainer).
Scores: April 6, at Boston – Toronto 1, Boston 2; April 9, at Boston – Toronto 3, Boston 2; April 11, at Toronto – Toronto 1, Boston 3; April 13 at Toronto – Toronto 0, Boston 2; April 16, at Boston – Toronto 1, Boston 3.

1937-38 – Chicago Black Hawks – Art Wiebe, Carl Voss, Hal Jackson, Mike Karakas, Mush March, Jack Shill, Earl Seibert, Cully Dahlstrom, Alex Levinsky, Johnny Gottselig, Lou Trudel, Pete Palangio, Bill MacKenzie, Doc Romnes, Paul Thompson, Roger Jenkins, Alf Moore, Bert Connolly, Virgil Johnson, Paul Goodman, Bill Stewart (manager-coach), Eddie Froelich (trainer).
Scores: April 5, at Toronto – Chicago 3, Toronto 1; April 7, at Toronto – Chicago 1, Toronto 5; April 10 at Chicago – Chicago 2, Toronto 1; April 12, at Chicago – Chicago 4, Toronto 1.

1936-37 – Detroit Red Wings – Normie Smith, Pete Kelly, Larry Aurie, Herbie Lewis, Hec Kilrea, Mud Bruneteau, Syd Howe, Wally Kilrea, Jimmy Franks, Bucko McDonald, Gordon Pettinger, Ebbie Goodfellow, Johnny Gallagher, Scotty Bowman, Johnny Sorrell, Marty Barry, Earl Robertson, Johnny Sherf, Howard Mackie, Jack Adams (manager-coach), Honey Walker (trainer).
Scores: April 6, at New York – Detroit 1, NY Rangers 5; April 8, at Detroit – Detroit 4, NY Rangers 2; April 11, at Detroit – Detroit 0, NY Rangers 1; April 13, at Detroit – Detroit 1, NY Rangers 0; April 15, at Detroit – Detroit 3, NY Rangers 0.

1935-36 – Detroit Red Wings – Johnny Sorrell, Syd Howe, Marty Barry, Herbie Lewis, Mud Bruneteau, Wally Kilrea, Hec Kilrea, Gordon Pettinger, Bucko McDonald, Scotty Bowman, Pete Kelly, Doug Young, Ebbie Goodfellow, Normie Smith, Jack Adams (manager-coach), Honey Walker (trainer).
Scores: April 5, at Detroit – Detroit 3, Toronto 1; April 7, at Detroit – Detroit 9, Toronto 4; April 9, at Toronto – Detroit 3, Toronto 4; April 11, at Toronto – Detroit 3, Toronto 2.

1934-35 – Montreal Maroons – Marvin (Cy) Wentworth, Alex Connell, Toe Blake, Stew Evans, Earl Robinson, Bill Miller, Dave Trottier, Jimmy Ward, Larry Northcott, Hooley Smith, Russ Blinco, Allan Shields, Sammy McManus, Gus Marker, Bob Gracie, Herb Cain, Tommy Gorman (manager), Lionel Conacher (coach), Bill O'Brien (trainer).
Scores: April 4, at Toronto – Mtl. Maroons 3, Toronto 2; April 6, at Toronto – Mtl. Maroons 3, Toronto 1; April 9, at Montreal – Mtl. Maroons 4, Toronto 1.

1933-34 – Chicago Black Hawks – Taffy Abel, Lolo Couture, Lou Trudel, Lionel Conacher, Paul Thompson, Leroy Goldsworthy, Art Coulter, Roger Jenkins, Don McFayden, Tommy Cook, Doc Romnes, Johnny Gottselig, Mush March, Johnny Sheppard, Chuck Gardiner (captain), Bill Kendall, Tommy Gorman (manager-coach), Eddie Froelich (trainer).
Scores: April 3, at Detroit – Chicago 2, Detroit 1; April 5, at Detroit – Chicago 4, Detroit 1; April 8, at Chicago – Detroit 5, Chicago 2; April 10, at Chicago – Chicago 1, Detroit 0.

1932-33 – New York Rangers – Ching Johnson, Butch Keeling, Frank Boucher, Art Somers, Babe Siebert, Bun Cook, Andy Aitkinhead, Ott Heller, Ozzie Asmundson, Gord Pettinger, Doug Brennan, Cecil Dillon, Bill Cook (captain), Murray Murdoch, Earl Seibert, Lester Patrick (manager-coach), Harry Westerby (trainer).
Scores: April 4, at New York – NY Rangers 5, Toronto 1; April 8, at Toronto – NY Rangers 3, Toronto 1; April 11, at Toronto – Toronto 3, NY Rangers 2; April 13, at Toronto – NY Rangers 1, Toronto 0.

1931-32 – Toronto Maple Leafs – Charlie Conacher, Harvey Jackson, King Clancy, Andy Blair, Red Horner, Lorne Chabot, Alex Levinsky, Joe Primeau, Hal Darragh, Hal Cotton, Frank Finnigan, Hap Day, Ace Bailey, Bob Gracie, Fred Robertson, Earl Miller, Conn Smythe (manager), Dick Irvin (coach), Tim Daly (trainer).
Scores: April 5 at New York – Toronto 6, NY Rangers 4; April 7, at Boston* – Toronto 6, NY Rangers 2; April 9, at Toronto – Toronto 6, NY Rangers 4.

* Ice was unavailable in Madison Square Garden and Rangers elected to play the second game on neutral ice.

1930-31 – Montreal Canadiens – George Hainsworth, Wildor Larochelle, Marty Burke, Sylvio Mantha, Howie Morenz, Johnny Gagnon, Aurel Joliat, Armand Mondou, Pit Lepine, Albert Leduc, Georges Mantha, Art Lesieur, Nick Wasnie, Bert McCaffrey, Gus Rivers, Jean Pusie, Léo Dandurand (manager), Cecil Hart (coach), Ed Dufour (trainer).
Scores: April 3, at Chicago – Montreal 2, Chicago 1; April 5, at Chicago – Chicago 2, Montreal 1; April 9, at Montreal – Chicago 3, Montreal 2; April 11, at Montreal – Montreal 4, Chicago 2; April 14, at Montreal – Montreal 2, Chicago 0.

1929-30 – Montreal Canadiens – George Hainsworth, Marty Burke, Sylvio Mantha, Howie Morenz, Bert McCaffrey, Aurel Joliat, Albert Leduc, Pit Lepine, Wildor Larochelle, Nick Wasnie, Gerald Carson, Armand Mondou, Georges Mantha, Gus Rivers, Léo Dandurand (manager), Cecil Hart (coach), Ed Dufour (trainer).
Scores: April 1 at Boston – Montreal 3, Boston 0; April 3 at Montreal – Montreal 4, Boston 3.

1928-29 – Boston Bruins – Cecil (Tiny) Thompson, Eddie Shore, Lionel Hitchman, Perk Galbraith, Eric Pettinger, Frank Fredrickson, Mickey Mackay, Red Green, Dutch Gainor, Harry Oliver, Eddie Rodden, Dit Clapper, Cooney Weiland, Lloyd Klein, Cy Denneny, Bill Carson, George Owen, Myles Lane, Art Ross (manager-coach), Win Green (trainer).
Scores: March 28 at Boston – Boston 2, NY Rangers 0; March 29 at New York – Boston 2, NY Rangers 1.

1927-28 – New York Rangers – Lorne Chabot, Taffy Abel, Leon Bourgault, Ching Johnson, Bill Cook, Bun Cook, Frank Boucher, Billy Boyd, Murray Murdoch, Paul Thompson, Alex Gray, Joe Miller, Patsy Callighen, Lester Patrick (manager-coach), Harry Westerby (trainer).
Scores: April 5 at Montreal – Mtl. Maroons 2, NY Rangers 0; April 7 at Montreal – NY Rangers 2, Mtl. Maroons 1; April 10 at Montreal – Mtl. Maroons 2, NY Rangers 1; April 12 at Montreal – NY Rangers 1, Mtl. Maroons 0; April 14 at Montreal – NY Rangers 2, Mtl. Maroons 1.

1926-27 – Ottawa Senators – Alex Connell, King Clancy, George (Buck) Boucher, Ed Gorman, Frank Finnigan, Alex Smith, Hec Kilrea, Hooley Smith, Cy Denneny, Frank Nighbor, Jack Adams, Milt Halliday, Dave Gil (manager-coach).
Scores: April 7 at Boston – Ottawa 0, Boston 0; April 9 at Boston – Ottawa 3, Boston 1; April 11 at Ottawa – Boston 1, Ottawa 1; April 13 at Ottawa – Ottawa 3, Boston 1.

1925-26 – Montreal Maroons – Clint Benedict, Reg Noble, Frank Carson, Dunc Munro, Nels Stewart, Harry Broadbent, Babe Siebert, Dinny Dinsmore, Bill Phillips, Hobart (Hobie) Kitchen, Sammy Rothschild, Albert (Toots) Holway, Shorty Horne, Bern Brophy, Eddie Gerard (manager-coach), Bill O'Brien (trainer).
Scores: March 30 at Montreal – Mtl. Maroons 3, Victoria 0; April 1 at Montreal – Mtl. Maroons 3, Victoria 0; April 3 at Montreal – Victoria 3, Mtl. Maroons 2; April 6 at Montreal – Mtl. Maroons 2, Victoria 0.

The series in the spring of 1926 ended the annual playoffs between the champions of the East and the champions of the West. Since 1926-27 the annual playoffs in the National Hockey League have decided the Stanley Cup champions.

1924-25 – Victoria Cougars – Harry (Happy) Holmes, Clem Loughlin, Gordie Fraser, Frank Fredrickson, Jack Walker, Harold (Gizzy) Hart, Harold (Slim) Halderson, Frank Foyston, Wally Elmer, Harry Meeking, Jocko Anderson, Lester Patrick (manager-coach).
Scores: March 21 at Victoria – Victoria 5, Montreal 2; March 23 at Vancouver – Victoria 3, Montreal 1; March 27 at Victoria – Montreal 4, Victoria 2; March 30 at Victoria – Victoria 6, Montreal 1.

1923-24 – Montreal Canadiens – Georges Vezina, Sprague Cleghorn, Billy Couture, Howie Morenz, Aurel Joliat, Billy Boucher, Odie Cleghorn, Sylvio Mantha, Bobby Boucher, Billy Bell, Billy Cameron, Joe Malone, Charles Fortier, Léo Dandurand (manager-coach).
Scores: March 18 at Montreal – Montreal 3, Van. Maroons 2; March 20 at Montreal – Montreal 2, Van. Maroons 1. March 22 at Montreal – Montreal 6, Cgy. Tigers 1; March 25 at Ottawa* – Montreal 3, Cgy. Tigers 0.

*Game transferred to Ottawa to benefit from artificial ice surface.

1922-23 – Ottawa Senators – George (Buck) Boucher, Lionel Hitchman, Frank Nighbor, King Clancy, Harry Helman, Clint Benedict, Jack Darragh, Eddie Gerard, Cy Denneny, Harry Broadbent, Tommy Gorman (manager), Pete Green (coach), F. Dolan (trainer).
Scores: March 16 at Vancouver – Ottawa 1, Van. Maroons 0; March 19 at Vancouver – Van. Maroons 4, Ottawa 1; March 23 at Vancouver – Ottawa 3, Van. Maroons 2; March 26 at Vancouver – Ottawa 5, Van. Maroons 1; March 29 at Vancouver – Ottawa 2, Edm. Eskimos 1; March 31 at Vancouver – Ottawa 1, Edm. Eskimos 0.

1921-22 – Toronto St. Pats – Ted Stackhouse, Corb Denneny, Rod Smylie, Lloyd Andrews, John Ross Roach, Harry Cameron, Bill (Red) Stuart, Cecil (Babe) Dye, Ken Randall, Reg Noble, Eddie Gerard (borrowed for one game from Ottawa), Stan Jackson, Nolan Mitchell, Charlie Querrie (manager), Eddie Powers (coach).
Scores: March 17 at Toronto – Van. Millionaires 4, Toronto 3; March 20 at Toronto – Toronto 2, Van. Millionaires 1; March 23 at Toronto – Van. Millionaires 3, Toronto 0; March 25 at Toronto – Toronto 6, Van. Millionaires 0; March 28 at Toronto – Toronto 5, Van. Millionaires 1.

1920-21 – Ottawa Senators – Jack McKell, Jack Darragh, Morley Bruce, George (Buck) Boucher, Eddie Gerard, Clint Benedict, Sprague Cleghorn, Frank Nighbor, Harry Broadbent, Cy Denneny, Leth Graham, Tommy Gorman (manager),Pete Green (coach), F. Dolan (trainer).
Scores: March 21 at Vancouver – Van. Millionaires 2, Ottawa 1; March 24 at Vancouver – Ottawa 4, Van. Millionaires 3; March 28 at Vancouver – Ottawa 3, Van. Millionaires 2; March 31 at Vancouver – Van. Millionaires 3, Ottawa 2; April 4 at Vancouver – Ottawa 2, Van. Millionaires 1

1919-20 – Ottawa Senators – Jack McKell, Jack Darragh, Morley Bruce, Horrace Merrill, George (Buck) Boucher, Eddie Gerard, Clint Benedict, Sprague Cleghorn, Frank Nighbor, Harry Broadbent, Cy Denneny, Price, Tommy Gorman (manager), Pete Green (coach).
Scores: March 22 at Ottawa – Ottawa 3, Seattle 2; March 24 at Ottawa – Ottawa 3, Seattle 0; March 27 at Ottawa – Seattle 3, Ottawa 1; March 30 at Toronto* – Seattle 5, Ottawa 2; April 1 at Toronto* – Ottawa 6, Seattle 1.

*Games transferred to Toronto to benefit from artificial ice surface.

1918-19 – No decision, Series halted by Spanish influenza epidemic. Five games had been played when the series was halted, each team having won two and tied one. The results are shown:
Scores: March 19 at Seattle – Seattle 7, Montreal 0; March 22 at Seattle – Montreal 4, Seattle 2; March 24 at Seattle – Seattle 7, Montreal 2; March 26 at Seattle – Montreal 0, Seattle 0; March 30 at Seattle – Montreal 4, Seattle 3.

1917-18 – Toronto Arenas – Rusty Crawford, Harry Meeking, Ken Randall, Corb Denneny, Harry Cameron, Jack Adams, Alf Skinner, Harry Mummery, Harry (Happy) Holmes, Reg Noble, Sammy Hebert, Jack Marks, Jack Coughlin, Neville, Charlie Querrie (manager), Dick Carroll (coach), Frank Carroll (trainer).
Scores: March 20 at Toronto – Toronto 5, Van. Millionaires 3; March 23 at Toronto – Van. Millionaires 6, Toronto 4; March 26 at Toronto – Toronto 6, Van. Millionaires 3; March 28 at Toronto – Van. Millionaires 8, Toronto 1; March 30 at Toronto – Toronto 2, Van. Millionaires 1.

1916-17 – Seattle Metropolitans – Harry (Happy) Holmes, Ed Carpenter, Cully Wilson, Jack Walker, Bernie Morris, Frank Foyston, Roy Rickey, Jim Riley, Bobby Rowe (captain), Peter Muldoon (manager).
Scores: March 17 at Seattle – Montreal 8, Seattle 4; March 20 at Seattle – Seattle 6, Montreal 1; March 23 at Seattle – Seattle 4, Montreal 1; March 25 at Seattle – Seattle 9, Montreal 1.

1915-16 – Montreal Canadiens – Georges Vezina, Bert Corbeau, Jack Laviolette, Newsy Lalonde, Louis Berlinguette, Goldie Prodgers, Howard McNamara, Didier Pitre, Skene Ronan, Amos Arbour, Skinner Poulin, Jack Fournier, George Kennedy (manager).
Scores: March 20 at Montreal – Portland 2, Montreal 0; March 22 at Montreal – Montreal 2, Portland 1; March 25 at Montreal – Montreal 6, Portland 3; March 28 at Montreal – Portland 6, Montreal 5; March 30 at Montreal – Montreal 2, Portland 1.

1914-15 – Vancouver Millionaires – Kenny Mallen, Frank Nighbor, Fred (Cyclone) Taylor, Hughie Lehman, Lloyd Cook, Mickey MacKay, Barney Stanley, Jim Seaborn, Si Griffis (captain), Jean Matz, Frank Patrick (playing manager).
Scores: March 22 at Vancouver – Van. Millionaires 6, Ottawa 2; March 24 at Vancouver – Van. Millionaires 8, Ottawa 3; March 26 at Vancouver – Van. Millionaires 12, Ottawa 3.

1913-14 – Toronto Blueshirts – Con Corbeau, F. Roy McGiffen, Jack Walker, George McNamara, Cully Wilson, Frank Foyston, Harry Cameron, Harry (Happy) Holmes, Alan M. Davidson (captain), Harriston, Jack Marshall (playing-manager), Frank and Dick Carroll (trainers).
Scores: March 7 at Montreal – Montreal 2, Toronto 0; March 11 at Toronto – Toronto 6, Montreal 0; Total goals: Toronto 6, Montreal 2. March 14 at Toronto – Toronto 5, Victoria 2; March 17 at Toronto – Toronto 6, Victoria 5; March 19 at Toronto – Toronto 2, Victoria 1.

1912-13 – Quebec Bulldogs – Joe Malone, Joe Hall, Paddy Moran, Harry Mummery, Tommy Smith, Jack Marks, Russell Crawford, Billy Creighton, Jeff Malone, Rocket Power, M.J. Quinn (manager), D. Beland (trainer).
Scores: March 8 at Quebec – Que. Bulldogs 14, Sydney 3; March 10 at Quebec – Que. Bulldogs 6, Sydney 2.

Victoria challenged Quebec but the Bulldogs refused to put the Stanley Cup in competition so the two teams played an exhibition series with Victoria winning two games to one by scores of 7-5, 3-6, 6-1. It was the first meeting between the Eastern champions and the Western champions. The following year, and until the Western Hockey League disbanded after the 1926 playoffs, the Cup went to the winner of the series between East and West.

1911-12 – Quebec Bulldogs – Goldie Prodgers, Joe Hall, Walter Rooney, Paddy Moran, Jack Marks, Jack McDonald, Eddie Oatman, George Leonard, Joe Malone (captain), C. Nolan (coach), M.J. Quinn (manager), D. Beland (trainer).
Scores: March 11 at Quebec – Que. Bulldogs 9, Moncton 3; March 13 at Quebec – Que. Bulldogs 8, Moncton 0.

Prior to 1912, teams could challenge the Stanley Cup champions for the title, thus there was more than one Championship Series played in most of the seasons between 1894 and 1911.

1910-11 – Ottawa Senators – Hamby Shore, Percy LeSueur, Jack Darragh, Bruce Stuart, Marty Walsh, Bruce Ridpath, Fred Lake, Albert (Dubby) Kerr, Alex Currie, Horace Gaul.
Scores: March 13 at Ottawa – Ottawa 7, Galt 4; March 16 at Ottawa – Ottawa 13, Port Arthur 4.

1909-10 – Monteal Wanderers – Cecil W. Blachford, Ernie (Moose) Johnson, Ernie Russell, Riley Hern, Harry Hyland, Jack Marshall, Frank (Pud) Glass (captain), Jimmy Gardner, R. R. Boon (manager).
Scores: March 12 at Montreal – Mtl. Wanderers 7, Berlin (Kitchener) 3.

1908-09 – Ottawa Senators – Fred Lake, Percy LeSueur, Fred (Cyclone) Taylor, H.L. (Billy) Gilmour, Albert Kerr, Edgar Dey, Marty Walsh, Bruce Stuart (captain).
Scores: Ottawa, as champions of the Eastern Canada Hockey Association, took over the Stanley Cup in 1909 and, although a challenge was accepted by the Cup trustees from the Winnipeg Shamrocks, games could not be arranged because of the lateness of the season. No other challenges were made in 1909. The following season – 1909-10 – however, the Senators accepted two challenges as defending Cup Champions. The first was against Galt, and the second against Edmonton. Results: January 5 at Ottawa – Ottawa 12, Galt 3; January 7 at Ottawa – Ottawa 3, Galt 1. January 18 at Ottawa – Ottawa 8, Edm. Eskimos 4; January 20 at Ottawa – Ottawa 13, Edm. Eskimos 7.

1907-08 – Montreal Wanderers – Riley Hern, Art Ross, Walter Small, Frank (Pud) Glass, Bruce Stuart, Ernie Russell, Ernie (Moose) Johnson, Cecil Blachford (captain), Tom Hooper, Larry Gilmour, Ernie Liffiton, R.R. Boon (manager).
Scores: Wanderers accepted four challenges for the Cup: January 9 at Montreal – Mtl. Wanderers 9, Ott. Victorias 3; January 13 at Montreal – Mtl. Wanderers 13, Ott. Victorias 1; March 10 at Montreal – Mtl. Wanderers 11, Wpg. Maple Leafs 5; March 12 at Montreal – Mtl. Wanderers 9, Wpg. Maple Leafs 3; March 14 at Montreal – Mtl. Wanderers 6, Toronto (OPHL) 4. At start of following season, 1908-09, Wanderers were challenged by Edmonton. Results: December 28 at Montreal – Mtl. Wanderers 7, Edm. Eskimos 3; December 30 at Montreal – Edm. Eskimos 7, Mtl. Wanderers 6. Total goals: Mtl. Wanderers 13, Edm. Eskimos 10.

1906-07 – (March) – Montreal Wanderers – W. S. (Billy) Strachan, Riley Hern, Lester Patrick, Hod Stuart, Frank (Pud) Glass, Ernie Russell, Cecil Blachford (captain), Ernie (Moose) Johnson, Rod Kennedy, Jack Marshall, R. R. Boon (manager).
Scores: March 23 at Winnipeg – Mtl. Wanderers 7, Kenora 2; March 25 at Winnipeg – Kenora 6, Mtl. Wanderers 5. Total goals: Mtl. Wanderers 12, Kenora 8.

1906-07 – (January) – Kenora Thistles – Eddie Geroux, Art Ross, Si Griffis, Tom Hooper, Billy McGimsie, Roxy Beaudro, Tom Phillips.
Scores: January 17 at Montreal – Kenora 4, Mtl. Wanderers 2; Jan. 21 at Montreal – Kenora 8, Mtl. Wanderers 6.

1905-06 – (March) – Montreal Wanderers – H. Menard, Billy Strachan, Rod Kennedy, Lester Patrick, Frank (Pud) Glass, Ernie Russell Ernie (Moose) Johnson, Cecil Blachford (captain), Josh Arnold, R. R. Boon (manager).
Scores: March 14 at Montreal – Mtl. Wanderers 9, Ottawa 1; March 17 at Ottawa – Ottawa 9, Mtl. Wanderers 3. Total goals: Mtl. Wanderers 12, Ottawa 10. Wanderers accepted a challenge from New Glasgow, N.S., prior to the start of the 1906-07 season. Results: December 27 at Montreal – Mtl. Wanderers 10, New Glasgow 3; December 29 at Montreal – Mtl. Wanderers 7, New Glasgow 2.

1905-06 – (February) – Ottawa Silver Seven – Harvey Pulford (captain), Arthur Moore, Harry Westwick, Frank McGee, Alf Smith (playing coach), Billy Gilmour, Billy Hague, Percy LeSueur, Harry Smith, Tommy Smith, Dion, Ebbs.
Scores: February 27 at Ottawa – Ottawa 16, Queen's University 7; February 28 at Ottawa – Ottawa 12, Queen's University 7; March 6 at Ottawa – Ottawa 6, Smiths Falls 5; March 8 at Ottawa – Ottawa 8, Smiths Falls 2.

1904-05 – Ottawa Silver Seven – Dave Finnie, Harvey Pulford (captain), Arthur Moore, Harry Westwick, Frank McGee, Alf Smith (playing coach), Billy Gilmour, Frank White, Horace Gaul, Hamby Shore, Bones Allen.
Scores: January 13 at Ottawa – Ottawa 9, Dawson City 2; January 16 at Ottawa – Ottawa 23, Dawson City 2; March 7 at Ottawa – Rat Portage 9, Ottawa 3; March 9 at Ottawa – Ottawa 4, Rat Portage 2; March 11 at Ottawa – Ottawa 5, Rat Portage 4.

1903-04 – Ottawa Silver Seven – S.C. (Suddy) Gilmour, Arthur Moore, Frank McGee, J.B. (Bouse) Hutton, H.L. (Billy) Gilmour, Jim McGee, Harry Westwick, E.H. (Harvey) Pulford (captain), Scott, Alf Smith (playing coach).
Scores: December 30 at Ottawa – Ottawa 9, Wpg. Rowing Club 1; January 1 at Ottawa – Wpg. Rowing Club 6, Ottawa 2; January 4 at Ottawa – Ottawa 2, Wpg. Rowing Club 0. February 23 at Ottawa – Ottawa 6, Tor. Malboros 3; February 25 at Ottawa – Ottawa 11, Tor. Marlboros 2; March 2 at Montreal – Ottawa 5, Mtl. Wanderers 5. Following the tie game, a new two-game series was ordered to be played in Ottawa, but Wanderers refused unless the tie game was replayed in Montreal. When no settlement could be reached, the series was abandoned and Ottawa retained the Cup and accepted a two-game challenge from Brandon. Results: (both games at Ottawa), March 9, Ottawa 6, Brandon 3; March 11, Ottawa 9, Brandon 3.

1902-03 – (March) – Ottawa Silver Seven – S.C. (Suddy) Gilmour, P.T. (Percy) Sims, J. B. (Bouse) Hutton, D. J. (Dave) Gilmour, H. L. (Billy) Gilmour, Harry Westwick, Frank McGee, F. H. Wood, A. A. Fraser, Charles D. Spittal, E. H. (Harvey) Pulford (captain), Arthur Moore, Alf Smith (coach.)
Scores: March 7 at Montreal – Ottawa 1, Mtl. Victorias 1; March 10 at Ottawa – Ottawa 8, Mtl. Victorias 0. Total goals: Ottawa 9, Mtl. Victorias 1; March 12 at Ottawa – Ottawa 6, Rat Portage 2; March 14 at Ottawa – Ottawa 4, Rat Portage 2.

1902-03 – (February) – Montreal AAA – Tom Hodge, R.R. (Dickie) Boon, W.C. (Billy) Nicholson, Art Hooper, W.J. (Billy) Bellingham, Charles A. Liffiton, Jack Marshall, Jim Gardner, Cecil Blachford, George Smith.
Scores: January 29 at Montreal – Mtl. AAA 8, Wpg. Victorias 1; January 31 at Montreal – Wpg. Victorias 2, Mtl. AAA 2; February 2 at Montreal – Wpg. Victorias 4, Mtl. AAA 2; February 4 at Montreal – Mtl. AAA 5, Wpg. Victorias 1.

1901-02 – (March) – Montreal AAA – Tom Hodge, R.R. (Dickie) Boon, W.C. (Billy) Nicholson, Art Hooper, W.J. (Billy) Bellingham, Charles A. Liffiton, Jack Marshall, Roland Elliott, Jim Gardner.
Scores: March 13 at Winnipeg – Wpg. Victorias 1, Mtl. AAA 0; March 15 at Winnipeg – Mtl. AAA 5, Wpg. Victorias 0; March 17 at Winnipeg – Mtl. AAA 2, Wpg. Victorias 1.

1901-02 – (January) – Winnipeg Victorias – Burke Wood, A.B. (Tony) Gingras, Charles W. Johnstone, R.M. (Rod) Flett, Magnus L. Flett, Dan Bain (captain), Fred Scanlon, F. Cadham, G. Brown.
Scores: January 21 at Winnipeg – Wpg. Victorias 5, Tor Wellingtons 3; January 23 at Winnipeg – Wpg. Victorias 5, Tor. Wellingtons 3.

1900-01 – Winnipeg Victorias – Burke Wood, Jack Marshall, A.B. (Tony) Gingras, Charles W. Johnstone, R.M. (Rod) Flett, Magnus L. Flett, Dan Bain (captain), G. Brown.
Scores: January 29 at Montreal – Wpg. Victorias 4, Mtl. Shamrocks 3; January 31 at Montreal – Wpg. Victorias 2, Mtl. Shamrocks 1.

1899-1900 – Montreal Shamrocks – Joe McKenna, Frank Tansey, Frank Wall, Art Farrell, Fred Scanlon, Harry Trihey (captain), Jack Brannen.
Scores: February 12 at Montreal – Mtl. Shamrocks 4, Wpg. Victorias 3; February 14 at Montreal – Wpg. Victorias 3, Mtl. Shamrocks 2; February 16 at Montreal – Mtl. Shamrocks 5, Wpg. Victorias 4; March 5 at Montreal – Mtl. Shamrocks 10, Halifax 2; March 7 at Montreal – Mtl. Shamrocks 11, Halifax 0.

1898-99 – (March) – Montreal Shamrocks – Joe McKenna, Frank Tansey, Frank Wall, Harry Trihey (captain), Art Farrell, Fred Scanlon, Jack Brannen, Dalby, C. Hoerner.
Scores: March 14 at Montreal – Mtl. Shamrocks 6, Queen's University 2.

1898-99 – (February) – Montreal Victorias – Gordon Lewis, Mike Grant, Graham Drinkwater, Cam Davidson, Bob McDougall, Ernie McLea, Frank Richardson, Jack Ewing, Russell Bowie, Douglas Acer, Fred McRobie.
Scores: February 15 at Montreal – Mtl. Victorias 2, Wpg. Victorias 1; February 18 at Montreal – Mtl. Victorias 3, Wpg. Victorias 2.

1897-98 – Montreal Victorias – Gordon Lewis, Hartland McDougall, Mike Grant, Graham Drinkwater, Cam Davidson, Bob McDougall, Ernie McLea, Frank Richardson (captain), Jack Ewing. The Victorias as champions of the Amateur Hockey Association, retained the Cup and were not called upon to defend it.

1896-97 – Montreal Victorias – Gordon Lewis, Harold Henderson, Mike Grant (captain), Cam Davidson, Graham Drinkwater, Robert McDougall, Ernie McLea, Shirley Davidson, Hartland McDougall, Jack Ewing, Percy Molson, David Gillilan, McLellan.
Scores: December 27 at Montreal – Mtl. Victorias 15, Ott. Capitals 2.

1895-96 – (December) – Montreal Victorias – Gordon Lewis, Harold Henderson, Mike Grant (captain), Robert McDougall, Graham Drinkwater, Shirley Davidson, Ernie McLea, Robert Jones, Cam Davidson, Hartland McDougall, David Gillilan, Reg Wallace, Stanley Willett.
Scores: December 30 at Winnipeg – Mtl. Victorias 6, Wpg. Victorias 5.

1895-96 – (February) – Winnipeg Victorias – G.H. Merritt, Rod Flett, Fred Higginbotham, Jack Armitage (captain), C.J. (Tote) Campbell, Dan Bain, Charles Johnstone, H. Howard.
Scores: February 14 at Montreal – Wpg. Victorias 2, Mtl. Victorias 0.

1894-95 – Montreal Victorias – Robert Jones, Harold Henderson, Mike Grant (captain), Shirley Davidson, Bob McDougall, Norman Rankin, Graham Drinkwater, Roland Elliot, William Pullan, Hartland McDougall, Arthur Fenwick, A. McDougall. Montreal Victorias as champions of the Amateur Hockey Association were prepared to defend the Stanley Cup. However, the Stanley Cup trustees had already accepted a challenge match between the 1894 champion Montreal AAA and Queen's University. It was declared that if Montreal AAA defeated Queen's University, Montreal Victorias would be declared Stanley Cup champions. If Queen's University won, the Cup would go to the university club. In a game played March 9, 1895, Montreal AAA defeated Queen's University 5-1. As a result, Montreal Victorias were awarded the Stanley Cup.

1893-94 – Montreal AAA – Herbert Collins, Allan Cameron, George James, Billy Barlow, Clare Mussen, Archie Hodgson, Haviland Routh, Alex Irving, James Stewart, A.C. (Toad) Waud, A. Kingan, E. O'Brien.
Scores: March 17 at Mtl. Victorias – Mtl. AAA 3, Mtl. Victorias 2; March 22 at Montreal – Mtl. AAA 3, Ott. Capitals 1.

1892-93 – Montreal AAA – Tom Paton, James Stewart, Allan Cameron, Alex Irving, Haviland Routh, Archie Hodgson, Billy Barlow, A.B. Kingan, J. Lowe. In accordance with the terms governing the presentation of the Stanley Cup, it was awarded for the first time to the Montreal AAA as champions of the Amateur Hockey Association in 1893. Once Montreal AAA had been declared holders of the Stanley Cup, any Canadian hockey team could challenge for the trophy.

Scoring Leaders, Standings, and Overtime

Stanley Cup Standings

1918-92
(ranked by Cup wins)

Teams	Wins	Yrs.	Series	Wins	Losses	Games	Wins	Losses	Ties	For	Against	%
Montreal	22*	67	125*	80	44	590	355	227	8	1835	1445	.608
Toronto	13	54	82	43	39	374	177	194	3	961	1024	.477
Detroit	7	41	70	36	34	337	162	174	1	903	918	.482
Boston	5	53	93	45	48	449	220	223	6	1333	1325	.497
Edmonton	5	13	37	29	8	180	120	60	0	770	579	.667
NY Islanders	4	15	39	28	11	196	119	77	0	687	563	.607
Chicago	3	47	81	37	44	364	168	191	5	1066	1175	.468
NY Rangers	3	44	75	34	41	327	149	170	8	905	954	.468
Philadelphia	2	20	43	25	18	223	116	107	0	715	688	.520
Pittsburgh	2	12	22	12	10	107	60	47	0	356	348	.561
Calgary***	1	18	28	12	16	132	61	71	0	439	475	.462
St. Louis	0	22	38	16	22	195	86	109	0	571	656	.441
Los Angeles	0	18	25	7	18	118	42	76	0	366	477	.356
Minnesota	0	17	31	14	17	166	80	86	0	554	579	.482
Buffalo	0	17	26	9	17	123	54	69	0	390	420	.439
Vancouver	0	12	16	4	12	71	27	44	0	205	256	.380
Washington	0	10	16	6	10	86	40	46	0	284	284	.465
Winnipeg	0	9	11	2	9	50	15	35	0	150	212	.300
Hartford	0	8	9	1	8	49	18	31	0	143	177	.367
Quebec	0	7	13	6	7	68	31	37	0	212	242	.456
New Jersey****	0	5	7	2	5	42	19	23	0	134	147	.452
San Jose	0	0	0	0	0	0	0	0	0	0	0	.000

*1919 final incomplete due to influenza epidemic.
**Montreal Canadiens also won Stanley Cup in 1916.
***Includes totals of Atlanta 1972-80.
****Includes totals of Colorado 1976-82.

Ten Longest Overtime Games

Date	City	Series	Score				Scorer	Overtime	Winner
Mar. 24/36	Mtl.	SF	Det. 1	Mtl. M. 0			Mud Bruneteau	116:30	Det.
Apr. 3/33	Tor.	SF	Tor. 1	Bos. 0			Ken Doraty	104:46	Tor.
Mar. 23/43	Det.	SF	Tor. 3	Det. 2			Jack McLean	70:18	Det.
Mar. 28/30	Mtl.	SF	Mtl. 2	NYR 1			Gus Rivers	68:52	Mtl.
Apr. 18/87	Wsh.	DSF	NYI 3	Wsh. 2			Pat LaFontaine	68:47	NYI
Mar. 27/51	Det.	SF	Mtl. 3	Det. 2			Maurice Richard	61:09	Mtl.
Mar. 27/38	NY	QF	NYA 3	NYR 2			Lorne Carr	60:40	NYA
Mar. 26/32	Mtl.	SF	NYR 4	Mtl. 3			Fred Cook	59:32	NYR
Mar. 21/39	NY	SF	Bos. 2	NYR 1			Mel Hill	59:25	Bos.
May 15/90	Bos.	F	Edm. 3	Bos. 2			Petr Klima	55:13	Edm.

All-Time Stanley Cup Playoff Goal Leaders

since 1893
(40 or more goals)

Player	Teams	Yrs.	GP	G
*Wayne Gretzky	Edm., L.A.	13	156	95
*Jari Kurri	Edm., L.A.	11	150	93
*Mark Messier	Edm., NYR	13	177	87
Mike Bossy	NY Islanders	10	129	85
Maurice Richard	Montreal	15	133	82
*Glenn Anderson	Edmonton	11	164	81
Jean Béliveau	Montreal	17	162	79
Bryan Trottier	NYI, Pit.	16	219	71
Gordie Howe	Det., Hfd.	20	157	68
*Brian Propp	Phi., Bos., Min.,	14	160	64
Yvan Cournoyer	Montreal	12	147	64
*Bobby Smith	Min., Mtl.	13	184	64
Frank McGee	Ottawa	4	22	63
Bobby Hull	Chi., Hfd.	14	119	62
Phil Esposito	Chi., Bos., NYR	15	130	61
Jacques Lemaire	Montreal	11	145	61
Stan Mikita	Chicago	18	155	59
Guy Lafleur	Mtl., NYR	14	128	58
Bernie Geoffrion	Mtl., NYR	16	132	58
*Denis Savard	Chicago, Mtl.	12	123	58
Denis Potvin	NY Islanders	14	185	56
*Joe Mullen	St.L., Cgy., Pit.	10	112	55
Rick MacLeish	Phi., Pit., Det.	11	114	54
Bill Barber	Philadelphia	11	129	53
*Cam Neely	Bos.	6	84	51
*Esa Tikkanen	Edm.	8	114	51
Frank Mahovlich	Tor., Det., Mtl.	14	137	51
Steve Shutt	Mtl., L.A.	12	99	50
*Dino Ciccarelli	Min., Wsh.	10	94	49
Henri Richard	Montreal	18	180	49
Reggie Leach	Bos., Phi.	8	94	47
Ted Lindsay	Det., Chi.	16	133	47
Clark Gillies	NYI, Buf.	13	164	47
Dickie Moore	Mtl., Tor., St.L.	14	135	46
Rick Middleton	NYR, Bos.	12	114	45
*Steve Larmer	Chicago	10	103	45
*Mario Lemieux	Pittsburgh	3	49	44
*Paul Coffey	Edm., Pit., L.A.	10	123	44
Lanny McDonald	Tor., Cgy.	13	117	44
*Ken Linseman	Phi., Edm., Bos.	11	113	43
*Brett Hull	Cgy., St.L.	7	57	42
Bobby Clarke	Philadelphia	13	136	42
John Bucyk	Det., Bos.	14	124	41
*Tim Kerr	Phi., NYR	10	81	40
Peter McNab	Bos., Van.	10	107	40
Bob Bourne	NYI, L.A.	13	139	40
*John Tonelli	NYI, Cgy., L.A.	13	172	40

* – Active player.

All-Time Stanley Cup Playoff Assist Leaders

since 1893
(60 or more assists)

Player	Teams	Yrs.	GP	A
*Wayne Gretzky	Edm., L.A.	13	156	211
*Mark Messier	Edm., NYR	13	177	142
Larry Robinson	Mtl., L.A.	20	227	116
Bryan Trottier	NY, Pit.	16	219	113
*Jari Kurri	Edm., L.A.	11	150	112
Denis Potvin	NY Islanders	14	185	108
*Glenn Anderson	Edmonton	11	164	102
Jean Béliveau	Montreal	17	162	97
*Bobby Smith	Min., Mtl.	13	184	96
*Ray Bourque	Boston	13	135	95
Gordie Howe	Det., Hfd.	20	157	92
*Paul Coffey	Edm., Pit., L.A.	10	123	92
Stan Mikita	Chicago	18	155	91
Brad Park	NYR, Bos., Det.	17	161	90
*Denis Savard	Chi., Mtl.	12	123	89
*Brian Propp	Phi., Bos., Min.	14	160	84
Henri Richard	Montreal	18	180	80
Jacques Lemaire	Montreal	11	145	78
*Ken Linseman	Phi., Edm., Bos.	11	113	77
Bobby Clarke	Philadelphia	13	136	77
Guy Lafleur	Mtl., NYR	14	128	76
Phil Esposito	Chi., Bos., NYR	15	130	76
Mike Bossy	NY Islanders	10	129	75
*John Tonelli	NYI, Cgy., L.A.	13	172	75
*Chris Chelios	Mtl., Chi.	9	122	74
*Peter Stastny	Que., N.J.	10	84	70
Gilbert Perreault	Buffalo	11	90	70
Alex Delvecchio	Detroit	14	121	69
Bobby Hull	Chi., Hfd.	14	119	67
Frank Mahovlich	Tor., Det., Mtl.	14	137	67
Bobby Orr	Boston	8	74	66
*Adam Oates	Det., St.L., Bos.	6	78	66
Bernie Federko	St. Louis	11	91	66
Jean Ratelle	NYR, Bos.	15	123	66
*Al MacInnis	Calgary	8	82	65
Dickie Moore	Mtl., Tor., St.L.	14	135	64
Doug Harvey	Mtl., NYR, St.L.	15	137	64
*Steve Larmer	Chicago	10	103	63
Yvan Cournoyer	Montreal	12	147	63
*Craig Janney	Bos., St.L.	5	75	62
*Charlie Huddy	Edm., L.A.	11	144	62
John Bucyk	Det., Bos.	14	124	62
*Doug Wilson	Chicago	12	95	61

* – Active player.

All-Time Stanley Cup Playoff Point Leaders

since 1893
(100 or more points)

Player	Teams	Yrs.	GP	G	A	Pts.
*Wayne Gretzky	Edm., L.A.	13	156	95	211	306
*Mark Messier	Edm., NYR	13	177	87	142	229
*Jari Kurri	Edm., L.A.	11	150	93	112	205
Bryan Trottier	NYI, Pit.	16	219	71	113	184
*Glenn Anderson	Edmonton	11	164	81	102	183
Jean Béliveau	Montreal	17	162	79	97	176
Denis Potvin	NY Islanders	14	185	56	108	164
Mike Bossy	NY Islanders	10	129	85	75	160
Gordie Howe	Det., Hfd.	20	157	68	92	160
*Bobby Smith	Min., Mtl.	13	184	64	96	160
Stan Mikita	Chicago	18	155	59	91	150
*Brian Propp	Phi., Bos., Min.	14	160	64	84	148
*Denis Savard	Chi., Mtl.	12	123	58	89	147
Larry Robinson	Mtl., L.A.	20	227	28	116	144
Jacques Lemaire	Montreal	11	145	61	78	139
Phil Esposito	Chi., Bos., NYR	15	130	61	76	137
Guy Lafleur	Mtl., NYR	14	128	58	76	134
Bobby Hull	Chi., Hfd.	14	119	62	67	129
Henri Richard	Montreal	18	180	49	80	129
Yvan Cournoyer	Montreal	12	147	64	63	127
Maurice Richard	Montreal	15	133	82	44	126
*Ray Bourque	Boston	13	135	30	95	125
Brad Park	NYR, Bos., Det.	17	161	35	90	125
*Ken Linseman	Phi., Edm., Bos.	11	113	43	77	120
Bobby Clarke	Philadelphia	13	136	42	77	119
Bernie Geoffrion	Mtl., NYR	16	132	58	60	118
Frank Mahovlich	Tor., Det., Mtl.	14	137	51	67	118
*John Tonelli	NYI, Cgy., L.A.	13	172	40	75	115
Dickie Moore	Mtl., Tor., St.L.	14	135	46	64	110
Bill Barber	Philadelphia	11	129	53	55	108
*Steve Larmer	Chicago	10	103	45	63	108
Rick MacLeish	Phi., Pit., Det.	11	114	54	53	107
Alex Delvecchio	Detroit	14	121	35	69	104
John Bucyk	Det., Bos.	14	124	41	62	103
*Peter Stastny	Que., N.J.	10	84	33	70	103
Gilbert Perreault	Buffalo	11	90	33	70	103
Bernie Federko	St. Louis	11	91	35	66	101
Rick Middleton	NYR, Bos.	12	114	45	55	100

* – Active player.

All-Time NHL Playoff formats

1917-18 – The regular-season was split into two halves. The winners of both halves faced each other in a two-game, total-goals series for the NHL championship and the right to meet the PCHA champion in the best-of-five Stanley Cup Final.

1918-19 – Same as 1917-18, except that the Stanley Cup Final was extended to a best-of-seven series.

1919-20 – Same as 1918-19, except that Ottawa won both halves of the split regular-season schedule to earn an automatic berth into the best-of-five Stanley Cup Final against the PCHA champions.

1921-22 – The top two teams at the conclusion of the regular-season faced each other in a two-game, total-goals series for the NHL championship. The NHL champion then moved on to play the winner of the PCHA–WCHL playoff series in the best-of-five Stanley Cup Final.

1922-23 – The top two teams at the conclusion of the regular-season faced each other in a two-game, total-goals series for the NHL championship. The NHL champion then moved on to play the PCHA champion in a best-of-three Stanley Cup Final. The winner played the WCHL champion in an additional best-of-three Stanley Cup Final.

1923-24 – The top two teams at the conclusion of the regular season faced each other in a two-game, total-goals series for the NHL championship. The NHL champion then moved on to play the loser of a PCHA–WCHL playoff in a best-of-three Stanley Cup Final. The winner of this series met the PCHA–WCHL playoff winner in an additional best-of-three Stanley Cup Final.

1924-25 – The first-place team (Hamilton) at the conclusion of the regular season was supposed to play the winner of a two-game, total-goals series between Toronto and Montreal, the second- and third-place clubs. However, Hamilton refused to abide by this new format, demanding additional compensation. Thus, Toronto and Montreal played their two-game, total-goals series, and the winner (Montreal) earned the NHL title and then played the WCHL champion (Victoria) in a best-of-five Stanley Cup Final.

1925-26 – The format which was intended for 1924-25 went into effect. The winner of the two-game, total-goals series between the second- and third-place teams squared off against the first place team in the two-game, total-goals NHL championship series. The NHL champion then moved on to play the WHL champion in a best-

of-five Stanley Cup Final.

After the 1925-26 season, the NHL took sole control of Stanley Cup competition.

1926-27 – The 10-team league was divided into two divisions – Canadian and American – of five teams apiece. In each division, the winner of a two-game, total-goals series between the second- and third-place teams faced the first-place team in a two-game, total-goals series for the division title. The two division title winners then met in a best-of-five Stanley Cup Final.

1928-29 – Both first-place teams in the two divisions played each other in a best-of-five series. Both second-place teams in the two divisions played each other in a two-game, total-goals series as did the two third-place teams. The winners of these latter two series then played each other in a best-of-three series for the right to meet the winner of the series between the two first-place clubs. This Stanley Cup Final was a best-of-three.

Series A: First in Canadian Division versus first in American (best-of-five)
Series B: Second in Canadian Division versus second in American (two-game, total-goals)
Series C: Third in Canadian Division versus third in American (two-game, total-goals)
Series D: Winner of Series B versus winner of Series C (best-of-three)
Series E: Winner of Series A versus winner of Series D (best-of-three) for the Stanley Cup

1931-32 – Same as 1928-29, except that Series D was changed to a two-game, total-goals format and Series E was changed to best-of-five.

1936-37 – Same as 1931-32, except that Series B, C, and D were each best-of-three.

1938-39 – With the NHL reduced to seven teams, the two-division system was replaced by one seven-team league. Based on final regular-season standings, the following playoff format was adopted:

Series A: First versus Second (best-of-seven)
Series B: Third versus Fourth (best-of-three)
Series C: Fifth versus Sixth (best-of-three)
Series D: Winner of Series B versus winner of Series C (best-of-three)
Series E: Winner of Series A versus winner of Series D (best-of-seven) for the Stanley Cup

1942-43 – With the NHL reduced to six teams (the "original six"), only the top four finishers qualified for playoff action. The best-of-seven Semi-Finals pitted Team #1 vs Team #3 and Team #2 vs Team #4. The winners of each Semi-Final series met in a best-of-seven Stanley Cup Final.

1967-68 – When it doubled in size from 6 to 12 teams, the NHL once again was divided into two divisions – East and West – of six teams apiece. The top four teams in each division qualified for the playoffs (all series were best-of-seven):

Series A; Team #1 (East) vs Team #3 (East)
Series B: Team #2 (East) vs Team #4 (East)
Series C: Team #1 (West) vs Team #3 (West)
Series D: Team #2 (West) vs Team #4 (West)

Series E: Winner of Series A vs winner of Series B
Series F: Winner of Series C vs winner of Series D
Series G: Winner of Series E vs Winner of Series F for the Stanley Cup

1970-71 – Same as 1967-68 except that Series E matched the winners of Series A and D, and Series F matched the winners of Series B and C.

1971-72 – Same as 1970-71, except that Series A and C matched Team #1 vs Team #4, and Series B and D matched Team #2 vs Team #3.

1974-75 – With the League now expanded to 18 teams in four divisions, a completely new playoff format was introduced. First, the second- and third-place teams in each of the four divisions

were pooled together in a Preliminary Round. These eight clubs were ranked #1 to #8 based on regular-season record:

Series A: Team #1 vs Team #8 (best-of-three)
Series B: Team #2 vs Team #7 (best-of-three)
Series C: Team #3 vs Team #6 (best-of-three)
Series D: Team #4 vs Team #5 (best-of-three)

The winners of this Preliminary Round were then pooled together with the four division winners. These eight teams were again ranked #1 to #8 based on regular-season record:

Series E: Team #1 vs Team #8 (best-of-seven)
Series F: Team #2 vs Team #7 (best-of-seven)
Series G: Team #3 vs Team #6 (best-of-seven)
Series H: Team #4 vs Team #5 (best-of-seven)

The four Quarter-Finals winners were then ranked #1 to #4 based on regular-season record:

Series I: Team #1 vs Team #4 (best-of-seven)
Series J: Team #2 vs Team #3 (best-of-seven)
Series K: Winner of Series I vs winner of Series J (best-of-seven) for the Stanley Cup

1977-78 – Same as 1974-75, except that the Preliminary Round consisted of the second-place team in each division and the four teams finishing with the next-highest regular-season point totals.

1979-80 – With the addition of four former WHA franchises, the league expanded its playoff structure to include 16 of its 21 teams. The four first-place teams in the four divisions automatically earned playoff berths. Among the 17 other clubs, the top 12, according to regular-season record, also earned berths. All 16 teams were then pooled together and ranked #1 to #16 based on regular-season record:

Series A: Team #1 vs Team #16 (best-of-five)
Series B: Team #2 vs Team #15 (best-of-five)
Series C: Team #3 vs Team #14 (best-of-five)
Series D: Team #4 vs Team #13 (best-of-five)
Series E: Team #5 vs Team #12 (best-of-five)
Series F: Team #6 vs Team #11 (best-of-five)
Series G: Team #7 vs Team #10 (best-of-five)
Series H: Team #8 vs Team #9 (best-of-five)

The eight Preliminary Round winners, ranked #1 to #8 based on regular-season record, moved on to the Quarter-Finals:

Series I: Team #1 vs Team #8 (best-of-seven)
Series J: Team #2 vs Team #7 (best-of-seven)
Series K: Team #3 vs Team #6 (best-of-seven)
Series L: Team #4 vs Team #5 (best-of-seven)

The four Quarter-Finals winners, ranked #1 to #4 based on regular-season record, moved on to the Semi-Finals:

Series M: Team #1 vs Team #4 (best-of-seven)
Series N: Team #2 vs Team #3 (best-of-seven)
Series O: Winner of Series M vs winner of Series N (best-of-seven) for the Stanley Cup

1981-82 – The first four teams in each division earn playoff berths. In each division, the first-place team opposes the fourth-place team and the second-place team opposes the third-place team in a best-of-five Division Semi-Final series (DSF). In each division, the two winners of the DSF meet in a best-of-seven Division Final series (DF). The two winners in each conference meet in a best-of-seven Conference Final series (CF). In the Prince of Wales Conference, the Adams Division winner opposes the Patrick Division winner; in the Clarence Campbell Conference, the Smythe Division winner opposes the Norris Division winner. The two CF winners meet in a best-of-seven Stanley Cup Final (F) series.

1986-87 to date – Division Semi-Final series changed from best-of-five to best-of-seven.

Team Records

1918-1992

MOST STANLEY CUP CHAMPIONSHIPS:
22 – Montreal Canadiens 1924-30-31-44-46-53-56-57-58-59-60-65-66-68-69-71-73-76-77-78-79-86
13 – Toronto Maple Leafs 1918-22-32-42-45-47-48-49-51-62-63-64-67
7 – Detroit Red Wings 1936-37-43-50-52-54-55

MOST CONSECUTIVE STANLEY CUP CHAMPIONSHIPS:
5 – Montreal Canadiens (1956-57-58-59-60)
4 – Montreal Canadiens (1976-77-78-79)
– NY Islanders (1980-81-82-83)

MOST CONSECUTIVE PLAYOFF APPEARANCES:
25 – Boston Bruins (1968-92, inclusive)
23 – Chicago Black Hawks (1970-92, inclusive)
22 – Montreal Canadiens (1971-92, inclusive)
21 – Montreal Canadiens (1949-69, inclusive)
20 – Detroit Red Wings (1939-58, inclusive)

LONGEST OVERTIME:
116 Minutes, 30 Seconds – Detroit Red Wings,
Mtl. Maroons at Montreal, March 24, 25, 1936. Detroit 1, Mtl. Maroons 0. Mud Bruneteau scored, assisted by Hec Kilrea at 16:30 of sixth overtime period, or after 176 minutes, 30 seconds from start of game, which ended at 2:25 a.m. Detroit won best-of-five SF 3-0.

SHORTEST OVERTIME:
9 Seconds – Montreal Canadiens, Calgary Flames, at Calgary, May 18, 1986. Montreal won 3-2 on Brian Skrudland's goal and captured the best-of-seven F 4-1.

MOST CONSECUTIVE PLAYOFF GAME VICTORIES:
12 – Edmonton Oilers. Streak began May 15, 1984 at Edmonton with a 7-2 win over NY Islanders in third game of F series, and ended May 9, 1985 when Chicago defeated Edmonton 5-2 at Chicago. Included in the streak were three wins over the NY Islanders, in 1984, three over Los Angeles, four over Winnipeg and two over Chicago, all in 1985.

FASTEST THREE GOALS, ONE TEAM:
23 Seconds – Toronto Maple Leafs at Toronto, April 12, 1979, against Atlanta Flames. Darryl Sittler scored at 4:04 of first period and again at 4:16 and Ron Ellis at 4:27. Leafs won 7-4 and best-of-three PR 2-0.

FASTEST FOUR GOALS, ONE TEAM:
2 Minutes, 35 Seconds – Montreal Canadiens at Montreal, March 30, 1944, against Toronto. Toe Blake scored at 7:58 of third period and again at 8:37; Maurice Richard, 9:17; Ray Getliffe, 10:33. Montreal won 11-0 and best-of-seven SF 4-1.

FASTEST FIVE GOALS, ONE TEAM:
3 Minutes, 36 Seconds – Montreal Canadiens at Montreal, March 30, 1944, against Toronto. Toe Blake scored at 7:58 of third period and again at 8:37; Maurice Richard, 9:17; Ray Getliffe, 10:33; and Buddy O'Connor, 11:34. Canadiens won 11-0 and best-of-seven SF 4-1.

Individual Records

1918-1992

MOST YEARS IN PLAYOFFS:
20 – Gordie Howe, Detroit, Hartford (1947-58 incl.; 60-61; 63-66 incl.; 70 & 80)
– **Larry Robinson, Montreal, Los Angeles** (1973-92 incl.)
19 – Red Kelly, Detroit, Toronto
18 – Stan Mikita, Chicago
– Henri Richard, Montreal

MOST CONSECUTIVE YEARS IN PLAYOFFS:
20 – Larry Robinson, Montreal, Los Angeles (1973-1992, inclusive).
17 – Brad Park, NY Rangers, Boston, Detroit (1969-1985, inclusive).

16 – Jean Béliveau, Montreal (1954-69, inclusive).

MOST PLAYOFF GAMES:
227 – Larry Robinson, Montreal, Los Angeles
219 – Bryan Trottier, NY Islanders, Pittsburgh
185 – Denis Potvin, NY Islanders
184 – Bobby Smith, Minnesota, Montreal
182 – Bob Gainey, Montreal

MOST GAME-WINNING GOALS IN PLAYOFFS (CAREER):
18 – Maurice Richard, Montreal
– **Wayne Gretzky, Edmonton, Los Angeles**
17 – Mike Bossy, NY Islanders
15 – Jean Béliveau, Montreal
– Yvan Cournoyer, Montreal

MOST OVERTIME GOALS IN PLAYOFFS (CAREER):
6 – Maurice Richard, Montreal (1 in 1946; 3 in 1951; 1 in 1957; 1 in 1958.)
4 – Bob Nystrom, NY Islanders
– Dale Hunter, Quebec, Washington

MOST POWER-PLAY GOALS IN PLAYOFFS (CAREER):
35 – Mike Bossy, NY Islanders
27 – Denis Potvin, NY Islanders
26 – Jean Béliveau, Montreal

MOST THREE-OR-MORE-GOAL GAMES IN PLAYOFFS (CAREER):
7 – Maurice Richard, Montreal. Four three-goal games; two four-goal games; one five-goal game.
– **Wayne Gretzky, Edmonton.** Five three-goal games; two four-goal games.
– **Jari Kurri, Edmonton.** Six three-goal games; one four-goal game.

MOST SHUTOUTS IN PLAYOFFS (CAREER):
15 – Clint Benedict, Ottawa, Mtl. Maroons
14 – Jacques Plante, Montreal, St. Louis
13 – Turk Broda, Toronto
12 – Terry Sawchuk, Detroit, Toronto, Los Angeles

MOST MINUTES PLAYED BY A GOALTENDER (CAREER):
7,645 – Billy Smith, NY Islanders
6,899 – Glenn Hall, Detroit, Chicago, St. Louis
6,846 – Ken Dryden, Montreal
6,651 – Jacques Plante, Montreal, St. Louis, Toronto, Boston

MOST POINTS, ONE PLAYOFF YEAR:
47 – Wayne Gretzky, Edmonton, in 1985. 17 goals, 30 assists in 18 games.
44 – Mario Lemieux, Pittsburgh, in 1991. 16 goals, 28 assists in 23 games.
43 – Wayne Gretzky, Edmonton, in 1988. 12 goals, 31 assists in 19 games.
38 – Wayne Gretzky, Edmonton, in 1983. 12 goals, 26 assists in 16 games.

MOST POINTS BY A DEFENSEMAN, ONE PLAYOFF YEAR:
37 – Paul Coffey, Edmonton, in 1985. 12 goals, 25 assists in 18 games.
31 – Al MacInnis, Calgary, in 1989. 7 goals, 24 assists in 18 games.
25 – Denis Potvin, NY Islanders, in 1981. 8 goals, 17 assists in 18 games.
– Ray Bourque, Boston, in 1991. 7 goals, 18 assists in 19 games.
24 – Bobby Orr, Boston, in 1972. 5 goals, 19 assists in 15 games.

MOST POINTS BY A ROOKIE, ONE PLAYOFF YEAR:
21 – Dino Ciccarelli, Minnesota, in 1981. 14 goals, 7 assists in 19 games.
20 – Don Maloney, NY Rangers, in 1979. 7 goals, 13 assists in 18 games.

MOST GOALS, ONE PLAYOFF YEAR:
19 – Reggie Leach, Philadelphia, 1976. 16 games.
– **Jari Kurri, Edmonton,** 1985. 18 games.

MOST GOALS BY A DEFENSEMAN, ONE PLAYOFF YEAR:
12 – Paul Coffey, Edmonton, 1985. 18 games.
9 – Bobby Orr, Boston, 1970. 14 games.
– Brad Park, Boston, 1978. 15 games.

MOST GOALS BY A ROOKIE, ONE PLAYOFF YEAR:
14 – Dino Ciccarelli, Minnesota, 1981. 19 games.
11 – Jeremy Roenick, Chicago, 1990. 20 games.
10 – Claude Lemieux, Montreal, 1986. 20 games.

MOST ASSISTS, ONE PLAYOFF YEAR:
31 – Wayne Gretzky, Edmonton, 1988. 19 games.
30 – Wayne Gretzky, Edmonton, 1985. 18 games.
29 – Wayne Gretzky, Edmonton, 1987. 21 games.
28 – Mario Lemieux, Pittsburgh, 1991. 23 games.

MOST ASSISTS BY A DEFENSEMAN, ONE PLAYOFF YEAR:
25 – Paul Coffey, Edmonton, 1985. 18 games.
24 – Al MacInnis, Calgary, 1989. 22 games.
19 – Bobby Orr, Boston, 1972. 15 games.

MOST WINS BY A GOALTENDER, ONE PLAYOFF YEAR:
16 – Grant Fuhr, Edmonton, 1988. 19 games.
– **Mike Vernon, Calgary,** 1989. 22 games.
– **Bill Ranford, Edmonton,** 1990. 22 games.
– **Tom Barrasso, Pittsburgh,** 1992. 21 games.

LONGEST SHUTOUT SEQUENCE:
248 Minutes, 32 Seconds – Norm Smith, Detroit, 1936. In best-of-five SF, Smith shut out Mtl. Maroons 1-0, March 24, in 116:30 overtime; shut out Maroons 3-0 in second game, March 26; and was scored against at 12:02 of first period, March 29, by Gus Marker. Detroit won SF 3-0.

MOST POINTS, ONE GAME:
8 – Patrik Sundstrom, New Jersey, April 22, 1988 at New Jersey during 10-4 win over Washington. Sundstrom had 3 goals, 5 assists.
– **Mario Lemieux, Pittsburgh,** April 25, 1989 at Pittsburgh during 10-7 win over Philadelphia. Lemieux had 5 goals, 3 assists.

MOST GOALS, ONE GAME:
5 – Newsy Lalonde, Montreal, March 1, 1919, at Montreal. Final score: Montreal 6, Ottawa 3.
– **Maurice Richard, Montreal,** March 23, 1944, at Montreal. Final score: Montreal 5, Toronto 1.
– **Darryl Sittler, Toronto,** April 22, 1976, at Toronto. Final score: Toronto 8, Philadelphia 5.
– **Reggie Leach, Philadelphia,** May 6, 1976, at Philadelphia. Final score: Philadelphia 6, Boston 3.
– **Mario Lemieux, Pittsburgh,** April 25, 1989 at Pittsburgh. Final score: Pittsburgh 10, Philadelphia 7.

MOST ASSISTS, ONE GAME:
6 – Mikko Leinonen, NY Rangers, April 8, 1982, at New York. Final score: NY Rangers 7, Philadelphia 3.
– **Wayne Gretzky, Edmonton,** April 9, 1987, at Edmonton. Final score: Edmonton 13, Los Angeles 3.

Early Playoff Records

1893-1918

MOST GOALS, BOTH TEAMS, ONE GAME:
25 – Ottawa Silver Seven, Dawson City at Ottawa, Jan. 16, 1905. Ottawa 23, Dawson City 2. Ottawa won best-of-three series 2-0.

MOST GOALS IN PLAYOFFS:
63 – Frank McGee, Ottawa Silver Seven, in 22 playoff games. Seven goals in four games, 1903; 21 goals in eight games, 1904; 18 goals in four games, 1905; 17 goals in six games, 1906.

MOST GOALS, ONE PLAYOFF GAME:
14 – Frank McGee, Ottawa Silver Seven, Jan. 16, 1905 at Ottawa in 23-2 victory over Dawson City.

Index

Overleaf: Maurice Richard (left) and Butch Bouchard hoist a jubilant Elmer Lach, whose overtime goal gave the Canadiens a 1–0 win and the Stanley Cup championship in game five of the 1953 finals. This was Lach's only goal in post-season play in 1953, and would prove to be the last playoff goal of his career.